Mad about Belief

Mad about Belief

Religion in the Life and Thought of Bertrand Russell

LARRY D. HARWOOD

⁌PICKWICK *Publications* · Eugene, Oregon

MAD ABOUT BELIEF
Religion in the Life and Thought of Bertrand Russell

Copyright © 2024 Larry D. Harwood. All rights reserved. Except for brief quotations in critical publications or reviews, no part of this book may be reproduced in any manner without prior written permission from the publisher. Write: Permissions, Wipf and Stock Publishers, 199 W. 8th Ave., Suite 3, Eugene, OR 97401.

Pickwick Publications
An Imprint of Wipf and Stock Publishers
199 W. 8th Ave., Suite 3
Eugene, OR 97401

www.wipfandstock.com

PAPERBACK ISBN: 978-1-62564-494-7
HARDCOVER ISBN: 978-1-4982-8647-3
EBOOK ISBN: 978-1-7252-4916-5

Cataloguing-in-Publication data:

Names: Harwood, Larry D. [author].

Title: Mad about belief : religion in the life and thought of Bertrand Russell / Larry D. Harwood.

Description: Eugene, OR: Pickwick Publications, 2024 | Includes bibliographical references and index.

Identifiers: ISBN 978-1-62564-494-7 (paperback) | ISBN 978-1-4982-8647-3 (hardcover) | ISBN 978-1-7252-4916-5 (ebook)

Subjects: LCSH: Russell, Bertrand, 1872–1970. | Religion—Philosophy. | Philosophers—Biography. | Atheism.

Classification: B1649.R91 H379 2024 (paperback) | B1649.R91 (ebook)

05/20/24

For DJ

Hear, O heavens, and give ear, O earth; for the Lord has spoken:
Sons have I reared and brought up, but they have rebelled against me.

Isaiah 1:2
The Holy Bible, English Standard Version

Contents

	Preface	ix
	Acknowledgments	xvii
	Permissions	xxi
	Abbreviations	xxiii
	Introduction	xxv
1	Russell's Trek from Religion	1
2	Russell's Hesitations with Religion	32
3	Russell on Belief and Unbelief	60
4	Russell Religion, Past and Present	87
5	Religion in the Early Adult Life of Bertrand Russell	126
6	Religion in Early Friendships of Russell	158
7	Religion with the Mistresses	194
8	Russell in Contention over Religious Belief	239
9	Conclusions	270
	Bibliography	317
	Index	331

Preface

Sometime while a university undergraduate I first heard mention of Bertrand Russell. Like not a few students in their initial foray into philosophy, scrutiny of various beliefs prompted reading critics of religious belief, and so I took up Russell. I encountered first the provocatively entitled book *Why I am Not a Christian*, edited by Paul Edwards. In Russell I found an apostle of reason seemingly unwilling to concede even a tiny thimble of truth or goodness or beauty to anything religious. In Russell I nevertheless discovered a superbly penetrating and often entertaining writer, though I remained undecided about some judgements he made about religion. This suspicion arose because his verdicts seemed negative to the point of overwhelmingly derisive toward that subject. Almost right away I was curious about his criticisms, particularly his frequent vehemence on the subject of religion.

With some suspicion that Russell claimed too much in his plentiful criticisms of religion, I nevertheless encountered Russell advocates who esteemed the agnostic Russell as thoroughly reasonable on the subject. Though without expressly saying as much, partisans of Russell urged students like myself—deemed deliberately hiding in the cowardice of religious safety—to undertake a study of Russell on the subject of religion. Understandably, such advice and the estimation of Russell on the subject of religion generally issued from secular people, often academics. Most seemed confident in pointing to Russell's refutations on a subject they disdained presumably as much as seemed apparent in Russell. Sometimes the insinuation was that the case for atheism made by a famous mathematician and noted philosopher and a Nobel Prize winner, simply could not to be taken lightly or worse, ignored. In many ways this was the impetus of my initial interest in Russell on religion. A thinker of such standing as Russell was deserving of due attention. Russell's advocates are, I think, manifestly correct on this point.

A great amount of the respect for Russell's point of view on religion issued from the way Russell said what he did, for he had an extraordinary gift for words and for memorable ways of putting things. However, sometimes very arresting or commanding prose enables both the writer and his listener to glide over complications that a tidy or stellar phrase ignores or skates past, and little did I know at the time that critics did arise who took issue with Russell for some of his terse criticisms of religion. To a general public, however, the prestigious voice of this celebrated thinker tended to overshadow such criticisms. Moreover, readers who appreciated Russell for his notable and popular writings on religion were ready to enlist him and his words in the charge against religious belief. Russell, on religion anyway, was the voice needed to wipe away the residue of religion still breathing in an otherwise secular culture. He was, therefore, often appreciated as a scrappy Voltaire for striking out against the superstitions and follies of religion past and present.

In subsequent reading I was pleasantly surprised to discover that Russell had written a variety of pieces on religion and that his judgements were not always negative on the subject, though most certainly were. Just as I had wondered if Russell had religion right with the overwhelmingly negative and bombastic tone of some of his writing on that subject, I now wondered if students of this thinker had rightly understood his position on religion. Perhaps Russell's strongly worded and negative verdicts on the subject effectively submerged other things he had written. I began to wonder if one could piece together most of what Russell had said on the subject and thus perhaps systematize this philosopher's thought on religion.

Soon aware of C. D. Broad's often quoted comment about Russell coming up with a new philosophy every few years, I wondered if Russell's view on religion, like his philosophy, had been rather constantly on the move. That being said, and as I started to read more of the voluminous writings, I saw that Russell had emphasized various aspects of the subject of religion at different times in his life and writings, for there were some clearly detectable ebbs and flows to be found in following his estimations of religion. Russell was most assuredly reticent with religion, but he was also restless at times to have one; in time I came to see this is the primary enigma posed in getting at Russell on religion. Furthermore,

PREFACE

these two facets of Russell, I would discover, could work in tandem at times, though rarely. No wonder many readers of Russell on religion had thought his estimation of religion only negative.

Both as a professional or technical philosopher, though also as a social critic, Russell nevertheless was for many the most notably influential thinker among twentieth-century philosophers in the Anglo-American tradition. Certainly the life he lived was noteworthy for a multitude of reasons, and partly for this reason I also took notice of Russell's life as a subject as colorful and intriguing as what he often wrote in his essays and books. Furthermore, I was discovering that Russell wrote quite a bit of autobiography within his voluminous writings, culminating in his three-volume autobiography, regarded by many as a classic in the genre of autobiography. Any study of Russell, however, must confront just how forbiddingly massive was the Russell body of writing. Roughly there were seventy books, 2500 or so essays, articles and reviews, and approximately 40,000 surviving letters.[1] Despite the colossal mountain of Russell's corpus, however, Russell was simply too fascinating for me to set aside, and so in graduate school, my interest in Russell on the subject of religion peaked, and I selected as my thesis topic, Bertrand Russell's philosophy of religion. My primary reader, the late Dr. Stewart Hackett, was hugely helpful to my project, though primarily in guiding me through points of Russell's technical philosophy. He nevertheless once remarked to me that it was Russell's work *The Philosophy of Leibniz* that Hackett judged as presenting the most acute criticisms of Leibniz's philosophy. This I duly noted at the time, particularly as this judgement was the estimation of a Leibnizian, as Hackett proudly considered himself to be. Hackett also told me of stimulating conversations with Fr. Frederick Copleston, the Jesuit historian of philosophy concerning Copleston's debate with Russell on the existence of God on BBC Radio in 1948, an event I was unaware of at that time. (In Copleston's monumental *A History of Philosophy* he devotes three chapters to Russell's philosophy and dedicates not a few pages to the origin and legacy of analytic philosophy as it is found in G. E. Moore and Russell.) Now hastily reading the exchanges in that debate, I realized that however much Russell could be considered primarily a polemicist on the subject of religion by many—for which one can make something of a reasonable though not a particularly strong case—he nevertheless was thoroughly comfortable and indeed appeared

---

1. At present, and as of 2021, the number of letters approaches 50,000. https://russell.humanities.mcmaster.ca/brletters.html.

unflappable debating the subject of religion with anyone, including as able and noteworthy a critic as Copleston. In the debate Russell hardly offered only weak polemical points with Copleston. That is, the author of the essays in the volume *Why I am not a Christian* could also advance sophisticated argument.[2]

Despite the rigors of studying a thinker as massively prolific as Russell, I remained interested in Russell and religion after my thesis was accepted and now ventured a visit to the Russell Archives at McMaster University in Hamilton, Ontario. At that time Chief Archivist Kenneth Blackwell ably managed a massive collection of things Russell, and Dr. Blackwell and his staff were hugely helpful during my initial month stay at McMaster, but that too-brief time only provoked more wonder and questions about Russell. Nevertheless, for most of my time in the Russell Archives, I concentrated on letters and Russell essays in out of the way publications. (This was before the BR Editorial Project had produced any of the magnificent volumes excepting the first volume of *Collected Papers of Bertrand Russell*.) In time I discovered how the treasures of Russell's letters and, though less often, largely forgotten essays could serve to fill out some particulars of Russell's posture toward religious belief and things religious. Moreover, as impressively clear as Russell was in his published writings, oftentimes his letters provided particular qualification enormously helpful to inquiry. I returned in a few years for another visit to the Archives and then marriage and children and more graduate school pushed me into other areas of interest and my interest in Russell, though never quite dormant, was now only infrequently mined. Nevertheless, whenever anyone brought up Russell, I could never avoid

---

2. In Russell's arguments in the debate with Copleston, he exhibits a firm and familiar commitment to reason, while reflecting a scientific and secular mindset in his maintenance of a perspective which sees at no point any need for a theistic explanation of anything. When debating the foundation of moral obligations and feeling, Russell contends, "I'm inclined to think that 'ought,' the feeling that one has about 'ought' is an echo of what has been told one by one's parents or one's nurses." Copleston responds by saying, "Well, I wonder if you can explain away the idea of the 'ought' merely in terms of nurses and parents. I really don't see how it can be conveyed to anybody in other terms than itself. It seems to me that if there is a moral order bearing upon the human conscience, that that moral order is unintelligible apart from the existence of God." Russell will have no such metaphysical flights of fancy, but if they are insisted upon, Russell is prepared to lay out the consequences of that view: "Then you have to say one or other of two things. Either God only speaks to a very small percentage of mankind—which happens to include yourself—or He deliberately says things that are not true in talking to the consciences of savages." "A Debate on the Existence of God: Bertrand Russell and F. C. Copleston," in Hick, *Existence*, 186.

chiming into the conversation. When an occasional inquirer asked me about my interest in the philosopher, my usual response was that to study Russell was to study the twentieth century.

Years later and after reading Ray Monk's impressive biography of Russell while on a trip in China, I was irresistibly drawn to seriously consider the subject of Bertrand Russell and religion again. I soon read with great interest some of the work of intervening years on this topic, but found no overarching work on Russell's religious views other than small though still significant and sometimes penetrating monographs, like those of Pitt, Griffin, Andersson, Greenspan, Grayling, Kuntz and others. I think this lack mainly due to the immensity of Russell's writings, though another difficulty is that many of Russell's writings on religion, as indicated already, were written for popular audiences, and therefore rarely commended themselves to scholars working the province of philosophy of religion.

In this book, I propose evaluative assessments of Russell's views on religion and religious belief, while venturing possible ways in which circumstances and details of Russell's life contributed to his views on religion. Therefore, and as already indicated, not only the intellect of Russell, but something of his life will be under scrutiny in this study, though the latter for purposes of grappling with the former. Biographical considerations certainly have some relevance to Russell's views on religious belief, though one can certainly consider the views of any thinker on a subject without any reference to the life, familial and otherwise, of the thinker. However, such division would be to separate the man from his thinking. To insist upon a dichotomy or even a wall between the life of the man and the thinking of the man disallows the real possibility of understanding at least some of Russell's argumentation about religion. Furthermore, it is a rare case where the thought of a thinker on particular subjects may not be better understood knowing something of the life behind the words. In a study of Russell something of the latter is required, beginning with the youthful Russell taking issue with the beliefs and culture of his upbringing at Pembroke Lodge, largely provided by his Grandmother Russell. Some account of that experience, as only one example, contributes some light to Russell's position on religion. It is chiefly for such reasons that I have included biographical material about Russell, rather than simply considering the essayed thoughts of Russell.

Though Russell may be one of the most religiously minded thinkers among secular companions—a point which Russell not infrequently notes of himself in letters—he also appears among the most adamant of the irreligious with little hesitation in giving grave offense to the religiously inclined. How he can be both is a central question I have set out to address in this book, as already suggested. In attempting to bring some systemization to my subject, I nevertheless have not intended to produce a meticulously tidy study or a study so constrained as to be only for specialists. Rather, my intent is to make some contribution to the study of Russell on religion for readers who have been fascinated by this great philosopher, though somewhat offended by (or even in agreement with) his generally bombastic tone when he turns to religion. In this book I try to throw some light on the frequently critical tone in Russell on the subject, while at the same time accounting for a lesser and respectful tone Russell on occasion manifested with it.

The idea and some contours of this book were prompted in great part because Ray Monk's biography on Russell exposed something of the persona of the man Russell that I found suggestive for this study of Russell and religion. Monk had the gall—perhaps more politely put, the candidness or frankness—to make some judgements of Russell that were for some readers simply too severe. At the same time Monk acknowledged Russell as almost hands down the greatest philosopher of the past century. Of course Monk's overall thesis about the fear of madness in Russell's life has been questioned (as of course was to be expected) but equally as intriguing in Monk's work was how he presented Russell. That is to say, however much this thinker was a towering giant of twentieth century philosophy, Monk portrayed him as a man somewhat overcome by his own foibles, not to say at times follies, despite the great authority which followed the name and pen of Bertrand Russell. Monk may have also suggested—again too much for some critics— that a kind of adulation for Russell presumed impeccable and flawless reason followed Russell on well-nigh every topic he took up, and I would venture, especially when he assailed religion and religious belief. The story of Russell's life and philosophy, therefore, must include more than the tale of Russell's logical acumen and stellar successes. It needs to include some disappointments, and among these, Russell's efforts to construct a religion viable for himself and the few secularists who also manifested that desire.

Understandably, Monk has had his critics, and none perhaps more severe than Prof. Stone, who charged Monk with presuming to judge much of Russell's life and writing from a more or less conservative perspective.[3] To Prof. Stone this was illicit. However, I suspect some admirers are simply too close or too adoring of their subjects to submit them to particular kinds of assessments, fearing a kind of sacrilege. Taking offense at the scrutiny of a venerated figure, a critic may contend that the blows received only count from the perspective of a partisan, and therefore unfair, perspective. Such alleged partisan criticism can be castigated as most unworthy of such a subject.

I rather prefer what Russell remarked about the all-too-human hesitancy to acknowledge what may be a fact when the fact is perceived as annoying to the point of being unwelcome. Such a stilted perception or evaluation, however, Russell contended, may be a reason to resent, but not to reject. As Russell was fond of saying, truth is a ruthless taskmaster. The requirement of admitting the truth remains, even when the truth is deemed unpleasant or even unflattering about a subject or person from whom we might have wished for better.

Soli Deo Gloria.
Larry D. Harwood
La Crosse, Wisconsin, USA
November 2023.

---

3. Stone, Review of *The Ghost of Madness*, 88–89.

Acknowledgments

A generous year-long sabbatical from Viterbo University in academic year 2015–16 enabled me to spend much of that time doing final research and writing for the present book. I wish to thank former Viterbo President Dr. Glena Temple, Dr. William Reese, and Dr. Andrew Hamilton—all of Viterbo University—for their patient and unflagging support for this project. A most special thanks is in order to Dr. Temple, who was for many years a source of unflinching inspiration and support. I am additionally grateful for her genuine support of the small cluster of faculty in philosophy at Viterbo over past years. Sincere thanks are also in order to Caitlyn Konze, Information Services Manager at Viterbo University Library. She spent not a little time chasing down books and articles requested with interlibrary loan at Viterbo and always evidenced willingness to help.

To present and past staff at the Russell Archives in Hamilton, Ontario, and particularly Kenneth Blackwell, Carl Spadoni, and Shelia Turcon, I am exceedingly grateful for help and suggestions during the decade of the 1980s. I am thankful for the aid provided me during my 2016 and 2019 trips to the Archives by Beverly Bayzat, Library Assistant, and, as always, to Kenneth Blackwell, now Honorary Russell Archivist. Thanks are also extended to Bridget Whittle, Digital Archives Librarian, who was most helpful in running down some final pieces of Russell writing for me. Thanks are also due to Rick Stapleton, Archives and Research Collections Librarian during my 2019 visit and now Head, Archives & Research Collection at McMaster University Library, for his aid in matters of copyright. I am particularly grateful to the William Ready Division of Archives and Research Collections for a Research Travel Grant awarded to me in 2020 for further work in the Russell Archives.

ACKNOWLEDGMENTS

As indicated in the preface, a main catalyst for this book was my reading of Professor Ray Monk's two-volume biography of Russell. Except for Professor Monk's stimulating and provocative work on Russell I perhaps would never have written the present book. To my editors at Pickwick Publications, Stephanie Hough and Revd. Dr. Robin Parry, and assistant managing editor, Matthew Wimer, I am thankful for reassuring aid and encouragement in the writing of this book, as well as their gracious willingness to extend deadlines.

Thanks are in order to Dr. Peter Harland of Cambridge University in the UK for arranging for me some weeks as a visiting scholar during Easter Term 2016 at the School of Divinity at Cambridge University. I am especially thankful to Dr. Douglas Hedley of the School of Divinity for our conversations on Russell during that time. Thanks are in order to Mr. Chris Gravett, former curator at Woburn Abbey and Gardens at Bedfordshire, UK, who kindly gave a most informative tour in autumn of 2015 of Bedford Chapel at Chenies, where many Russell family members are buried. I of course wish also to thank His Grace, the 15th Duke of Bedford, for his kind permission allowing me to tour the Bedford Chapel. Additional thanks are due to Rev David Allsop, Rector, The Chenies Benefice, for his generous help in arranging my visit.

To Principal Michael Lloyd at Wycliffe Hall, Oxford University, I am very grateful to have been given opportunity to read portions of my work and for stimulating questions while at Wycliffe as a visiting scholar in Michaelmas term of 2015. For aid in logistical matters while at Wycliffe I would also like to thank John Michaux, Admissions Officer; Chris Leftley, Librarian; Andy Butterworth, Bursar; Robyn Wyncoll, Assistant Busar; Trish Coleman, Finance Manager; Andy Hamilton, IT Manager; and Kerstin Jeapes, Receptionist. The time and efforts extended to me by each of these people to expedite my research and writing are warmly appreciated and fondly remembered.

I am grateful to Judy Ulland of Viterbo University for having read critical portions of the manuscript and for having provided needed corrections. Her scrutiny has greatly benefitted the final product, and I am grateful to her for meticulous devotion to expressing the English language well. To Carol Taylor, who read the entire manuscript and gave numerous and needed suggestions for improvement, sincere thanks are due. I have also had the benefit of conversations about Russell with students from two decades of teaching at Viterbo University. For conversations on religious belief and Russell's views on religious belief, I am

ACKNOWLEDGMENTS

grateful to former students and still friends, Gwen St.Marie, Sara Weibel, and David Booman. The questions of a student are oftentimes as helpful for a developing project as the critique of a colleague. Additionally, I wish to sincerely thank my brother for always asking me how "the book" was coming in countless Saturday phone conversations over the past years. Happily, now we will have other subjects to chat about. I have also greatly benefited from innumerable conversations with many other and uncountable persons interested in the famous philosopher and his position on things religious. I hope this book provides some answers to some of their questions.

Most importantly, I wish to thank members of my immediate family for their patience with this project. Particularly, I am grateful to my wife for her willingness to accommodate the tremendous expenditure of time needed to compose this book. I thank her also for undertaking travel with me in pursuance of this and other projects. Her unflagging support has not gone unnoticed nor unappreciated over the past many years. With her needed encouragement, I have managed to see this book to the end. Accordingly, to her this book is gratefully and deservedly dedicated.

It goes without saying—yet I will state it here—that the judgements and opinions on Russell expressed in this book, both the ordinary and the outrageous, are entirely my own.

Permissions

I am grateful for permission to quote from unpublished letters of Russell for which copyright is held by the Bertrand Russell Archives, William Ready Division of Archives and Research Collections, McMaster University Library, Hamilton, Ontario, Canada, and referenced in the writing of this book. Though a very valuable and revealing selection of Russell's correspondence is found within his three volume *Autobiography of Bertrand Russell*, the quantity of letters published in the *Autobiography* is dwarfed by an estimated forty thousand letters penned by Russell. This mammoth number excludes letters penned to him. Therefore, the quantity of Russell letters for study can be daunting to a researcher, though the task of consulting them is aided by the fact that McMaster University holds the copyright on virtually all of them. I am particularly grateful to the Permissions Committee of the Bertrand Russell Archives at McMaster University, for permission to quote from the letters in Maria Forte's dissertation, "Bertrand Russell's Letters to Helen Thomas Flexner and Lucy Martin Donnelly."

Though the vast majority of letters referenced in this book are penned by Russell, two exceptions are the letters of Gilbert Murray to Russell and letters of Russell's grandmother, Lady Frances Anna Maria Elliot, to her son Rollo Russell and to her daughter in-law Gertrude Russell, concerning the young Bertrand Russell. For permission to print excerpts from the letters of Russell's grandmother, I am grateful to Russell's grandson John Francis Russell, 7th Earl Russell. For permission to quote excerpts from Murray's letters I am grateful to Murray's grandson, Prof. Alexander Murray. Both sets of letters were made available for my use by Special Collections, Bodleian Library, Oxford University, UK, and I am

PERMISSIONS

especially grateful to Oliver House, Superintendent, Special Collections Reading Rooms at the Bodleian, for his assistance in using these letters.

I gratefully acknowledge permission from *Russell* journal editor Kenneth Blackwell to print in this work an article of mine from the journal *Russell*, "Russell's Reticence with Religion," *Russell* 17 (1997) 27–41. The article has been substantially revised in the present work.

For permission to quote an excerpt from a letter of Fr. Frederick Copleston to Russell I am grateful to Rebecca Somerset and the British Jesuit Archives in Britain. For permission to quote from letters of Dora Winifred Russell I am grateful to Andrew Tait and Harriet Ward and to the International Institute of Social History at Amsterdam, Netherlands. For permission to quote from a letter of Kenneth Blackwell to Dora Russell I am grateful to Kenneth Blackwell. I gratefully acknowledge permission from the Russell Archives at McMaster University to quote from letters written by Russell to Lady Ottoline Morrell. For quotations from those letters I am also grateful to the Harry Ransom Humanities Center, the University of Texas at Austin, as owners of the physical letters.

Abbreviations

Russell, 1872–1914	*The Autobiography of Bertrand Russell, 1872–1914*. London: George Allen and Unwin, 1967.
Russell, 1914–1944	*The Autobiography of Bertrand Russell, 1914–1944*. London: George Allen and Unwin, 1968.
Russell, 1944–1969	*The Autobiography of Bertrand Russell, 1944–1969*. New York: Simon and Schuster, 1969.
Russell, *AP* I	*The Amberley Papers,* Vol. 1. London: George Allen and Unwin, 1937 (co-edited with Patricia Russell).
Russell, *AP* II	*The Amberley Papers,* Vol. 2. London: George Allen and Unwin, 1937 (co-edited with Patricia Russell).

Letters quoted from in the above works (*The Autobiography* and *The Amberley Papers*), to include all letters referenced from other works and correspondents, are dated uniformly in the present book by month, day, and year sequence.

Russell, *CP* 1	*The Collected Papers of Bertrand Russell,* Vol. 1: *Cambridge Essays, 1888–99,* edited by Kenneth Blackwell, Andrew Brink, Nicholas Griffin, Richard A. Rempel, and John G. Slater. London: George Allen and Unwin, 1983.
Russell, *CP* 6	*The Collected Papers of Bertrand Russell,* Vol. 6: *Logical and Philosophical Papers, 1909–13,* edited by John G. Slater with the assistance of Bernd Frohmann. London: Routledge, 1992.

ABBREVIATIONS

Russell, CP 8	*The Collected Papers of Bertrand Russell*, Vol. 8: *The Philosophy of Logical Atomism and Other Essays, 1914–19*, edited by John G. Slater. London: George Allen and Unwin, 1986.
Russell, CP 9	*The Collected Papers of Bertrand Russell*, Vol. 9: *Essays on Language, Mind and Matter, 1919–26*, edited by John G. Slater with the assistance of Bernd Frohmann. London: Unwin Hyman, 1988.
Russell, CP 10	*The Collected Papers of Bertrand Russell*, Vol. 10: *A Fresh Look at Empiricism, 1927–42*, edited by John G. Slater with the assistance of Peter Kollner. London: Routledge, 1996.
Russell, CP 11	*The Collected Papers of Bertrand Russell*, Vol. 11: *Last Philosophical Testament, 1943–68*, edited by John G. Slater with the assistance of Peter Kollner. London: Routledge, 1997.
Russell, CP 12	*The Collected Papers of Bertrand Russell*, Vol. 12: *Contemplation and Action, 1902–14*, edited by Richard A. Rempel, Andrew Brink, and Margaret Moran. London: George Allen and Unwin, 1985.

Introduction

Some of Russell's most notable essays on religion, written in the initial decades of the twentieth century, evidence a serious and sobering consideration of religion. For the most part that kind of posture toward religion weakened in Russell in subsequent decades, though never entirely vanishing. Broad's remark about oscillation in Russell's philosophy, moreover, was most true for Russell's technical philosophy. That is, changes of emphasis regarding religion were certainly present in Russell, but they were hardly any seismic or substantial revolutions in his thinking on religion. Still, one must exercise caution, for Russell lived a very long life which gave him ample opportunity for change of viewpoint.

For study of Russell on religion, it is necessary to concede that Russell's life and the times in which he lived were too turbulent for a restless philosopher such as him to stay put or consolidate. Russell was most always eager to move on to the next thing, rather than to wrap his prior thoughts into systematic bundles. In this respect, Russell was rather like Leibniz, a philosopher Russell held up as one of his favorites, and about whom Russell wrote the second of his seventy books in 1900. That is, to reconstruct Leibniz's philosophy one has to piece together various portions from multiple places in his writings, substantially including his letters. To more fully understand Russell at times one must do much of the same.

Spinoza was more favored by Russell than Leibniz.[1] From Spinoza's notion of the intellectual love of God Russell tried to salvage a philosophy

---

1. However, neither was his favorite. In a letter to Lucy Donnelly of February 20, 1914, Russell writes, "I find that of all the men that ever lived, Heraclitus is the most intimate to me—" In Forte, *Letters*, 218.

INTRODUCTION

of life that he could embrace, while steering clear of unbelievable religious and metaphysical ideas that Spinoza exuded. On this last point, one discovers an insistent point of Russell on religion or philosophers who gravitated toward religion or specifically religious belief. For Russell the honest inquirer or seeker should not antecedently prejudice any investigation for truth by allowing his preferred beliefs to bias his study. On thinkers Russell deemed both illicitly deferring to religious beliefs and resisting neutrality, he was relentlessly and loudly critical. This point of view Russell never veered from in his long life.

If Russell had philosophers like Leibniz and Spinoza that he admired, he had others he disdained, and he was not always oblique in his judgements against their person or their philosophy. Russell thoroughly disliked Kant's philosophy and thought ill of him for it, calling Kant more than once one of the great misfortunes in the history of philosophy. On philosophers and philosophies like Kant's that Russell thought slavishly obedient to personal prejudices or predilections he took particular aim, a feature of Russell's judgements not lost to John Hermann Randall, the American historian of philosophy, who went so far as to say that on philosophers whom Russell thought ill, "he is no safe guide."[2] Russell, on the other hand, was a thinker with strong opinions and little to no fear in stating them.[3] In his is most negative judgements on religion and in his most vehement denunciations of religion, it may appear that religion is the chief promulgator of evils and thus bears responsibility for the most cruel and blood-soaked episodes of human history. However, there are other figures and institutions and human proclivities aside from religion that suffer no light castigation by Russell. The full list of the guilty nevertheless does not lighten the responsibility of religion for its gigantic falsities and foibles. All the same, Russell often does represent religion as the worst offender against truth and goodness in human history.

In his aspirations for a future better than the present, Russell not infrequently exhibited both impatience and strong judgement against religion evoked by his judgments of the adamant refusal of religious bodies

2. Randall, Review of Russell's *History of Western Philosophy*, 32.

3. As an indication of this demeanor in Russell, he writes to friend Lucy Donnelly about her (and also Russell's) friend, Helen Flexner, "who wrote me quite a serious remonstrance, which amused me. I should have thought she would have known by this time that social caution in the expression of opinion is not my strong point. If she had known Christ before he delivered the Sermon on the Mount she would have begged him to keep silence for fear of injuring his social position in Nazareth." Russell to Lucy Donnelly, February 10, 1916, in Russell, *1914–1944*, 69.

to turn and pursue another course. Furthermore, in his writings Russell often presents his better options for the future as rather blindingly clear and self-evident, except to those duped by religion and religious belief, as well as other malefactors. However, the Russell proposals for the future not infrequently had little effect upon the accused, as Russell charged with lament and disdain. In great degree this is why he is so vehemently critical of things religious and religious belief; that is, Russell was out to chart another course for humanity and the world for the better, but old obstacles continued to block the new and better way. Against such obstacles Russell would be relentless, though also frustrated.

To study Russell's life and thought gives notice to how hugely influential some of his ideas were—to advocates and critics. This was certainly true for his contributions to technical philosophy, but perhaps even more true for his work and writing as a public intellectual. Here Russell's ideas cost him employment as he was impugned by some while praised by others. As one noteworthy example, he was blamed as well as heralded for his part in bringing about the sexual revolution of the twentieth century. Russell thus had his successes as well as his frustrations in attempting to reroute the ways of the world, and frequently the battleground was traditional notions of right and wrong. This necessarily prompted Russell into fights with religious belief.

Though much of Russell's writing on religion was polemical, and on his own admission sometimes propagandistic, he could also broker sophisticated argument, as is evident in the debate between Russell and Copleston. Furthermore, the Russell corpus provides some protracted discussions between other intellectual critics and Russell on the subject of religion, such as William James and Ludwig Wittgenstein, as well as Gilbert Murray and T. S. Eliot. In such contentions, one glimpses Russell with his sleeves sometimes rolled up on the subject and in general with the same sort of confidence he exuded in his debate with Copleston. Nonetheless, in Russell's interactions with these and other thinkers, one can discern unifying though at times also complicating details on his views on religion and religious belief.

In the debate with Copleston, Russell seems singularly unmoved by any of Copleston's arguments or counter-arguments: in fact there is perhaps at least a tad of talking down to Copleston from Russell. For starters, Russell is insistent that there is not any metaphysical bedrock from which our moral values are derived: "I should say that the universe is just

INTRODUCTION

there and that's all."[4] The universe, conceived in any anthropomorphic fashion, is simply a conceptual legacy of the past, its residual upholders refusing to concede the point. The impression one receives from Russell's demeanor in this debate with Copleston is thus not dissimilar at times to the tone of his more popular works. The air of confidence with which he marshals his case against religious belief and religion is strikingly similar in both, for Russell sees little to give deference to in religion, given its historic errors, or, for that matter, false visions of this world or a beatific world to come.

According to Russell, the broad truth is that ignorance has prompted and sustained religion and religious belief, and cruelty has been the consequence most often. The viability of an enlightened view of the world, not couched in fear anymore, lies within human grasp for Russell, but only if humans will shake themselves free of bondage to past antiquated beliefs quite unworthy of modern people. This refusal is manifestly cowardly belligerence, with Russell informing his fiancée Alys Pearsall Smith, "I cannot get over a sort of contempt for a Xtian in our generation."[5] Furthermore, for anyone willing to look and consider the findings of science, such as those of Copernicus and Darwin, the impossibility of the previous religious conception of the world is blindingly evident. However, despite such a barrage of negative assessment of religion and the implausibility of trustworthy religious belief in modernity, Russell's positive thoughts on religion evidence some hope for a religion enabling the modern human to negotiate life with some courage. Russell's efforts to maintain these two estimations of religion will be the subject of this book.

4. "A Debate," in Hick, *Existence*, 175.
5. Russell to Alys Pearsall Smith, September 22, 1894. Document no. 300151, Box no. 6.52, Bertrand Russell Archives, McMaster University Library.

1

Russell's Trek from Religion

A. RUSSELL AS PUBLIC FIGURE AND PHILOSOPHER

Born into an English family prominent in politics during the centuries of modernity, Bertrand Russell in his first book tackled a political subject. This book, *German Social Democracy*, turned up as Russell developed interest in the particular topic while visiting Berlin in 1895 during his first married months with his wife Alys. Political subject matter, however, was not something new to Russell. In the household where he grew up, at Pembroke Lodge, politics were always close at hand, and Russell would eventually take his turn in the political and social arena like some notable familial predecessors, but first he took up with mathematics and then philosophy. His second book, written on the philosophy of Leibniz, came four years later. The strong political atmosphere at Pembroke Lodge inevitably stoked political and social interests in him, though its solitariness also nudged him toward mathematics and philosophy. He later wrote:

> When I had finished my student years at Cambridge, I had to decide whether to devote my life to philosophy or to politics. Politics had been the habitual pursuit of my family since the sixteenth century, and to think of anything else was viewed as a kind of treachery to my ancestors. Everything was done to show that my path would be smooth if I chose politics. John Morley, who was Irish Secretary, offered me a post. Lord Dufferin, who was British Ambassador in Paris, gave me a job at our Embassy

there. My family brought pressure to bear upon me in every way they could think of. For a time I hesitated, but in the end the lure of philosophy proved irresistible.[1]

Not included in this brief account by Russell is the added complication that Russell's family also desired for him to take the political post at Paris to distance him from his fiancée Alys before the two could finalize any plan to wed. Like the attempt to push Russell toward politics rather than philosophy, this familial effort also failed. At Pembroke Lodge not a few fractures between young Bertrand and Russell family members would occur, though Russell's older brother Frank provoked even more consternation.

The obligation of political duty was strong in the Russell family, and Bertrand never gave up political interests for any extended period as an adult. For much of the long life that lay ahead of him, Russell would oscillate between technical philosophy and social topics. He would sometimes take leave of one for the other until he tired of it and would return to his former love. Both gave him something of what he found intellectually absorbing and something of what he felt his duty as a Russell, but he was never entirely committed to one to the exclusion of the other. Russell evidenced many interests—though politics and philosophy predominated. The sheer variety and number of subjects attracting his attention are evident in his many books, essays, articles, interviews, speeches, and letters. A man whose literary output, aside from his seventy books, would encompass thirty-five volumes in *The Collected Papers of Bertrand Russell*, is scarcely comprehensible.

Accordingly, to put the robust life and voluminous work of Bertrand Russell in a nutshell for the sake of brevity or for the reader scarcely acquainted with Russell's work is difficult to nearly impossible. His life was long and his literary output almost unbelievable for a man who spent as much time as Russell did outside his study and away from his desk.

---

1. Russell, "Adaptation: An Autobiographical Epitome," 5. On the other hand, in "From Logic to Politics," 32, Russell wrote of his increasing interest in social and political questions but also the difficulty of negotiating such subject matter after having devoted himself to mathematics and philosophy previously: "Although I did not completely abandon logic and abstract philosophy, I became more and more absorbed in social questions and especially in the causes of war and the possible ways of preventing it. I have found my work on such subjects much more difficult and much less successful than my earlier work on mathematical logic. It is difficult because its utility depends upon persuasion, and my previous training and experience had not been any help toward persuasiveness."

As something of an introduction to a life spanning ninety-seven years, we could start by enumerating a few of the people with whom the long-lived Russell crossed paths, both physically and in letters. Ronald Clark, Russell's first biographer after his death, put it pointedly when he noted that Russell was born during the American presidency of Ulysses Grant and died during the presidency of Richard Nixon.[2] As a youngster of five, Russell met British Prime Minister Gladstone at Pembroke Lodge. On the other end of his life, American President Kennedy and Soviet Premier Khrushchev received letters from Russell in his last decade of life at a time most people would have withdrawn from public view. In fact, he lived so long that many of his notable former students, friends, and colleagues—many younger than him—predeceased him. In terms of this longevity and coupled with his often controversial views, Russell calls to mind Thomas Hobbes. Both philosophers had a love of mathematics and maintained some distance and diffidence toward religion. Both could provoke significant sectors of the public to oppose them, though in Russell's case opposition could also make of him a hero. Like the long-lived Hobbes also, Russell continued writing in his later years, though his work in technical philosophy significantly ebbed. Nevertheless, some observers surmised the man would be around forever. Russell's daughter, Katharine Tait, remarks in her brief and endearing story, *Carn Voel, My Mother's House*: "My father lived to be 97 and my mother 92 and I used sometimes to think they could not bear to die before they had straightened out the world."[3] Straightening out the world and exposing dubious philosophical method and castigating errant philosophers is one way to interpret the life work of Russell, and perhaps equally fitting as a description of Russell's crusading work outside the university, as well as inside. In the later years of his life, the prestigious philosopher remained increasingly absorbed with pressing world affairs. As such, it is hardly surprising that the majority of Russell's corpus is written outside his expertise as a technical philosopher.

From Russell's voluminous writings on social topics his reputation with the public became increasingly established, though these writings could jeopardize employment as a philosopher in the university: he was dismissed from his lectureship at Cambridge University in 1916 for political statements and in 1940 Russell was prevented from taking up an

---

2. Clark, *Life*, 19.
3. Tait, *Carn Voel*, 28.

academic position at City College of New York in America, over community contentions that Russell was morally unfit to be a teacher. Russell's chafing at various Victorian mores prompted him to contest many social conventions of his day as he sought for a rational human future.

However, the trenchant social critic would first be drawn to mathematics and philosophy. The young Russell and his Cambridge colleague G. E. Moore would change the direction of subsequent generations of philosophers when both were young men at Cambridge. Their philosophical motivation was to see the world as the world was, and in so doing the two men produced a new vision for philosophy in their time. Russell and Moore, though with different angles of critique taken with the Cambridge thinking of their day and with different personalities, the two moved the mode of English philosophy away from adulation of the German Hegel and idealist philosophy to a focus on analysis rather than grandiose metaphysical schema. From this standpoint Russell would go on to make lasting contributions to the field of technical philosophy with his emphasis on logic and his never quenched appetite for epistemology. With Moore, Russell had a substantial role in turning Anglo-American philosophy into a new direction still present in English-speaking philosophy to this day. This is not to say—particularly in the case of Russell—that the two men would approve of all directions their heirs took philosophy, nor that either man approved of the other personally.

There had been a few critics of the Hegelian philosophy in Britain before Russell and Moore, but this pair would in time turn British philosophy back toward its historical empiricist tradition. The two would now mock the Hegelian philosophy that had previously blinded them and their peers, and would turn toward a picture and account of the world termed at times "realism." It was a view of the world not so foreign or far afield from the ordinary view of the world embraced by people other than philosophers, and so was sometimes referred to as "common sense realism." After rejection of his previous allegiance to idealism, Russell never spoke with anything but disdain for the philosophy he and Moore had once held. Though youthful religious beliefs disowned as an adolescent could occasionally be readmitted for Russell's attention later, this was never the case with idealism after Russell's rejection of that philosophy.

With only these sparse facts about Russell's adult life duly noted, one might reasonably expect that Russell nearly always and typically pushed against the grain. This, however, is only partially true, as Russell could be among the loudest critics of new trends in philosophy. That is, despite his propensity to provoke controversy on many occasions even in the field of philosophy, Russell always retained and defended something of the standard or older notion of philosophy. Furthermore, he complained over some of the deviating directions the philosophical method he and Moore had inspired took and in this frustration Russell remained particularly perturbed by the way some philosophers would take the track of analyzing language for the sake of language. Russell irksomely referred to this infatuation as "the cult of common usage," and never ceased to pillage the position and its practitioners. Russell himself never relented in refusing to give up on the traditional goal of philosophy as an effort to present a justified explanation for positions taken on the great and difficult questions of philosophy. The reason he changed his philosophy so often—recalling the remark of C. D. Broad—was because philosophical questions presented difficult challenges that provoked not just vision, but revisions. The cult of common usage was a case of philosophy turned in on itself, and thus it was too ingrown and humanistic for Russell in its study of the silly ways silly people say silly things, as Russell would contend.[4] Russell wanted to bring precision and clarity to philosophy, while the cult of common usage had an opposite and virtually useless purpose in Russell's estimation. He was trying to diminish the usual murkiness in which most of our talk is invested; his antagonists seemed bent in the opposite direction.

While working to clean up the vagaries and wrong turns of philosophy, past and present, Russell likewise evidenced much of the same aim when he turned to social topics. As a technical philosopher in the earlier part of his career, in great part because of his love of mathematics and the consequent desire to bring something of the sureties of mathematics to the murkiness often belonging to philosophy, Russell's movement toward topics of interest to a general public showed something of the same aggravated motivations. That is, with his political and social interests absorbing a greater part of his life, Russell invoked a stringent analysis of common social notions that he claimed rarely endured the scrutiny of unbiased investigation or permitted the admission of reason. Though such topics might have the sanction and safe-keeping of tradition and convention and the respect of otherwise thinking people, Russell stood prepared to question them. These topics included morality, happiness,

---

4. Russell, "Cult of 'Common Usage,'" 166–72.

marriage, science, religion, education, politics, and freedom in a modern society, among others.

Interestingly, G. E. Moore shared little interest in such topics in comparison to Russell, while Russell's most famous student, Ludwig Wittgenstein, castigated Russell rather severely for writing on some of these subjects. A tantalizing detail concerning the relationship between Russell and his student was that Wittgenstein did not presume that *nobody* should write on such topics; he seemed to think, however, that *Russell* should not. To a degree, however, and though perhaps overstated, Wittgenstein may have regarded Russell as something of a rogue rather than a simple radical.[5]

Meanwhile, Russell joined himself to a host of social movements of his day, and interests provoked in significant part by his aristocratic Russell family heritage, which included some very notable predecessors, among whom was Bertrand's grandfather, Lord John Russell (1792–1878). Bertrand, moreover, was proud of the Russell heritage and not infrequently displayed his continuing allegiance to many of the things his family had stood for in the past. However, the Victorian world at Pembroke Lodge put Russell at odds with many of the mores of his time and at odds with some of his own family members—a point that will be duly noted in this book. Meanwhile, Russell relentlessly critiqued that world and its ways, with his logic providing public audiences and increasing acclaim for Russell.[6] To great degree and sometimes to great fanfare as well as contentious controversy, Russell would largely assume the role of a public intellectual with his many forays into the topics previously mentioned. Such ventures would mark Russell as a different and versatile thinker compared to most of his closest peers.[7] To understand Russell,

---

5. Possibly Moore regarded Russell in some way similar to Wittgenstein on Russell.

6. An example from Russell's *Marriage and Morals*, 83, provides the following: "The women of the Victorian age were, and a great many women still are, in a mental prison. This prison was not obvious to consciousness, since it consisted of subconscious inhibitions. The decay of inhibitions, which has taken place among the young of our own time, has led to the reappearance in consciousness of instinctive desires which had been buried beneath mountains of prudery. This is having a very revolutionary effect upon sexual morality, not only in one country or in one class, but in all civilized countries and in all classes."

7. Nicholas Griffin sums up this aspect of Russell quite well: "Quite apart from his work in philosophy, Russell was one of the twentieth century's most colourful and controversial intellectuals. Throughout a very long life he took up a great many causes, most of them unpopular. He was certainly never afraid to take a stand, and some of those he took got him into quite spectacular amounts of trouble. Few philosophers have led as

therefore, requires understanding a man who crossed traditional and tidy boundaries in being both a cloistered intellectual and a public figure. In the latter role, he very rarely hesitated to argue his point of view on social matters and manners even when this put him at odds with friends and authorities of the day. This is one reason that one of Russell's very good and longtime friends, the classicist Gilbert Murray, urged Russell to take up the writing of an autobiography. In a letter of August 16, 1949, Murray writes to Russell, "You are one of the few people who really ought to write an autobiography. You have deservedly great influence. You have been much misunderstood and attacked. Consequently you need to be explained, and no one could do the explaining as well as yourself."[8] Part of the reason for Murray's push was that Russell was frequently controversial, and controversy could easily provoke misunderstandings of the man making for the controversies. Part of the controversies were aroused because Russell treated his chosen topics in a radical manner; the shorter list of such topics would include marriage and politics, sex and religion. Russell tended to be frank, candid, and no-nonsense on such things and inclined to think of himself as wielding logic on subjects hopelessly mired in superstition and thus in dire need of reason rather than justified by obscurantist mystification or blind concession.

So, unlike most of the Cambridge University dons, Russell began to write on topics of social interest and accordingly was drawn into the purview of a public and extended audience who found Russell's words and work commanding attention and often entertaining. One reason not often pointed out for Russell's captivated audiences has been articulated by Crawshay-Williams, a close friend of Russell in the last decade of Russell's life. He contends that

> It was this superstructure of extreme feeling on a rational basis which gave Russell his force and influence as a polemicist. It is after all a truism that the entirely reasonable man, whose opinions are not convictions, will seldom get things done. The courses of action that he advises may be right, but they are not carried out. In this sense Russell was not an entirely reasonable man. He was a man of passion and action. All the same, he was by no means the *ordinary* excitable man. The great difference between him and

---

adventurous a life as Russell, and none have engaged with the world in so many different ways. In one way or another he involved himself with most of the important political and intellectual concerns of the twentieth century." Griffin, *Cambridge Companion*, 2.

8. Gilbert Murray to Russell, August 16, 1949, Oxford, Bodleian Libraries, MS. Gilbert Murray 166, fol. 87.

most polemicists was that he could usually be pulled back from his extreme position, and indeed he would often come back of his own accord when seriousness was in order.[9]

Moreover, in the beginning of his efforts at public speaking, Russell's manner was hardly adapted to his audience until he became acclimated to public delivery. Russell's written words, however, suffered no such need for adjustment. His popularity as a writer did not go unrecognized at the popular or professional level,[10] and in 1950 he was awarded the Nobel Prize for Literature. Russell's earlier and continuing political work had given him impetus to write and speak even more and not least on political matters. After a pamphlet he had written which authorities took to be offensive to Britain's American allies during World War I, Russell found himself sentenced to six months in jail during that war. Russell would run for a seat in the English Parliament on four occasions, something his father, Lord Amberley, did only once.[11] Russell, therefore, was no cloistered academic nor only a technical philosopher. Of his seventy books—a relatively small portion of that number are written by Russell the technical philosopher, though some of the fewer number do have pride of place beside other Russell titles. However, Russell's last technical work, *Human Knowledge: Its Scope and Limits*, written in 1948, was not one of them. Beleaguered by some negative reviews of that work, Russell seemed to perceive that among the newer generation of British philosophers, his student Wittgenstein had eclipsed his own prior popularity. Russell, therefore, would go where he was wanted: that is, if not the philosophers in the academy, his larger reading public.

Because most of Russell's non-technical works are written on topics of interest to a general public, Bertrand Russell is apt to be a name most everyone has heard of, even if they have never ventured into philosophy or mathematics. Furthermore, it is as the public intellectual that Russell's writings and notoriety on the subject of religion and such subjects

9. Crawshaw-Williams, *Russell*, 25. Much of Crawshaw-Williams's basic point, as applied to Russell's views on religion, will be in evidence in our second chapter.

10. Stewart Candlish aptly describes Russell's communicative ability as no less than "Writing with a literary style of unsurpassed crispness . . ." Candlish, *Russell-Bradley Dispute*, 2. George Santayana, a friend and sometimes adversary of Russell, wrote of Russell that "He has written abundantly and, where the subject permits, with a singular lucidity, candour, and charm." Santayana, *Winds*, 111.

11. Russell's second son, Conrad, however, upon the death of his older half-brother John in 1987 took his seat in the House of Lords and was quite active in that body for some years.

was established, even though Russell's second book, written on Leibniz in 1900, evidences acute criticism of the arguments for the existence of God as found in Leibniz's work. Only professionals and specialists usually read such a work as this, however. As in our day, the general public is largely not acquainted, at least directly, with the professional work of academics or scholars; however, if an academic veers toward the public sector with a subject of interest sometimes the public notices. Russell's writings and habits were such. The point is not so much that Russell was adept at simplifying complex ideas—though he did do that with his books *The A B C of Atoms* and *The A B C of Relativity*, published in 1923 and 1925, respectively. Russell was simply capable of provoking attention by a no-nonsense way of putting things and with little fear of or inhibition about offending. In other words, Russell was serious in what he said, or for that matter critically minded, and therefore did not just talk or write for a pastime or even money—though on his own admission, this was often necessary—but for feeling he had something plausible and pertinent even if not profound to say. Coupling such tendencies with an extraordinarily gifted way of wording things, Russell never needed to beg for readers and audiences.

The noticeable indifference of Russell toward conventional opinion was impressive to many. His daughter Kate remarks how Russell's third wife, Patricia Spence, in the beginning of her relationship with Russell, "must have been flattered by the stop-at-nothing passion of a famous man she greatly admired. (Like my mother before her.)"[12] To others of course such behavior could be counted repulsive. Thus, Russell could offend sensibilities almost as easily as he could inspire courage. G. E. Moore, as one example of the former, certainly took offense at some incidents of Russell's life, with Moore appearing to think of Russell as having few moral scruples, for Russell seemed to ignore and repudiate convention in ways that he lived and in some things that he wrote. In fairness to Russell, he could hardly compete in any comparison with Moore, who was not infrequently revered as something of a philosophical saint and described as possessing purity of soul. Russell was never described this way, with the exception of sometimes suffering description as a "secular saint," a reference to his reasonableness and not his moral sagacity, however. Russell was striving for solutions, not sainthood, and cared little for reverence bought at the cost of intellect. For example, when Russell was

12. Tait, *My Father*, 158.

asked in 1965 what he thought about Mahatmas Gandhi's views of sex, his reply was tart: "superstitious and harmful."[13]

Nevertheless, in an attempt to get at ultimate motivations of her father Russell, Tait suggests that if the man had lived in a more believing age, he would have been a saint.[14] It is certainly true that Russell possessed a spiritual appetite, though often obscured because he most often disciplined any such appetite with a regimen virtually suffocating any such desire. Furthermore, the possibility of a religious and saintly Russell in a believing age must also contend with the rebel or confrontational streak in Russell. Admittedly, Russell could on occasion present himself in an opposite manner and various comments may seem to insinuate an aversion to confrontation and conflict. As one example, in speaking of the difficulty of choosing between philosophy and politics as a career after his student days in Cambridge, and with the familial pressure exerted upon him to take the road of politics, he wrote, "This was my first experience of conflict, and I found it painful. I have since had so much conflict that many people have supposed that I must like it. I should, however, have preferred to live at peace with everybody. But over and over again profound convictions have forced me into disagreements, even when I least desired them."[15]

However, Russell did not have peace because he did not run from the public controversies that sometimes followed him. Miles Malleson (who married Lady Constance in 1915), while contending of Russell that "he's been wrong a great many times," added that "The only thing I'd say in defence of that is that he's never hesitated to say what he thought without wondering whether it was going to get him into prison. Whereas all the other great men it's been my privilege to brush up against in my

---

13. Russell, "Gandhian Way," 34. In a piece written by Russell in Fall, 1952, he justifies such an answer, contending that "You have to ask yourself a question here that is of fundamental importance: which is better for mankind, a saint or an intelligent man?—assuming them to be incompatible. I don't think they are incompatible, but if you had to choose between a silly saint and an intelligent man who was not particularly wicked but not particularly saintly either, which is likely to do more good for the community? For my part, I don't think that the saintly type is the one that is most useful." Russell, "Medieval Mind of Gandhi," 89.

14. "He was by temperament a profoundly religious man, the sort of passionate moralist who would have been a saint in a more believing age." Tait, *My Father*, 184; "He should have been a saint; he had the passion, the intemperate longing for truth and justice, the yearning for a world of peace and love. Perhaps he was a saint, even without the faith." Tait, *My Father*, 189.

15. Russell, "Adaptation: An Autobiographical Epitome," 5.

life on the stage and in writing plays—people like Shaw and Wells—they *always* wondered whether they were saying the popular thing."[16] However, though Russell makes the claim that his audiences had frequently but falsely assumed he preferred controversy since it had been so much a part of his life, such a contention—a not an uncommon overstatement by Russell—obscures the component of fearlessness often prompting Russell into controversy. His statement minimizes the extent, put forward by Tait, that Russell not infrequently delighted in mischievous antics.[17] All in all, Russell hardly seemed the spiritual supplicant. Furthermore, he rather seemed to prefer something of the opposite trait in others and conveys this idea rather pointedly when he wrote "I do like people to be willing to shoot Niagara."[18] A certain kind of reckless vitality seemed to appeal to Russell and must account in some part for his eventual negative feelings toward his first wife Alys, who seemed to him almost totally lacking in such a quality.[19] Russell, as Tait correctly suggest, desired the robustness of a personality he apparently seldom encountered among otherwise religious people.

With the trait of fearlessness of course went the propensity of Russell to tread on subjects which others might have avoided or spoken less stridently about. As an example, Russell seemed to relish few things as much as undermining the presumed lofty status of the religious. He particularly seemed to enjoy a habit of less than the habitual deference

16. Crawshaw-Williams, *Russell*, 152.

17. "My father was a notably irreverent and mischievous man, not above using his children to provoke people in ways that would not be quite acceptable from conventional adults. Later, when we traveled more by car, he suggested that we might lean out of the windows when we passed other cars and shout out: 'Your grandfather was a monkey!' This was to convince them of the correctness of Darwin's theory of evolution, but usually they could not hear clearly enough to get the message." Tait, *My Father*, 4. Later, in describing some of the exterior changes in her father through the years, she nonetheless contends that he was "always ready to outrage conventional sensibilities" (72). Crawshaw-Williams, however, contends that "Although Russell held many anti-establishment views, this was in his case due much more than usual in a reformer to the clarity of his thinking: he usually rebelled rather because he saw that the *status quo* was indefensible than simply because he felt rebellious. He was not therefore the type of reformer (like D. H. Lawrence and some educationalists) who are right for the wrong reasons—because the *status quo* is so horrible that anything different could not help being an improvement." Crawshaw-Williams, *Russell*, 91.

18. Russell to Ottoline Morrell, October 1, 1915, quoted in Monk, *Russell*, 1:392.

19. Writing to Ottoline, he complains that "I wish I could explain to you what I feel about spiritual companionship. Most people, even when I am very fond of them, remain external to me. Alys, even when I was most in love with her, remained outside my inner life." Russell to Ottoline, June 24, 1914, in Clark, *Life*, 238.

extended to members of the clergy by non-clergy. As recounted by Tait, he forthrightly stated on introduction to a member of the clergy, that he was an atheist or agnostic when he could have simply said that he was the adherent of no religious creed. Indicative of Russell's caustic manner in such situations, he was not averse to pointing out the ineptitude or mistakenness of clergy, even those placed rather highly. He said for example, "The Pope, while infallible, has made some grievous errors."[20] Russell simply permitted few things to miss his pen, and armed with an argument, he would knock virtually anything down that obstructed what he desired to demonstrate. Russell's toleration of the risk of trouble from his words as well as from his actions seemed to feed an appetite indifferent to controversy. I am not suggesting that Russell was far from a somber saint in terms of the adjective or noun, nor that he was more like a frolicking hedonist. I am suggesting, however, that because he presumes and argues that there are few fixed things in the world, his allegiances are ultimately few. However, the strength of Russell's allegiances, to reason for example, may function so as to be capable of undermining many if not most of the allegiances of others not as dutiful to reason as Russell required. This is to say that Russell was prone to critique a motivation to do or not do something if the reason is deemed one of fear. Religion, of course, on the common Russellian analysis provided such an example: "Religion is based, I think, primarily and mainly upon fear. It is partly the terror of the unknown and partly, as I have said, the wish to feel that you have a kind of elder brother who will stand by you in all your troubles and disputes. Fear is the basis of the whole thing—fear of the mysterious, fear of defeat, fear of death. Fear is the parent of cruelty, and therefore it is no wonder if cruelty and religion have gone hand in hand. It is because fear is at the basis of those two things."[21]

One result of a desired life lived largely without fear was that often Russell found himself able to do and live much as he wished. To a

---

20. Eisler, *Quotable*, 145.

21. Russell, *Why*, 22. While the reader may feel that Russell is attacking a dated notion of sin or wrongdoing, Russell offers the following example to make his point that many persons who consciously believe they have thrown off such morbidness, and in fact traditional morals too, still in fact retain them in their subconscious: "I wish it were possible to institute a statistical enquiry, among men who believe themselves emancipated from such nursery tales, as to whether they would be as ready to commit adultery during a thunderstorm as at any other time. I believe that ninety percent of them, in their heart of hearts, would think that if they did so they would be struck by lightning." Russell, *Marriage and Morals*, 274–75.

substantial degree he found happiness in so doing. Much of this felicity derived from having abandoned beliefs he thought no longer defendable, including religious beliefs. Not infrequently, therefore, and unsurprisingly, his consequent persona and demeanor came across as one possessing an unusual degree of happiness to some observers. In a letter of 1931, Russell's publisher W. W. Norton writes to Russell, "You have always seemed to me to be about the happiest person I have ever known."[22] However, when Norton goes on to ask what influences have made for that happiness and suggests that perhaps it is Russell's insistence upon the scientific outlook, Russell concedes something of the point, but also contends that "An appreciation of the ends of life is something that must be superadded to science if it is to bring happiness."[23] There might be some ground or basis for religion.

B. RUSSELL AS SUSPICIOUSLY RELIGIOUS

That Russell did desire something that proved elusive is apparent on even a cursory look at his life and writings. Indeed, some readers of Russell have found within his writings indications that, as Copleston observed, "Sometimes indeed, in spite of all philosophical differences, Russell writes more like an existentialist than a 'rationalist.'"[24] With a larger picture of Russell on the subject of religion, we see the philosopher straining and at times even conceding some legitimacy to the religious appetite, which he has, for the most part, derided and mocked in his writings as a whole. On rare occasions both sentiments occur in the same work. However, aside from the notably few essays he wrote mainly in the initial decades of the twentieth century, there are admittedly scant sympathetic appraisals of religion to be found in his later writings. Nonetheless, there are occasional and brief digressions to the subject that prove resourceful in trying to systematize a subject that Russell never systematized.

---

22. W. W. Norton to Russell, January 14, 1931, Box no. 1.26, Bertrand Russell Archives, McMaster University Library.

23. Russell to W. W. Norton, January 27, 1931, Russell, *1914–1944*, 301–2.

24. Copleston, review of *Russell, 1872–1914*, 314–15. Alan Wood, in his biography of Russell, written a decade before Russell's death, and to some degree written under Russell's watch, writes concerning Russell's famous essay, "A Free Man's Worship," that despite the blatant atheism of the piece, "the reader will discover, among other things, that some of Russell's precepts read like paraphrases of texts from the New Testament." Wood, *Bertrand Russell*, 75–76.

Russell's desire to find something firm in the world to buttress oneself from the world persisted. However, virtually nothing—to include in time his revered mathematics in platonic form—survived hard scrutiny. That is, Russell leaned upon presumed immovable fixtures long enough to see them move, while prior hopes gave way to a reality befriending no able candidates. Closing the distance to "the ends of life" referenced in the previous noted letter to Norton escaped him.

As indicated, Russell's quest for a religion was most exercised in the first two decades of the twentieth century. Within this effort, however, Russell would rebuke a whole coterie of thinkers for gross neglect of Russell's insistence on an unbiased search for truth. This requirement Russell first imposed upon himself as an adolescent, and such a stricture never left him. Later, in an undergraduate talk he gave in the form of an address to The Apostles in 1897, entitled "Seems Madame, Nay It Is," Russell charged that most philosophers, religionists, romantics, and the like, let the desired result of their inquiry intrude upon the result found. The popularity of the Bergsonians of the second decade of the twentieth century, as one pernicious example, accordingly committed such an error, and Russell accordingly and relentlessly made such a charge against them. Russell's frequent criticisms of a multitude of these guilty thinkers can scarcely be overstated in understanding a primary reason why Russell could not embrace religious belief. That is, many faint-hearted thinkers, for fear of finding a true but devastatingly unhappy answer to their religious inquiry, neglected a proper approach to the question in their haste to arrive at the preferred answer. This is precisely why Russell often appears and frequently is so scathing toward such persons.

Russell attempted to see the world as it was; he was not after safety at all costs, but rather the truth of the matter or problem under consideration. While he searched for a way of incorporating religion into a modern conception of the world, Russell resented those who claimed to have found what eluded him, in great part because their journey evidenced bias in what they claimed to find. Russell would have none of it—at least most of the time.

Religion was not just another subject to Russell. Granted, on the one hand Russell was confrontational toward religion on most occasions. On the other hand, though on fewer occasions, but with noticeable tenacity, he sought for a rightful place for it—something that many secular-orientated and generally like-minded associates of Russell seemed very rarely to desire. In other words, Russell is noticeably quite unlike the typical secular critic of religion. Though Russell could often be deemed too dismissive toward religion, he sometimes could and would pause with lament over how scientific thinking eroded the religious fabric of a prior age. Thus, Russell is a critic on two fronts: he criticizes those who evoke religion with a faulty methodology benefitting the desired destination, but also secular-oriented people indifferent toward religion. Russell was unlike either, most of the time. On the one hand, he could be a most bellicose and virtually unrelenting critic of religion, while on the other hand and very differently, he spent some time considering how a proper religion could lift humanity out of a barbarism to which religion had often contributed.

Russell's religious journey, which began in adolescence, soon toppled the framework of religious beliefs held by his relatives at Pembroke Lodge. Indeed, much of Russell's adult position on religion was already growing in his private writings during these early years. Russell's initial doubts and then disbelief provoked him for a time afterward into regret for having lost those things that many around him still possessed. However, his grief was lessened by the time he went to Cambridge at eighteen years of age. Later in life and in his writings, he would contend, not always accurately, that the initial pain of such disassociation from religious belief was only temporal. Such a contention is rather typical of Russell's usual eagerness to disassociate happiness and contentment from religion. Moreover, his attempt to retain something religious would not conclude as early as he would often insinuate, for he would later try his hand at mysticism of various sorts. His hope was for a religion permitting him to be religious without religious belief, for religious belief, he would always contend, could not be vindicated. The resulting unbelief is why Russell could on occasion make the boast that his views on religion were established when he was sixteen years of age—a statement not entirely untrue. However, a remark as implicating about a subject as this, lent credibility to the perception that for Russell religion could not bear up under rational scrutiny. Russell himself would often indicate as much. That is, in his view, the blatant errors and crimes of religion in human history were open for all to see and judge accordingly. Russell did just that, but he also had desire for a religion. In part, the evidence of this is Russell's own acknowledgment that he was not among the happy secularists that he often perceived many of his associates to be—and that they sometimes mistakenly took Russell to be.

When he felt compelled to accept Wittgenstein's verdict about mathematics as tautologies, the admission approached another religious loss for Russell and prompted from him the admission that his journey with mathematics had undergone exasperating episodes culminating in the "long retreat from Pythagoras." By way of comparison, Russell's assessment of his rejection and consequent retreat from any religious belief, he generally presented as positive and any initial pain as only temporary.[25] Most interesting for finer comparison is the religious satisfaction he had derived from the earlier view of mathematics. Such an admission goes part of the way in revealing that Russell had sought something of a surrogate religion in mathematics. Ultimately, what Russell was searching for in each case, both in religion and mathematics, he found in neither.

While Russell's general public presumed this public figure was uncompromisingly negative in his judgements on religion, a variety of circumstances, both inside and outside his life, provoked Russell to return to the subject of religion, though most often treated negatively. From time to time, in some of his books and essays and in not a few of his letters, however, it is abundantly clear that he has not entirely given up on the subject. It may be, and as earlier asserted, that the strictures Russell placed on an acceptable religion whether intended or not, are too severe and choking to permit one. Partly in consequence, his search is a search and never a seizure. At the same time, Russell concedes some legitimacy and even provides some accolades, however miniscule, to some things religious, alongside his diatribes against religion. Compliments are certainly comparatively few in comparison to the manifest sins alleged by Russell as the outcome of the religious instinct. However, to understand the imbalance, one must discern that the negative image of things religious is scarcely ever far from Russell's pen or from his words. At full throttle, therefore, Russell's writing on religion can appear to leave no room for anything positive concerning this subject.

Studying Russell's writings on religion might suggest that Russell's penchant for offense against religion is possibly rooted in his own predicaments in life, such that much of his posture toward religion is formed out of grievances conceivably born from the tragedies of his

---

25. Russell's judgment on the effect of his lost religious beliefs varies. As one example, in a March 8, 1959 interview with John Freeman on BBC television, after Freeman asked if Russell had been a skeptic since childhood, Russell responded, "Oh, I wasn't a sceptic [sic] when I was very young, no. I was very deeply religious and lost my conventional beliefs slowly and painfully." "Russell Reflects," 503.

youth, namely, the early deaths of both parents and a sister. However, to my knowledge, there is no place in Russell's work, where, when calling attention to the ills and calamities of human existence—of which Russell affirms many—he offers up his own misfortunes as fuel to add fire to his critique of religious beliefs.[26] In this respect, Russell seems to permit himself no self-pity, even as he does insinuate judgment on the maker of the world who could, according to Russell, only be a fiend by the callous nature of his handiwork and superintendence of the world.

Possibly his loss of religious belief prompted a kind of anger toward people retaining the religious beliefs he had presumed to have seen through. His animus toward believers whose company he otherwise enjoyed, most notably perhaps Lady Ottoline Morrell, might be such a case. Russell's chagrin at the unbending believer is a posture often witnessed in following his statements of loves and hates and annoyances. Though Russell is at times drawn to the mystical side of religion, partly through the influence of Ottoline, at the same time Russell never goes back to consider the metaphysical contentions of religious belief as viable as a result of any such influence. To a significant degree adolescent musings for the most part seem to have settled the matter. On various theological points Russell's adolescent reading of his godfather John Stuart Mill finalized the issue. Thus, while consideration of reason had felled Russell's earlier religious beliefs, Russell seems to reason that believers still believing incredulously, had simply refused to submit to reason, as he had dutifully done.

Probing of Russell on the complexities of his positions on religion reveals that he held something of two conflicting views of the world and appears to have oscillated between them, though hardly as an individual unable to make up his mind. Nor is it the case that the move between them can be counted in terms of years of even a decade or decades of his life. Rather, on many occasions he holds both views on the same day. One view we might call the tragic view of life, and the other, the utopian view of the world. Among some audiences and among some friends he exhibited one more than the other. In his affiliation with the Bloomsbury

---

26. One significant incident stands out, however, in which Russell's wrath toward dubious theological beliefs was evident. In a letter of February 17, 1929, to Ottoline, he wrote: "'On Tuesday, the critical day, I had come to London to debate the Xtian religion against Bishop Gore,' he says. 'I was told that suffering is sent as a purification from sin. Poor little John never sinned in his life. I wanted to spit in their faces—they were so cold & abstract, with a sadistic pleasure in the tortures their God inflicts.'" Quoted in Clark, *Life*, 413.

literary group, for example, he was uppermost the rationalist, and the people in the group tended predominantly to see him as such and stood in awe of him for brandishing a deadly reason against murkiness. Here was a man with the genius to fix the world and so bold as to castigate a world indifferent to any such real possibility. This made of Russell something of a colossal intellect, one whose path an adversary did not cross for fear of the capacity of Russell's razor-like reason to wound and incapacitate the less fit. Consequently, most of that prestigious Bloomsbury group both revered and feared Russell. As the exemplary rationalist, he exuded optimism, because reason lays conundrums bare and prompts the suggestion and surmise that reason having cleared the air, now one can see. One need not delay to act because the previous clouds have been cleared away and no excuse for inaction or indecisiveness remains. Russell's powers as an analyst, so honed by a philosophical method and program he employed after abandoning Hegelian philosophy, prompted the stalwart reason living in him to cut down and through any unworthy position. This kind of feat could result in a perhaps excessive exuberance and thus was the source of J. M. Keynes criticism that Russell seemed to hold two incompatibles: "He held that in fact human affairs were carried on after a most irrational fashion, but that the remedy was quite simple and easy, since all we had to do was to carry them on rationally."[27] Katherine Tait makes a similar complaint about Russell when she writes, in the aftermath of her own religious conversion in adulthood, "I found no message in his books but failure and despair (for me): men *can* be . . . men *should* be . . . men rightly brought up *will* be . . . the world *might* be . . . . But what about *is*? The world was not what he hoped it might be, and neither was I, nor could I believe that men would ever become the intelligent paragons of his imagination."[28]

The other side of Russell—Russell's tragic view of life—stood prompted in part by another kind of reflection on the world he lived in, to include his own life. Both the state of his life and the actual state of the world could sometimes provoke doubt against the optimism that he could on occasion evidence, chiefly as the aforementioned rationalist. More importantly, this tragic view of life was often Russell's default position, in part because what he wanted in his own life on most occasions seemed mocked by life itself. From this tragic view of life, therefore, often

---

27. Keynes, *Collected Writings*, 10:449.
28. Tait, *My Father*, 188.

came his barbs of pessimism. Russell wanted desperately to see the world as it was, but he also desperately wanted to find something stable and enduring. For the majority of his life this kind of goal eluded Russell and he complained at times loudly about it. What he complained against or about in its absence were varied culprits: sometimes God, sometimes Man as exalted by men, sometimes spiritless and blind matter—often unthinking people preparing unknowingly for certain death because they refused to think. One must keep both the rational optimist and the tragedian sides of Russell in view when reading Russell.

If Russell intended in his popular works on religion to divest religion of any remaining and presumed cogencies, he nevertheless wanted in a smaller voice to treat religion of the helpful kind with some rightful and deserved respect. However, despite Russell's interest in the positive possibilities for religion, he simply could not bear his own critique and suspicions of religious belief. In other words, at times it appears as though Russell is straining for something that he knows in the last analysis he cannot have. At the same time, he would nevertheless on occasion and in some periods of his life be drawn to try the impossible again.

C. THE ROLE OF EPISTEMOLOGY IN RUSSELL'S RELIGIOUS VIEWS

A chief part of Russell's chagrin with religious belief and traditional religious people was simply that in his mind, they lacked adequate grounds for the edifices of belief they had constructed or followed. At the same time, however, Russell contended that the appetite for something religious need not die with admission of discredited religious beliefs, a point to which disinterested secularists might give notice. By contrast, most religious people naively assumed the religious appetite sufficiently strong to justify the inference that there must be somewhere or something to provide satisfaction for such a strong or even voracious appetite. In his reply to Edgar Brightman in 1944, Russell offers an argument from analogy, however, to indicate that such logic often found among religious people is fallacious. Russell counters Brightman by comparing the thirst for God to being thirsty in a desert and faults the presumption of wrongly assuming that water or God will be found simply because there is a thirst for water or God. For Russell, this presumed something of a cozy and compliant reality fitted to meet our every need. For Russell, such a surmise was too obviously false.

At the same time, Russell admits and acknowledges aspirations for things that are not "real," in that human values or spiritual desires can presume no fulfillment or vindication from the sciences nor metaphysics. Having to acknowledge this incongruence, I think, provoked resentment in Russell. Water does quench and in so doing satisfies the prior thirst. By contrast, human values deemed absent in larger reality reflect a discrepancy between the world as it is and how we should wish it to be. That is, however clever his answer—"You did not provide us with sufficient evidence for your existence"—was to an interviewer's question about what Russell might say to God in the afterlife, it also possibly reflects Russell's dismay and disappointment, not to say anger, over the fact that there is no guarantee of finding water to satiate thirst or a spiritual food and reality to satiate religious appetites. That is, why would the Supplier make himself or the water so difficult to find? Russell clearly thinks the liability in this equation lies with God. When asked after his 1939 lecture at Ann Arbor about the possibility of God being beyond the comprehension of the human mind, Russell replies, "My answer to that would be that so far as it is true, God becomes quite irrelevant to our thinking, and those who say that God is beyond comprehension of the human mind profess to know a great deal about God."[29] Noteworthy in this sentence is Russell's charge that in such a circumstance we can return the favor to God. That is, we reciprocate and affirm God's indifference to ourselves by our lack of knowledge of God that God could have clearly provided, but did not, according to Russell.

Russell resented an absent God, while much of his battle with religious belief issues from the quagmire of questions of epistemology in his philosophy. That is, as orientated as Russell is toward the metaphysical question of what is real, he is even more driven by epistemological desires. In 1911, in a letter to his close confidant Lady Ottoline Morrell he wrote, "It was largely the hope of getting a religion out of philosophy that led me to take it up. . . . When I adopted Moore's view, the last hope of getting any creed out of philosophy vanished. This of course was a great disappointment, and helped to turn me back to mathematics. Since

---

29. Russell, "Evidence and Nature of God," *CP* 10:264.

then I have only hoped that philosophy could show that we do know something; and to find out whether it is so has been my main business."[30]

Russell wants a satisfactory argument for how we know what we claim to know—in this he resembles the chief philosophers of early modernity, each of them, from Descartes to Kant, fixed on the epistemological questions accentuated by skeptics of the Renaissance and the presumed knowledge of the Scientific Revolution. One might even say there is epistemological obsession over this question of knowledge and the associated family of questions for many modern philosophers, Russell included. Indeed, the noticeable changes one finds in Russell's seemingly ever-changing philosophy are by and large changes to his epistemological position on human knowledge. Unlike Whitehead, whose later interests are dominated by metaphysical problems, Russell continues working underneath, wanting to find something that will provide surety for our claims to knowledge.

The penchant for epistemology fits with Russell's voracious appetite for grounding mathematics, seen early on in Russell's youthful inquiry to his elder brother Frank over the desired proof of the axioms of geometry. Much later, too, his attempt to improve upon the thesis that mathematics was derivative and dependent upon logical notions was a herculean effort to cement the basis of knowledge securely. The often quoted line from Russell about his "retreat from Pythagoras," however, has not been always seen for all that this shift produced, or failed to produce. That is, in witnessing his desire for certainty collapse, he will speak on occasion in a self-chastising manner of a "misspent youth" chasing certainty. In effect such remarks place Russell at the end of his philosophical journey close to where he had begun. That is, little of what he hoped to prove as sure or certain had succeeded, for Russell's life of searching largely

---

30. Russell to Ottoline, September 28, 1911. Document no. 199, Box no. 2.55, Bertrand Russell Archives, McMaster University Library/Ottoline Morrell Collection, Box 19, Folder 5, Harry Ransom Center, University of Texas, Austin.

Russell's friend Rupert Crawshaw-Williams, contends that "Russell, as a philosopher (rather than a pure logician), was primarily a skeptical epistemologist; that is, a man whose intellectual concern was to investigate the ways in which we attain knowledge and to search out, in order to eliminate, any false notions about how much we know. As he makes clear in his *Autobiography*, he had started out as a child with a passionate desire to find objective (and logical) certainty in our knowledge of the empirical world, but had been gradually forced to accept that this certainty was unattainable. Having thus been disappointed, he naturally wanted to make sure that no one else should be bamboozled by traditional ideas, as he had been, into assuming that knowledge was reliable when it was nothing of the sort." Crawshaw-Williams, *Russell*, 86.

proved disappointing. Scholars commonly point to Russell's list of "What I have lived for" in his *Autobiography*, while drawing comparatively little attention to his own admission of disappointment in achievement. I suspect this is because one does not like to hear a great man lament even when he does. Though his hopes for philosophy had disappointed the great man, Russell was nonetheless unflinching in maintaining the traditional reason for philosophy. That reason was to get to the root of things; this most accounts for his criticism of the later Wittgenstein and his disciples. He vehemently writes in his *My Philosophical Development*, "The later Wittgenstein, on the contrary, seems to have grown tired of serious thinking and to have invented a doctrine which would make such an activity unnecessary."[31] To Russell they have given up even the pretense of doing philosophy.

Moreover, when Russell speaks in his *Autobiography* of a life spent in the "vain search for God," he is speaking from the perspective of the traditional and modern epistemologist chasing for bedrock certainty and not as a Pascalian supplicant searching for the "God of Abraham, Isaac and Jacob." However, and again, despite Russell's candid admission of philosophical disappointments, he still ardently believes the goal of real knowledge is worthy of the human chase, even though he has closed in on it very little. Having identified the longing for love as his first and lifelong passion, he wrote in his prologue, "[W]ith equal passion I have sought knowledge. I have wished to understand the hearts of men. I have wished to know why the stars shine. And I too have tried to apprehend the Pythagorean power by which number holds sway above the flux. A little of this, but not much, I have achieved."[32]

The continuing effort to reach the things not attained, though striven for over a very long lifetime, is thus undaunted. Moreover, his effort is not relinquished nor is any apology necessary or needed for continuing and applauding the pursuit. Such a position indicates Russell's distance from Lessing's famous contention that it is not possession of the truth that he prizes but instead the pursuit of truth. Russell will persist in the search, but not for the reason Lessing modeled.[33] Even less so could Russell affirm Lessing's contentment at falling short of the prize of pure truth, while humbly relegating such only to God. Russell, by contrast,

---

31. Russell, *My Philosophical Development*, 161.

32. Russell, *1872–1914*, 3–4.

33. Russell's notion of the aim of philosophy does, however, clearly have some affinities to Lessing's conception, but not in the aforementioned aspect.

sought the truth that God as omniscient alone possessed. This truth was the prize that Russell ardently sought, and he searched doggedly to find a way to get there; in that effort, his failures are largely epistemological failures. As earlier suggested, having to discipline emotions straining for warranted belief because they lacked the elusive epistemological bedrock may have provoked a resentment, indeed anger, over the elusive and absent justification. Because the desire for warranted belief was unmet, it was as though an absent God was faulted for not having provided an available justification for things unseen that humans yearned to find. If there is a God, this being owes his ruminating creatures an explanation. While Russell wrote, "Every man would like to be God, if it were possible; some few find it difficult to admit the impossibility,"[34] he did not desire to be God, though he did desire to know the mind of God, in terms of the knowledge possessed by God alone.

Feeling himself the dutiful though unrewarded seeker of truth, Russell exhibits in himself an element of the tragic along with some rage. He had served to some degree an unknown god and had stoically persisted in what largely amounted to a vain search. This kind of disappointed and unrewarded courage could provoke Russell to a kind of shrillness that he perhaps felt was something of a rejoinder to those who proclaimed finding metaphysical bedrock from positions Russell regarded as permitted only by dubious epistemological practice. In effect, they had no right for their belief, and yet, he too had been a seeker, but without their happy though tainted result. He perceived that most inquirers lacked the humility that Russell thought a prerequisite of intellectual inquiry. Indeed, this is why, for all of Russell's own voracious epistemological desires, he nevertheless sought to keep epistemology in a humble rather than elevated position.

> I reverse the process which has been common in philosophy since Kant. It has been common among philosophers to begin with how we know and proceed afterwards to what we know. I think this is a mistake, because knowing how we know is one small department of knowing what we know. I think it a mistake for another reason: it tends to give to knowing a cosmic importance which it by no means deserves, and thus prepares the philosophical student for the belief that mind has some kind of supremacy over the non-mental universe, or even that the non-mental universe is nothing but a nightmare dreamt by mind in

---

34. Russell, *Basic Writings*, 15.

its un-philosophical moments. This point of view is completely remote from my imaginative picture of the cosmos.[35]

This passage connotes Russell's frustration with the human inquirer's inability to set himself aside in his search for a truthful picture of the world. Russell's desire is to produce a firm account of reality and thus one divested of the biases evident in a human effort to paint a metaphysical picture congenial to human vanities. Russell would have none of that. One contention in this book is that while most of Russell's work on the topic of religion was in large part motivated by his desire to move philosophy and indeed most all things toward a scientific method of sorts, he was routinely too dismissive, and too hostile, toward the subject of religion to do the matter justice. For example, he was incensed when the physicists James Jeans and Arthur Eddington presumed to argue for their religion from science, or at least to deem it commensurate with the findings of science. Russell seemed to believe the falsities of religious belief sufficiently established that a contention for the truth of religious belief were particularly galling to him.[36] Russell could hardly take seriously modern religious apologists. He himself dabbled in the effort to find something that would make life more tolerable, but he never gave himself wholly to any candidate. At the same time, Russell on occasion conceded that the verdicts of reason against religious belief did not wholly settle the question of religion. However, such an admission granted no license or reprieve to defenders of religion presuming to give credence to religious truth by dubious means. In his criticism of this kind of effort, Russell is a thoroughgoing modernist, because he took it to be the case that the sovereignty of reason, though banished for a time or stalled occasionally, could and would always disrobe any pretenders to the throne except itself. Truth, as indicated earlier, was for Russell a neutralizing medium and therefore a ruthless taskmaster. However, throughout his long life, Russell himself could succumb to various temptresses rivaling rational truth as he tried to be allegiant to reason, but found it difficult to do so continuously. Russell, like the weakened and tempted prisoner Boethius, could permit the invitations of diversions from elsewhere to occupy him—only to be rebuked by the rational philosopher on return.

---

35. Russell, *My Philosophical Development*, 12.

36. Russell frequently remarks to Ottoline (and others) that no one in the academy at Cambridge believed orthodox theology any longer.

D. THE ROLE OF METAPHYSICS IN RUSSELL'S RELIGIOUS VIEWS

Despite Russell's aversion to Kant, frequently voiced in his writing and lecturing,[37] it is notable that somewhat like Kant, Russell extends his thoughts onto topics which each deems outside the province of philosophy proper.[38] However, most uncongenial to Russell about Kant and other philosophers like him, is the illicit conveyance of the importance of the human mind and the human, often against the backdrop of the indifferent and silent cosmos, that elevates the importance of humans for such thinkers. In this vein of critique of Kant and other like offenders, Russell attacks such presumptions of human importance as an unscientific vestige lingering in the minds of thinkers presuming to inhabit modernity. Part of the reason that Russell is so insistent that philosophy attempt to emulate the neutrality of science and scientific method is to overcome such a tendency. In maintaining this perspective Russell wants to keep the human in his humble place, whereas offending thinkers are prepared to skew reality by their illicit inferences as it concerns the human position in reality. Thus they fabricate a host of false and grandiose cosmological conceptions of the human. Russell will have none of this—at least most of the time. In Russell's contrasting posture, he is repulsed by any metaphysic providing false aid to human self-conception, in great part because such a view cannot be epistemologically vindicated or justified. Furthermore, any presumed union of the world of the cosmos and the human world is for Russell evidence of a vainly presumptuous human will. The divide between the human world and the cosmos is simply much of the time too grievous for the human to bear and from fear and cowardice the fearful human resorts to unjustified religious or similar

---

37. In his lecture at Ann Arbor Russell affirms his dislike of Kant: "You remember that Kant, who is conventionally considered the greatest of philosophers—but whom I have been guilty of calling in print a misfortune...." Russell, *CP* 10:262.

38. Speaking of the first months of his marriage to Alys, Russell records that "During this time my intellectual ambitions were taking shape. I resolved not to adopt a profession, but to devote myself to writing. I remember a cold, bright day in early spring when I walked by myself in the Tiergarten, and made projects of future work. I thought that I would write one series of books on the philosophy of the sciences from pure mathematics to physiology, and another series of books on social questions. I hoped that the two series might ultimately meet in a synthesis at once scientific and practical. My scheme was largely inspired by Hegelian ideas. Nevertheless, I have to some extent followed it in later years, as much at any rate as could be expected. The moment was an important and formative one as regards my purposes." Russell, *1872–1914*, 184–85.

hope, masquerading as knowledge. The truth about human life is simply for many so tragic as to beckon the soothing falsities of religion. Russell frequently seems to think such a religious response is evidence of a cowardice that cannot face the world as it is; preferred is an agnostic humanism refusing to succumb to defeat. Thus, Russell's opposite insistence was that the "constitution of the universe" took no account of humans and this fact must be admitted as the most humbling facet of human existence. Moreover, Ray Monk rightly noticed the lack of attention paid to Russell's insistence on needed rebuke for such wishes: "The emotional importance to Russell of picturing life as an unimportant speck in a vast, impersonal universe is little understood in the published work written on him, though he himself made innumerable efforts to convey it."[39]

Russell rarely tired of denouncing the presumption of a metaphysic which attributed cosmic importance to the human world and in one of his short stores, entitled "The Theologian's Nightmare," Russell lampoons this belief mercilessly.[40] In this story a confident theologian having recently endured death presents himself at the door of heaven for his presumed rightful reward by way of admission, only to find that the learned gatekeepers nevertheless know nothing of him or of his species, or for that matter anything about his previous locality in the enormity of space. This theologian grows increasingly impatient while waiting for researchers to establish what "man" is. One investigator finally returns—years later—though with very unwelcome news for his guest: "'I have,' he said, 'at last discovered the particular star concerning which inquiries have been made, but I am quite at a loss to imagine why it has aroused any special interest. It closely resembles a great many other stars in the same galaxy. It is of average size and temperature, and is surrounded by very much smaller bodies called 'planets.' After minute investigation, I discovered that some, at least, of these planets have parasites, and I think that this thing which has been making inquiries must be one of them.'"

Russell scoffs at the enraged theologian for his vain presumption. With added relish Russell formulates the pathetic confession of this shocked and abject theologian in an impotent speech indicating he had lived a mistaken life in the erroneous opinion that he had lived for the purposes of a Creator who cared for him. The disappointed candidate for heaven, for having shown this kind of outrageous impiety, is now

---

39. Monk, *Ghost*, 73.
40. Russell, *Collected Stories*, 260.

rewarded with an even bleaker future and sent to the "Other Place," to spend his eternity.

Russell could not embrace the theologian's metaphysical presumptions—though he could hardly drop the matter of religion. Hence, Russell extends significant effort toward some resolution in the conflict besetting the human finding himself in an alien world. So as to not be overwhelmed by this grave realization, Russell gave articulate expression to this desire in the early essays "A Free Man's Worship," "The Essence of Religion," and "Mysticism and Logic" and in a couple chapters of *Principles of Social Reconstruction*. During subsequent decades his virulence against things religious increases, and he never again wrote anything comparable to these early and notable essays on the subject of religion. Furthermore, one might plausibly contend that these early pieces are simply Russell pushing his limits in an effort to configure an appropriate religious response to a world lacking any consoling religious metaphysic. One might add, however, that a later work, Russell's *The Conquest of Happiness*, written in 1930, does share in some of the same themes as th earlier essays, but it also provides some warnings against religious motivations, warnings that in the other and earlier works are, by comparison, more muted.

The Conquest of Happiness begins to signal what Russell will do in subsequent years and decades: he will tend to castigate things religious with more intensity and frequency. Nevertheless, despite his lessening keenness for finding something religious to enable living in the world— the search so evident in earlier essays—the quest did not die in Russell. Moreover, something akin to religious experience continued to resonate with Russell, for he sometimes speaks of it as having provided some of his most exalted states of life and being. In the prologue of his *Autobiography*, quoted earlier, he states that " . . . in the union of love I have seen, in a mystic miniature, the prefiguring vision of the heaven that saints and poets have imagined."[41] The philosophers are conspicuously not mentioned.

Sometimes, as noted by John Maynard Keynes in a letter of 1905, Russell is deemed to be "fundamentally religious."[42] Russell, however, did not share the affirmation of Keynes that "We had the best of both worlds. We destroyed Xty& yet had its benefits."[43] Russell, to my knowledge,

41. Russell, *1872–1944*, 3.
42. Lubenow, *Apostles*, 406.
43. Lubenow, *Apostles*, 409.

never expressed a sentiment parallel to this in Keynes, though it is notable that when Gilbert Murray in correspondence with Russell vied for something of a return to Christendom during the worst days of World War II, Russell expressed some shared sympathy with Murray, though of course with caveats.

The two postures of Russell on religion, as friend but mainly foe, were never easy to hold together, as Russell tended to favor reproving religion. The dilemma is that the pride of Russell's humanism is constrained by a governing scientific view of the world—his view of the world—that does not permit the paltry human to stride about as if Lord of the Universe. Russell's lampooned theologian was guilty of such presumption, for the theologian arrogantly imagines that the human creature is the darling of the adoring Creator. Russell cannot affirm either of these conceptions in their entirety. He must therefore side with the humanist, even if begrudgingly.

In J. M. Keynes's earlier referenced surmise that Russell's social philosophy had two incompatibles, Russell expresses something of an oscillating judgment about his absentee god. That is, the correctives to the problems of the world should be no problem for the maker of the world; the fact, however, that there are so many manifest and horrifying problems in the world is indication that this god is abysmally indifferent to the plight of the world and the people within it. Epistemologically, as Russell frequently contended, he cannot claim to know with any degree of certainty that no god exists, though often in the same breath he would contend with taunting statement that there is nevertheless not the least reason to think God exists. To presume that God exists, given the predicaments in the world with an absentee god doing nothing about them, is simply too outrageous to believe. Russell's barbs, therefore, portray such a god as an indifferent and implacable foe of humans, and indeed, a being more like the traditional celestial opponents of God than a righteous God. Thus, in 1911, and just as he had begun to experience happiness with Lady Ottoline, he is told he might have cancer in his mouth, and reports that he proceeded to "congratulate the deity on having got me after all just as happiness seemed in sight."[44] Similarly, he states in his lecture at Ann Arbor in 1939, "I should say in conclusion that it is possible that there may be an omnipotent God. He would have had to create

---

44. Russell, *1872–1914*, 336.

evil without any temptation for creating evil. He must be infinitely weak, an absolute fiend."[45]

However, if the world can be judged as negatively so as to impugn any purported Maker of that world because of its miseries and problems, why have the vast human populations of the earth maintained belief in God? Russell suggests that ignorance goes a long way by way of answering this question, though just as powerful is his stipulation that fear also provokes belief. Cobbling such motivations together may indicate for Russell why cowardice is ultimately the trigger for religious beliefs and religious lives. However, such conjecture explains little in Russell's own life and writing that evidences an interest in religion.

On the one hand, Russell takes umbrage against religious belief and believers because they have simply not played by the rules. That is, they are almost analogous to thieves who have taken what they have no justification to possess, and worst of all, they end up lauded for the beliefs they possess, as if the belief issued from courage rather than from fear and cowardice. By way of contrast, according to Russell his student Wittgenstein delighted in proving something wrong, because it narrowed the field of what was possibly true. People of religious belief, however, who have no commendable allegiance to truth, simply skirt the gate of admission out of fear of discovering their belief false.

It seems undeniable that humans under duress are more willingly believers. This observation, however, prompts religious unbelievers to contend that this causal connection weakens the plausibility of religious belief being true. That is, when a man is down, he is least likely to reason. Most often a serious dilemma may provide a tempting and powerful occasion for him to take leave of reason. Such a contention saddles religious belief with the liability of admitting that particular circumstances provoke looking for God. The cogency of belief in God is therefore naturally to be weighed as dubious under conditions which provoke it.

However, one could plausibly argue for something of the opposite contention. That is, one's reason is most acute and awakened when under the most strain. Furthermore, there is nothing quite like awaiting an execution in the morning to clear one's head and thinking the night before. In addition, Russell himself evidences some steps toward things religious on infrequent occasions when life was most traumatic, and more specifically when he felt an immense strain from the burdens of his life. That

---

45. Russell, "Evidence and Nature of God," *CP* 10:263.

one is to be suspicious of what comes from such times because of the times in which they are cast, is hardly just cause for dismissing the belief because of the circumstances giving rise to it.[46]

Thus, Russell is suspicious of a believer in the truth of religious contentions because he judges the act of believing suspect since he presumes such believed doctrines too congenial to human desires. Hence, because such "truths" are desired, the human falls prey to believing without sufficient reasoning; on a subject not so bound up with human emotions, one would require more reasoning. Moreover, there is an ever-present tendency for humans to sacrifice the restraint of objectivity when dealing with truths desired. Russell is therefore not only critical of the grounds of assent to the truth of any religious doctrines; the truths themselves are rendered suspect by the fact that they are too cozily congenial, given the desires of human nature.

In "A Free Man's Worship," after enumerating many "facts" about the universe, all summed up in a contention about the purposelessness of the universe, Russell pauses to assure the hesitant reader, ". . . .all of these things, if not quite beyond dispute, are yet so nearly certain, that no philosophy which rejects them can hope to stand."[47] However, though Russell's readiness to speak of the purposelessness of the universe was often his counterargument against suspiciously pleasant religious belief, in his more careful moments he was prepared to admit that "From a scientific point of view, optimism and pessimism are alike objectionable: optimism assumes, or attempts to prove, that the universe exists to please us, and pessimism that it exists to displease us. Scientifically, there is no evidence that it is concerned with us either one way or the other. The belief in either pessimism or optimism is a matter of temperament, not of reason, but the optimistic temperament has been much commoner among Western philosophers."[48] It is, therefore, the "optimistic temperament" that Russell finds most objectionable among Western philosophers, and even more so, the religiously inclined.

46. As something of a parallel example, historical reliability is not necessarily impugned by extraordinary circumstances surrounding purported historical testimony. One can thus believe that a witness to an event does not have to be dispassionate necessarily to be truthful. "One accepts, for instance, that the first witnesses of Auschwitz were both truthful and passionate, even if in some circles they were at first easily dismissed because of their passion. But in retrospect, merely dispassionate witness regarding Auschwitz would be obscene." Carson, *John*, 40.

47. Russell, "Free Man's Worship," *CP* 12:67.

48. Russell, *History*, 759.

However, Russell could on occasion concede the unsettledness of such matters: "What science has to say of the subject of immortality is not very definite."[49] At the same time, Russell's general criticism of religious belief amounts to a claim that religious knowledge-claims exceed experience, and hence they are not susceptible of confirmation. However, Russell is no positivist, and he noted the chief deficiency of an empiricist epistemology as the inability of empiricism to account for, on empirical premises, the belief that all our knowledge is derived solely from experience.

At the same time Russell is much more apt to chastise a scientific thinker for a descent into religion, as he did A. J. Balfour, James Jeans, Arthur Eddington, and others. The idea that religious belief can infiltrate and inform scientific understanding, Russell found abhorrent. By contrast, scientific beliefs can undermine religious belief and in the process render them specious. This realization will occur early on in the adolescent Russell. However, that was not the end of the matter of religion for Russell. That is, though religious belief can claim no vindication from science, as Balfour, Jeans, and Eddington tried to insinuate, there are other routes that Russell will pursue. Religion for Russell is simply too important to be left to die. A personal religion can and should posit itself, though religious appetites cannot presume metaphysical vindication. Reason could not approve that union, nor could Russell.

---

49. Russell, *Religion and Science*, 137.

2

Russell's Hesitations with Religion

A. RELIGION AS NEGATIVE IN RUSSELL

My views on religion remain those which I acquired at the age of sixteen. I consider all forms of religion not only false but harmful. My published works record my views.[1]

These words are indicative of Russell's chagrin at being thought on the side of religion. Though coming from Russell himself, they scarcely do justice to his religious views, for Russell's irreligion was not areligious, nor was it monolithic. When his views on religion were at issue Russell's responses reveal conspicuously little of the complexity of a viewpoint that was not wholly negative, nor do his responses in any substantial way indicate the protracted nature of his own struggle for a personal religion. Neither of these characteristics is indicated in the above statement, however, or from the majority of his polemic against religion.

The brief words quoted above came when Russell was 95 to combat the recurring rumor of his reconciliation with religion. Though the suggestion of reconciliation was false, Russell himself contributed to the perception of his religious views as entirely negative. Furthermore, such perception apparently bothered him very little, as Russell only rarely contested the interpretation of himself as opposed to religion on all counts. In fact, as in the above response, he shows a willingness to allow such a misconception.

---

1. Russsell, "Bertrand Russell on the Afterlife," 29.

In reviewing Russell's very popular *A History of Western Philosophy*, the noted historian of ideas John Hermann Randall, Jr., observed that on thinkers whom Russell found uncongenial, he was "no safe guide."[2] If Randall's criticism is fair critique of Russell on such thinkers, a similar appraisal might suggest itself in Russell's treatment of subjects he found unfavorable. Religion would be a likely candidate, given Russell's disgruntlement with a subject arousing some of his most passionate, though primarily negative, feelings. However, fuller answer to the question of why Russell is not a reliable guide on himself when the subject is religion seems required, for consideration of Russell's broader published works does not reveal a view that considers "all forms of religion not only false but harmful."

The complexity of Russell's religious views comes across nicely in a single sentence of response to the personalist philosopher Edgar Brightman, who noted in 1944 that Russell's view of religion was not entirely negative. Conceding Brightman's interpretation in his reply Russell explained that

> What makes my religious views complex is that although I consider some form of personal religion highly desirable, and feel many people unsatisfactory through lack of it, I cannot accept the theology of any well-known religion and I incline to think that most churches at most times have done more harm than good.[3]

In this passage Russell finds organized religion, on balance, having provoked more harm than good in the world, and, on balance, finds no theology truthful, though he finds people unsatisfactory who lack some form of a religion. The distinctions put down here are repeatably helpful in understanding the specifics of Russell's position on religion—and also work in tandem in understanding his own religious quest. For example, one might erroneously infer that in Russell a denunciation of religious metaphysics or organized religious bodies is a criticism of all religion, and that religion, in toto, is of no value. Indeed, Russell's condemnations of religion typically pass over his desire to commend a form of personal religion. However often in his negative polemic Russell did not observe his own distinctions, they are nonetheless distinctions that undergird his position on religion for the most part throughout his life. Too, the

---

2. Randall, Review of Russell's *History of Western Philosophy*, 32.
3. Russell, "Reply to Criticisms," *CP* 11:53.

distinctions become evident in trying to unify what Russell had to say on religion, and to make sense of a plethora of statements which may seem initially to cancel each other. Consider, for example, two often-quoted statements, particularly the latter, from Russell's three-volume *Autobiography*:

> Throughout the long period of religious doubt, I had been rendered very unhappy by the gradual loss of belief, but when the process was completed, I found to my surprise that I was quite glad to be done with the whole thing.[4]
>
> The sea, the stars, the night wind in waste places, mean more to me than even the human beings I love best, and I am conscious that human affection is to me at bottom an attempt to escape from the vain search for God.[5]

In the first passage the culmination of rejecting religious beliefs gives rise to some surprise. That is, on the occasion of actual loss, unhappiness did not result, but rather its opposite: not grief, but unexpected relief. In the second quotation Russell bespeaks a more sobering consequence to the absence of God and the consequent lack of belief. Unlike the early adolescent quest of which Russell contended later that "loneliness had much more to do with my unhappiness than theological difficulties," the disappointment depicted in the latter quotation is more severe and long lasting and lacks any hint of triumphalism as in the earlier quotation.[6] We cannot infer from the second quotation, in contrast to the first, that Russell's religious quest and loss of God evoked no anxiety in him. Though the adolescent religious quest sloughed off various components of traditional theism, the result was hardly a celebration for Russell. The second statement, however, though indicative of the fact that the desire for some form of religion did survive, does not revoke or undo the earlier theological critique of religion: Russell never rescinded his judgments on the theological tenets of the existence of God, the immortality of the soul, and the freedom of the will.[7] A search for some form of personal religion continued over the rubble of a rejected religious metaphysic and despite the absence of the traditional components of creed and church.

---

4. Russell, *1872–1914*, 50.

5. Russell, *1914–1944*, 36.

6. Russell, "My Religious Reminiscences," *Basic Writings*, 31.

7. These were the theological tenets Russell subjected to intense criticism at the time of his adolescent religious crisis.

Russell's desire for a religion could at times mimic the desire to penetrate the core of mathematical certainty—and prove as disappointing. His ultimate desire was to ground his religious appetite in something his intellect could embrace. After Pembroke Lodge, this would require the aid of philosophy, for theology scarcely retained any more promise. In time, however, as a student at Cambridge, Russell would subject philosophy to the same scrutiny that he had earlier directed toward theological doctrines. That is, in time Hegelianism and later Pythagorean number mysticism would fail after Moore and Wittgenstein, respectively, with Russell writing in the aftermath that he had "never since found religious satisfaction in any philosophical doctrine that I could accept."[8] Nonetheless, between these two decades and after his earlier religious quest Russell wrote, "Yet when the dogmas have been rejected, the place of religion in life is by no means decided."[9] That is, the demise of any cogent theological tenets in his adolescent quest coupled with the failure of any philosophical doctrine to serve a religious purpose would compound the problem of finding a religion for himself.

Russell's frequent and fervent attacks on religion often prompted readers to surmise that Russell conceived of religion solely as a misfortune of the human experience and a facet of human life that would hopefully die out.[10] Certainly Russell did believe that religion, in the main, had more often been a detriment to individual and social well-being than it had been a positive force contributing to good. Nevertheless, Russell desired for a personal religion to be normative. While many thinkers past and present believed the undermining of religious beliefs sealed the fate of religion, Russell did not. Russell valued highly some of the impulses that had given rise to religion and expressed his belief that "if they were to die most of what is best would vanish out of life."[11] And, at the supposed height of anti-religious feeling in his life, he still managed

---

8. Russell, "Why I Took to Philosophy," *Portraits*, 18.

9. Russell, "Essence of Religion," *CP* 12:112.

10. Russell in fact stated on numerous occasions such a view, as, for example in his *Let the People Think*, 22: "I am a dissenter from all known religions and I hope that every kind of religious belief will die out. I do not believe that, on the balance, religious belief has been a force for good." As seen in his reply to Edgar Brightman, Russell makes a very important distinction, one essential to understanding his view, between the religious belief spoken of here, and religious feeling, being opposed to the former, but not necessarily the latter.

11. Russell, *Principles of Social Reconstruction*, 144.

to affirm in 1944 his response to Brightman that, "I consider some form of personal religion highly desirable."[12]

Meanwhile, Russell continued to maintain that the rejected theological beliefs of religion were blatantly false, perhaps the chief of which was belief in God, a belief Russell contended was virtually always held on inadequate grounds and largely for emotional reasons. He considered religion to be a primary and influential source of evil in the world, mainly through the cruelty it fostered,[13] and as an impediment to intellectual and social progress. Religion, in its base forms, had been born of fear, and hence was the "parent of cruelty." Despite often overstated criticisms of religion, Russell could also express hope that religion might eventually be shorn of false beliefs and cruel practices so that, as he put it, "the good alone may remain."[14]

Though Russell remained relentlessly critical of the abuses of religion in the world, and at the same time sympathetic to a personal religion, his sympathy was often obscured by his contention of the harm religion could do. That contention, sometimes well-nigh to an infatuation, seems to provoke a reluctance on his part to be more vocal about his sympathies to religion, especially as Russell worked with an overriding motive of attempting to "set the world right."[15] The mire into which much religious belief and institutional religion had sunk humanity seemed so deep that he consequently felt little justification for commending religion

---

12. Russell, "Reply to Criticisms," *CP* 11:53.

13. For readers unacquainted with Russell it may not be immediately evident how religion could foster cruelty. Russell, writing in 1932, provides the following example: "The law of marriage and divorce, though not quite what most ecclesiastics would wish, retains absurdities and cruelties—such as the refusal of divorce for insanity—which would not survive a week but for the influence of Christian churches." Russell, *Education and the Social Order*, 67.

14. Russell, *Religion and Science*, 189.

15. The first sentence of Russell's three volume *Autobiography* reads as follows: "Three passions, simple but overwhelmingly strong have governed my life: the longing for love, the search for knowledge, and unbearable pity for the suffering of mankind." Russell, *1872-1914*, 3. On Russell's view, organized religion had historically been one of the major culprits responsible for much unnecessary suffering in the world and would continue fulfilling that role if permitted. This point of view is the source of some exaggerations in Russell's denunciations of religion, and he at times tries to evoke a similar feeling of aversion in his readers by using an imagery that anyone would find repulsive to their sympathies. His daughter, in commenting on this trait observed: "Once Russell had convinced himself that an opponent was wicked (which usually meant willing to allow the suffering of others), he would attack with absolute ferocity and small regard for truth." Tait, review of Clark, *The Life*, in *Russell*, 21, 53.

in much of any form. To give a more systematic and sustained expression to his views on religion perhaps would attract too much attention to his religious sympathies, while detracting from the needed rehabilitation of the wrongs of the world. Such seems to account for his manner on the subject of religion. Nevertheless, Russell's belief that a personal religion was needful for the world is also evident, though rarely stated forthrightly and easily buried beneath Russell's overarching criticisms of religion.

Somewhat typical of this manner was an occasion when Russell was lecturing in 1949 at Columbia University. Speaking on the inability of science alone to remove certain evils in the world, chiefly wrongs that men and nations commit against each other, he made the point that something besides science was needed—the same point Russell had made to Unwin in 1931.

> The root of the matter is a very simple and old-fashioned thing, a thing so simple that I am almost ashamed to mention it, for fear of the derisive smile with which wise cynics will greet my words. The thing I mean—please forgive me for mentioning it—is love, Christian love, or compassion. If you feel this, you have a motive for existence, a guide in action, a reason for courage, an imperative necessity for intellectual honesty. If you feel this, you have all that anybody should need in the way of religion.[16]

The ensuing dilemma found Russell flooded, as he puts it, "with a deluge of letters from free-thinkers deploring my adoption of orthodoxy, and from Christians welcoming me to the fold."[17] His reaction follows.

> When, ten years later, I was welcomed by the Chaplain of Brixton Prison with the words, "I am glad that you have seen the light," I had to explain to him that this was an entire misconception, that my views were completely unchanged and that what he called seeing the light I would call groping in darkness. I had thought it obvious that, when I spoke of Christian love, I put in the adjective 'Christian' to distinguish it from sexual love, and I should certainly have supposed that the context made this completely clear. . .It seems to me totally inexplicable that anybody should think the above words a description of Christianity, especially in view, as some Christians will remember, of how very rarely Christians have shown Christian love. I have done my best to console those who are not Christians for the pain that

---

16. Russell, *Impact of Science*, 92.
17. Russell, *1944–1969*, 24.

I unwittingly caused them by a lax use of the suspect adjective. My essays and lectures on the subject have been edited and published in 1957 by Professor Paul Edwards along with an essay by him on my New York difficulties of 1940, under the title *Why I Am Not a Christian*.[18]

In Russell's response to this situation he desires to make clear that his previous hostility towards religion is still intact and unmoved, and that he was merely commending a Christian principle of love, of which there had been noticeable absence on the part of Christian practitioners. The misunderstanding could have been avoided if his listeners had been more careful students of history and been aware, as some of them were, of the irony of Christian love and Christians. Russell does not want to be misunderstood and so he commends to the attention of the reader some of his further writing on the subject of religion.

However, if Russell desired to avoid any misrepresentation of himself on the subject, he is hardly recommending the appropriate volume, for the notorious *Why I Am Not a Christian* is as misrepresentative of Russell's religious views as one might find. Apparently, however, Russell does not mind. Religion for Russell had been too much of a help in evil-doing to spend an inordinate amount of time in praise of admirable ethical principles that few persons followed anyway: better to expurgate religion of its misdeeds than to applaud unheeded though praiseworthy ethical axioms. Accordingly, Russell himself is in large part responsible for the perception of himself as exclusively a negative critic of religion.[19]

Sympathetic devotees of Russell on the subject of religion utilized Russell's bombasts against religion to promulgate the cause of free-thought, and in such context found it hardly fitting to reprint any essay that might not denounce religion. However, such a skewed selection contributed to the prevailing perceptions of Russell as exclusively critical of

18. Russell, *1944-1969*, 24-25.

19. As further evidence that Russell was not being wholly fair to his own views in this instance, note what he had said fourteen years earlier in his otherwise polemical *Religion and Science*, 246-47, concerning Christians and Christian love: "The warfare between science and Christian theology, in spite of an occasional skirmish on the outposts, is nearly ended, and I think most Christians would admit that their religion is the better for it. Christianity has been purified of inessentials inherited from a barbarous age, and nearly cured of the desire to persecute. There remains, among the more liberal Christians, an ethical doctrine which is valuable: acceptance of Christ's teaching that we should love our neighbours, and a belief that in each individual there is something deserving of respect, even if it is no longer called a soul. There is also, in the Churches, a growing belief that Christians should oppose war."

religion. Paul Edwards, the editor of Russell's *Why I Am Not a Christian*, for example, makes his purposes in editing that work plain in what Russell calls "his admirable prefatory observations": "A book by Bertrand Russell on religion would be worth publishing at any time. At present, when we are witnessing a campaign for the revival of religion which is carried on with all the slickness of modern advertising techniques, a restatement of the unbeliever's case seems particularly desirable."[20]

And so the resulting picture of Russell some acolytes have fostered: the heroic voice raised to advance free inquiry against the assaults of superstition. As indicated, Russell willingly gave his own powerful voice to that impression, though for readers venturing deeper into Russell on religion, the surmise could be different. As one example, Ronald Jager noted that "What is of value in Russell's writings on religious subjects is not that for which he is known best. . . ."[21]

Russell was admittedly an agnostic on the chief assertion of religion, that there is a God—for he contended that atheism was as presumptuous as theism—though Russell was, by his own admission, practically speaking an atheist. While no notoriety need attach itself to an intellectual in our modern age for unorthodox religious opinions, Russell's habit of speaking unabashedly about his views on religion earned him the well-known reputation as a formidable enemy of religion. Scores of freethinkers—many of whom shared much of Russell's thinking on religion—relished the fact that Russell was not content to keep his views inside the ivory tower or even on the printed page. Meanwhile, Russell stood ready to lend his weight to the cause of free thought most especially it seems when his opposition to religion was suspect. Thirty years after he had delivered a talk at the Battersea Town Hall in 1927, entitled "Why I am Not a Christian," that speech became the lead essay in the volume of essays by that title, with Russell in the preface expressing annoyance at rumors of his lessening hostility towards religion while reiterating his insistence that religion remained "both untrue and harmful." Furthermore, after the inadvertent comment about "Christian love" at Columbia University he recommends to the reader that same volume of denunciatory essays.[22]

If Russell had desired his readers to have the "essential Russell" on religion, however, he would not have chosen *Why I Am Not a Christian*.

20. Russell, *Why*, xii.
21. Jager, *Development*, 484.
22. Russell, *1944–1969*, 24–25.

His views on religion were most often articulated as his views on wrong religion because most religion was wrong religion in Russell's view. Good religion was difficult to commend when an abundance of bad religion was present. However, writing to Lady Ottoline Morrell in 1911, with whom he often crossed swords on religion, he says:

> But it interests me far more to try to preserve what I value than to attack what I disagree with. Only, I think the absolute fearless pursuit of truth is the first condition of right-thinking for me and for all who spend much time on abstract thought. And so attacking what seems to me comfortable fictions is bound up with my positive beliefs, and has to be done along with the rest.[23]

Nevertheless, it was Russell's predominantly negative assessment of religion that prompted Edgar Brightman to contend that Russell's religious sympathies were a "side of Russell that is unsuspected by many of his readers." Russell attempted to hold both sides together—a rather difficult task as it might be for anyone who militantly attacks religion in Russell fashion. However, as noted by Russell in the above letter to Ottoline, his positive beliefs remain the foundation of his attacks on religion. His irreligion, then, can hardly be separated from the things he valued. Understandably, however, he habitually found the attack on "comfortable fictions" a consuming task, forging his legacy as one of the most persistent and offending critics of religion. This was a reputation that, though not preferred by him early in his public life, in time he rather came to savor, especially after World War I. Attacking comfortable fictions took on more importance and urgency in an uncomfortable world.

When George Santayana leveled the charge of "religious conservatism" at Russell's views, the occasion might have proved a valuable one for Russell to have divulged something besides his opposition to religion.[24] Instead he only countered the charge of Santayana by adding to the prevailing view of himself as a mocker of religion: "I will leave the reader to form his own judgment on that matter."[25] The high calling he expounded in his remark to Lady Ottoline was typically lost in his opposition to religion and could easily be missed and ignored. It was missed in the essays in *Why I Am Not a Christian*, where religion manages only two dubious credits: fixing the calendar and aiding the chronicling of

---

23. Russell to Ottoline, April 10, 1911, quoted in Clark, *Life*, 158–59.
24. Admittedly, the meaning of such a charge is difficult to discern.
25. Russell, *Portraits*, 98.

eclipses. After this paltry list Russell adds: "but I do not know of any others."[26] A positive place for religion in negative contexts was typically not mentioned. Russell's extraordinary intellect and his skill as a writer, moreover, could provoke in some readers an impression of Russell as having effectively silenced any defender of religion.

B. ACADEMIC HESITATIONS WITH RUSSELL ON RELIGION

As a persistent and virtually unwavering critic of religion, Russell was therefore scarcely motivated to write much of anything in a neutral vein, much less flattering toward religion after the 1930s. Nevertheless, Russell still conceded on rare occasions that religion could provide laudable counsel instead of only provoking condemnation. Nevertheless, the notable and often anthologized essays Russell wrote on the topic of religion in the initial decades of the twentieth century would cease, though these early essays are Russell's best writing on the subject. In them something like a search for a religion is evident, though Russell thereafter would complain that his lauded rhetoric lacked much by way of cogent argument, especially in the case of his most famous essay on the subject, "A Free Man's Worship." The possibility of a religion in secular modernity is nevertheless sought by Russell in these essays as he tries to capture something nearly impossible, for Russell's unbelief is so constrained by how little he allows himself to believe that the ring of despair sometimes overwhelms the whisper of hope. Said another way, his exhortation in that famous essay may sound more like a weakened but persistent expression of hope in a hopeless situation.

Meanwhile, with Russell on the attack against religion, his reading public savored essays and books by Russell as popular to them as they were profitable to him. Free-thinking readers gratefully gathered his ammunition against religion and enjoyed entertainment provided by a famous philosopher who needed no introduction. The flavor of the earlier essays, where he had struggled to bring a viable religion in some form forward, is now significantly weakened, as Russell rather easily suspended the earlier effort for the different effort of advancing more bristly and bombastic rhetoric against religion. As a renowned intellectual whose religious views were more well-known by sectors of the public than

26. Russell, *Why*, 24.

perhaps any other intellectual during his time, he frankly welcomed this task. Russell's popular and public works on religion, though with little nuance on this subject, were for agreeable audiences a welcomed critique of a phenomenon deemed hardly viable in the modern secular world.

While Russell stood ready in almost all situations to champion and defend the rationale of religious unbelief, and however much he relished such work, little of Russell's thought on religion found itself as a resource for scholarly work in the philosophy of religion, excepting, as indicated, the earlier essays. Today there is no school of religious philosophy that derives from Russell, in contrast to his student Wittgenstein, who penned essays that philosophers of religion ruminated on and wrote about, or his colleague Whitehead, whom Russell veered far from, taking contention with Whitehead's later philosophy, called process theology. Similarly, for the influential school of religious pragmatism arising from the work of William James and the pragmatic humanist F. C. S. Schiller, Russell had little but criticism, contending that pragmatists gave unworthy deference to religious hopes without justifiable philosophical warrant.

Russell never conceded that his views on religion as found in his popular writings lacked more finessed and sophisticated argument. Certainly, and as indicated earlier in the Introduction, in his famous debate with Copleston in 1948, he defends his case as ably as any thinker critical of religious beliefs. Indeed, in a letter to Russell after the debate, Copleston relates how nervous he became before the debate, realizing just who his debater was: "It was for me a highly embarrassing occasion, to find myself engaged in debate with the most celebrated living British philosopher. But your friendly talk when we were entertained by the B. B. C. greatly helped to diminish the embarrassing aspect of the situation."[27] Here Copleston, rather than Russell, indicates some trepidation over his opponent. The popularizer Russell did not shrink from sophisticated debate.

Even as a popularizer, Russell proved as astute as any critic of religion, though he rarely bothered with the subject outside popular contexts after the 1930s.[28] However, though Russell's name is scarce commodity

27. Frederick Copleston to Bertrand Russell, May 18, 1962, Document no. 110395, Box no. 10.47, Bertrand Russell Archives, McMaster University Library.

28. In Russell's lecture of February of 1939 at the University of Michigan at Ann Arbor, familiar Russell themes on religion and religious belief are articulated with customary wit and incisiveness. While conceding there are "Christian virtues I most wholeheartedly accept, and wish to see perpetuated," a dominating criticism in his lecture is directed at the provincial view of God that God-believers often assume. Early on in the lecture he tells his audience that "For my own part, while my own position

within the field of philosophy of religion, important exceptions occur in the application of Russell's theory of descriptions to the ontological argument for God's existence, and Russell's analysis of cause and infinite number as applied to the cosmological argument for the existence of God. Much of this was due to Russell's work on Leibniz, undertaken to teach McTaggart's course on the German philosopher and culminating in Russell's book on Leibniz in 1900. What Russell found in Leibniz would thereafter be hugely significant for how Russell conceived metaphysics and by implication, how he assessed the arguments for God's existence.[29] Russell would now argue that there were other logical relations besides subject-predicate, and that such a discovery had a "dire effect upon metaphysics."[30] Previously always willing "to listen to a metaphysical argument for or against God or immortality," that willingness now changed: "It was only after acquiring a new logic that I ceased to think such arguments worth examination."[31] Nor does Russell's view of where the deficiencies of the arguments rest seem to change. Almost a half century after his book on Leibniz, in his debate with Copleston on the issue of the cosmological argument, Russell still contends that the argument depends on "a logic that I reject."[32] Before that realization, however, the

---

is agnostic, if I were in any degree orthodox—if I did believe in God—I should be ashamed to deduce his existence from our terrestrial needs on this planet, which seems too petty a point of view for so cosmic a conclusion. I think that when you are thinking of God you must not think of God as the God of this planet or the God of some chosen race on this planet. You must take the matter up, thinking of God as a Universal God and consider us as unimportant as we are." Russell, *CP* 10:255–56.

29. Russell puts it this way: "Leibniz, in his private thinking, is the best example of a philosopher who uses logic as a key to metaphysics. This type of philosophy begins with Parmenides, and is carried further in Plato's use of the theory of ideas to prove various extra-logical propositions. Spinoza belongs to the same type, and so does Hegel. But none of these is so clear as Leibniz in drawing inferences from syntax to the real world. This kind of argumentation has fallen into disrepute owing to the growth of empiricism. Whether any valid inferences are possible from language to non-linguistics is a question as to which I do not care to dogmatize; but certainly the inferences found in Leibniz and other *a priori* philosophers are not valid, since all are due to a defective logic." Russell, *History*, 595.

30. Russell, *1872–1914*, 212.

31. Russell, *Basic Writings*, 35.

32. Hick, *Existence*, 170. The immediate context of this part of the debate is disagreement over alluding to "contingent" and "necessary" being: "Russell: The difficulty of this argument is that I don't admit the idea of a necessary being and I don't admit that there is any particular meaning in calling other beings 'contingent.' These phrases don't for me have a significance except within a logic that I reject. Copleston: Do you mean that you reject these terms because they won't fit in with what is called 'modern

contentions of religious belief were already undermined by his own musings and various influences recorded in his adolescent writings. As one such example, he informs a questioner in his audience at the University of Michigan in 1939: "When I was adolescent, I was very much influenced by the argument of the first cause and believed in the existence of God because of that argument, until I read John Stuart Mill's autobiography in which he remarked, 'my father told me that the question 'who made me?' cannot be answered because it supposes the question 'who made God?' That is a complete answer."[33]

Such an assertion may present Russell, in one manner, as a thoroughly convinced modernist, that is to say, a secular agnostic. He was hardly a happy one—his various and periodic protests aside. Moreover, and adding to the earlier point about Russell's willingness to advance the argument against religion, Russell could also seem strongly annoyed with the subject. Thus, in his exchange with Brightman in 1944, Russell commends Brightman for Brightman's professionalism in discussing Russell's criticism of a religion that Brightman upheld, while Russell remarks that he does not know if he could have reciprocated, had he been in Brightman's position. Truthfully, probably not, because the subject of religious belief often provoked Russell often to strong reaction with his inveterate use of reason. Again, part of Russell's annoyance was simply over the refusal of thinkers congenial to religious belief to admit what Russell regarded as the irrevocable case for unbelief. Russell takes the case against religious belief to be substantially settled, such that Russell's patience with religious beliefs, and by extension to religious believers, could be short.

Some academics, taking account of Russell on religion, have regarded him as antiquated on the subject. As a notably example, the American theologian and academic Harvey Cox, writing in 1966 in his well-known book *The Secular City*, began that work with a synopsis of how secularism has so permeated the modern mind that interest in religious issues was seldom anymore evoked among the populace. Cox instanced the lack of attention paid to Russell's criticisms of religion to support his thesis that secularism was the present and unstoppable future of the West. For Cox, Russell's attacks found only a tiny audience among religious unbelievers sufficiently secular to be indifferent toward religion and already sold on

---

logic'? Russell: Well, I can't find anything that they could mean. The word 'necessary,' it seems to me, is a useless word, except as applied to analytic propositions, not to things."

33. Russell, "Existence and Nature of God," *CP* 10:258.

the secular cause.[34] Russell, Cox insinuated, was behind the times. However, and contra Cox, many secular academics sympathetic to Russell's views on religion have continued to commend these writings by Russell with an easy confidence quite astonishing.[35]

In his later book, *Religion in the Secular City*, written almost two decades later in 1985, Cox admitted to earlier overestimating the security and strength of secularism in the face of undeniable growing religious movements, though hardly in academia. Belonging to a more or less insular academic environment where secularism did thrive and continues to thrive, Cox had not surprisingly misread the religious landscape of the outside world. In addition, one can also doubt Cox's contention that readers of Russell's writings on religion were as few as he thought, for Cox was too quick to think persons indifferent to Russell's criticism because they had already conceded the points made by Russell against religion. Consequently, more orthodox religious believers (whose numbers intellectuals such as Cox are usually either prone to grossly underestimate or to grossly exaggerate) have not viewed Russell as pummeling only the religious beliefs of obscurantists. Russell, in other words, was deemed still relevant on the subject.

As is evident, Russell was primarily a negative critic of religion—whether a dated critic or not—with his bombasts against religion being the predominant perception of Russell on the subject. On the popular level, while this has certainly been the impression of Russell,[36] scholarly opinion, likewise, has been scarcely more congenial to viewing Russell as having anything positive to say on the subject of religion.[37] This opinion among

---

34. Cox, *Secular City*, 2.

35. As example, note Griffin, "Bertrand Russell as a Critic of Religion," 47–58.

36. As indication of how far Russell's reputation on religion extended, during 1921–22 Russell was a lecturer at the University of Peking in China and while there he became severely ill and erroneous news was circulated of his death, of which he remarks: "One missionary paper, I remember, had an obituary notice of one sentence: 'Missionaries may be pardoned for heaving a sigh of relief at the news of Mr. Bertrand Russell's death.'" Russell, *1914–1944*, 182–83.

37. As example, Paul Edwards, author of "Ethics and the Critique of Religion" in the article on Russell in *The Encyclopedia of Philosophy*, also edited by Edwards, remarks, "No such doubt as Russell has expressed about his subjectivism in ethics mark his views on religion." Edwards then proceeds with commentary on Russell's negative criticisms of religion without mention of Russell's sympathies with religion. William P. Alston, in his article "Problems of Philosophy of Religion," also in the *The Encyclopedia of Philosophy*, likewise exhibits a similar unawareness. While discussing various attitudes to religion, Alston remarks: "In the other major group we can distinguish between those who simply reject traditional religion (Holbach and Russell) and those who in addition try to put something in its place."

scholars has understandably and easily been engendered because of Russell's frequent virulent hostility to religion in his writings. A sampling from that writing reveals statements reflecting this perspective by Russell:

> The harm that theology has done is not to create cruel impulses, but to give them the sanction of what professes to be a lofty ethic, and to confer an apparently sacred character upon practices which have come down from more ignorant and barbarous ages.[38]
>
> No man treats a motorcar as foolishly as he treats another human being. When the car will not go, he does not attribute its annoying behavior to sin; he does not say, 'You are a wicked motorcar, and I shall not give you any more petrol until you go.' He attempts to find out what is wrong and to set it right. An analogous way of treating human beings is, however, considered to be contrary to the truths of our holy religion.[39]

When an author writes about religion in the manner found in these quotations and becomes as notoriously famous for it as did Russell, then any other writings on the same subject, perhaps less vehement, are apt to be overlooked. For most of his long life this is what occurred when others took stock of Russell's religious views. The attention given to his scathing criticisms of religion[40] left many critics ignorant of his contention that religion can serve positive purpose.

A few scholars during Russell's lifetime occasionally alluded to Russell's religious sympathies.[41] E. I. Watkin, who detected sufficient religious sympathies in Russell's writings to refer to him as a "religious atheist," wrote: "But it is even more useful to gather together the witness to religion contained in admissions scattered here and there through

---

38. Russell, *Religion and Science*, 106.

39 Russell, *Why*, 40.

40. Because Russell wrote predominantly at a popular level on the subject of religion and usually with considerable lucidity against religion, such writings are sometimes presumed to be all Russell penned on the subject. Accordingly, Frederick Copleston wrote: "To look for a profound philosophy of religion in his writings would be to look in vain." Copleston, *History of Philosophy*, 241. By contrast, when Copleston reviewed the first volume of Russell's *Autobiography*, he wrote,"And though there is in his opinion no intellectual justification for belief in God, while in any case the evil and suffering in the world make it impossible to believe in a God who is both omnipotent and good, he obviously admits and values what might be described as a religious dimension in a man." Copleston, *Month*, 314-15.

41. Watkin, "Bertrand Russell—Religious Atheist," 742; Pringle-Pattison, "Consideration of Mr. Bertrand Russell's Views on Religion," 63.

Mr. Russell's writings, a witness naturally scant and obscure, as being the witness of a man whose thought is, in its main trend so hostile to religion, and to bring into the light the affirmation by an intellectual skeptic of personal experience of God and communion with Him." A. S. Pringle-Pattison makes virtually the same observation as Watkin: "And when one considers the theory of 'the universal soul' or 'the divine part of man' which he so inconsistently attempts to graft upon the materialistic dogma, it is easy to see how far the latter is from expressing his full mind as to the nature of reality."

However, it was chiefly and largely only after his death that some scholars opted to reconsider Russell's views on religion.[42] Moreover, immediately prior to his death, Russell's publication of his three-volume autobiography, particularly the first two volumes, provided readers with something of a contrast to the man who so often appeared in other writings simply to dismiss religion. When more comprehensive work began on Russell's vast corpus, as opposed to piecemeal evaluations which easily lent credence to the prevailing perceptions of Russell, Jack Pitt underlined the conclusion of this reconstructive work by contending that "we can no longer subscribe to customary evaluations of Russell's approach to religion which assert it to be one of cynical criticisms or uninvolved

---

42. Ronald Jager was one of the first scholars to suggest that religious concerns played a role in the development and alterations of Russell's philosophy. Writing two years after Russell's death he says: "So long, and to the degree that, Russell turned a part of his intellectual life upon the interior concerns that engage the quest for individual salvation, so long his religious ideas are intrinsically interwoven with his philosophical outlook. It was when, and to the degree that, he began to look at religion externally, merely as a social and historical phenomenon, that he lost his grip upon its inner dynamic; he then sought in the outer idiom of logic and analysis for something to speak to the fire in his soul." Jager, *Development*, 506. Louis Greenspan in *The Incompatible Prophecies*, 15, summarizes this reconstruction of Russell on religion: ". . .there is an interpretation of Russell which seems to be gaining adherents, the view that Russell was essentially a religious man. No doubt the author of *Why I Am Not a Christian* would have been appalled at this suggestion, but it is put forward by admirers of Russell such as Jager and Cranston. The most convincing statement of Russell's religiosity is given in the excellent memoir by his daughter Katherine Tait." However, Greenspan fails to distinguish between Russell's assaults on organized religion, religious metaphysics and religious belief as opposed to his sympathies with personal religion, a point made by both Jager and Tait. Inasmuch as this new assessment of Russell is merely discovering what was for the most part ignored in Russell's writing, the author of *Why I Am Not a Christian* would not be appalled by this new interpretation of his religious views. He would, however, very likely object on the ground that it detracts from our awareness of the harmful influences of religious belief and institutions.

dismissal."[43] Nevertheless, Russell's impatience with religion and religious belief made the headlines, while his life manifested a frustrated quest for a religion he could embrace.

C. RELIGION AS HARMFUL IN RUSSELL

What did Russell set out to do when the subject was religion? Answering this question makes more intelligible the apparent indifference on his part for a more holistic perception of his religious views. The general answer to this question, already outlined, is that religion generally constituted a problem and obstacle to reforming human people and institutions. In a more disciplined world, religion could maintain a rightful place, but in the world we live in, religion overwhelmingly blocks and stalls human progress according to Russell.

Thus, many of Russell's negative criticisms of religion are primarily due to his notion of the failings of religion, namely its lack of truth and the harm it provokes. Russell was willing to criticize religion so severely precisely because he saw much of religion as not encouraging persons to "stand upon our own feet and look fair and square at the world—its good facts, its bad facts, its beauties, and its ugliness, see the world as it is and be not afraid of it."[44] The resulting false beliefs were coupled with another culprit emanating from religion: the great harms that resulted from false beliefs. This dual criticism of religion by Russell is the source of most of his negative critique of religion, and it occupies so much of his writings on religion because, from his view, religion had scorched the world with both falsities and cruelties.

So, despite Russell's belief that religion provided something essential for the human and thus religion was of prime importance in the human experience, he more often castigated religious belief as a source of untold human misery. Nevertheless, Russell sometimes sought to draw from the religious propensity of humans something favorable and essential to human betterment, rather than, as he more often did, excoriating religious belief as damningly indicative of human fears and cowardice.

In this negative vein Russell tended to criticize religious beliefs as a source of harm to the potential happiness and well-being of both individuals and society. Organized religion, though a frequent culprit in this

43. Pitt, "Russell on Religion," 52.
44. Russell, Why, 23.

regard, nevertheless need not bear all blame on this score, for founders share in at least a portion of the responsibility for the harms done.[45] Furthermore, he also suggests that followers are bound to get some of their teacher's teaching wrong.

Russell delineated in his book *On Education, Especially in Early Childhood* four traits he considered essential to ideal character: vitality, sensitiveness, courage, and intelligence.[46] These traits are often presented in contrast to traditional religious beliefs that deprive the individual from the opportunity of acquiring any and all of these traits, according to Russell. So, for example, he contends that conventional religious morality sufficiently sapped any vitality that an individual might initially possess. The belief in original sin, the Calvinist horror of "natural man,"[47] and obedience to ten commandments that told one what not to do[48] were effective if one's desire was to be rendered morbidly impotent, but if not, an obvious reversal in the teaching of "virtue" was required:

> The first and greatest change that is required is to establish a morality of initiative, not a morality of submission, a morality of hope rather than fear, of things to be done rather than things to be left undone. It is not the whole duty of man to slip through the world so as to escape the wrath of God.[49]

In Russell's view, traditional religion had suppressed the instinctive life of man to a consequent listlessness[50] and driven him to think he could do his whole duty to God in solitude.[51] This resulted in a morbid self-absorption, with individuals imagining that the most important thing in the universe was that they should be virtuous.[52] Contrary to the Calvinist claim that the "natural man" was absorbed in self, quite the reverse was true.[53] To Russell, the natural man was the desired man, for he had an exuberance about life that issued from a natural vitality. However, with religious self-absorption came a related propensity to seek humbleness

---

45. Russell, *Why*, 18.
46. Russell, *On Education*, 35.
47. Russell, *Mysticism and Logic*, 37.
48. Russell, *Human Society*, 32.
49. Russell, *Principles of Social Reconstruction*, 141.
50. Russell, *Principles of Social Reconstruction*, 141.
51. Russell, *Marriage and Morals*, 176.
52. Russell, *Conquest of Happiness*, 176–77.
53. Russell, *Marriage and Morals*, 291.

before God, for to be humble was both right and prudent, for God would punish pride.⁵⁴ Quiet submission was the goal. This tendency stifled man's creative innovativeness, for he felt himself always under the jealous eye of God,⁵⁵ fearful that to enjoy and make his life here below too comfortable, he would perhaps lose the desire for God's heaven.⁵⁶ Thus, most religious people saw the futility of their earthly existence in comparison to a greater heaven, and so the betterment of this world and the evils in it were minimized: no one would expend exorbitant labor in a habitat they were certain to vacate later.⁵⁷

Furthermore, Russell asserted that along with a mentality afflicted by fear of wrongdoing before God came a hesitancy to be sensitive to the well-being of others. Religious believers had buffered whatever natural sympathy they might have by a fear that their extended sympathies might undo some of God's fit chastisements for sin. Accordingly, Russell noted that the use of anesthesia at childbirth was initially opposed by clergymen who reminded medical men that God had told Eve her children would be brought forth in sorrow.⁵⁸ Similarly, according to Russell, many religious believers had objected to efforts to alleviate the afflictions of venereal diseases on the ground that they were punishments by God for sin.⁵⁹ In Russell's own time this lack of sensitivity was depicted by a Catholic and Anglican endorsement of the "harsher" of the two pronouncements in the New Testament on divorce.⁶⁰

> The consequent improvement in health and increase of longevity is one of the most remarkable and admirable characteristics of our age. Even if science had done nothing else for human happiness, it would deserve our gratitude on this account. Those who believe in the utility of theological creeds would have difficulty in pointing to any comparable advantage that they have conferred upon the human race.⁶¹

54. Russell, *History*, 538.

55. Russell makes much in his writing of how an absorption in the awareness of sin is not conducive to good mental health, nor to happiness. This is one of the main points of his *Conquest of Happiness*, a book which "won very high praise" from professional psychiatrists. Russell, *1914–1944*, 219.

56. Russell, "Religion and Happiness," 714–15.

57. Russell, *Education and the Social Order*, 72.

58. Russell, *Religion and Science*, 105.

59. Russell, *Marriage and Morals*, 149.

60. Russell, *Human Society*, 14.

61. Russell, *Religion and Science*, 108–09.

One of the chief objections to religion for Russell is that its moral precepts date from a more barbarous age and would die out but for the support of religion.[62] The softening of the "ferocious" doctrine of Calvinism[63] and the decay of belief in hell has been due to a lessening of men's brutality toward one another in comparison to the barbarous ages in which those reprehensible doctrines were formulated.[64] While the orthodox have lamented this loss of belief, religious liberalism was fond of boasting of the mildness of their religious beliefs and practices in comparison to those of past ages, failing to note, however, that this "mildness" was not due to religion, but to the assaults of freethinkers.[65]

Inasmuch as "fear is the source of all that is bad in the world,"[66] Russell is contemptuous of a religion based on fear, when religion could be inculcating courage. However, men had largely been driven to belief in God out of fear,[67] and belief in immortality would probably have never arisen if they had not feared death.[68] Men have paid dearly for their fears in the past: under the impression that the gods were angry with them, they had often attempted appeasement by human sacrifices; under the biblical injunction to "suffer not a witch to live," innocent women met their end because of fear of failing to heed God's commandments.[69] In this vein of criticism, Russell's position is perhaps best summarized though also exaggerated by himself: "My own view of religion is that of Lucretius. I regard it as a disease born of fear and as a source of untold misery to the human race."[70]

In Russell's view intelligence was the cure of these human ills, but traditional religion had minimized the role of intelligence in promoting well-being. Russell counts it a liability of the New Testament that there is not one word in the Gospels in praise of intelligence.[71] In fact religion

---

62. Russell, *Why*, 30.
63. Russell, *History*, 365.
64. Russell, *Religion and Science*, 135–36.
65. Russell, *Why*, 37, 198.
66. Russell, *How to Be Free and Happy*, 28.
67. Russell, *How to Be Free and Happy*, 28.
68. Russell, *Why*, 53.
69. Russell, *Religion and Science*, 90.
70. Russell, *Why*, 24.
71. Russell, *Education and the Social Order*, 73. Russell writes of his father that "He, as appears in his letters ... did not believe in the divinity of Christ, whose ethic seemed to him defective in not laying enough stress on intelligence." Russell, *AP* I:35.

spread the idea that thought was not necessary to virtue: the ignorant could as readily attain favor with God as the learned.[72] While an element of virtue was necessary for good-will, without intelligence good-will was "impotent and transient."[73]

Continuing his charges against religion, Russell contends that religion had another reason, however, for minimizing the role of intelligence besides its infatuation with virtue. Intellect was prone to attack religious beliefs as little more than comfortable myths designed to placate man's fears. Religious believers, under the guise of defending religion, were in fact seeking to maintain the prestige of the human in a universe they feared had no such feeling.[74] Intellect refused to patronize such fears and prejudices, and hence was frequently castigated by religion for exalting itself above God. Intellect had been the great dispeller of fear, but, as might be expected, religion opposed it.

Russell's identification of religion as one of the major culprits responsible for much unnecessary cruelty in the world made him ferociously averse to the harm that he reckoned religion had produced. Though the power of religion has subsided over past centuries, Russell claimed that, if unchecked, religion and its authorities would resume the quest for power unabated. However, Russell's relentless and public quest against harm and cruelty could mask his underlying motivation in such an endeavor. Readers of Russell on the harmfulness of religion may suspect him in the same way that one reviewer of Russell's *Unpopular Essays* did: as a man to whom "nothing is holy." This assessment could hardly reveal a greater misunderstanding. Russell is so irreverent because he does regard some things as in some manner sacred, and his commentary on the failures of religion is due to his desire to remove the religious obstacles that he saw as impediments to the well-being and indeed the felicity of individuals and society. This singular motivation is at the same time both the source of his own desire for a religion and his own irreverence toward much established religion. In Russell's view religion had in a convoluted manner simultaneously provided for but also prevented the realization of traits he valued in individuals and in society. This dual nature of religion is not to be deemed mysterious or impenetrable. Rather, the religious instinct is conceived by Russell as extremely pliable, tending either to good or to evil. Religion, then, is not an unalloyed good, nor is

---

72. Russell, *Human Society*, 63.
73. Russell, Review of *Pagan and Christian Creeds*, 118.
74. Russell, *Scientific Outlook*, 43.

it an unmitigated evil. This balanced view of the potential in religion was a point of view Russell sought to bring to his readers and audiences.

However, Russell's tremendous aversion to our inhumanity to one another found focus in those forms of religion conceived and nourished by fear. In *Why I Am Not a Christian*—a work of pure agnostic apology without one good word for religion in any of the fifteen essays—we are told in the most famous essay of the group that "Fear is the basis of the whole thing—fear of the mysterious, fear of defeat, fear of death."[75] Russell's own search for a personal religion and any accolades for it had to be tempered with his recognition that religion could crush civilization as easily as it might guide it.

Brandishing philosophical weapons and with oratory reminiscent of Tom Paine in 1789, Russell's writings on religion bristle with condemnations of any religion that impedes the progress of civilizing a human race only too prone to totter toward barbarism. In *Why I Am Not a Christian*, certainly his most widely read book on religion, he charges that:

> The knowledge exists by which universal happiness can be secured; the chief obstacle to its utilization for that purpose is the teaching of religion. Religion prevents our children from having a rational education; religion prevents us from removing the fundamental causes of war; religion prevents us from teaching the ethic of scientific co-operation in place of the old fierce doctrines of sin and punishment. It is possible that mankind is on the threshold of a golden age; but, if so, it will be necessary first to slay the dragon that guards the door, and this dragon is religion.[76]

In light of denunciations such as these, Russell has justifiably been compared to Voltaire on religion. This kind of legacy has been nourished by champions and assailants of Russell and flourishes in the focus on his penchant for criticizing the failings of religion, with few qualifications. Any sympathies for religion held by Russell, moreover, have been overshadowed by his own skill and relentlessness at chronicling the falsities and foibles of religion. The resulting interpretation of Russell on religion, again, owes its ultimate origins to Russell's belief that there were things wrong with the world, and that on balance religion was a major contributor to this state of affairs and a comparatively negligible contributor to progress. Russell's concern about the perception of his religious views,

75. Russell, *Why*, 22.
76. Russell, *Why?*, 47.

therefore, fell to favoring his opposition to religion. In this opposition his castigations and his repudiations appear with scant qualifications, thus seeming to exhibit no sympathy for religion.

D. RELIGION AS FALSE BUT POSSIBLE IN RUSSELL

On rare occasions, the positive and the negative in Russell's view of religion can be found together. In *Principles of Social Reconstruction*, a work written during World War I and before Russell began to gain notoriety for his negative views on religion, he expressed a view of religion that even at the time of his response to Brightman in 1944 Russell still referred to as the "least unsatisfactory." However, there are two passages in this work where Russell may appear to express two different—perhaps even contradictory—thoughts about his subject. These statements thus may appear to be in conflict, but on inspection they interface at some points while clarifying some distinctions within Russell's religious views. The first statement is on thinking:

> Men fear thought as they fear nothing else on earth—more than ruin, more even than death. Thought is subversive and revolutionary, destructive and terrible; thought is merciless to privilege, established institutions, and comfortable habits; thought is anarchic and lawless, indifferent to authority, careless of the well-tried wisdom of the ages. Thought looks into the pit of hell and is not afraid. It sees man, a feeble speck, surrounded by unfathomable depths of silence; yet it bears itself proudly, as unmoved as if it were the lord of the universe. Thought is great and swift and free, the light of the world, and the chief glory of man.[77]

What makes thought so feared is that it reveals truth to be as fearsome as itself. Indeed, thought and truth are interchangeable in the first half of the paragraph; in the last half ethical prescriptions are laid upon thought in the face of truth. Truth, as revealed by thought, is hard for man because it takes no thought of him or of anything else. Man, however proudly, stares into the pit of hell, not the beatific vision. Thus, though thought be unafraid, it is hardly felicitous. Because truth is usually painful rather than pleasant, the temptation for religion is present; here, however, support for thought takes place with religious imagery

---

77. Russell, *Principles of Social Reconstruction*, 165–66.

pressed into secular service. In this extraordinary paragraph, Russell the liberal, the freethinker and the humanist, exalts man's grandeur in religious phraseology: lord of the universe, light of the world. Though thought in the passage is merely free thought, it sounds like Hegelian Thought or Reason. The passage could have been part of an address to the National Secular Society. Eighty pages later is a passage on man the feeble speck. It could have been delivered from a pulpit:

> The world has need of a philosophy, or a religion, which will promote life. But in order to promote life it is necessary to value something other than mere life. Life devoted only to life is animal, without any real human value, incapable of preserving men permanently from weariness and the feeling that all is vanity. If life is to be fully human it must serve some end which seems, in some sense, outside human life, some end which is impersonal and above mankind, such as God or truth or beauty. Those who best promote life do not have life for their purpose. They aim rather at what seems like a gradual incarnation, a bringing into our human existence of something eternal, something that appears in imagination to live in a heaven remote from strife and failure and the devouring jaws of Time. Contact with this eternal world—even if it be only a world of our imagining—brings a strength and fundamental peace which cannot be wholly destroyed by the struggles and apparent failures of our temporal life.[78]

In this passage the speaker suggests that thought attach itself to one of the transcendentals: God, truth, or beauty. Thought is noble to the extent that it is emancipated from the thought of self and attached to one of these three. To make a better world the objects of one's thought cannot be of this world—though they regrettably are. The world, having been deprived of a theological metaphysic or a suitable philosophical substitute, points humanity back toward itself. Russell is reticent to assign the locus of value in the universe to its human inhabitants because he fears that they may never rise higher than themselves. But they need something larger than themselves in order to give themselves significance. A theological or a philosophical doctrine might have provided this, but in their absence an eviscerated transcendental will have to do.

What Russell writes here, though veering toward the transcendent, must nonetheless weather the realization that the transcendentals are but

---

78. Russell, *Principles of Social Reconstruction*, 245.

the creations of humans finding themselves as feeble specks in the silent universe. With this hardly happy realization one can nevertheless choose to salvage transcendentals as guiding lights for human life, or one can choose to acknowledge that all the light there is in the world is human light, and thus humanity is indeed the light of the world. The latter choice is one that gave Russell considerable pause and reticent acquiescence:

> Those who attempt to make a religion of humanism, which recognizes nothing greater than man, do not satisfy my emotions. And yet I am unable to believe that, in the world as known, there is anything that I can value outside human beings, and, to a much lesser extent, animals. Not the starry heavens, but their effects on human percipients, have excellence; to admire the universe for its size is slavish and absurd; impersonal nonhuman truth appears to be a delusion. And so my intellect goes with the humanists, though my emotions violently rebel. In this respect, the "consolations of philosophy" are not for me.[79]

Some form of personal religion, however evil the larger history of religion, was needed for good, and evidence for this need is found scattered across Russell's writings. It was a notion that the circumstances of Russell's life did not permit him to develop, but neither to abandon, although sympathy for religion seems to progressively diminish during his long life. The increasing negativity toward religion, however, might as easily be seen as frustration with the human inability to direct human life towards goodness rather than committing evils. The rub is that Russell frequently contends that religion makes man out to be worse than he actually is, but when man is worse than what Russell thought him capable, religion is made responsible for the difference. Into such a dichotomy slips the implication that religion is blameworthy and its opponent laudatory and that the opponent of religion is pointing to a world that religion and the traditional allies of religion obstinately refuse to concede. Thus, the impediments that religions impose on the rise of civilization are brazenly as bad as religion's untruths. Nevertheless, Russell's combating of bad religion could and did mask his sympathies for a form of religion, while his predominantly negative writings require some careful sifting to find any form of religion that could pass muster. Such complexity in a thinker as prolific in writing as Russell is one reason that Katharine Tait, who knew her father Russell better than virtually anyone

---

79. Russell, *Basic Writings*, 49.

else writing about him in 1975, could draw a portrait of Russell contrary to and therefore surprising to the presumed legacy of Russell as only a mocker of religion.

Russell's writings surely did castigate religion, even as he sometimes conceded there was the germ of something commendable in it. The sins of religion, however, vastly predominant in Russell's writings:

> The principles of the Sermon on the Mount are admirable, but their effect upon average human nature was very different from what was intended. Those who followed Christ did not learn to love their enemies or turn the other cheek. They learned instead to use the Inquisition and the stake, to subject the human intellect to the yoke of an ignorant and intolerant priesthood, to degrade art and extinguish science for a thousand years.[80]

Historically, the founders of religions have had very little to do with what their purported followers have taught or practiced,[81] to the degree, in the instance of Christianity, that its founder would be astounded at it today.[82] Religious organizations have had a life of their own—apart from the intentions of their founders[83]—and it has been organized religion that has influenced civilization, not, for the most part, the founders[84]: "The world owes something to the Gospels, though not so much as it would if they had had more influence...."[85]

For Russell, this trajectory of influence has impeded real progress in matters religious. That is, with the organized religions that have grown up around their founders has also grown an indifference to personal religion. Historically the laity has been the main source of moral renovation in the Catholic Church, but on most occasions has found itself labeled as an antagonist by the Church.[86] This dichotomy has increasingly solidified to the point that little of what is of real value in religion comes from those who are eminent in organized religion: "This division has weakened the force of religion: religious bodies have not been strengthened by the enthusiasm and single-mindedness of the men in whom personal

---

80. Russell, *Bolshevism*, 17.
81. Russell, *Bertrand Russell Speaks His Mind*, 27.
82. Russell, *History*, 378.
83. Russell, *History*, 378.
84. Russell, *Why*, 25.
85. Russell, *Power*, 241.
86. Russell, *Education and the Social Order*, 71.

religion is strong, and these men have not found their teaching diffused and made permanent by the power of ecclesiastical institutions."[87]

This failure of organized religion to maintain the trust of its position has been largely due to its preoccupation with the power vested in it,[88] and in the desire to maintain that authority, the Church has historically been instinctively conservative, with the regrettable consequence of opposing any increase in individual or social betterment that might deprive the Church of its authority. In fact, the ". . .Churches, everywhere, opposed as long as they could practically every innovation that made for an increase of happiness or knowledge here on earth."[89] In its effort to preserve power why had the Church succeeded so well? Predominantly for the reason that the final appeal to the authority of the Church rested in exploiting fear, the main source of the motivation of ill-gotten religion. The Catholic Church had so effectively dangled the keys of heaven because they patronized this culpable human trait of fear.

However, such an assertion by Russell also indicated that he could ascribe mixed motivations in the origin of religious feeling; fear need not be the only motivation to religion. This perspective is typified in a passage from Russell's *A History of Western Philosophy*:

> There are two sorts of saints: the saint by nature, and the saint by fear. The saint by nature has a spontaneous love of mankind; he does good because to do so gives him happiness. The saint from fear on the other hand, like the man who only abstains from theft because of the police, would be wicked if he were not restrained by the thought of hell-fire or of his neighbour's vengeance.[90]

---

87. Russell, *Principles of Social Reconstruction*, 138.

88. Russell is opposed to a number of other social institutions and ideas besides those of religion, and it is essential to keep this fact in mind in attempting to understand specifically what he opposes. That is, many of the vices so blatantly exhibited by religion are not unique to that institution. Russell's criticism here of the church's misuse of power, he also applies to communism: "I think the most important thing that is wrong in communist doctrine is the belief in benevolent despotism. A belief which is really ancient and existed in all sorts of communities, but has always proved itself wrong, because when you take a benevolent man and make him a despot, his despotism survives but his benevolence rather fades away." Russell, *Speaks His Mind*, 55. Pitt in "Russell on Religion," 43, makes the following perceptive comment in reference to Russell's castigations of organized religion: "It is the charge that the churches have sinned." Ultimately, however, this criticism by Russell boils down to a criticism of the faults of human beings.

89. Russell, *History*, 529.

90. Russell, *History*, 768.

According to Russell it was the latter type of saint who had the greater share in the history of religion. Without minimizing the contribution to civilization of the preferred kind of saint—and Russell sometimes conceded their contribution—it was not they who proved a menace to humanity. Since the saints by fear greatly outnumbered the saints by nature, Russell gave more of his time to writing against the former than he did commending the latter. In a world which had misused the religious impulse, commending religious sympathies would be at the risk of neglecting a weightier priority. Russell's choice of emphasis is more a matter of expediency rather than of personal choice—as indicated in his April 1911 letter to Lady Ottoline quoted earlier. Thus, the same Russell who charged religion with being "a source of untold misery to the human race" and "hoped it would die out," also wrote that if the feelings giving rise to religion should die "most of what is best would vanish out of life."[91] With the latter assessment of religion Russell is, of course, speaking of the saint by nature, not the saint by fear—but also of religion divorced from erroneous theologies and powerful institutions.

In contending that Russell's concern about the perception of his religious views favored his opposition to religion, we thus cannot lose sight of the other component of his thinking—that religion is vital to humanity. Nevertheless, he regarded religion in its organizational and theological or metaphysical aspects as having brought a preponderance of inhumanity to the world. Moreover, the fight against bad religion rarely gave Russell pause to indicate his belief that there could be religion of another kind. Under the weight of confronting the problems of his world—problems to a great degree, in Russell's view, created or sustained by religion—he spoke much more about religion as contributing to the problems and rather less as contributing to any betterment of humanity. Russell's criticism of religion proved to be a formidable, though necessary, task in his eyes, but it resulted in less attention given to any positive view or place for religion in his life and in his thought. This is why he more often shows scant concern to speak of religion as a positive influence on humanity than as an obstacle to increasing human progress.

---

91. Russell, *Principles of Social Reconstruction*, 208.

3

Russell on Belief and Unbelief

A. RELIGIOUS BELIEF

According to Russell, the vast majority of religious believers courted religious belief on emotional grounds and scarcely bothered with intellectual arguments. However, a few believers professed to base their belief in God on such arguments.[1] Though Russell oftentimes was critical of the sincerity of their aims,[2] he much preferred an actual argument for God's existence to a sentimental religious apologetic attempting to validate belief in God by what Russell regarded as subversive means:

> For my part, I prefer the ontological argument, the cosmological argument, and the rest of the old stock-in-trade, to the sentimental illogicality that has sprung from Rousseau. The old arguments at least were honest: if valid, they proved the point; if invalid, it was open to any critic to prove them so. But the new theology of the heart dispenses with argument; it cannot be refuted, because it does not profess to prove its points. At bottom, the only reason offered for its acceptance is that it allows us to indulge in pleasant dreams. This is an unworthy reason, and if I

---

1. "Of course I know that the sort of intellectual arguments that I have been talking to you about are not what really moves people. What really moves people to believe in God is not any intellectual argument at all. Most people believe in God because they have been taught from early infancy to do it, and that is the main reason." Russell, *Why*, 13–14.

2. Russell's claim is that religious believers frequently presume belief and adduce reasons afterward.

had to choose between Thomas Aquinas and Rousseau, I should unhesitatingly choose the Saint.[3]

In Russell's day, a particular kind of argument that lent specious clout to the affirmation of God's existence had arisen in pragmatism and Russell maintained some of his harshest criticisms for this philosophy, counting it the most recent example of intellectual deviousness. His disdain for pragmatism was most evident regarding religious belief, with Russell mockingly asserting that "The advantage of the pragmatic method is that it decides the question of the truth of the existence of God by purely mundane arguments, namely, by the effects of belief in His existence upon our life in the world. But unfortunately this gives a merely mundane conclusion, namely, that belief in God is true, i.e., useful, whereas what religion desires is the conclusion that God exists, which pragmatism never even approaches."[4]

For Russell the fault of pragmatism was to forego any honest and genuine attempt to answer questions by diverting the real issue of truth; this fault compromised the possibility of ascertaining the real truth and served as a covert and devious ploy to permit religious belief entry by a back door. Russell's contention was that the supposed results of such a dubious inquiry were vitiated by a bias calculated for one's own liking. With desired religious beliefs precluding any actual reasoned justification to support those beliefs, such claims are suspect.[5] In this regard, Russell calls attention to Bradley's statement that metaphysics is the finding of bad reasons for what one believes by instinct.[6] Therefore, for Russell the claims of religious belief are vitiated and made suspect by

---

3. Russell, *History*, 694.

4. Russell, *Philosophical Essays*, 125.

5 Russell makes the following statement in that regard in *ABC of Relativity*, 135: "When men began to reason they tried to justify the inferences that they had drawn unthinkingly in earlier days. A great deal of bad philosophy and bad science resulted from that propensity." Russell makes the same charge against the Catholic Church in *Why*, 5: "...the Catholic Church has laid it down as a dogma that the existence of God can be proved by the unaided reason. That is a somewhat curious dogma, but it is one of their dogmas. They had to introduce it because at one time the free-thinkers adopted the habit of saying that there were such and such arguments which mere reason might urge against the existence of God, but of course they knew as a matter of faith that God did exist....Therefore they laid it down that the existence of God could be proved by the unaided reason and they had to set up what they considered were arguments to prove it."

6 The implication is not that Russell believed that this was the proper way to do metaphysics, but rather that the subject should be pursued in a neutral and disinterested fashion.

uncritical assumptions about our own desires; by contrast, science has produced methodologies excluding vested interests and has had consequent extraordinary success in the acquisition of knowledge. Philosophers desiring to acquire answers to difficult questions should adopt the methodology of science. Moreover, according to Russell religious beliefs are suspect by failing to take account of what constitutes a sufficient reason for assent to truth-claims. Russell's view of why religious beliefs elicit assent, though he admits overstatement on occasion, is as follows:

> Orthodoxy and a virtuous life, I am told, will enable me to go to heaven when I die; there is pleasure in believing this, therefore I shall probably believe it if it is forcibly presented to me. The cause of belief, here, is not, as in science, the evidence of fact, but the present feelings derived from belief, together with sufficient vigor of assertion in the environment to make the belief seem not incredible.[7]

The desire to attain truth, without reservations, as opposed to the desire to arrive at edifying results, is virtually as much a rarity among philosophers as the assent to religious beliefs among the religious. Russell therefore sees any such failure to distinguish between the world or truth as we would like it to be and the world and truth as it in fact is, as perhaps the chief vice infecting knowledge-claims since its introduction by Plato: Russell thus lays this charge at the feet of not a few thinkers beyond the Athenian philosopher.

> Philosophers, from Plato to William James, have allowed their opinions as to the constitution of the universe to be influenced by the desire for edification: knowing, as they supposed, what beliefs would make men virtuous, they have invented arguments, often very sophistical to prove that these beliefs are true. For my part I reprobate this kind of bias, both on moral and on intellectual grounds.[8]

---

7 Russell, *Power*, 139–40.

8 Russell, *History*, 834–35. Russell's warning against this kind of intrusion is not only found in his more popular works, but also in his more technical philosophy. In the last chapter of *Our Knowledge of the External World* such warnings are given: "The desire to know philosophical truth is very rare—in its purity, it is not often found even among philosophers." Russell, *Our Knowledge*, 183; "The desire to establish this or that result, or generally to discover evidence for agreeable results, of whatever kind, has of course been the chief obstacle to honest philosophizing. So strangely perverted do men become by unrecognized passions, that a determination in advance to arrive at this or that conclusion is generally regarded as a mark of virtue, and those whose studies lead to an opposite conclusion are thought to be wicked. No doubt it is commoner to wish

Accordingly, philosophers congenial toward religion are guilty of biased investigation. Persuaded that religious beliefs gives credence to our wish for high standing in the cosmos, these philosophers have been prepared to defend dubious religious assertions. However, as might be guessed, any arguments propelled from such a perspective are designed to present positive and agreeable conclusions, and are thus subject to severe criticisms by Russell. Such arguments are surreptitiously legislating ontology on the basis of desires prejudicial to the results of inquiry. Plato's Socrates, because he was "determined to prove the universe agreeable to his ethical standards . . . we may believe him admitted to the communion of saints; but as a philosopher he needs a long residence in scientific purgatory."[9] Kant, perceiving that Hume's criticisms of traditional religion made much that he wished to believe in difficult, introduced various postulates he thought necessary for virtue under the rubric of "practical reason," which of course, should have been called, not "practical reason," in distinction from pure reason, but prejudice.[10] Some philosophers, however, have not seen any need for such facades, such as the idealist McTaggart, who by his own admission did metaphysics for the "cheerful conclusions" he expected. On this matter, one of Russell's milder rebuffs is for his friend Whitehead, who built a superstructure of metaphysics, according to Russell, in an attempt at "escaping from belief in a merely mechanistic universe."[11] All such thinkers, to one degree or another, have let their emotions, intuitions, and other unworthy suppliers finesse their "arguments."

The assumption of such thinkers is to assume belief in advance of inquiry; for how do they know that reality, or the universe, has purposes congenial with our own? That is, there is an epistemological quantum-leap made without providing any legitimate justification for this belief according to Russell. The attempts at justifying this belief, when any actual attempts have been made, have been sadly deficient in the reasons adduced. As an example, when Edgar Brightman claimed that the appetite of religious impulse in humans was justification for belief in God, Russell's reply was pointed and uncompromising: "I cannot agree. The fact that I

---

to arrive at an agreeable result than to wish to arrive at a true result. But only those in whom the desire to arrive at a *true* result is paramount can hope to serve any good purpose by the study of philosophy." Russell, *Our Knowledge*, 184.

9 Russell, *History*, 143.
10 Russell, *Let the People Think*, 63.
11 Russell, *1872–1914*, 201.

feel a need for something more than human is no evidence that the need can be satisfied, anymore than hunger is evidence that I shall get food. I do not see how any emotion of mine can be evidence of something outside me."[12] Much religious and philosophical thought has, nevertheless, presumed that the universe provides for the ultimate desires of man. Because of the tremendous and unarguable success of science in such areas as the physical sciences, however, religious believers have been forced to fight a defensive battle for their cherished notions, though they have lost their battle inch by inch, until finally religious thinkers hit upon the idea of using the results of science so as to adduce religion.[13] Scientific thought, however, Russell contends, favors no such conclusions.

Thinkers congenial toward religion nonetheless continue to covet the idea that the universe embodies a purpose that includes humanity, however weak their failed arguments.[14] While such persons would never regard a physician's diagnosis of terminal cancer as untrue simply because it was unwelcome, religious apologists nonetheless refuse to accept the pronouncement that the universe is indifferent to our desires solely because they find that assertion unpleasant.[15] Science has found our ethical wishes, as it found the search for final causes, an impediment to the acquisition of real knowledge, and today we find it unconscionable to erect parameters upon the results of scientific investigation. Nevertheless, religious beliefs maintain a defense not by real argument, but by people's wants and desires. In this exhibition of lacking legitimate reasons, Russell finds the illicit influence of human desires evidenced in most thinkers inclined toward religion, and because of it their thinking is infected with a resulting "optimistic bias"[16] with no basis in reality.

The initial issue for any religious belief, then, is to advance a cogent argument for believing that reality reveals a purpose congenial to our own desires. Such a task is much greater than the advocates of traditional religion are willing to acknowledge, for the scope and limitations

---

12 Russell, "Reply to Criticisms," *CP* 11:52.

13 Typical of the manner in which Russell condemns such a move is the first sentence of his review of a work by Julian Huxley, who sought to substantiate his liberal theology with the results of science: "In the time of Mr. Huxley's grandfather, biology was a new enemy to religion; now they are allies." Russell, Review of *Essays of a Biologist*, 223.

14 Russell claimed that religiously-minded persons, however liberal, whether scientists or not, were all one in their belief in "Cosmic Purpose." Accordingly, in his *The Scientific Outlook* he devotes a full chapter to attacking the belief.

15 Russell, *Fact and Fiction*, 47.

16 Russell, "Reply to Criticisms," *CP* 11:53.

of our knowledge prevent acceptance of most, if not all, of the usual time-honored convictions and contentions of religious belief. Theology has of course professed to give answers to some of our most ultimate questions, but its very definiteness has cast doubt on its reliability.[17] Meanwhile, theologians have lived in apparent ignorance or suppression of the fact that deductive reasoning about the world, in their case from "an unquestionable text,"[18] has not been accepted since the time of Galileo.

Therefore, even if any religious truth-claims were factually true, it is a doubtful whether "this fortunate fact could be discovered by the faculties of the human mind."[19] On the question of the existence of God, therefore, whether it be the Christian God or any other, inquiry is virtually futile, for such questions "lie outside the region of even probable knowledge."[20] Thus, while admitting the inability to precisely and definitively refute the truth-claims of religion,[21] Russell's more frequent charge is the inability to confirm them. By contrast, science is buttressed by a methodology of observation and inferences that one with the requisite knowledge and means can undertake to verify or prove.

In this particular charge, that is, of theological claims being unverifiable, Russell shows some relatedness to the logical positivists, though he remained critical of some perspectives of the positivists despite the affinities he shared with them. As an example of the difference between Russell and the positivists, the positivists regarded the raising of the question of God's existence as asking a "meaningless" question. Russell did not, and parted company with positivism on their analysis of "God exists":

> The orthodox and the unorthodox alike will feel a certain reluctance to accept the view that the words "God exists" are a mere meaningless noise, like 'Abracadabra.' Whatever may be the logical definition of the deity, the word "God" is one which arouses certain emotions, and the question in people's minds is whether there is an object to which these emotions are appropriate. This question is not disposed of by Mr. Ayer's arguments.[22]

---

17 Russell, *History*, xiv.
18 Russell, *History*, 199.
19 Russell, *Power*, 225.
20 Russell, *Why*, 51.
21 Russell, *Religion and Science*, 145.
22 Russell, Review of *Language, Truth and Logic*, 542.

However, despite Russell's claim that the pragmatist and the positivist—though in different ways— merely skirted the real question of God's existence, he nonetheless deemed that when the arguments for God's existence were subject to logical and empirical scrutiny and not fanciful caveats, the existence of God could be deemed highly unlikely.

B. SCIENTIFIC BELIEF

To what should appeal be made in attempting to ascertain the truth on any matter? According to Russell whether we think that among various beliefs one tends to edification more than the others, or is more morally desirable, is irrelevant. Traditions of revelation presumed from God are hardly acceptable, because there are multiple claimants to such revelation, with no apparent sufficient criterion to distinguish authenticity among them.[23] Neither is intuition acceptable. As suggestive of possible truth, intuition might serve a purpose, but as an arbitrator of truth and falsity it is faulty. For this purpose reason is needed. What is meant by reason?

> I think that what we mean in practice by reason can be defined by three characteristics. In the first place, it relies upon persuasion rather than force; in the second place, it seeks to persuade by means of arguments which the man who uses them believes to be completely valid; and in the third place, in forming opinions, it uses observation and induction as much as possible and intuition as little as possible.[24]

Russell also acknowledges that in assessing knowledge claims it is necessary to begin with premises lacking proof, and hence a consideration has to be made of what premises we are warranted in accepting in this role:

> We must therefore ask ourselves: What sort of thing is it reasonable to believe without proof? I should reply: The facts of sense-experience and the principles of mathematics and logic—including the inductive logic employed in science. These are things which we can hardly bring ourselves to doubt and as to which there is a large measure of agreement among mankind. But in matters as to which men disagree, or as to which our own

---

23 Russell, *Outline of Philosophy*, 236.
24 Russell, *Let the People Think*, 64.

convictions are wavering, we should look for proofs, or, if proofs cannot be found, we should be content to confess ignorance.[25]

Relatedly, according to Russell, all definite knowledge belongs to science, whereas "all dogma as to what surpasses definite knowledge belongs to theology."[26] Theology is therefore hardly anything more than a spurious and error-laden enterprise for Russell. At the same time, while Russell recognizes that what merits the status of "knowledge" is something of a contentious matter in terms of degree,[27] nevertheless, the evidence of scientific beliefs exceeds those of either theology or philosophy. Science, however, "as the defenders of religion emphatically assert,"[28] cannot make pronouncements on values. Against these defenders of religion, however, Russell claims that questions of value lie wholly outside the realm of knowledge. Therefore, these "defenders of religion" possess no privilege denied to others.

Russell made protracted attempts to bring scientific method to philosophy, and in one stage of his career as a philosopher this was his predominant message. Russell tended to think philosophy lacking in having followed theology in its vices, rather than following science in its virtues. That is, the philosopher, like the theologian, had tended to brashly assert himself ahead of his evidence by a crude methodology that gave credence to his wishes ahead of his dubious conclusions. Therefore, while the unrepentant or defiant theologian may entertain his illusion and delusions because his faith in theology is greater than his faith in science, this cannot be the position of any self-respecting philosopher in an age of science. The picture that science paints of the world and the sobering picture of our resultant place in it, however, remained of great interest to Russell and from that consideration he produced some of his best writing. In a single and often quoted sentence from Russell's essay, "The Free Man's Worship," in speaking of the bifurcated world of which we humans are an interested party, Russell wrote:

> A strange mystery it is that nature, omnipotent but blind, in the revolutions of her secular hurrying's through the abysses of space, has brought forth at last a child, subject still to her power,

---

25 Russell, *Atheism*, 4.
26 Russell, *History*, xiii.
27 Russell, *Human Knowledge*, 98.
28 Russell, *Religion and Science*, 230.

but gifted with sight, with knowledge of good and evil, with the capacity of judging all the works of his unthinking Mother.[29]

For Russell this issue or problem was the supreme paradox of the human situation. Russell never found any answer, but spoke with magisterial eloquence of this paradox as the supreme dilemma of human existence. While Russell admits that he finds this "arrangement" odd and particularly so in regard to the presence of human values in an indifferent amoral world, he refused to accept the view that the content of our moral sensibilities is not the result of the accidental contingencies of our world, and in time he relinquished his prior belief in objective values as found in "The Free-Man's Worship." This shift was in part his concession to the reigning scientific picture of the world. For those religious thinkers and people refusing to acknowledge this account of the universe we live in, Russell had only contempt.

While scarcely another thinker of the twentieth century clamored as loudly and as often against religion as Russell, there is an opposite pole in the man, for Russell is intent, as many secularists were not, to find some place for religion in a secular age. Together, these two facets of Russell present perhaps the greatest conundrum about the esteemed philosopher. On the one hand, Russell presents himself much in the mould of the rationalistic thinkers of the Enlightenment, particularly the French, but with shades of a romanticism that he was highly critical of, especially in the philosophy of Rousseau. Moreover, unlike the typical French philosophe, Russell on occasion could be more in the stream of the German Herder, both men giving attention to the spiritual life of humans as against the rationalistic tendency of pummeling religion so strong in the Enlightenment.

Nevertheless, for Russell the success of science tended to mitigate against mystical or religious possibility, however much the latter were desired. Furthermore, as previously pointed out, Russell regards the tremendous success of science in the discovery of knowledge as attributable to disregard of ethical prerogatives on any question: "The kernel of the scientific outlook is the refusal to regard our own desires, tastes and interests as affording a key to the understanding of the world."[30] This methodology has shown itself time and time again as the key to knowledge, often in the teeth of opposition from contentious religious

---

29. Russell, "Free-Man's Worship," CP 12:67.
30 Russell, "Place of Science in a Liberal Education," 40.

beliefs. Benjamin Franklin, for example, regarded electricity as a natural phenomenon to be harnessed for the benefit of man, but his experiments were regarded by some as impious attempts to thwart the will of God by the obstacles of lightning rods. Similarly, no progress was made in the treatment of persons with mental aberrations until such sickness was treated as natural phenomenon not due to the wickedness of the patient.

The mentality of science has largely been confined to such places as the laboratory, and its absence is most evident in such domains as religion, Russell contends. The reason is simple and undeniable according to Russell: the scientific mentality is not natural to and therefore not easy for human nature, as can be seen even among scientific men, who, when discussing something outside their own province of knowledge, are apt to resort to emotional or vested interest arguments they would never tolerate much less accept in scientific discussions.[31] Consequently, in science, while anticipated results are the reason and stimulus for inquiry, in a very real sense, the more important factor is not what is believed but how it is believed, because the latter is indicative of the trustworthiness of the former.[32]

To the religiously or mystically inclined, however, secular scientific procedures may be deemed futile and without efficacy in the arena of religion, a contention that Russell often squared off against. To the mystic something of an emotion must be worked up, that emotion permitting a confirmation of the mystic's perceived vision. However, even if one does make the requisite attempt, there is no guarantee that one will experience a confirmation of the claims of the mystic, according to Russell.[33] Nevertheless, for all of Russell's derisive comments about the mystic and the mystical experience, he was himself tempted by mysticism, seeming in his essay "Mysticism and Logic" to try to create some ground of

31 Russell, *Scientific Outlook*, 14.

32 Russell, *Human Society*, 184.

33. By the time of Russell's 1939 lecture on religion at Ann Arbor, his efforts with mysticism are largely spent. In his remarks to a questioner having asked Russell to "say a word, please, about mysticism and modern religion . . ." Russell responds that "Again it is difficult to say a word. A volume would seem more appropriate. I should say this about mysticism, that it has two different aspects. On the one hand it is an emotion. On the other hand as a result of that emotion people come to certain beliefs. Now, the emotion I value. I think it is a very important emotion indeed. I think the people who have experienced it are likely to be able to reach a higher level in certain respects than people who never reach it. But the beliefs that are based on that emotion vary according to the time and place. . . . I attach no truth whatever to the beliefs which mystics say result from their mystic insight." Russell, "Existence and Nature of God," *CP* 10:265–66.

legitimacy for mysticism to operate, while also singling out for criticism thinkers who have dubiously extended the legitimacy of the mystical domain. On the other hand, moreover, Russell finds no thinker so excessively antagonistic to mysticism as to suffer any rebuke by Russell. This is an indication, I think, that Russell's treatment of mysticism, despite what might be called its promise, is largely parallel to his treatment of religion. That is, though largely a critic of both, he at the same time permits each some, though guarded, and indeed very guarded, legitimacy. Any concessions to legitimacy, however, are oftentimes crushed by the rational undercurrents in Russell's thought.

Russell's inclination is to protect and defend reason and rational science against those persuaded by intuition of a mystical revelation, rather than protecting a mystical haven against rationalist critics. One motivation of the essay on "Mysticism and Logic" is to position the mystical vision and feeling into a quarter where science and real knowledge are not impeded by its presence. So Russell contends:

> In such matters as self-preservation and love, intuition will act sometimes (though not always) with a swiftness and precision which are astonishing to the critical intellect. But philosophy is not one of the pursuits which illustrate our affinity with the past: it is a highly refined, highly civilized pursuit, demanding, for its success, a certain liberation from the life of instinct, and even, at times, a certain aloofness from all mundane hopes and fears. It is not in philosophy, therefore, that we can hope to see intuition at its best. On the contrary, since the true objects of philosophy, and the habits of thought demanded for their apprehension, are strange, unusual, and remote, it is here, more almost than anywhere else, that intellect proves superior to intuition, and that quick analyzed convictions are least deserving of uncritical acceptance.[34]

If, however, Russell disassociates philosophy from intuition and mystical propensities, it might seem that such an assertion counters his larger contention in the essay, namely, that the best philosophy and philosophers exhibit some of both propensities. Nevertheless, his point here is that philosophy requires some needed distance in the interest of objectivity, whereas intuition works too closely to the self and too quickly for objective self-appraisal. In expanding in his next paragraph on this tension Russell contends that:

34. Russell, "Mysticism and Logic," *CP* 12:168.

> In advocating the scientific restraint and balance, as against the self-assertion of a confident reliance upon intuition, we are only urging, in the sphere of knowledge, that largeness of contemplation, that impersonal disinterestedness, and freedom from practical preoccupations which have been inculcated by all the great religions of the world. Thus our conclusion, however it may conflict with the explicit beliefs of many mystics, is, in essence, not contrary to the spirit which inspires those beliefs, but rather the outcome of this very spirit as applied in the realm of thought.[35]

In this passage, Russell suggests that the mystical mindset might be aligned with the spirit of the great religions and that possibly aligned with the origins of scientific thinking. However, in the previous passage, his intimation is that intuition by itself is faulty by being simply too close to its subject to maintain any objectivity. Because Russell's concession to the mystic is a concession to the emotional world of the mystic, at the same time it is loaded with caveats. That is, the human can be profitably instructed in the way of the mystic by way of self-enlargement, though not for acquiring truthful knowledge of the world. "It reveals a possibility of human nature—a possibility of a nobler, happier, freer life than any that can be otherwise achieved. But it does not reveal anything about the non-human, or about the nature of the universe in general. Good and bad, and even the higher good that mysticism finds everywhere, are the reflections of our own emotions on other things, not part of the substance of things as they are in themselves."[36]

Mysticism, therefore ends, much like religion, by suffering more rebuke than commendation in Russell's estimation, though Russell does contend that the religious and scientific viewpoint share something valuable.

> [A] philosophy which does not seek to impose upon the world its own conceptions of good and evil is not only more likely to achieve truth, but is also the outcome of a higher ethical standpoint.... In religion, and in every deeply serious view of the world and of human destiny, there is an element of submission, a realization of the limits of human power, which is somewhat lacking in the modern world.... The submission which religion inculcates in action is essentially the same in spirit as that

---

35. Russell, "Mysticism and Logic," *CP* 12:168.
36. Russell, "Mysticism and Logic," *CP* 12:174.

which science teaches in thought; and the ethical neutrality by which its victories have been achieved is the outcome of that submission.[37]

As previously noted, however, Russell charged religious followers with favoring their own desired view of the world by resisting a scientific enterprise attempting to see the world as it is, not as we should wish it to be. In Russell's time and to his chagrin, religious and implicit theological considerations had slighted reason and philosophy, while producing dubious philosophical systems, such as the kind much vaunted in Russell's day by the followers of Bergson. Meanwhile, Russell was engaged in strenuous efforts to make philosophy more like science, short of the excesses of the positivists, who left little room for philosophy in their conception of science.

> Plato produced a divorce between philosophy and science, from which, in my opinion, both have suffered ever since and are still suffering. The man of science, whatever his hopes may be, must lay them aside while he studies nature; and the philosopher, if he is to achieve truth, must do the same. Ethical considerations can only legitimately appear when the truth has been ascertained: they can and should appear as determining our feeling towards the truth, and our manner of ordering our lives in view of the truth, but not as themselves dictating what the truth is to be.[38]

This is a tendency that Russell never ceases to reiterate, simply because it continues to compromise the work of many.

Coupled with this vice is Russell's contention that intuition and its ally, instinct, "seems on the whole to diminish as civilization increases. It is greater, as a rule, in children than in adults, in the uneducated than in the educated. Probably in dogs it exceeds anything to be found in human beings. But those who see in these facts a recommendation of intuition ought to return to running wild in the woods, dyeing themselves with woad and living on hips and haws."[39] With this kind of swipe at the opposing position, Russell would seem to have little to no sympathy with the Counter-Enlightenment mentality of a Rousseau and of course he does not, for Russell often awards to Rousseau the prize of introducing into the modern world the error of trying to disestablish and

---

37. Russell, "Mysticism and Logic," *CP* 12:176.
38. Russell, "Mysticism and Logic," *CP* 12:161.
39. Russell, "Mysticism and Logic," *CP* 12:166–67.

revoke the rule of reason. At the same time Russell's sentiments toward romanticism, somewhat like his sentiments toward religion, are not all negative. Nonetheless, except for some youthful and adolescent strivings to incorporate a view of the natural world that would ease the rigidity of a feared determinism, in adulthood Russell virtually always shrinks from any perceived compromise to the scientific picture of the world. Thus, any argument for religious belief or life must come to terms and not evade the scientific picture of nature. Accordingly, the scientific view cannot be overturned by fanciful and concocted religious revisions to that view or picture. A religious life lived in modernity must acknowledge the fact that human values and goals are admittedly at variance with the picture modern science provides of the world. For Russell, this is a necessary admission that no religion can ignore, to include the great mystics. Furthermore, the maintenance of our all-too-human values in the face of an indifferent universe is a kind of rebellion against an antagonistic world. At the same time, this is why Russell sought for something outside the world providing the human some respite from his struggle.[40]

C. PHILOSOPHICAL BELIEF

In one characterization of philosophy, Russell describes the subject as a "No-Man's Land" lying intermediately between science and theology.[41] Like science it makes use of scientific method as much as possible, but unlike science, it makes pronouncements on questions about which science, thus far, has been unable to ascertain definite knowledge. In this latter feature philosophy is also like theology, except for the fact that the conclusions of philosophy are always tentative, like those of science, whereas theology, Russell asserts, requires dogmatic belief. Herein lies the value of philosophy, for science on its own admission cannot provide answers to our most sought-after questions, such as whether life has a

---

40. That having failed, so largely too did restlessness badger and distress Russell at the human level. This is the meaning of his contention that "I have since had so much conflict that many people have supposed that I must like it. I should, however, have much preferred to live at peace with everybody. But over and over again profound convictions have forced me into disagreements, even when I least desired them." Russell, *Portraits*, 5.

41. Russell, *History*, xiii. "All *definite* knowledge—so I should contend—belongs to science; all *dogma* as to what surpasses definite knowledge belongs to theology. But between theology and science there is a No Man's Land, exposed to attack from both sides; this No Man's Land is philosophy."

meaning, or, what man's position in the universe is. Science, moreover, is apt to forego these questions and may in fact undermine attention to them. Philosophy, however, keeps interest in these questions alive, or so Russell contends. On the other hand, impatience with questions remaining unanswered may provoke a temptation to extend knowledge claims to realms in which there is in fact no knowledge, as is typical of theology. Philosophy, to prevent this, keeps the limitations of human knowledge in proper perspective. Hence, philosophy has at the same time both an imaginative and a restrictive function.

When attempting to provide further specifics to Russell's conception of philosophy, the reader encounters conflicting statements in Russell's writings. However, some perceived inconsistencies in Russell's thought are more apparent than real, and as both Wood[42] and Copleston[43] point out, some of the ambiguities and apparent contradictions in Russell's writings are resolvable when it is recognized that Russell, when expounding his view on a certain matter, is at the same time often arguing against other viewpoints. Hence, he often exaggerates a point, almost exclusively a negative one. An awareness of this fact is a prerequisite for ascertaining Russell's views. This is not to say that in accounting for this factor, perfect consistency can be discovered in Russell's writings, as Russell himself never made claim that a definition of philosophy was easy to formulate.[44] Nevertheless, while Russell's variant pronouncements on philosophy cannot be subsumed into a perfectly consistent thread, we have already seen that Russell defined the limits of knowledge as restricted to science, and in this vein he is prepared to admit that philosophical thinking is not

---

42 Russell, *My Philosophical Development*, 204–5. Appended to the end of this book by Russell are a few pages of Alan Wood's draft of a work on Russell that was interrupted by Wood's death. Russell thought Wood's work valuable enough to include at the end of his book.

43 Copleston, *History of Philosophy*, 243.

44 For example, Russell begins his *Outline of Philosophy* with these words: "Perhaps it might be expected that I should begin with a definition of 'philosophy,' but, rightly or wrongly, I do not propose to do so. The definition of philosophy will vary according to the philosophy we adopt; all that we can say to begin with is that there are certain problems, which certain people find interesting, and which do not, at least at present, belong to any of the special sciences." Alan Wood claims that Russell finally gave up the attempt to define what philosophy was or what philosophers did. "For an illustration, we may consider the word 'philosophy' itself, which Russell finally gave up the attempt to define . . . . " Wood, "Cautionary Notes," appended in Russell's *My Philosophical Development*, 204.

such as would be admitted in a "strictly scientific treatise,"[45] and that the introduction of metaphysics into a discussion is an implicit admission that a point cannot be proved, for otherwise one would not resort to metaphysics.[46] Indeed, Russell at times went so far as to express doubt that philosophy, as a study distinct from science, "is anything more than an unfortunate legacy from theology."[47]

This derisive view of philosophy, however, was never predominant in Russell, despite the many changes in Russell's philosophy and in particular his technical philosophy over the decades of his life, but rather evidences the constraints of epistemology that Russell was aware of and never forgot throughout his life as a philosopher.[48] In consequential weighty practical matters, however, such as Russell's opposition to Hitler, Russell's opposition to the man stood firm, despite the element of skepticism that runs through Russell's philosophy. For Russell, even the skeptic still lives in the world; he felt compelled not to be bound by admitted ignorance to the point of dangerous inaction.

Russell often calls upon philosophy to address questions such as the meaning of life that science cannot make pronouncement upon. In fact, the province of philosophy as the addressing of ultimate questions is one normative function of philosophy that remains present with Russell throughout his varied philosophical emphases and changes. Russell sees the value of philosophy as directing our interest to these questions; however, does philosophy possess a methodology capable of advancing an answer to such questions?

Russell insists frequently that it does not, both in his polemical and non-polemical writings. In the Introduction to his *History of Western Philosophy* he prefaces his enumeration of many of the questions of most interest to humans with the statement that "The studying of the questions, if not the answering of them, is the business of philosophy," but the

---

45 Russell, Review of *Life and Finite Individuality*, 646.

46 Russell, *Freedom versus Organization*, 197.

47 Russell, *Logic and Knowledge*, 324–25. Such remarks as these must not, however, be taken in isolation from Russell's appreciation of the fact that most scientific knowledge has been preceded by philosophical contemplation or wonder, which led to science.

48. As an affirmation of the epistemological quest of Russell, in his autobiographical book, *My Philosophical Development*, 9, in the first paragraph of that work he writes: "My philosophical development may be divided into various stages according to the problems with which I have been concerned and the men whose work has influenced me. There is only one constant preoccupation: I have throughout been anxious to discover how much we can be said to know and with what degree of certainty of doubtfulness."

last page of that book concludes by saying that the philosophical school of logical analysis, to which he belongs, "confess[es] frankly that the human intellect is unable to find conclusive answers to many questions of profound importance to mankind . . . ."[49] The contention of the inability of philosophy to answer questions about the universe that "religious feeling made me think important," was not updated with the publication of his *History* in 1945, for in his 1914 work, *Our Knowledge of the External World*, which had the dual purpose of condemning most previous philosophy for attempting to arrive at edifying proposals and of commending the amoral methodology of science to philosophy, he had repeatedly expressed the conviction that the ultimate questions of human existence were incapable of solution. In the case of Russell's *History*, written three decades after the earlier work, he still defined one province of philosophy as the addressing of these ultimate questions, and to quote again, "if not the answering of them." He continues, as mentioned, in the last pages of that work to relegate many of these problems to the category of the insoluble, just as he had done thirty years earlier in *Our Knowledge of the External World*. Over the course of his career Russell remained skeptical of philosophy's ability to provide conclusive answers.

Russell judges many philosophers as attempting to forego this admission of the inability of philosophy to answer such questions by instead contending that the results of science vindicates their truth-claims about religious beliefs. However, in Russell's view, religion must abandon this futile endeavor, as must philosophy. That is, both of these disciplines by such ploys make themselves susceptible to refutation by the next bit of acquired scientific knowledge. To avoid this pitfall, philosophy must aim at a methodology which, while it does not utilize the results of science, does use appropriate scientific methods, insofar as this is possible. In this regard philosophy should appropriate the neutral method of science, as had his own school of logical analysis, which Russell sees as one of that school's great merits.[50]

According to Russell, the crucial aspect of philosophy that always accompanies the enterprise is sustained analysis. In the first part of his philosophical career, Russell was known for his assertion that logic was the essence of philosophy, and he continued to hold that logic had an important role in philosophy, though it had, on his view, for the most part

49 Russell, *History*, xiv, 835.
50 Russell, *History*, 835.

been misused by his predecessors.[51] The philosophical method Russell advocated did not, as Parmenides and Hegelian logic did, attempt to legislate ontology by using logic to condemn all other alternatives and then pronouncing one's own to be instantiated in the world.[52] Rather, it "liberates imagination as to what the world may be, while it refuses to legislate as to what the world is."[53] If it be thought that this methodology would result in a certain trivialness in philosophy, Russell maintains this is not so, as the problem of space and time, and perception, as examples, can be fruitfully worked on. To be noted, however, here there is absence of allusion to philosophy as working on the larger problems of existential human interest. In fact, there may be pronouncement of the effort as futile:

> The consideration that philosophy, if there is such a study, must consist of propositions which could not occur in the other sciences, is one which has very far-reaching consequences. . . . Philosophers have too often, in the past, permitted themselves to pronounce on empirical questions, and found themselves, as a result, in disastrous conflict with well-attested facts. We must, therefore, renounce the hope that philosophy can promise satisfaction to our mundane desires. What it can do, when purified from all practical taint, is to help us to understand the general aspects of the world and the logical analysis of familiar but complex things. . . . It offers, in its own domain, the kind of satisfaction which the other sciences offer. But it does not offer, or attempt to offer, a solution to the problem of human destiny or the destiny of the universe.[54]

It would seem, then, that while science admittedly cannot give us answers to these ultimate questions, neither can philosophy nor religion. The value of philosophy is not seen by Russell in its results, at least in relation to these metaphysical questions. In 1912, after speaking of the inability of philosophy to prove the truths of religious beliefs, he says:

> We cannot, therefore, include as part of the value of philosophy any definite set of answers to such questions. Hence, once more, the value of philosophy must not depend upon any supposed body of definitely ascertainable knowledge to be acquired by

---

51 Russell, *Mysticism and Logic*, 107.
52 Russell, *Our Knowledge*, 15.
53 Russell, *Our Knowledge*, 15
54 Russell, *Our Knowledge*, 22.

those who study it. The value of philosophy is, in fact, to be sought largely in its very uncertainty.[55]

Admitting that unless the range of the human intellect is radically altered[56] such questions as those raised by philosophy will remain unanswered, Russell at the same time maintains that ignoring them for that reason would disregard questions deserving of attention. Russell had made this very point in something of a conciliatory manner in a letter to Lowes Dickinson in 1904: "And I do not altogether wish mankind to become too firmly persuaded that there is no road from philosophy to religion, because I think the endeavor to find one is very useful, if only it does not destroy candor."[57]

Lacking answers to ultimate questions is one obstacle in philosophy, but if the embrace of a particular metaphysics is due to the temperament of the individual, the legitimacy of metaphysics is additionally undermined. It is true that Russell usually makes this suggestion by way of a parenthetical aside. Such is the comment in Russell's *Autobiography* that Whitehead's later metaphysical endeavors and Russell's own philosophical bent were due to differences in temperament, which pure reason could not resolve.[58] Following on such an explanation and in reviewing Santayana's *Skepticism and Animal Faith* in 1923, Russell commends the absence of extended metaphysical reasoning in the author's work, asserting that "This is a gain, since it has become clear that metaphysical reasoning is fallacious reasoning, and that metaphysical opinions ought to be frankly stated as dogmas or assumptions."[59] Metaphysics, in other words, may have its place, but flights of imaginative fancy are just that and should not claim the kind of justifications so often given in the past by its practitioners. Moreover, in a review of Joad's *Essays in Common-Sense Philosophy* Russell writes: "He points out quite convincingly that a man's philosophical opinions, however they may seem to rest upon argument, are really an embodiment of his temperament, and he inclines to generalize this view so as to make it apply to all opinions."[60] Furthermore, regarding his change of view on objective ethical values, Russell stated

55 Russell, *Problems*, 155.
56 Russell, *Problems*, 155.
57 Russell, *1872–1914*, 307.
58 Russell, *1872–1914*, 201.
59 Russell, Review of *Mephistopheles and The Brute*, 429.
60 Russell, Review of *Essays in Common-Sense Philosophy*, 652.

in the preface of the 1929 edition of *Mysticism and Logic*: "Perhaps the change in my outlook is only due to the fact that the passing of the years leaves one more wedded to the actual than one is in youth. It is true that as a logician I can give many intellectual grounds for the change which appear to me theoretically adequate; but if I were a psycho-analyst, I could no doubt show that they all have emotional sources."[61] Russell would continue to express agreement with Bradley that metaphysics is generally a case of concocting reasons for what one believes by instinct, though certainly not fully, for then philosophy would be trapped in a prison of subjectivism. Moreover, instincts incline to self-preservation as well as presumption and not infrequently to vanities. As seen repeatedly in Russell, such motivations have produced much bad philosophy.

D. PROPER BELIEFS

Russell's disdain of the religion evidenced during his upbringing at Pembroke Lodge was in great part disdain for the Victorian piety and religious sensibilities that persisted alongside dubious religious beliefs. Moreover, with one of his earliest essays, first delivered in 1897 to the Apostles, "Seems, Madame? Nay It Is," implied are criticisms of the atmosphere of his grandmother's world, both religiously, morally, and intellectually, even though his criticism of Hegelianism in paramount in this essay. Nonetheless, Russell's mental reaction to his grandmother's mocking of his philosophical questions, somewhat like the general silence greeting his questions about his parents, pushed him to infer that his grandmother's religion rested on something of an unsure foundation. Although Russell's grandmother was not a philosophical pragmatist, she did believe that the purpose and practice of one's religion should put one to work in the right direction. For Russell, however, who felt the pull of thinking strongly, such an emphasis could not satisfy his questions about religion.

Russell viewed the Victorians as suffering an intellectual deficit in that "The Victorians had many merits, and were in numberless ways our superiors. But they lacked the sense of truth, and could not distinguish between their own emotions and the constitution of the universe."[62] This was Russell's complaint against more than the Victorians of course, for such a fault was not unique to them—the great mass of humanity shared

---

61 Bertrand Russell, *Mysticism and Logic*, v.
62. Russell, Review of *The Principle of Citizenship*, 270.

such a weakness and a vice. The philosophical idealism of the young Russell at Cambridge was sufficient for a short time afterward, until Russell and Moore began their attack upon Hegelian philosophy. After that, Russell never let this presumptuous philosophy out of his sights, simply because, for him, it possessed a most pernicious error—the error of believing that the universe is in some way friendly to us. When years later the astronomer Arthur Eddington suggested a conception of reality resembling an idealist metaphysic, Russell immediately aimed his philosophical arsenal against the astronomer, for Russell could not subscribe to Eddington's path to God anymore than he could the mystical path. Though Russell tried to give some space to mysticism in his manner of looking at the world, in the end he never succeeded. Like the religious beliefs he gave up before going to Cambridge, such frustrations and disappointments were not unfelt and is one reason that Russell in his autobiographical writings could on occasion read like a disappointed existentialist of sorts. The angst of living in an indifferent universe is admitted and so courage is needed, nay required, to face life as life is. This assessment of the human situation should be acknowledged by free men, as it was by the Greek tragedians, who dispensed with senseless moaning. Essentially the rub is that the human is a foreigner in a universe not made for him. He simply shows up (as Sartre later says) and is confronted by the realization that the universe does not stand ready to welcome him or accommodate his wishes, whether trivial or profound.

While Russell did not precisely place his friend Whitehead in the camp of the religiously misguided, he did indicate lack of agreement with his older colleague over how Whitehead attempted to provide some room for interface of human values with the world at large in metaphysical schema. Whitehead, unlike many in the analytic tradition spawned by Moore and Russell, continued to work in the field of metaphysics. As such, he was a trenchant critic and opponent of the logical positivists. The positivists' inordinate suspicion of speculation particularly drew Whitehead's wrath, while he contended that the positivists conception of philosophy was small and narrow for fear of making a mistake. Whitehead expressed this criticism in a few economical words meant for these adversaries: "Panic of error is the death of progress; and love of truth is its safeguard."[63]

---

63. Whitehead, *Modes of Thought*, 22.

However, in contrast to the metaphysician Whitehead, Russell was supremely cautious toward any appearance of interjecting our human values into the fabric of the universe. As noted earlier, he approvingly quotes from Bradley's contention that as a subject metaphysics is simply the conjuring up of pathetic reasons for what one believes from visceral instinct, a trajectory of belief that is hardly rational. Russell, however, almost from the very beginning of his adult life, did sometimes admit that his own views were hardly easy to bear. In a letter to Gilbert Murray of December 12, 1902, and composed right after his "Free Man's Worship," he writes, "But the coldness of my own doctrine is repellent to me; except at moments when the love of God glows briefly."[64] But the glows were dim and infrequent for Russell. Moreover, as cynical as Russell would become about God, his cynicism about Man was often greater. In a letter of April 20, 1913, Russell wrote to his friend Lowes Dickinson that

> Human energy being limited, most of us have to choose between the universal and the particular—I don't know any exception except Plato. For my part I prefer the universal, because it is not created by God. I haven't seen Benn's Short History. I think you are wrong in saying it is God's fault, not ours, that we have found so little truth. Hardly any of the men who spin cobwebs desire truth—they desire a reason for believing that what pleases them is truth. I dare say if we tried to find truth, God would defeat us, but so far I think he has not had to interfere much."[65]

Two of Russell's more frequent themes in his writing on religion are found here. On the one hand, he finds the desire for truth as simply truth lacking among most inquirers, while on the other hand, he depicts God as envious and vain, particularly if humans prove to be strong competition for the Deity. Whether Descartes's evil demon or Russell's God presents more difficulty in the quest for truth remains a question.

While Russell made early attempts to undergird his religious feelings and emotions with philosophical justifications and to derive religious satisfactions from philosophical positions, in the end he admitted defeat. In *Portraits from Memory* he wrote that

> When I first became interested in philosophy, I hoped that I should find in it some satisfaction for my thwarted desire for a

---

64. Russell, *1872–1914*, 260.
65. Russell to Lowes Dickinson, April 20, 1913, Document no. 049239, Box no. 5.12, Bertrand Russell Archives, McMaster University Library.

religion. For a time, I found a sort of cold comfort in Plato's eternal world of ideas. But in the end I thought this was nonsense and I have found in philosophy no satisfaction whatever for the impulse toward religious belief. In this sense I have found philosophy disappointing, but as a clarifier I have found it quite the opposite.[66]

Amplifying upon this admission, in his essay "Why I Took To Philosophy" he wrote that

> For a time I found satisfaction in a doctrine derived, with modification, from Plato. According to Plato's doctrine, which I accepted only in a watered-down form, there is an unchanging timeless world of ideas of which the world presented to our senses is an imperfect copy. Mathematics, according to this doctrine, deals with the world of ideas and has in consequence an exactness and perfection which is absent from the everyday world. This kind of mathematical mysticism, which Plato derived from Pythagoras, appealed to me. But in the end I found myself obliged to abandon this doctrine also, and I have never since found religious satisfaction in any philosophical doctrine that I could accept.[67]

In light of such statements by Russell, we can infer that for him while religious belief maintains no philosophical (or scientific) footing, neither can philosophy produce a satisfactory religion. Therefore, any religion must issue solely from a feeling disattached from any supposed fact. Indeed, in Russell's mind philosophical (and scientific) analysis of religious beliefs decimates their factual believability. In other words, the basis of religion rises no higher than religious feeling or emotion, having found, according to Russell, no vindication in science or philosophy. Russell is adamant that one cannot elevate religious emotions to the role of conferring legitimacy on religious belief.

Even with a person whom he cared for as much as he did Lady Ottoline, Russell was frequently and generally prone to impugn and resent her religious belief, even as he sometimes admired her spiritual finesse, and indeed on some occasions sought (or fought with himself) for it, though without any significant success. This is yet another example of Russell as mad about religious belief—he can scarcely tolerate those possessing religious belief, because it is denied to him. Moreover, those

66. Russell, *Portraits*, 11–12.
67. Russell, *Portraits*, 17–18.

possessors are justly castigated for their sleight of hand, for they have not paid the price of any resultant pain as the religious unbeliever incurs for his unhappy nonbelief. Most unjustly, the seeker who has paid the price for knowing there is no God in effect receives nothing, while the one who has paid nothing, ends up, nevertheless, with what he came for and the answer he presumed to find. That is, for Russell believers can only maintain their belief illicitly by working outside the pale of reason, while Russell has dutifully put reason in charge of all of his beliefs, going back to his adolescent commitment to Clifford that it is always and forever wrong to turn a blind eye toward reason, no matter how excruciating the result. So to the philosopher Russell, what the theologian has done in the absence of any commitment to reason, violates reason and is in effect philosophically criminal. Such a presumptuous path of faith is to Russell inexcusable for having cheated on what Russell deems a legitimate question, the question of the existence of God, for an answer is allowed to assume itself without the vindication or validation of reason.

Despite such objections to religious beliefs, religious expression and feelings could still resonate with Russell because admirable forms of religious life had something to contribute to humanity:

> What is of most value in human life is more analogous to what all the great religious teachers have spoken of.[68]
> In art and literature and religion, some men have shown a sublimity of feeling which makes the species worth preserving.[69]

These sentiments are on occasion wrapped in some of Russell's writings most hostile to religion. For example, in *Religion and Science* Russell paused to say:

> I cannot admit any method of arriving at truth except that of science, but in the realm of the emotions, I do not deny the value of the experiences which have given rise to religion. Through association with false beliefs, they have led to much evil as well as good; freed from this association, it may be hoped that the good alone will remain.[70]

Here the religious instinct is treated with respect when distanced from false beliefs and harmful consequences. Thus, the mottled record of religion is improved by discarding false beliefs, which in the past provided

---

68. Russell, *Power*, 302.
69. Russell, "Man's Peril," *Portraits*, 238.
70. Russell, *Religion and Science*, 189.

"much evil as well as good." Similarly, in *A History of Western Philosophy*, not a work known for any charity toward religion, Russell writes that

> In the sphere of thought, sober civilization is roughly synonymous with science. But science, unadulterated, is not satisfying; men need also passion and art and religion. Science may set limits to knowledge, but should not set limits to imagination.[71]

Here religion, along with passion and art, is not set in the usual adversarial relationship with science, but portrayed as something needful for civilization. Religion thus displays again an ambiguous position in relation to civilization. One of Russell's most revealing statements of his considered position on religion is found in a letter written before the notoriety of his anti-religious views eclipsed the attention given to the positive possibilities of religion. The letter conveys an attitude that I believe Russell never repudiated, though in the pressure of confronting religion as he encountered it, it was an attitude scarcely audible over his denunciations of religion.

> It seems to me that our attitude on religious subjects is one which we ought as far as possible to preach, and which is not the same as that of any of the well-known opponents of Christianity. There is the Voltaire tradition, which makes fun of the whole thing from a common-sense, semi-historical, semi-literary point of view; this, of course, is hopelessly inadequate, because it only gets hold of the accidents and excrescences of historical systems. Then there is the scientific, Darwin-Huxley attitude, which seems to me perfectly true, and quite fatal, if rightly carried out, to all the usual arguments for religion. But it is too external, too coldly critical, too remote from the emotions; moreover, it cannot get to the root of the matter without the help of philosophy. Then there are the philosophers, like Bradley, who keep a shadow of religion, too little for comfort, but quite enough to ruin their systems intellectually. But what we have to do, and what privately we do do, is to treat the religious instinct with profound respect, but to insist that there is no shred or particle of truth in any of the metaphysics it has suggested: to palliate this by trying to bring out the beauty of the world and of life, so far as it exists, and above all to insist upon preserving the seriousness of the religious attitude and its habit of asking ultimate questions.[72]

71. Russell, *History*, 16.
72. Russell to G. Lowes Dickinson, July 16, 1903, in Russell, *1872–1914*, 303.

However, it was in the Voltairean tradition that Russell took his place, pushed there in great part by the circumstances that he found in the world. Russell would have preferred I think not to have taken that stance, as indicated in his letter to Lady Ottoline referenced in Chapter 2, footnote 23, and also here in the letter to Dickinson. That is, in the context of a better world than the world inherited, Russell might have been a more vocal advocate for religion, but in the world of disappointments that he encountered, he swung significantly in the other direction. To some not insignificant degree, Russell was energized by the falsity and inhumanity that accompanied bad religion into a fight against religion itself. This fight he could relish as one of his chief contributions to a world gone awry.

Russell's manner with religion though previously discussed as in contrast to Whitehead, can also suggest a profitable comparison to him. In his *Religion in the Making*, Whitehead punctuates that work periodically with his view that "Religion is the last refuge of human savagery. The uncritical association of religion with goodness is directly negated by plain facts." But in the sentence following this warning Whitehead presents a contrasting claim: "Religion can be, and has been, the main instrument for progress."[73] How could he maintain both views and could Russell have admitted as much? Russell does say by way of some implicit agreement with Whitehead that "He was at all times deeply aware of the importance of religion."[74] But the fact is that Whitehead presents something of a tenuous equilibrium on the relations of religion, cruelty, and progress, whereas Russell most often presents religion and cruelty in contrast and counterbalance to human progress, though, as earlier highlighted, not always. Moreover, Russell's view, considered in its entirety, and drained of notoriety, might not be substantially different from the more positive view expressed by Whitehead.

However, and again, on questions of the truth of any religious belief, Russell regards the desires of human emotions as in the end misleading. Venturing beyond even this contention, however, Russell in effect takes his precautions in maintaining "disinterested inquiry" to an extreme, such that any ontology, any religious metaphysic, or any religious belief is suspect to the degree that is might lend credence to our desires. Starting out in childhood with a precaution against letting his desires unduly

---

73. Whitehead, *Religion in the Making*, 36, 22.
74. Russell, *Portraits*, 103.

influence any assessment of the truth of religion, he ends up taking those desires as indicative of what the world is not like. We witness this in Russell's suspicion that any purported orderliness found in nature or the world was really a mirror of the human desire for orderliness foisted onto the world, so that for him the belief in the order and unity of the world was one of his most fundamental disbeliefs, a belief he regards as "rubbish."[75] Likewise, none of the anthropologically significant doctrines of Christian orthodoxy, i.e., that there is a God who loves and cares for humans, who lowered Himself to redeem humans, can be entertained by Russell because they are simply too preferential to human desires and presumed human vanities to be true. For Russell, humankind's readiness to accept such doctrines without reasoning scrutiny was enough to make religious belief suspect. Russell hardly permitted the contention that if there is a God, and humans were God's creation, a relationship with God would come somewhat naturally and easily for those creatures. H. G. Wood made a point pertinent to Russell here: "The disinterested love of truth largely consists in a readiness to recognize disagreeable facts. It may easily degenerate into an unwillingness to build on agreeable ones."[76] A methodology of disinterested inquiry, pushed too far, would deflect the acquisition of any knowledge that relates to humans in a way that religion does. As Russell travelled far down that road, he escaped from his grandmother's world, to a world that was alien to the human living therein.

---

75. Russell, *Scientific Outlook*, 95.
76. Wood, "Logic and Pessimism," 46.

4

Russell Religion, Past and Present

A. RADICALISM IN THE RUSSELL ANCESTRY

Given Russell's aristocratic ancestry, the atmosphere at Pembroke Lodge bespoke the past and to great degree instilled familial traditions that left an indelible mark on Russell. However, while adherence to older tradition sometimes distinguished Russell from his contemporaries, Russell also instinctively had an eye on the future. In fact, the values the Russell family possessed often made them radicals planning the future in the present. As a group, the Russells were thus not slavish toward the past. Furthermore, Russell's parents, Katharine Stanley (1842–1874) and John Russell [Lord Amberley] (1842–1876) had made a vigorous break with much of the heritage of the past. It was this kind of thinking that shocked Russell's Grandmother Russell upon the deaths of Bertrand's parents after her perusal of Amberley and Kate's papers.

Because Russell's deceased parents were radicals going beyond their elders, the couple at times proved suspicious to some family members, both Russells and Stanleys. Following the example of his deceased parents, Russell called into question key elements of Western civilization, both in his manner of living and in his manner of thinking. Convinced that much of the past is marred by grievous errors precipitated by largely unreasoned emotions, Russell endeavored to start from a refurbished slate, and to significant degree, cautiously assumed nothing from the past without first weighing it by reason. For Bertrand Russell, a housecleaning of the present was in order. Much of the culture and ideas permeating Pembroke Lodge prodded Russell into rebellion against the staid ways permeating his childhood home. This would make of Russell, much in the mould of his parents, a radical, with his eyes on the future.

A notable example of Russell's critique of traditional society is found in his thoughts toward marriage. Though Russell's parents championed progressive sexual ethics, women's suffrage, and emancipation from conventional religion, Russell moved significantly beyond them. In his later compiling of *The Amberley Papers*, the papers of his parents, he came across and drew inspiration from their ideas, as he took issue with how much of the psychological as well as sociological structure of the Western mind and indeed the world was beholden to religious and more specifically Christian beliefs binding the world he was attempting to set free. Russell had to empty the world of many stubbornly old but fundamentally wrong notions. Thus, virtually everything was up for grabs in the attempt to remake the human world, while the revisioning process would be a product of reason and rational thought. With strenuous effort Russell tried to provide himself a reference point to do this and generally looked to mathematics and philosophy and later to "scientific philosophy" in his attempts. When some attempts were less than successful, Russell still continued to sail in the waters of changing the world. From his perspective, he had every reason to do this, because one could no longer appeal to any Christian or Kantian transcendent reason. Russell in effect would be something of a Descartes, trying to construct a new philosophy for the world, or more accurately, a new way of thinking and living in the world.

Belief in a better day to come, common from a progressive perspective on history, belonged to both the Russells and the Stanleys. The Russells had particular pride in the accomplishments of their familial forebearers, while the radicalness of Russell's parents and Russell himself was often pitted against a past from which even greater liberation would be sought. Certainly the Reform Bill of 1832, advanced by Russell's grandfather Lord John Russell (1792–1878) stood as evidence of the Russell determination to extricate England from some past wrongs. If Russell's parents went farther in their own causes in the estimations of their parents, the radical couple nevertheless reflected the Russell impetus to do their part in moving the world from their corner of it. To some the Russells might look antiquated, though as indicated here, the Russell family often stood for values significantly beyond the ken of many of their contemporaries. The Russells would be public figures because it was part of their calling to lead from the present toward the future.

Historian John Morrill, writing in the *Oxford Dictionary of National Biography* on Russell's second son and third child, Conrad, wrote of the Russell legacy in precisely such terms. That is, despite the tumultuous relationship that would transpire between father and son, with a delayed visit in 1968 by Conrad to see his father, Morrill surmised that "[it] is difficult not to conclude that he was drawn not to his father but to what his father represented—400 years of aristocratic radicalism: the Russell tradition of self-conscious progressivism that had seen the fourth earl of Bedford stand up to Charles I, William Lord Russell die on the scaffold for plotting against Charles II, the fourth duke of Bedford as the leading Foxite in the Lords, Lord John Russell the epitome of nineteenth-century reforming whiggery, and his own father as a firebrand pacifist and social radical."[1]

This was not precisely a religious calling, but certainly effected shades of it, no more apparent than the verse that Russell's grandmother wrote in her gift to her grandson Bertrand of a Bible, and from which Russell frequently quoted, Exodus 23:2: "Follow not a multitude to do evil."[2] J. A. Froude, writing in *Woburn Abbey and Chenies*, contended that "The claims of the Russells to honourable memory the loudest Radical will acknowledge. For three centuries and a half they have led the way in what is called progress. They rose with the Reformation. They

---

1. Morrill, "Russell, Conrad."

2. Russell Library, Call no. 0579, Bertrand Russell Archives, McMaster University Library. There are other verses also penned in the Bible by Lady Russell, but to my knowledge these other verses are not mentioned by Russell in any of his writings. However, he does write, "She gave me a Bible with her favourite texts written on the fly-leaf." Russell, *1872–1914*, 19. The verse from Exodus, however, is given prominence as it is mentioned often in Russell's writings, I presume because of Russell's willingness to not infrequently champion unpopular causes. On the Bible fly leaf are the words, "For dear Bertie—From Granny." The date inscribed is May 18, 1884, and though not mentioned, the date is also Russell's birthday. On the next page are written the following words and verses from the Bible along with the date of May 8, 1888, though the date intended might be instead, May 18, 1884:

"The eternal God is thy refuge, & underneath are the everlasting arms.

Thou shalt not follow a multitude to do evil.

Be strong and of a good courage; be not afraid, neither be thou dismayed; for the Lord thy God is with thee whithersoever thou goest.

God is love.

You shalt love the Lord thy God with all thy heart and with all thy soul and with all thy mind.

You shalt love thy neighbour as thyself.

Stand fast in the liberty wherewith Christ hath made us free."

furnished a martyr for the Revolution of 1688. The Reform Bill is connected for ever with the name of Lord John."[3]

Very soon after Russell's parents married in 1844, politics came into their world. However, some family members, and not least of which was Amberley's father, Lord John, aware of the very notable liberalism of Amberley, warned and worried that his son's positions on issues might make him unviable as a political candidate. As example, Lord John advised that "I cannot advise you to commit yourself with what is certainly the more radical portion of the liberal party so early in your life."[4] This attitude, or one close to it, seems to have been a rather common familial estimation of Amberley and Kate. Moreover, neither of them appear to rethink any of their radicalness because of it. Rather, as indicated by Russell himself, they seemed somewhat strangely aloof from such pressures.

Little of this scarcely mattered, because Amberley's political fortunes were not to be and when Amberley lost an election in South Devon, he gave up politics for good. Kate was happy to have him home and away from the fray of having to answer to distortions of his political views. For other men it might be viewed as an odd time to take up Amberley's next task, but Amberley now turned to the writing of his book *Analysis of Religious Belief*. Furthermore, about the time Amberley becomes involved in politics he falls under the influence of John Stuart Mill, as does Kate. Moreover, in Kate's case, the influence of Mill's step-daughter Helen Taylor, seems equally pronounced. Furthermore, the appearance

---

3. Froude, *Woburn Abbey*, 97. Interestingly, Georgiana Blakiston, *Woburn and the Russells*, 3, in referring to Russell writes: "A black sheep in the family, he was not invited to Woburn Abbey until he was over seventy, when his position as the second best-known living Englishman was recognized."

4. Lord John to Amberley, January 20, 1865, in Russell, *AP* I:351. Similarly, and right about the same time, Kate's Aunt Louisa voices something of the same caution in a letter to Kate: "And so Amberley is going to follow in his Father's footsteps & speak up for Reform—I know he is very liberal & at his age I consider it the right side to exceed on but I hope he will not go too far in a public speech . . . ." Louisa Stanley to Kate, January 28, 1865, in Russell, *AP* 1, 353. In the next month, moreover, this aunt writes a similar letter, expanding upon her reservations with Amberley's political stances and stating, "I do not think you could expect that I should for you know I am an old Whig by education & have been from my earliest years trained to Whig Politics but *not* to Radicalism & though I was quite aware that Amberley was of the ultra Liberal School, yet I trusted that he might have enough prudence not to give out at a public meeting the full flow of his *Liberalism*. . . . Give my love to Amberley & tell him I shall not despair of a *Reform* in his principles & shall console myself for the present by thinking how young he is & how much must be Theoretical & imaginary in his creed. . . ." Louisa Stanley to Kate, February 9, 1865, in Russell, *AP* I:440–41.

of near retirement at their home at Ravenscroft in Wales, seemed almost too retiring for Lady Russell, who writes her son about the advantages of one "mixg with his fellow man—even when he has so happy a home that he never wishes to leave it."[5] Despite Lady Russell's observation, the couple continued to interface with some few others, sometimes revealing their own religious preferences.[6] Invited to one event, and on meeting a bishop, Kate expressed in her journal that "neither of us cared for him; he looked like a man of the world & not like an ascetic."[7]

Ravenscroft was thus much to the liking of the couple, and the sense of satisfaction they had in their home is abundantly evident in their letters

---

5. Lady John to Amberley, January 16, 1869, in Russell, *AP* II:253. Amberley and Kate were indeed quite happy and satisfied in their new environment. Even some time later when sickness came to prevail over the Amberley household, Kate records in her journal of November 25, 1870, "We are quite happy & rather enjoy our solitude." Russell, *AP* II:382. On the last day of the year 1870, she writes in her journal, "This new home has been the great event of our domestic year & has turned out a very happy one as we are well satisfied with it & much enjoy the feeling of being settled. We are as happy as ever & fonder of one another each year." Russell, *AP* II:388.

6. As an example, Kate records in her journal of August 28, 1870, "We went to church at Llandogo in the aft. & hear a sermon about the Devil being everywhere; we cd not go again. A [Amberley] said it was like going back 2 centuries to hear such things." Russell, *AP* II:368.

7. Kate's Journal, August 2, 1869, in Russell, *AP* II:273. On occasion a friend or correspondent could even mock the Amberley's radical social leanings, as when W. H. Lecky, in a letter to Kate of March 15, 1869, ends his letter after recommending "my great lord & Master [Edmund] Burke—especially his French Revolution," by saying "With best wishes for the success of your many arduous schemes for the regeneration of the universe." Russell, *AP* II:305. Kate kept up a robust correspondence with Helen Taylor, who sometimes offered advice on negotiating the political and religious terrain of their day. A significant comment from Taylor in a letter to Kate of September 11, 1869, probably addressed from Kate's having to interact with family members who were Catholic, "Politically one cannot too much detest Catholicism, but socially and personally I must admit that many of the nicest people I have known have been Catholics. If your sister-in-law is a very zealous Catholic it would certainly be a misfortune if she had children; although even this would not probably do as much mischief as the conversion of influential grown up people. . . . There is so much that is exquisitely beautiful and touching in Catholicism that I never think any one quite safe from becoming a Catholic who is not aware of it, and has not learnt to distinguish between it and the deadening crushing influences which make Catholicism as a whole so mischievous, because so fatal to the fine and singleminded love of truth—true piety." Russell, *AP* II:312–13. In something of a friendly but critical interaction with his kinsman, Arthur Russell, Amberley writes, April 10, 1871: "If I were to stigmatize all with whose religious or political beliefs I differ as profoundly as you do from Crompton's as fools, I tremble to think how limited would be the little remnant of wise men with whom I should find myself. Nothing to my mind can be more grossly absurd than the common Christian theology, yet I do not regard those who hold it as wanting in sense." Russell, *AP* II:463.

and journals during this time. In speaking of fixing up the study room for her husband, Kate writes, "It was a great pleasure to me doing the room for him to work in & live in I hope for ever—"[8] However, greater pleasure was to come, at least for a time, for on May 18, 1872, Amberley records in his journal the birth of a second son, eventually named Bertrand. Three days later, Lord John Russell pens a letter to his son Amberley expressing the hope that "the boy will be called William, in memory of our great ancestor, who gave his life for the liberty of his country." Moreover, as religion was never a subject far from the Russell minds, Lord John adds, in his next sentence of the same letter, "I am going to explain the origin & progress of christianity in a series of historical essays."[9]

On asking John Stuart Mill to act as the godparent of the newborn Bertrand, Helen Taylor writes to Kate that "Mr. Mill says if you wish it he does not think that it would conflict with his opinions to enter into that relation."[10] Tensions with family members over some oddities of Amberley and Kate, however, were apparent on occasion, as when Kate's aunt Louisa wrote to Kate, "I hope the Baby has been christened for one day I was asked whether it wd be so, I marveled that there could be a doubt."[11] Russell himself footnotes in the *Amberley Papers*, "I was not baptized until I was 11, many years after both my parents were dead."[12] This event, therefore, fell within the years he lived at Pembroke Lodge.

After Amberley's failed political ambitions—largely attributed by Russell to his father's honesty but also a certain naivety about the political world—Amberley devoted himself to study and writing his book on religion. This project made for a quiet life, and indeed, not least because

---

8. Kate Journal, September 6, 1870, in Russell, *AP* II:373.

9. Lord John to Amberley, May 21, 1872, Russell, *AP* II:490–91. This "series of essays" will become his book entitled *History of Christianity*. Perhaps this work was motivated by Lord Russell's knowledge that his son Amberley, in producing his own book, might treat the Christian religion somewhat more radically than his father might have wished?

10. Helen Taylor to Kate, July 1, 1872, in Russell, *AP* II:495.

11. Louisa Stanley to Kate, August 29, 1872, in Russell, *AP* II:526–27.

12. Russell, *AP* II:527. In the preceding paragraph from Aunt Louisa's letter to Kate, her aunt had extended an invitation to Kate to come for a visit and assured her niece that "you shd not have so uncivil a reception as the Duchess gave you." Nevertheless Kate's aunt apparently could not hold her tongue and continues, "But my dear Kate do not be angry with me if I say—She served you right & you deserve it for you have a strange turn for all sorts of queer company and since your exhibition at that very low place at Bristol where you stood up and harangued about Women's rights I shd wonder at *nothing* odd you may do."

of the temperament of the couple. Meanwhile, as already indicated, the Amberley couple were viewed warily by many. Russell himself describes their distinctiveness:

> The cumulative effect of free-thought, feminism, and the suspicion of 'Malthusianism' was to shock society. But the Amberleys had always, when possible, chosen their associates for brains, and in their later years they saw very little of the grand folk who figure in their early diaries. They were considered firebrands, and even semi-radical friends urged caution and prudence, but the Amberleys would have nothing to do with these vices. The records of their quiet, studious lives give no hint of the storm that raged about them or of the wild ways they were supposed to follow.[13]

Russell further comments, "But Amberley and Kate were so much absorbed in their work and their happiness that they hardly noticed that 'the world' was shocked."[14] Though some of that shock came from family members, it hardly came from Lord John, who, though not as radical in politics as his son, remained proud of Amberley. Thus Russell writes, for example, "My grandfather, born, like Shelley, in the first month of the first French Republic, was willing to support anti-governmental movements abroad, especially in Italy, though in English affairs, after the passing of the Reform Bill in 1832, he was far from Radical. Nevertheless his principles remained such as would naturally lead to Radicalism in his son, to which he never objected. His pride in my father's bold carrying on of the Russell tradition outweighed their disagreements."[15]

Family pride, however, could not protect the Amberleys from tragedy. The tragedies that were to come upon the family of Amberley and Kate in the next years would leave their two sons without their radical parents. After the couple died, the Russell grandparents at Pembroke Lodge made legal moves to take custody of the two boys, for the shock and abhorrence of Lord and Lady Russell over what they found in the private papers of the deceased couple is an indication of the cultural distance Amberley and Kate had moved from the prior generation, however liberal some of their preceding family members had been.

John Russell had married Kate Stanley in 1864, the young couple being twenty-one and twenty-two respectively at a time when Victorian

13. Russell, *AP* I:36–37.
14. Russell, *AP* I:38.
15. Russell, *AP* I:29.

culture largely did not permit a dismissive attitude toward religion or religious matters. Nevertheless, it was Russell's parent's generation, rather than Russell's generation, who suffered the greater experience of the Victorian crisis of faith. As noted by commentators on Russell, particularly Nicholas Griffin, Bertrand Russell's upbringing by his Russell grandmother, to a significant degree, placed him tardily "behind" some of his peers in the religious doubts that besieged him as a youth.[16] That is, he went through much of the same struggle that had shaken the prior generation. This difference occurred because Russell was largely reared by Lady Russell, rather than by his parents. If Russell's parents had lived and had brought Russell up with their own religious beliefs, attenuated as they were, perhaps many of Russell's religious anxieties in his youth and his later animosities toward religion could have been avoided, or at least ameliorated. However, because he was raised by Lady Russell, he ended up retreading some of the earlier religious battles his father and his father's generation had faced.

B. CONTRASTS BETWEEN THE RUSSELL AND STANLEY FAMILIES

Russell's Grandfather Stanley died before Russell was born, and it was his widowed wife who exuded considerable influence upon the Stanley family, including grandson Bertrand and his brother Frank. As a child, Russell felt guarded affection for his Stanley grandmother, for her forthrightness was sometimes stinging and frightful to the youthful and sensitive boy. The woman was a formidable personality and different from Grandmother Russell. One cannot read Russell's descriptions of his Grandmother Stanley without inferring how much he respected her, though in the beginning he understandably feared the woman. She possessed traits that as an adult Russell would greatly admire and, indeed, emulate. As depicted by Russell, she was a woman of the Enlightenment, while behind his various descriptions of her is the clear indication that she—culturally aligned with Russell's preference for the eighteenth century—was impatient with religion. "She was always downright, free

---

16. Griffin remarks that "With this parental background, and with the general secularization of British culture and intellectual life in the closing decades of the 19th century, one would have expected Russell's agnosticism to be more easily come by than it was. That this did not happen was caused in part by the death of both his parents by the time he was four." Griffin, "Russell as a Critic," 48.

from prudery, and eighteenth-century rather than Victorian in her conversation."[17] Speaking of her son and Russell's Stanley uncle, Algernon, who became a priest, first as an Anglican and then in the Roman Church, Russell wrote: "Orthodoxy, however, sat lightly on him. Like his mother, he belonged to the eighteenth century; the earnest strenuousness of his own age passed him by. Some of his brothers and sisters, it must be admitted, were strenuous; nevertheless the whole family, whatever their faults may have been, were free from many of the defects that are typical of the nineteenth century."[18] Russell might as well have been describing himself seeking to be set free from the staid and crusty Victorianism of Pembroke Lodge. Certainly it was under the influence of the family of his Stanley mother that Russell found some comforts, chiefly a robust vitality he felt sorely absent at Pembroke Lodge. Thus, he found among the Stanley relatives a culture preferable to the hushed tones of speaking and avoidance of certain topics at Pembroke Lodge, for it was a household mired in Victorian sentiment. Russell observed that his Grandmother Stanley's children, both as children and as adults, had genuine affection for their mother.[19] This was hardly a judgment that Russell could confer on his Grandmother Russell without needed qualification.

Russell clearly saw the veins of free-thinking in his Grandmother Stanley and some of her children, particularly her son Lyulph, whom Russell tags as his grandmother's favorite and also his mother's favorite sibling. Russell describes him as "the cleverest of the family," and the child of his grandmother in whom "his brains were gratifying to her intellectual ambitions." Speaking of this free-thinking uncle, Russell remarks, "It is difficult to judge how much he contributed to my parents' emancipation from orthodoxy."[20] Contribute, however, he did; nothing like him, moreover, could be found in the family Russell. That Russell's son Conrad Russell (1937–2004) gave one of his sons the name Lyulph is evidence of the respect and fondness for Lyulph Stanley by some of the Russell family.

Though the Russells were Whigs like the Stanleys, other similarities were weaker. One might therefore think that the wedding of a Russell to a Stanley could not have been the most promising indication of a happy union with two people who came out of distinctly different families. That,

17. Russell, *AP* I:17.
18. Russell, *AP* I:28.
19. Russell, *AP* I:18.
20. Russell, *AP* I:26.

however, would not be the case in the marriage of Russell's parents. Nonetheless, Russell would later recall, "But I remember being impressed, at a very early age, by the difference between the Stanleys and the Russells."[21] Even so, by all accounts, Russell's father and his Stanley mother each appeared to complement their partner in marriage considerably.

Russell's upbringing at Pembroke Lodge was thus supplemented and offset by a significantly different cultural atmosphere from his mother's side of the family. On the one hand this was a welcome relief to the youngster Bertrand, even though the Stanley relatives initially proved too boisterous for the sensitive and youthful boy. Compared to the descriptions Frank and Bertrand gave of the staid and quiet whisperings of Pembroke Lodge, the Stanley household can be realistically imagined as near bedlam to the young and quiet Bertrand, though precisely brother Frank's cup of tea. Indeed, this group of relatives seemed fearless, and were therefore fearsome to the young Bertrand. He could not at such an age perceive that he would later be much like them, nor could anybody else, including even his grandmother Stanley who, because this grandson was quiet, bemoaned the fact that "Bertie is just like his father," her son-in-law.[22] Meanwhile and understandably, Grandmother Stanley preferred the rambunctious Frank, a Russell on the outside, but virtually all Stanley within. Lady Russell's preferences went in an opposite direction, and Bertie noticed the difference early on. In the beginning, probably under the strain of Stanleys on a quiet youngster, Russell sought for some refuge in his Grandmother Russell, though the aforementioned strain would switch over time.[23]

---

21. Russell, *AP* I:13. Like his parents, Russell himself could fall afoul of family loyalties, and he remarks in the *Amberley Papers* how his uncle Lyulph stood with him in later years: "He was an ardent supporter of free trade, and (what is really remarkable) he took the chair for me at a meeting during the War, when my pacifism made me unpopular and many of my relations fought shy of me." So, however much Russell had experienced, in terms of the Stanleys, a certain vigor and willingness to listen to arguments—in which the famous Sunday lunches were one example—Russell could also clearly see in the case of his parents that pushing the envelope too much could be costly. Radical ideas that were too radical were not the penchant of the family, but like his parents before him, Russell would take them up; unlike the very short lives of his parents, however, Russell would have decades to follow in the footsteps of parents for whom he inevitably felt great respect. The publication of the *Amberley Papers*, with his third wife Peter Spence, at a difficult juncture of his life, is something of a testament to his gratefulness to them. Hardly a scintillating biography of the couple, the book nevertheless evokes an appreciation of the philosopher's parents.

22. Russell, *1872–1914*, 35.

23. Speaking of Lady Russell and her household, Russell writes: "After I reached the

Compared to the Russells, the Stanley family was hardly a particularly religious lot, or at least they exhibited little of the stifling religiosity of the Russell family at Pembroke Lodge.[24] The Russells, by reason of this difference, probably looked upon the Stanleys as a bit uncouth and irreverent. Frank remarks that the Russells were simply jealous of the Stanleys.[25] This perceived trait, however, probably issued from the aversion of Lady Russell to the plain speaking that was habitual in the Stanley family. Frank speculated, "I imagine that the relations between the two families were chiefly political. How my mother ever found the necessary courage to face it I cannot think . . . ."[26]

However less religious the Stanleys were in comparison to the Russells, the Stanley relatives exposed the young Bertrand to a plurality of

---

age of fourteen, my grandmother's intellectual limitations became trying to me, and her Puritan morality began to seem to me to be excessive; but while I was a child her great affection for me, and her intense care for my welfare, made me love her and gave that feeling of safety that children need." Russell, *1872–1914*, 18.

24. This comparison, however, is perhaps not as contrasting as implied. That is, while Russell proudly notes his Grandmother Stanley's rationalistic temperament and "contempt for everything that she regarded as silly," and contends that "She was an eighteenth-century type, rationalistic and unimaginative, keen on enlightenment, and contemptuous of Victorian goody-priggery," it is clear that her opposition to the building of a chapel at Girton Hall earns her high or even higher marks in Russell's eyes. However, even though this family culture, derived from the Stanleys, played itself out in such obvious ways, the Russells too could be found leery of religion if the association with politics gave too much hand to bishops, for example. In speaking of his first lessons in English Constitutional history, given to him by his Aunt Agatha at Pembroke Lodge, Russell recalls that in the conflict between Thomas Becket and Henry II, the murder of Becket by the King's men is not mentioned, and though the execution of Charles I is, blame is not attributed. Russell, *1872–1914*, 35; 23. Moreover, Russell adds a bit of further comment to this in his description of the political leanings of Pembroke Lodge, under the influence of Lord John and Lady Russell: "It might perhaps be admitted also that Cromwell had gone too far in cutting off the king's head but, broadly speaking, anything done against kings was to be applauded—unless indeed, it were done by priests, like Becket, in which case one sided with the king." Russell, "Adaptation: An Autobiographical Epitome," 3. Thus, however noticeable the piety at Pembroke Lodge, it was apparently cautious toward too much religious infusions into politics. Russell remarks of his Grandfather Russell's political stances, "My grandfather belonged to a type which is now quite extinct, the type of the aristocratic reformer whose zeal is derived from the classics, from Demosthenes and Tacitus, rather than from any more recent source. They worshiped a goddess called Liberty, but her lineaments were rather vague. There was also a demon called Tyranny. He was rather more definite. He was represented by kings and priests and policemen, especially if they were aliens." Russell, "Lord John Russell," 119.

25. Russell, *My Life*, 52.

26. Russell, *My Life*, 11.

religious beliefs, or lack thereof, for these relations represented Islam, Roman Catholicism, the Church of England, Unitarianism, Positivism, and free-thought. Russell relates that there were often "vehement arguments" among them, often so ferocious that he feared "the whole pack would turn upon me."[27] No such frays on religious topics, or even philosophical ones, were the usual order of the day in the Russell household at Pembroke Lodge. Whereas life there exuded quiet and hushed tones that both Russell brothers eventually grew impatient with, the Stanley household by comparison seemed fully alive and openly engaged with the world. On the one hand, the clan of Stanleys must have seemed indomitable to two young boys; one, Frank, admired them for it, while the other, Bertrand, initially feared them because of it. On the other hand, the Russell's solemnness naturally provoked some uneasiness and in time suspicion in two young and inquisitive boys. Russell's Stanley grandmother in particular possessed traits that the youngster Bertie being raised at Pembroke Lodge might fear, but would adopt in later life; Frank, however, confronted some of the morbid culture of Pembroke Lodge head on. He would be his own person, even as a youngster. The younger Bertie would escape the straitjacket of the Russell household only later, whereas elder brother Frank exhibited his defiance from a much earlier age. The boy's Grandmother Stanley would surely have noticed the much quieter Bertie and to some degree attempted to mitigate this with the more rambunctious Stanley spirit, which Frank welcomed naturally, but his brother Bertie only with some difficulties. However, with the Stanley spirit Bertie eventually took on in adulthood, Bertrand Russell could appear as intimidating and daunting to his friends as the relatives at the Stanley lunches were for him as a youngster. Indeed, Russell's intellect was sometimes spoken of as a cutting saw blade by observers and intimidated associates. Russell himself was aware of this perception of himself when he confessed a suspicion to Lady Ottoline Morrell about her Bloomsbury circle: "They put up with me because they know I can make any one look ridiculous—if I had less brains and less satire, they would all be down on me—as it is, they whisper against me in corners, and flatter me to my face. They are a rotten crew."[28]

A favorite story of Russell concerning his Stanley grandmother was her practice of derisive comment on some guests after they left. "It

27. Russell, *1872–1914*, 37.
28. Russell to Ottoline, August 1, 1918, in Griffin, *Selected Letters*, 2:166.

was her practice to sit in her large drawing-room every afternoon while streams of visitors, including the most eminent writers of the time, came to tea. When any of them left the room, she would turn to the others with a sigh and say: 'Fools are so fatiguin.'" Undoubtedly, Russell in later life would experience this same reaction, not just over people, but over beliefs too—religion included. All in all, moreover, Russell regarded his inheritance from the Stanleys as greater than that from the Russells and wrote in his *Autobiography*, "My brother, who had the Stanley temperament, loved the Stanleys and hated the Russells. I loved the Russells and feared the Stanleys. As I have grown older, however, my feelings have changed. I owe to the Russells shyness, sensitiveness, and metaphysics; to the Stanleys vigour, good health, and good spirits. On the whole, the latter seems a better inheritance than the former."[29] Lest appreciation for the Russell inheritance be eclipsed too much in favor of the Stanleys, in the *Autobiography*, Russell speaks of the positive imprint of Lady Russell on him, alongside his judgments against his Russell grandmother and her household:

> I remember when I was about four or five years old lying awake thinking how dreadful it would be when my grandmother was dead. When she did in fact die, which was after I was married, I did not mind at all. But in retrospect, as I have grown older, I have realized more and more the importance she had in moulding my outlook on life. Her fearlessness, her public spirit, her contempt for convention, and her indifference to the opinion of the majority have always seemed good to me and have impressed themselves upon me as worthy of imitation.[30]

If such traits were worthy of imitation, as Russell contends, it was by noticeable contrast that Grandmother Russell's religious beliefs provoked scathing criticism from Russell in years to come. These criticisms, nevertheless, were born and finessed while the youngster lived at Pembroke Lodge with a grandmother who influenced him with other qualities that did remain with him.

---

29. Russell, *1872–1914*, 38.
30. Russell, *1872–1914*, 18–19.

C. THE YEARS AT PEMBROKE LODGE WITH GRANDMOTHER RUSSELL

Indicative of the secular resolve of Kate and Amberley, their wills were made such that in the event of their deaths, Bertrand and his brother would be under the guardianship of two atheists, T. J. Sanderson and Douglas Spalding. After the death of parents Kate and Amberley, however, and after a legal battle brought by Russell's grandparents, the young Russell, as he facetiously put it, "enjoyed the benefits of a Christian upbringing,"[31] for Russell's grandparents were not emancipated from religion as were their free-thinking son and daughter-in-law. Russell's father had made his formal break with orthodox Christian religion at the age of twenty-one by his decision not to attend church on Christmas day, having previously decided he was not a Christian.

When aspects of the young couples' lives extending beyond political radicalism emerged after their deaths, Lady Russell took decisive steps to take custody of Russell and elder brother Frank. Moreover, from the perspective of these grandparents, the deviance from the reigning Victorian culture by the couple was one thing: the actual moral license with which the couple lived in their marriage was another, and the grandparents could not allow these appointed guardians to have charge of their grandsons. The most shocking fact to the Russell grandparents was the revelation that Russell's mother had apparently shared a bed with one of the designated guardians of her children, because he had not wished to die celibate on finding out that he was in an advanced state of tuberculosis.

Russell's grandmother spoke little about the dead couple in the boy's presence, and understandably the young Bertrand became suspicious about the people who were his parents. Moreover, when his grandmother later began to suggest that Bertrand and Frank were better off without their parents, her opinion fueled the flames of the youngster's curiosity even more and in time surely provoked resentment toward his grandmother. However, as remarked before, to my knowledge Russell never exhibits anything like self-pity in his descriptions of the upheaval of losing parents before age four, though as a child he did often wonder what his deceased parents were like. The insinuations his Grandmother made to him about them would inevitably have produced unwelcome results.

The first tragedy struck the young family soon after Bertrand, the last of three children of Amberley and Kate, was born in 1872. Within

---

31. Russell, *Basic Writings*, 38.

two years, in 1874, mother Kate and daughter Rachel died, and in another two years father Amberley died, in 1876. In such circumstances the young Bertrand and Frank might likely have ended up as orphans or could have been raised separately. This was not to be, however, for Lady Russell and her now elderly husband, Lord John, took the boys into their home at Pembroke Lodge in Richmond Park, northwest of London, for rearing. Lady Russell meanwhile received more than a few letters of condolence from friends and acquaintances with sympathies expressed over such a devastating loss within the Russell family.

Pembroke Lodge, where the two boys came to live, carried many of the marks of an aristocratic family, a family once particularly great in England. However, as earlier discussed, the boys' two deceased parents, Amberley, the eldest son of Lord John and Lady Russell, and his Stanley wife, Kate, were not fully chips off the block from which they had come, for Amberley and Kate were more radical than their predecessors, something Lady Russell discovered soon after their deaths. Even if these disconcerting revelations had not come to light for the surviving grandparents, there would have been other trouble with which to contend. The friendships and associations Amberley and Kate had maintained were simply not the kind the Russell grandparents could approve of, starting with the guardians whom Amberley and Kate had appointed for their children. The intended guardians, Sanderson and Spalding, were judged to be completely unfit and therefore unsatisfactory by the Russell grandparents, especially Lady Russell. A battle to bring the two grandsons to Pembroke Lodge was necessary and successful.

Young Bertrand at the time of course perceived nothing of this tumult, though in later years how and why the two boys came to Pembroke Lodge became clearer. Especially after reading the diaries and letters of his parents, Russell realized how much of his own young life repeated and indeed paralleled the conflicts his father had endured at the hands of Lady Russell. In his upbringing Russell was saturated like his father Amberley with ideas from a Victorian culture that Bertrand, like Amberley, would combat and ultimately reject. Young Bertrand would be reared in a culture he would later come to impugn, even more so than his parents.

In the beginning, however, the youngster remained innocent of his parent's ideas, for widening cracks in his relationship with his grandmother came later. In adulthood and after his first two marriages, Russell and third wife, Patricia or Peter Spence (1910–2004) assembled a two-volume work of letters and other documents of his parents entitled

The Amberley Papers. The books provide informative portraits of the couple through their writings and from Russell's frequent commentary. The reader begins to see how much young Bertrand would subsume his parent's thinking after breaking free of the Victorian world of his Russell grandparents.

To a substantial degree Russell's eventual rebellion against the religious beliefs of the adults at Pembroke Lodge was directed at what was believed, though the religious atmosphere and piety of the home for Russell and his brother seemed equally foreign to them. This unsuitable atmosphere was not merely imagined by vivacious boys too restless for staid traditions, for various visitors and acquaintances of the family not infrequently remarked on how uncongenial the home seemed for the rearing of two promising children. In speaking later of the experience, Russell contended that most lacking was a sense of robustness and forthright speech. Instead an atmosphere of broodiness pervaded the household and arrested any lively atmosphere that growing boys would have welcomed and savored.

> Every adult member of the household, including Lady Russell, her unmarried daughter Agatha, and an unmarried son, Rollo, seemed stuck in a world that in time provoked hostile reaction on the part of the two boys. The response of the younger Bertie, as he was called, to his environment was for the most part one of mental and silent retreat before a household sharing few of his real interests and often mocking his early philosophical interests. Russell's grandmother, upon finding Bertrand interested in philosophical questions, mockingly chided, "Mind never matter; matter never mind." After a number of repetitions of such sloganeering, Russell ceased to find it funny and deemed it annoying.

Elder brother Frank, relatively soon after coming to Pembroke Lodge, rebelled outright against such an uncongenial home atmosphere. In the beginning, however, Bertie absorbed some of the ambience at Pembroke Lodge, such that his rambunctious and rebellious brother remarked that Bertie was for a time "an unendurable prig." However, Frank reserved his harshest judgements for the adults who found him as difficult to raise as he found them unendurable in his raising. In his autobiography, suitably entitled *My Life and Adventures*, Frank Russell provided a sampling of his exasperation with his superiors. In that work he remarks, "An additional irritation was the tone of voice in which conversation was generally conducted, a sort of hushed and pained undertone, as if one were in church with a corpse where some vulgar person had just committed the indiscretion of speaking in a natural voice. I do not suppose my Uncle Rollo for one moment realized, or if he had realized, could possibly have understood, how passionately I desired to kick him in the shins when he adopted this voice."[32]

The ways of the household thus wore on both boys and provoked in both a reaction of willful rebellion, though negotiated differently in each boy. These reactions and the calculations of each on how to endure their plights also made the timing of their responses different. While Frank would very soon after the move to Pembroke Lodge exhibit overt rebellion, the reserve of Bertrand was consciously and perhaps unconsciously building for a more fruitful though delayed repudiation of many of the values and culture of such a household. Indeed, with his real interests unnourished in such a household, the youthful Bertie sought for mental escapes, as contrasted to brother Frank's physical escape from the dour Pembroke Lodge. Adult remembrance of the atmosphere probably contributed to some of the vehemence found in Russell's later writings as they concerned religion. For the time being, however, while brother Frank fashioned real escapes, and who on one occasion in 1877 ran away from his keepers, Bertrand sank down into himself and his thoughts—and books.[33]

As one consequence of these different behaviors, the boy's grandmother would place high hopes upon her youngest grandson. For her, Frank may have seemed irredeemable and more so the older he became. With Bertie's quieter manner, this youngster seemed more compliant and therefore teachable in a way scarcely possible with Frank. Russell remarks in his *Autobiography* with perhaps some exaggeration that his grandmother could not admit to herself that she hated the rebellious Frank.

---

32. Russell, *My Life*, 50.

33. Rather typical of his later critical depiction of his Grandmother Russell is a concession to her positive qualities, which, Russell contended, could stall rebellion against her: "She was anti-intellectual from belief in moral intuition; she encouraged a morbid scrupulosity; she had a Puritan dislike of vitality and of many innocent forms of enjoyment. She instinctively hated her children's marriages, both from maternal jealousy and from a horror of sex. She never for one moment doubted her own rightness, and met disagreement with ridicule that pretended to be playful. At the same time, she was so kind, so conscientious, and so affectionate that rebellion was very difficult." Russell, *AP* I:144.

In the raising of the two boys, the household adults became increasingly exhausted with the rambunctious youngster and would in time have him educated elsewhere, perhaps not least for the peace that would be restored to the previously quieter household. Most seemed happier after the decision, not least of all Frank. In the next year, 1878, Lord John Russell, died. Though grandson Bertrand was only six years old when he passed, posthumous influence upon his grandson was not minimal, for the life and accomplishments of Lord John Russell was an understandable source of pride to the Russell family of the nineteenth and twentieth century and indeed to the English nation. Furthermore, after thirty-five years of marriage, the influence of Lord John upon his wife Lady Russell was plentiful. Lord John had been a widower who had brought six children into his marriage with Frances (Fanny) Anna Maria Elliot in 1841. Previous to becoming Lady Russell, the woman had been an admirer of Lord John for some time, and their marriage seemed to be one of genuine affection for one another.[34] Days before his death, according to Lady Russell's diary, each expressed to the other gratitude for the many years spent together, and understandable regrets for not having loved one another more.

With Frank out of the house and the family patriarch passed, Lady Russell would now marshal greater energies toward her younger grandson for the promises and possibilities she envisioned. In him she could entertain expectations denied her with Frank. Chief among her dreams was that there could be another future prime minister from Pembroke Lodge, one reared under her supervision to succeed her deceased husband. Lady Russell, however, would have to groom the youngster. Because he was but a mere six years old, she had the benefit of an early start with the young and seemingly malleable boy for such a project. Lady Russell would pour much of herself into this work and broodingly watch over him. She expected to be made proud by his carrying on the

---

34. While Russell oftentimes speaks of his Grandmother Russell with affection and respect, he could also characterize her with his perception of her limitations: " Marrying Lord John made great demands upon her courage. He was twenty-three years older than she was, and already a distinguished statesman; five years after the marriage he became Prime Minister. He was a widower with two children, and his first wife, when he married her, was a widow with four children. All these six were in my grandmother's care from the moment she was married. She herself had four children. She loved and respected her husband, but was never physically in love with him. Indeed Puritan inhibitions probably made her incapable of passionate love." Russell, *AP* I:31. "Puritan inhibitions" are characteristically attributed by Russell to a malady of personal and societal shortcomings.

prestigious Russell legacy, particularly as it concerned politics.[35] However, while such aspirations must have surely been her hope, the youngster Bertrand was increasingly given to interest in philosophical questions and mathematics. For Bertrand, dislike of much of the environment at Pembroke Lodge had driven him to mathematics, because this subject offered something of a real escape from his living in such a home. The uncertainties and frustrations of life at Pembroke Lodge were diminished by the solace of a mathematical world seemingly impervious to earthly afflictions.

When the boy's care became predominantly the province of his grandmother, she made religious instruction and practice an integral part of Russell's upbringing. Russell's grandfather had been Anglican, but Lady Russell was a Scottish Presbyterian, who, according to Russell, shocked her friends by becoming a Unitarian at seventy years of age.[36] His grandmother, as described by Russell, was liberal in religion. Theological nuance and hair-splitting were not attractive to her, and Russell indicates that he was not indoctrinated with eternal punishment,[37] miracles,[38] the literal truth of the Bible,[39] or the claim that everything the Bible said was true.[40] The home nonetheless inoculated piety; there were family prayers at eight in the morning and Russell related years later that he knew "thousands of hymns," presumably learned during this time.[41] His brother Frank also records that "We used to have Moody and Sankey hymns at morning prayer."[42] Though the quantity of hymns is undoubtedly exaggerated by Russell, it was nevertheless not uncommon for Russell to quote a stanza from a hymn to make a point in his writings, though usually in a negative vein. A fair amount of reading of the Bible in the home surely occurred, for not a few of Russell's books

---

35. A political future, though perhaps her strongest desire, was not the only future envisioned by Lady Russell for Bertrand: "Her hope for me was that I should become a Unitarian minister." Russell, *1872–1914*, 57.

36. Russell, *1872–1914*, 15.

37. Russell, "How I Came by My Creed," 14.

38. Russell, "How I Came by My Creed," 14

39. Russell, "My Religious Reminiscences," *Basic Writings*, 31.

40. Russell, "How I Came by My Creed," 14.

41. Christopher Farley, Russell's last secretary, relates the following: "He could also produce the most unusual pieces of information, and long quotations from the Old Testament (complete with verse numbers) or from childhood hymns." Thomas and Blackwell, *Russell in Review*, 17.

42. Russell, *My Life*, 36.

provide the reader with biblical stories, frequently relating minute details from a portion of Scripture.[43] Chris Farley also relates that Russell would sometimes serenade his guests with long memorized passages from the Bible, with ridicule often interjected at points by Russell for his audience's amusement. Such exhibitions were a staple of the later adult Russell, for the mood at Pembroke Lodge for the rearing of two boys was serious and provided little place for frivolity or mocking. Frank writes, "The usual routine of my life at P.L. at this time began with prayers in the morning, which all the servants attended, a Moody and Sankey hymn, a portion of scripture, and a prayer read by my grandmother from a volume of her own compiling."[44]

Though Lady Russell was a formidable personality, she was also a winsome person, for accounts of her suggest that she was much loved. One indication of this from family is etched on a marker prominent at the place of her burial at Bedford Chapel at Chenies and provided by her daughter and Russell's aunt, Agatha Russell. It reads, "Blessed are the Pure in Heart: For They Shall See God. And now abideth Faith, Hope, Love: These Three; But the Greatest of These is Love." Beneath this inscription other words read: "The tablet was placed by her daughter Agatha Russell in Loving and Grateful memory of her noble life." Certainly grandsons Frank and Bertrand could and did speak of their grandmother in this way, despite their accumulating and escalating annoyances as they lived within the halls of Pembroke Lodge. Frank writes, "My grandmother Lady John . . . was one of the best women who ever lived. She was witty, amusing, kind, even devoted, full of a sense of duty . . . ."[45] Bertrand himself, in his youthful writings entitled "Greek Exercises" could turn to compliment her amidst his criticisms of the woman. For example, only days before his sixteenth birthday, when he was about to leave for some months of study at the crammer, his grandmother had prayed for him in his preparation for the exams to be taken for entry to Cambridge. He wrote after the evening of the prayer: "Hence I see no reason to believe in God's kindness towards me and even the whole prayer was more or

---

43. He occasionally relates biblical stories which he subjects to ridicule, as in the following example: "Jephthah sacrificing his daughter is a heroic figure, by the heroism and self-sacrifice which the myths call out. . . A God who can be pleased by the sacrifice of an innocent girl could only be worshipped by men to whom the thought of receiving such a sacrifice is not wholly abhorrent." Russell, *Principles of Social Reconstruction*, 76.

44. Russell, *My Life*, 50.

45. Russell, *My Life*, 33.

less a solemn farce to me, though I was truly much affected by the simple beauty of the prayer and her earnest way in saying it. What a thing it is to have such people! What might I be, had I been worse brought up!"[46] In the same month, he records, "My doctrines, such as they are, help my daily life no more than a formula in algebra. But *the* great inducement to a good life with me is Granny's love, and the immense pain I know it gives her when I go wrong."[47]

There are significant allusions to religion in the writings of Lord John and Lady Russell providing some picture of the theological leanings and religious ideas of these two people. All the same, for both of them a religious topic is frequently joined to a political topic, and indeed, grows out of it in the world of this couple. The Russells, as firm and unmistakable Protestants, retained a guarded suspicion of Catholics. Both were nevertheless firm in conviction that freedom of religious expression and worship should be upheld in England, for Catholics, as for other Dissenters. The union of political discussion with religious discussion was commonplace between the two people. In their eyes one purpose of heightened religious conviction is to further advance the political and civic freedoms of citizens. In other words, furthering religious freedom brings with it one goal of a desired political society which permits, because it protects, religious liberties. The idea seems to be that the infiltration of Christian ideas upon society will have as one effect a political impetus of increased democratization. There is at least the idea of the two working somewhat in tandem and union for the realization of a common purpose.

However, this relationship might prompt one to think, though erroneously, that the union of state and church, such as it was in England, would be affirmed and accordingly buttressed from this reciprocating

---

46. Russell, "Greek Exercises," *CP* 1:14. This appreciation seems confirmed by Russell in his next entry, dated May 20, 1888, where on his first visit home from the crammer, he complains about the boys he found there: "It seems a pleasant place, but it is sad really to see the kind of boys that are common everywhere. No mind, no independent thought, no love of good books, nor of the higher refinements of morality, it is really sad that the upper classes of a civilized and (supposed to be) moral country can produce nothing better. I am glad I didn't go away from home before, as I should never have come to my present state had I done so, but should have been merely like one of them." However, in aspiring to advance even further in his learning, the issue of religion presents difficulties, with Russell writing here, "I should like to believe my people's religion, which is just what I could wish, but alas, it is impossible." The acknowledged affinity for his family is simply not enough to move him toward their religion, for their beliefs are simply such as he cannot believe.

47. Russell, "Greek Exercises," *CP* 1:15 .

union. However, husband and wife seem to diverge on this point. Lady Russell leans toward disestablishment, maintaining that "the objections to the voluntary system diminish on reflection," while in Lord John's book on the history of Christianity, published in 1873, he contends that "[t]hose who wish to promote the ascendency of Roman Catholic superstitions, or of Calvinistic enthusiasm, are more restrained than they would be if the Church of England were disestablished."[48] At most other times, the suspicions of the couple often were the same—both, for example, disliked the burgeoning Oxford Movement of their time for overtly and obvious Catholic sympathies. Russell's grandmother, moreover, was the more religiously ardent of the pair, and Russell comments that "All her ancestry was vehemently Protestant."[49]

Lady Russell's general perspective on religion reflects the importance and centrality she attaches to personal and authentic inner religion and she extends much latitude to worshipers of God in religious traditions outside her own Christian religion. For her it is genuine religious duty that is important, not abstruse religious doctrines. In fact, and as example, she is very impatient, if not to say put off, by the Thirty-Nine Articles in the Anglican Book of Common Prayer and remarks in a letter of 1842 to her sister, "I have just been reading the Thirty-nine Articles for the first time in my life, and am therefore particularly disposed to prefer all that is simple in matters of religion. They *may* be true; but whether they are so or not, is what neither I, nor those who wrote them, nor the wisest man that lives, can judge; that they are presumptuous in the extreme, all who read may see. In short, I hate theology as the greatest enemy of true religion, and may therefore leave the subject to my betters."[50]

Such a perspective might partially explain Lady Russell's aversion to disputation in theology or philosophy with her grandson Bertrand, for Lady Russell tended to emphasize the childlike simplicity of religious

---

48. Lord John Russell, *History of Christianity*, 234.

49. Russell, *AP* I:30. It is to be noted, however, that some among the Russell family evidence a Protestantism every bit if not more "vehemently Protestant" than the religious ancestry of Russell's grandmother. Moreover, behind Russell family pride in the martyred William Russell of the seventeenth century is not a bigoted anti-Catholicism, but fear that political Catholicism once established might jeopardize English liberty. Inasmuch as the Russell politicians regarded ambitious and unsavory English monarchs as the greatest threat to Parliament and liberty, this could only be more so if the king was Catholic or evidenced too many Catholic sympathies.

50. Lady John to Lady Mary Abercromby, September 11, 1842, in MacCarthy, *Lady John*, 66.

faith and detested making it more complex and complicated than need be. We might conclude that she is hardly theologically minded at all, but rather sought to live out her religious faith without the complications and finery of adult religion, including that of the Church of England. Indeed, she argues that entrance into the forbidding life and forms of the Church is apt to dash the natural and childlike faith that a youngster had previously enjoyed. She writes in 1851 that "I can see with pain, but cannot help seeing, that from the time a child begins to go to church, the truth and candour of its religion are apt to suffer.... Oh, how far we still are from the religion of Christ."[51] If we ask what the religion of Christ is from Lady Russell's perspective, we find repeated on several occasions in her letters that it is love of God and man. Furthermore, she aligns this notion with the notion of progress and puts the two often together, such as she does in a letter of 1869 to her son William, called Willy: "It is a great misfortune that we have so few really eminent men among the clergy of England, Scotland, or Ireland—in any of the various communities. Such men are to take the lead in what I cannot but look upon as a noble march of the progress of mankind, the assertion of the right to think and speak with unbounded freedom on that which concerns us all more deeply than anything else—religion. I believe that by the exercise of such unbounded freedom we shall reach to a knowledge of God and a comprehension of the all-perfect spirit of Christianity such as no Established Church has ever taught by Creeds or Articles."[52]

This kind of animus toward theological systemization and formality was later noted by grandson Frank: "Curiously enough my grandmother Russell was almost more disturbed by my High Church phase than by my agnosticism: her Presbyterian spirit was opposed to forms and ceremonies and suspected them."[53] Moreover, Lady Russell was not insistent that the element of godliness or religious seeking necessarily manifest a Christian form. She could perceive authentic religion outside the Christian religion, because the piety of Christian devotees might be exceeded by those of other religions. Writing in 1848, she says, "I believe that whatever is *meant* as an act of devotion to God, or as an acknowledgement of His greatness and glory, whether expressed by the simple prayer of a Covenanter on the hill-side or by the ceremonies of a

---

51. Lady John to Lady Mary Abercromby, April 11, 1851, in MacCarthy, *Lady John*, 113.

52. Lady John to William Russell, June 3, 1869, in MacCarthy, *Lady John*, 220.

53. Russell, *My Life*, 336.

Catholic priesthood, or even by the prostrations of a Mahometan, or by the self torture of a Hindoo, may and ought to inspire us with respect and with a devout feeling, at least when the worshippers themselves are pious and sincere."[54] In her son Rollo's communication with her she was nudged a bit about her religious ideas. Rollo had apparently raised some points about religious belief that Lady Russell felt she needed to respond to with some sage words. In a letter to Rollo, penned in 1870, she writes, "No doubt we must always in the last resort trust to our own reason upon all subjects which our reason is capable of helping us."[55] Of course, Lady Russell could also assess excessive reason as perhaps complicating things religious. But her statement to Rollo does indicate that she is hardly willing to abandon all reason for the sake of believing things religious, though later in the year she would insist to Rollo that "I believe that many of those who deem themselves sceptics or atheists retain, after all, enough of the divine element within them practically to refute their own words."[56] Thus, for Lady Russell the presence of real and true religion could visit even people who resisted, for in some circuitous way they assumed what they opposed. On occasion she could be tolerant to the point of permitting and presuming in some unbelievers a kind of piety and life of searching exceeding that of many believers. Writing to her sister in 1873, she says, "I have, perhaps, more indulgence than you for some of the anti-Christian thinkers and writers of the day—those who love truth with all their souls, who would give their lives to believe that—"Dust thou art, to dust returnest, was not spoken of the soul," but who seek a kind of proof of this which never can be found. They are unhappy in this world, but I believe they are nearer heaven than many so-called believers, and will find their happiness beyond that death upon which they look as annihilation."[57]

However, Lady Russell had her limits, and so after she read a copy of Mill's *Autobiography* that Rollo had bought, she indicates to Amberley and Kate, knowing of course of the close relationship between them and Mill, some of her reservations. When she perused Mill's essays on the utility of religion, she complained that the author "dwells almost entirely on the ugly and malevolent side of Nature, leaving out of sight the beautiful

---

54. Lady John to Lady Mary Abercromby, January 13, 1848, in MacCarthy, *Lady John*, 112–13.
55. Lady John to Rollo Russell, March 17, 1870, in MacCarthy, *Lady John*, 225.
56. Lady John to Rollo Russell, November 3, 1870, in MacCarthy, *Lady John*, 231.
57. Lady John to Lady Dunfermline, July 3, 1873, in MacCarthy, *Lady John*, 239.

and benevolent side—whereas both abound, and suggest the notion of two powers at strife for the government of the world."[58] In her letter to Amberley after his beloved wife Kate and young daughter Rachel died, dated March 28, 1875, she sympathizes with his plight and assures him that she will do for him what he cannot do: "You have indeed been sorely tried, my child, and you have not—would that I could give it to you—the one and only rock of refuge and consolation, of faith in the wisdom and mercy of a God of love. But I trust in him for you, and I know that though clouds hide Him from your sight, He will care for you and not forsake you—and even here on earth I look forward to much peaceful happiness for you, in your children. . . . Kiss my two precious little boys and keep us in their memory. Is Bertrand as full of fun and merriment as he used to be?"[59] This heart-rending letter bespeaks the depth of love Lady Russell had for her family and something of her strong and sincere efforts to aid a grieving son in his direst valley of sorrow. That peaceable happiness spoken of by Lady Russell for his future was not to be, for Amberley's family would very soon suffer even more catastrophe, when Amberley would be taken from the two boys shortly by death. What began as a family of five ended as two.

The relatively mild-mannered Amberley and Kate, however, produced a son with less reservation than them on matters religious and less respect for what Lady Russell called "wise indifference." If Russell had been raised by his parents, perhaps he might have exhibited a gentler manner toward religion; instead, he seems to have exceeded his parents, and perhaps this difference was due to being raised by his Russell grandmother. Of course Amberley had been too, but Amberley only lived to the age of thirty-four, while his son Bertrand lived to write and speak until he was ninety-seven.

Even amongst the doubts and negative resolutions Russell had made as an adolescent plunged into religious crisis, he was still able to appreciate the genuineness with which his pious grandmother had prayed for him, as earlier noted, on the occasion of his leaving to go to the crammer before his sixteenth birthday. Furthermore, after he arrived and experienced the juvenileness and crassness of his schoolmates, he must have surely set aside for the moment some of his previously negative judgements against his upbringing by his Grandmother Russell. In fact, the

---

58. Lady John to Amberley, December 29, 1874, in MacCarthy, *Lady John*, 245.
59. Lady John to Amberley, March 28, 1875, in MacCarthy, *Lady John*, 245-46.

commending of his grandmother's prayer is set in the tone of gratefulness. Russell would note her request on his behalf for him as evidence of her love for him, irrespective of the fact that the young Bertrand would soon have little of her religious belief left in himself. In other words, gratefulness to his grandmother prompts his appreciation without any theological reversals on his part. He was soothed by the words of the prayer of his grandmother's love for him on leaving for the crammer and maintained gratitude for such a prayer despite his loss of the religion of Pembroke Lodge. Russell could hardly fault his grandmother for loving and caring for him; so too he can hardly fault her prayer. Much of what she prays for and to whom, are not congruent with the young Bertrand's thinking, but such qualification is somewhat beside the point of Russell's appreciation for his grandmother.

D. RELIGION UNDER SCRUTINY BY A FAVORED GRANDSON

Unable to discuss his inquiries over religion with anyone at Pembroke Lodge, save Uncle Rollo on occasion, Russell resorted to recording his thoughts in a diary written in Greek as a precaution against discovery and entitled "Greek Exercises." It is an extraordinary document for a mere fifteen-year old and testament to the intelligence and diligence of a youngster intent to evaluate weighty theological questions.[60] To be kept in mind, nevertheless, is that Russell belonged to a family and culture that habitually committed thoughts and events to paper. Lady Russell had kept a diary and Russell's deceased parents had both maintained diaries that Russell later referenced in the writing of *The Amberley Papers*. However, it has been usual for students of Russell to also attribute some of this habit of writing and the keeping of diaries to the strands of English Puritanism present earlier in the Russell family. However, the habit of devotional and introspective writing only partly issues from the English Puritan tradition, for this genre of writing is found in some earlier centuries where authors wrote of the struggles of a soul seeking some solace or peace with God. Much older than the distinctive Puritan quest and writing is of course Augustine's *Confessions*, where likewise his primary

---

60. In his first entry from the Greek Exercises, March 3, 1888, young Bertrand writes, "I have in consequence of a variety of circumstances come to look into the very foundations of the religion in which I have been brought up." Russell, *CP* 1:5.

intent in writing that piece of autobiography is to expound upon his travails in relationship to God. Returning to the Puritans, the Englishman John Bunyan's *The Pilgrim's Progress*, written in 1678, catalogues the spiritual struggles endured but surmounted to arrive at salvation.[61]

Diaries of the nineteenth century, however, shift significantly in focus from the likes of John Bunyan, for in that century secular alternatives to the prior religious understanding of the world, and those things in it, including humans—turns in the direction of a besieged or even absent religious faith. Earlier Puritan diaries by contrast were most often devotional pieces tending to highlight spiritual aspirations and struggles with reference to God. A different tendency of the nineteenth century is toward an introspective search for the identity of the self, and while soul-searching remains, there is now less of a grappling with or for God and more effort extended toward the human as freeing himself from God, for purposes of human autonomy. Whereas medieval treatises fix on such quandaries as the "dark night of the soul," nineteenth-century pieces not uncommonly grapple with whether there is a human soul or not, and for that matter, whether there is a god who hears prayers. Russell's "Greek Exercises" certainly fits into such a description.

In the "Greek Exercises," moreover, Russell frequently attaches comments about himself in light of what he discerns from his readings and reasonings. The main import of these jottings by Russell is "to put down my grounds for belief in God," and thus to evaluate whether his "grounds for belief" can hold up under his own scrutiny. While family members and others are sometimes mentioned in this writing, the "Greek Exercises" are an exercise in reasoning designed to evaluate the validity of belief in God. Indicative of Russell's lifelong attachment to and interest in epistemological justification, he desires to have sufficient grounds for anything he believed. This quest had not been a province of Puritan diaries, underlining again that the Puritan diary had sought to clarify or shed light on the relationship of the human to the divine and

---

61. Interestingly, in later years and prior to his marriage to Alys Pearsall Smith, Russell laments the fact that he had previously given heed to the recommendation of reading Thomas Kempis's book, *The Imitation of Christ*, a famous book of Christian devotional literature, but now wishes he had given his attention instead to the philosopher Spinoza. As remarked by Alfred Kazin, "The influence of Puritanism had created a habit of mind that had persisted into the 'American Renaissance' and the peculiarly personal reverberations in Emerson, Thoreau, Whitman and how many others—the need to present to God, the Eternal Reader and Judge of the soul's pilgrimage on earth, the veritable record of one's inner life." Zinsser, *Inventing the Truth*, 124.

how to adjust and live life accordingly. By contrast, Russell's youthful diary attempts to come to terms with his doubts, while also being attentive to anticipated negative consequences of any absence of such religious beliefs on his life, including the perceived impact his theological judgements may have on family members, should they become aware of his position.

As already indicated, Lady Russell had scarcely given her grandson opportunity to discuss such subjects with her, so he was driven to explore them without her and by himself. Only very brief opportunities to converse with anyone else about the subject had occurred in Russell's youth to this point. For a brief time he had had a religiously agnostic tutor with whom he was able to discuss the subject, but, according to Russell, his grandmother suspected her employee's irreligious propensities and he was dismissed.[62] Such were the limitations of scant opportunities the youngster had to exchange views on this subject with others.

In the course of his private investigations evidenced in the "Greek Exercises," Russell examined three beliefs he considered essential to religion, namely the existence of God, free-will, and the existence of the soul. Over the course of three years he rejected each as untenable. Nevertheless, an intruding desire for an outcome or result to one's liking was perceived as poison to Russell, for it allowed such a desire to skirt the only goal appropriate for such an inquiry: the intent to find out the truth of the matter, irrespective of preferences or desire. Therefore, Russell was adamant in an unwillingness to allow his own desires to influence his decisions on these questions, a methodology he repeatedly later charged lacking in many philosophers who wove huge metaphysical complexes from rather parochial desires, never bothering, according to Russell, to admit the distinction between what the world or truth was, as opposed to what we should like it to be.[63]

Russell thus fixed early on in his life the necessity of impersonal objectivity to insure a truth not biased by wishful thinking that defended

62. Russell, *1872–1914*, 51.

63. As an example, in a letter to Lucy Donnelly of February 4, 1907, Russell registers his astonishment when "'The other day I went into Oxford to read about 'the nature of truth' (a purely logical subject) before a society of undergraduates, & J.A. Smith, who was present, thought fit to point out that my views were inconsistent with 'beliefs which to many of us are very sacred', or words to that effect. I am very much shocked at his conduct, & shall not readily recover my belief that he is either a gentleman or an honest man. In Oxford, philosophy is the handmaid of superstition—it is really despairing." Forte, *Letters*, 119.

a desirable answer with scant respect for truth. The young Russell would therefore need to consider the tools to accomplish the desired task. W. K. Clifford's book entitled *Common Sense of the Exact Sciences* provided a starting place for Russell because Clifford dared to say unabashedly what the young Bertrand was already thinking. Clifford famously contended that "It is wrong always, everywhere, and for any one to believe anything upon insufficient evidence." Russell now devoured and relished such an idea with zest, for within Clifford's pages was an outline of the erroneous sleight of hand in much argumentation that passed for credibility at the hands of the credulous. Russell wanted to make no such colossal mistake and now became enamored of reason and arguments and argument forms that embodied reason, both logical and empirical. Russell's resolve was to give due accord to the rights of reason, and this resolve for now would admit of few constraints. Some years later and under the impetus of a different anthropology and sociology, and alongside his notion of himself reformulated under realization of components of his person previously left ignored and unnurtured, he conceded some retractions. A bit of the later eroding enthusiasm is captured in Russell's preface for a new edition of Clifford's book, written after almost a half century of experience of the self and the world after the "Greek Exercises" and after reading Clifford's book for the first time:

> It was possible without any blind act of faith to believe that the human species would become progressively more humane, more tolerant, and more enlightened with the consequence that war and disease and poverty and the other major evils of our existence would continually diminish. In this beneficent process rational knowledge was to be the chief agent, and mathematics, as the most completely rational kind of knowledge, was to be in the van. This faith was Clifford's, and it was mine when I first read his book; in turning over its pages again, the ghosts of old hopes rise to mock me.[64]

The youthful Russell, following in the steps of Clifford, however, would tout reason and its power with deserved respect, for it was presumed to provide a sure vehicle for bettering the world without any blind act of faith. In other words, reason would be vindicated by wielding an axe against the falsities believed and obstacles delaying prior attempts to construct a rational world. Counting on the necessity of reason for use

---

64. Russell, Preface to *Common Sense of the Exact Sciences*, new edition, ix; Russell, *CP* 2:320.

in the betterment of the world, the youthful Russell reveals not only an enthusiasm resonating with the energy of youth, but more importantly akin to expectations of the Enlightenment and boosted perhaps with an optimism imbibed from some of his Stanley relatives. The optimism bespeaks a work to be done and intellectual rubbish to be swept away.

However, Russell's sentences from the Clifford preface connote something of the difference of a time buoyed up by a naïve optimism, namely that of the late nineteenth century, compared to the subsequent century and its yet unimagined wars and tyrannies. Writing in the decade of 1950, Russell commented, "For those who are too young to remember the world before 1914, it must be difficult to imagine the contrast for a man of my age between childhood memories and the world of the present day."[65] Russell's later viewpoint brought on by the collisions of the twentieth century, is a partial admission that the line to a better world is not as straight or easily achievable as once thought. The vision of the heavenly city of the eighteenth-century philosophers, to borrow from Carl Becker's title, would become brittle and break.[66] Before that, however, and in the enthusiasm of youthful energy wielding the sword of reason, Russell would take stock of the world around him with eyes fastened on Clifford's conception of reason. With Clifford's no-nonsense rudder taken as a guide, Russell would consider without distracting sentiment the plausibility of theological beliefs that enveloped Pembroke Lodge.

The question of why religious belief would encounter such serious scrutiny from the youthful Russell is not easily answered, with Russell himself providing no clear suggestion, save for his comment in the "Greek Exercises" that "I have in consequence of a variety of circumstances come to look into the very foundations of the religion in which I have been brought up."[67] Certainly the political beliefs of the family were as fundamental to Pembroke Lodge as were religious beliefs, though sources from Russell at this time in his life reveal almost nothing of doubts and acidic ruminations arising or lodged against these political beliefs. Perhaps it was the question-begging tone of voice used in mention of theological matters at Pembroke Lodge that provoked in Russell suspicions prompting the desire to evaluate theological beliefs. Added to this is the fact that in the "Greek Exercises," the young Russell not infrequently speaks of a preacher at a church service whom Russell deems something of a

---

65. Russell, "Adaptation: An Autobiographical Epitome," 1.
66. Becker, *Heavenly City*.
67. Russell, "Greek Exercises," CP 1:5.

bumbling idiot. However, perhaps the most plausible reason for Russell's theological doubts might be after witnessing religious believers' resistance to scrutiny of their beliefs in order to safeguard that belief. Russell maintains that a strong human desire for religious beliefs to be true is reason enough to cast doubt on the validity of the belief held. That such theological questions were dealt with gingerly in the past is reason to deal with them forcibly now, that is, objectively, with subjective preferences excluded.

Previously, a younger Russell had encountered and endured the initial shock of being told by his older brother Frank that the mathematical axioms that Bertrand inquired about by way of proof must be accepted before one could proceed any further in the lesson. Because he was tantalized by the subject of mathematics and its possibilities, Russell relented with his request for proof—though only for a time. In comparison to the possible solace of religious belief compared to mathematics, Russell was already gauging the obstacle of subjectivity as applied to evaluating the truths of religion, or philosophy for that matter. That is, the realm of mathematical truths was decidedly and indeed majestically different, for the element of subjectivity possessed no validity on the question of truth in mathematics. The world of mathematics could provide solace for a questioning human in a way that neither religious or philosophical beliefs could. Neither religious nor philosophical beliefs were grounded or justified in the way that mathematical truths were and that made mathematics king in Russell's world for a time. Grave disappointment came to be Russell's lot, however, when his venerated mathematics, under the corrosive influence of his student Wittgenstein, were deemed tautological truths.

The youthful Russell's plight in the rather bleak world of Pembroke Lodge sent him in search of something that could sustain him. Religious beliefs would rather naturally suggest themselves, one might infer. Indeed, in the "Greek Exercises" Russell laments not only having to keep his heterodox religious opinions to himself, and the anxieties associated with facing his opinions alone—again, without a sympathetic tutor to hear him out—but also because he had indeed looked to those religious beliefs to give him strength. They were now being exposed and even some destroyed by his own reasoned thinking. Russell would have to look for solace and comfort elsewhere; the obvious candidate would be mathematics. However, Russell was not yet finished with religion.

Russell often repeats how he kept and needed to keep his religious opinions to himself at Pembroke Lodge, but there was another kind of reasoning for remaining mum on the subject. That is, Russell's upgraded and enlightened understanding presented him with other negative consequences from religious unbelief that he also found worrisome. Thinking the prior impetus for humans being good or moral now lost or at least changed, that is, if no God existed, Russell found in his new lack of belief as compared to his previous beliefs the extra need for silence because moral motivations must come from elsewhere than God. Complicating the situation was that the benefits and liabilities of his new understanding were mixed for Russell. For example, he writes, "Also it makes goodness a much finer thing, as it takes from it all possibility of reward beyond internal satisfaction. For this reason also it makes goodness harder to practice, and is therefore not a religion I should wish to spread among the masses, who might relapse into excesses of immorality."[68] This Voltaire surmise about the need to refrain from broadcasting truths that have potential for danger amongst the general population will be reneged upon later as the adult Russell becomes a severe critic of the various ways of hedging against truth-telling for the sake of human susceptibilities. Indeed, Russell would be anything but a so-called "low volume atheist" in his future, for he would undertake in the decades of the 1920s and 1930s to expose not only the speciousness of various religious beliefs, but also, as he insisted, the incredible hurt and ruin they brought to human persons and human civilization. However, for now, Russell thought differently.

Believing subjective bias significantly undermined the believability of theological doctrines made Russell dubious about those doctrines. Such a contention would be the charge from which Russell would fire most of his volleys in his objections against religious belief. The problem with the presumptuous theologian in "The Theologian's Nightmare" could be found in a thousand other theological niches. Succumbing to this temptation was evident in scores of intellectuals and as frequently in some intellectual circles. It was the error of many philosophers who confused what they found in their thinking with what they wanted in their hearts. Mathematical truth seemed a more rewarding ally and provided safeguards in its promise of greater objectivity. Russell therefore preferred mathematical inquiries to forays into religious or theological beliefs and admitted that he tended to think of mathematical truth as the

---

68. Russell, "Greek Exercises," *CP* 1:13.

stepchild of the religious quest, and that his adulation for mathematics at least in its platonic form sufficed for something like religious purposes. Having been unable to salvage a religion from suspect and doomed religious beliefs, Russell would have to look elsewhere and for an understandable reason. Mathematics kept the volatile human factor at bay. The weakness of subjective preference for a likable "truth" had vitiated the plausibility of religious and philosophical beliefs and dealt to them nearly fatal blows.

Meanwhile, Russell's desire to believe something with which to stabilize human life remained more or less steadfast. The perpetual problem, however, is keeping the interfering human in the background, for the eagerness for comforting beliefs must be checked by submission to uncompromising and often unpromising reason. In other words, the seeker must put himself and his wishes aside for the sake of the truth. Russell experienced considerable anxiety during the course of his youthful theological investigations, ardently desiring to establish a rationale for some morsel of religious belief but with efforts exasperated by the need for silence at home. With the results of his theological investigations more or less finished at age sixteen, the final result, Russell nevertheless claimed, was one of surprising relief and not the expected remorse:

> Throughout the long period of religious doubt, I had been rendered very unhappy by the gradual loss of belief, but when the process was completed, I found to my surprise that I was quite glad to be done with the whole subject.[69]

In writing about the same experience in other pieces of writing, Russell adds that "loneliness had much more to do with my unhappiness than theological difficulties."[70] Moreover, Russell is perhaps including a bit of personal biography in his *Conquest of Happiness*, forty years later, when he writes:

> Nothing is more fatiguing nor, in the long run, more exasperating than the daily effort to believe things which daily become more incredible. To be done with this effort is an indispensable condition of secure and lasting happiness.[71]

---

69. Russell, *1872–1914*, 50.
70. Russell, "My Religious Reminiscences," 31.
71. Russell, *Conquest of Happiness*, 174.

For Russell, what is most important and crucial for lasting happiness is to believe nothing that is unbelievable. For an individual content with such a requirement, a reasonable happiness was possible, that is, if truth is deemed a praiseworthy goal. This kind of happiness, and more, elation, was in Russell's future, but not yet in his life at Pembroke Lodge, and for a short period it seemed like Russell might venture backward to retrace his steps and recalculate his journey. Any such movement, however, could never return all the way back, and in some bouts of desperation over such quandaries the young Russell turned to poetry as he reminisced about mathematics. Nevertheless, there was little pleasure in this change, and indeed as he tried for a reconfiguring of his quest for a religion, he avoided the vexing conflicts with reason that he had previously encountered. He would therefore not be able to abide theologically with the discarded beliefs anymore, though in some of the poets and in the romantics, he sensed some possibilities that had escaped his earlier scrutiny.

While trying to maintain his allegiance to the reasonable thinking required by Clifford, the young Russell thus turned to poetry. While Russell was at the time certainly in some despair over his loss of religious faith—and far from exuberant about it, as he would sometimes later infer—he began to reach toward something that would return some of what he had lost. Indeed, if Russell's later adult life is some indication, the realm of the poetic and the mystical as something sought by him held fast—in some rare times. In his education at Pembroke Lodge, Russell had not been bereft of an education in these things. Could he court a religiously mystical motif without the usual accompanying religious beliefs that were false?

Perhaps poetry now became of great interest to him because Russell sought for a promising path out of the presumed scientific notions that had dogged and virtually destroyed his now rejected religious beliefs. Specifically, Russell resisted the implications of a scientific determinism which seemed, symbolically like Pembroke Lodge, to be sucking the very marrow out of life. The basis of this determinism for Russell seemed to be the notion of a uniformity of nature which excluded all spontaneity, creativity, and randomness, and of course freedom from the real world. For the young Russell this loss was a high price to pay and painful on a par with the pain of already receding religious beliefs. As such, then, truth really was, as Russell was often to remind readers, a "ruthless taskmaster." If there was any way to avoid being subsumed within a deterministic universe, then Russell would have at it. His last sentences of the "Greek

Exercises" confirm the expectation that poetry could revive or rescue what he feared losing, with due precaution: "Thus God has become a part of my life, an ever present influence, moulding my action and my thought, comforting me in dejection and soothing me in inquietude.— Whether this faith be mere poetic sentimentalism, as a year ago I should have pronounced it to be, I know not; but this I do know, that it brightens my life, and harmonizes with all my highest. Let it then remain and bear fruit."[72]

Russell now began to focus on nature with the aim of somehow buttressing his supposition and hope that human consciousness could not be reduced to exclusively material constituents as he desired to avoid the exceedingly painful confrontation with materialistic determinism. Moreover, he discovered a soul mate in Percy Shelley.[73] Russell came to love Shelley for the intensity of his thoughts and for the spiritual succor he found in Shelley's writings. Undoubtedly, one of these would have been Shelley's famous essay, "The Necessity of Atheism." Russell never abandoned Shelley, even when he often later castigated the romantics for their slippery play with the ruthless taskmaster of truth. However, Russell would hardly ever manage to live without the romantics for significant stretches of his life. For now, before going up to Cambridge, it would be by their threads that he would be sustained.

Within the solitariness and somberness of Pembroke Lodge, Russell and his brother Frank would have preferred another kind of childhood. The attempt to deal with the unpleasantness of the place partially formed and molded in Russell a temperament of some withdrawal, and later, resentments borne against such an atmosphere. Consequently, the transition from a Victorian home to worldly Cambridge was more than a mere physical move. Russell experienced a culture at Cambridge eventually nearly as closely familial as at Pembroke Lodge, but not somber and therefore virtually opposite his previous home. For example, Russell had been ridiculed by his grandmother for expressing agreement with utilitarian ethical principles, to the point that he eventually gave up speaking on any such subjects with her. He described his experience at Cambridge, by contrast, of being able to "say things that I thought and be answered with neither horror nor derision but as if I had said something quite

---

72. Russell, "Greek Exercises," *CP* 1:21.

73. Russell remarks of his grandmother Russell that while she could excuse the excesses of Lord Byron, "She extended no such tolerance to Shelley, whose life she considered wicked and whose poetry she considered mawkish." Russell, *1872–1914*, 17.

sensible" as "intoxicating."[74] Russell also implies that the religious beliefs of Pembroke Lodge had not been presented in the most effectual way: "In regard to religious belief, those who were concerned with my education did not perhaps adopt the best methods for producing an unquestioning acceptance of some orthodoxy."[75]

Frank Russell remarks that on arriving at Pembroke Lodge after the death of his parents he was sent to church for the first time ever. Frank implies that it was a repellent experience, and though Bertrand presumably had a milder reaction, strewn through Russell's writings are references to the bumbling idiocy of ministers. However, despite the two boys' reaction to their religious upbringing, then and later, Russell's grandmother was hardly a staid traditionalist in her religious or theological proclivities, as noted when she "shocked" her circle of friends by becoming a Unitarian at seventy years of age. However, before that her diary and her letters are sprinkled with references to Unitarian ministers and authors she commends to others. Indeed, to some degree, the move to Unitarianism had been in the making for some time, however shocked some of her friends might have been. Furthermore, the theological emphases of Unitarianism comported well with Lady Russell's impatience with theological hairsplitting. She writes to her daughter in a letter of March 28, 1868, "The voice of God may sometimes sound differently to you from what it sounds even to your father or to me; if so, never be afraid to say so—never close your mind against any but bad thoughts; for although we are all one in as far as we all partake of God's spirit, which is the breath of life, still the communion of each soul with him is, and must be, for that alone."[76]

It might seem that Lady Russell would permit this same latitude to the young Bertrand, at least occasionally. However, as reasonable as Lady Russell's toleration allowed her to be with most others, she seemed more hesitant with her grandson. Perhaps her desire to fit him to be a possible prime minister differentiated her grandson from others for her. Still, it was not that she presented no defense of her own religious beliefs precisely. Maybe she felt that she lacked sufficient theological expertise to answer the kinds of ideas or the critiques that her grandson might confront her with. On the other hand, she hardly could have imagined

---

74. Russell, *1872–1914*, 89.
75. Russell, "How I Came by My Creed," 14.
76. MacCarthy, *Lady John Russell*, 216.

the young Bertrand as ignorant of some of the theological currents of their time. If her reticence was in not feeling such knowledge or acumen really necessary in order to live a godly life, she did nevertheless presume that a godly life was the goal for all humans, irrespective of the God presumed. Indeed, at the conclusion of the letter to her daughter previously quoted, and after expressing her latitude amongst religious believers in their varying conceptions of God compared to her own, she puts that aside to say that "Nothing great is easy, and the greatest and most difficult of all things is to overcome ourselves . . . ."[77] Another way one might capture her meaning is to say that God is not the problem; we are. That is, our human piety is more important and therefore more urgent a task than our theological conundrums about God. For a youngster like her grandson, however, the habit of relegating hard thinking to secondary status simply could not suffice.

In his Uncle Rollo, Russell seems to have had something of a confidant to whom he could talk sometimes about theological matters, but only to a point. Having conversed with this uncle about the implication of selfishness being bound up with belief in an afterlife, the young Russell indicates: "He seemed doubtful whether the motives of Salvationists and of some Methodists could be selfish, but they seem to me as purely so as anybody's. As I once heard a Salvationist put it, 'you put down a penny and you take up a thousand pounds.' Uncle Rollo said such ideas made him glad that to thinking men there was no certainty or definiteness about a future state, by which I fancy he only meant about our mode of being, not about our being at all, for he always seems to have a firm belief in immortality of some kind. To me the absolute perfection which is usually attributed to angels does not seem such a beautiful idea as the gradual approach to perfection such as I believe the Buddhists affirm, ending at last in Nirvana or absolute repose and perfection."[78]

Nevertheless, despite Russell's divergences from his uncle within the family at Pembroke Lodge, Rollo seems to have been his best conversationalist on such matters, for almost a month later Russell reports in his "Locked Diary" that "When everybody else was in bed, Uncle Rollo and I had a most interesting talk about Faith and Reason, in which he agreed with me wonderfully, condemning Faith in its ordinary sense altogether and acknowledging only Reason."[79] However, at the same time,

77 MacCarthy, *Lady John Russell,*
78. May 31, 1890, "Locked Diary," *CP* 1:47.
79. June 20, 1890, "Locked Diary," *CP* 1:53.

the theological latitude of Lady Russell would have been commendable to the youngster, and indeed was such that he expected and insisted upon it in his own circle of young friends. So, for example, when he meets the sister of his friend Fitz, he writes in his "Locked Diary" that she "seemed to me the ideal of young womanhood. In her I found liberalism in politics and religion...."[80] Indeed the presence of theological diversity seems to have been a trait belonging to at least some of the people and atmosphere at Pembroke Lodge, despite a greater presence and reality in the household of grandmother Stanley. However, toleration extended to religious or theological latitude is one thing; agnosticism and atheism are quite another. The young Russell would eventually place himself completely outside the religious world of his Grandmother Russell and Pembroke Lodge, with such writings as encountered in *Why I am Not a Christian*. Lord John and particularly Lady Russell might have seen no reason to doubt that their grandson Bertrand would not share in their religious views as he grew. Instead, he distanced himself more and more from those beliefs, though by the time he goes up to Cambridge in 1890 he seems still hopeful for his religious inclinations,[81] despite often lending an opposite impression.[82] The school of philosophical idealism at Cambridge would assuage some of the sought yearnings for a brief while.

His grandmother was presumably scarcely aware that her grandson would in time reject most of his religious inheritance and upbringing—though not elements of the political inheritance that had sunk deeply into the Russell makeup. The experience of rejecting the theology at Pembroke Lodge left Russell still in search of a religion of sorts when he arrived at Cambridge. His soft agnosticism at the time was not entirely settled nor was it precisely happy. In his entry of August 31, 1890, Russell in his "Locked Diary" acknowledges a bleak present, though anticipating a brighter future, while still affirming belief that Russells would have their part in making the world better. Meanwhile, what had tipped Russell still further in the direction of loss of belief in God occurred after

---

80. September 1890, "Locked Diary," *CP* 1:61.

81. Interestingly, in a comment upon his political upbringing at Pembroke Lodge, Russell writes in "Adaptation: An Autobiographical Epitome" that "I imbibed certain political principles and expectations, and have on the whole retained the former in spite of being compelled to reject the latter." Russell, *Portraits*, 2.

82. Russell remarks with no suggestion of loss on making initial acquaintance with Chris Sanger at Cambridge that the two "agreed upon theology and metaphysics." Russell, *1872–1914*, 78.

reading Mill's *Autobiography*. Before that and with some hope for "an almighty First Cause," Russell wrote

> I still think that the hypothesis of an almighty First Cause affords a consistent explanation of the Universe, and therefore has the same kind of probability . . . [that] must depend upon its explanation of a large number of particular facts, on which I am not qualified to give an opinion.—The loss of certainty, is however the great pain which results from the change. To feel that the universe may be hurrying blindly towards all that is bad, that humanity may any day cease in progressive development and may continually lose all its fine qualities, that Evolution has no necessarily progressive principle prompting it; these are thoughts which render life almost intolerable.[83]

Such thoughts for the young Russell remained private thoughts, and thus not the sort that he could share with his grandmother. Lady Russell, however, was fairly widely read and she certainly entertained a variety of people and thinkers in her home, which indicates something of a willingness or tolerance toward alternative opinions. For example, a noted philosopher of her day, though one whose influence today is virtually nil, was Herbert Spencer. With him she remained respectful, but found herself with misgivings about the tenets of such thinkers like him, particularly those shading toward agnosticism and atheism.

---

83. August 31, 1890, "Locked Diary," *CP* 1:56.

5

Religion in the Early Adult Life of Bertrand Russell

A. RELIGION AT CAMBRIDGE UNIVERSITY

With his entrance to Trinity College at Cambridge, Russell rather soon fell under the purview of the group known as the Apostles, and clearly regarded his membership in the group then and later as an epochal experience at Cambridge. Furthermore, most of Russell's closest friends during his student years at Cambridge were also members of the Apostles and this combination made the attachment to this group all the more gratifying for Russell. The unorthodox and skeptical nature of the group Russell also found appealing. However, with Russell having shed many of the religious beliefs of his upbringing—something that not a few of his fellow Apostles had experienced—Russell still contemplated the possibilities for adopting a religion.[1] That being said, the work of the Apostles was on scrutinizing beliefs of any sort, and religious beliefs, like any others, required able defense to pass muster at the gate of the Apostles. Russell's attachment to the group is meaningfully contrasted to another circle he associated with, though with lesser enthusiasm on his part—the

---

1. W. C. Lubenow writes of the time of the Apostles nearing the twentieth century, "The history of the Apostles is inseparable from the history of religion in the time between Waterloo and the Great War. When the church offered the best professional opportunities, they became churchmen; when professional opportunities widened, they left the church's ambit. Throughout, the Apostles were skeptical and venturesome, contributing to reform when they were of the church and remaining sympathetic to religious impulses when they were not." Lubenow, *Cambridge Apostles*, 407.

Bloomsbury Circle. One might contend that some of the Bloomsbury circle presented themselves in a light that Russell regarded as more selfish than substantive. Russell felt himself tolerated by the circle, though without much genuine admiration accorded him, in contrast to and rather unlike that given to Russell's fellow philosopher G. E. Moore by Bloomsbury.

As an organization, the Apostles originated in 1820 and could boast of such Cambridge notables as Alfred Lord Tennyson. Some of the first friends Russell made at Cambridge came from the group. New members were recruited after their first year as a student, and only two were selected annually. During Russell's student years at Cambridge, the members had tended to be classicists and historians, mixed with some, but significantly fewer, philosophers. It was also comparatively rare for a mathematician to find his way into their ranks, though the mathematician Alfred North Whitehead, himself a member, put the group on notice to watch out for the new mathematics student Russell as a possibility for membership. As one of Russell's examiners on his entrance to Cambridge, Whitehead had been duly impressed with his ability and potential. Russell was elected in his second year and thereafter speaks of the group in nostalgic terms. The membership was notably irreverent, but not for the sake of simply or only being irreverent. Rather, no question nor any angle on a question was expunged from their talks and discussions, for they tended to be freethinkers in the generic sense of the word. Religion or something related to religion was not infrequently up for discussion among them and ethics even more. Indeed, the late nineteenth century was very much a time of religious intellectual ferment in England and coupled with the fact that some Apostle members came from noticeably religious families, particularly Dissenters, religion as a topic was not shunned nor unwelcomed by the Apostles.

The group had weekly Saturday night meetings and required attendance by members on pain of expulsion if absent for no good reason. The highlight of the evening meeting was presentation of a paper or essay read by a member and commented upon by the attendant members. Notably with Russell, though shared by some other members, was the group's penchant for mockery. Such an inclination on Russell's part is perhaps attributable to his reaction to Pembroke Lodge. In an early letter to Ottoline, Russell speaks of this frustration with his people, for "when I argued with them, I found they were perfectly stupid, and incapable of answering any questions except by an appeal to authority. They continued to chaff and to refuse to argue seriously, and I saw they were not only stupid but lacking in candour."[2] By contrast, the tendency of the culture of the Apostles remained open to almost anything as long as one marshalled a series of arguments to undergird a contention or point of view. Thus, having been disappointed and mocked by his relations at Pembroke Lodge, and particularly by his grandmother, Russell perhaps now felt satisfaction in poking fun at ideas he considered ludicrous, just as some of his own ideas had been considered ludicrous by his grandmother. Suddenly, at Cambridge he felt free, and that feeling of freedom surely meant substantial freedom from a family that often had been as constricting as a snake around an unwilling victim.

Still seeking a religion of sorts after going up to Cambridge, despite his theological disappointments at Pembroke Lodge, and despite the earlier verdicts on God's existence, human free-will and human immortality, Russell would now try at Cambridge another way for what had previously evaded him. Having been prodded into philosophy by questions on the foundations of both mathematics and religion, and finding Trinity College at Cambridge the place to study mathematics, he also found it, in 1890, offering something else:

> At Cambridge I was made aware of whole systems of thought of which I had previously been ignorant and I abandoned for a time the ideas which I had worked out in solitude. At Cambridge I was introduced to the philosophy of Hegel who, in the course of nineteen abstruse volumes professed to have proved something which would do quite well as an emended and sophisticated version of traditional belief.[3]

The abandonment "for a time" of the previous verdict against religious belief strongly suggests that Russell had not finished in his strivings for something religious and that, now, Cambridge provided Russell other opportunities. If studying of mathematics would teach Russell the habit of analysis, the reigning Hegelian philosophical school at Cambridge taught synthesis to the point of contending that all of reality is one conglomerate entity, and yet even the word "conglomerate" is misplaced because it implies conjunctive parts. At the end of the nineteenth century, English philosophy and English philosophers previously steeped in

2. Russell to Ottoline Morrell, September 28, 1911, Document no. 000199, Box no. 2.55, Bertrand Russell Archives, McMaster University Library/Ottoline Morrell Collection, Box 19, Folder 5, Harry Ransom Center, University of Texas, Austin.

3. Russell, *Portraits*, 17.

a long historical tradition of allegiance to empiricism, from John Locke to John Stuart Mill, had climbed onto the Continental bandwagon where the idealist philosophy of the German philosopher Hegel reigned. The most notable Hegelian amongst English philosophers was F. H. Bradley, the Oxford philosopher. Both Hegel's and Bradley's influence had spread to Cambridge by Russell's time. While Cambridge possessed no single individual of the stature of Bradley, at Cambridge, J. E. McTaggart, only a half dozen years older than Russell, proved to be its main exponent of Hegelian philosophy.[4]

At the root of the Hegelian philosophy, complementing its idea of "oneness," is its allied doctrine that reality is only naively conceived as material, for materialists of course argued that only matter was real. However, from the perspective of idealists, their philosophy emphasizes the intelligibility of the world and reality as coming through the lens of a human mind peering into something resembling cosmic Mind, often referred to by idealists as the Absolute. There is thus at least a resemblance to a pantheism of sorts, though some idealists like McTaggart, counted themselves atheists. For some, a conception of a non-material or spiritual reality seemed to present a possibility for blending philosophy and religion. The belief that reality was not at its base crude matter could suggest to the spiritually or religiously inclined that this was a possible philosophy for those despairing of the less attractive and even frighteningly deterministic alternatives. Such a possibility undoubtedly provided some promise to Russell for a time, however brief. The negative evaluation of religious beliefs while at Pembroke Lodge, however, would not be rescinded, for Russell was looking elsewhere for what his previous theological forays had denied him. This possibility did not mean that Russell

---

4. Since Russell and G. E. Moore and largely because of their criticism of Hegel and Idealism, Hegel has hugely fallen into disfavor, not to say contempt by nearly all Anglo-American philosophy, which has mocked Hegel as relentlessly as the later logical positivists mocked the language and philosophy of Martin Heidegger—each as example of how not to do philosophy. A sample of the derisive and contemptuous tone for much criticism of Hegel is exemplified in the first sentence of Morton White's *The Age of Analysis*, 13: "It is a remarkable tribute to an enormously muddled but brilliant German professor of the nineteenth century that almost every important philosophical movement of the twentieth century begins with an attack on his views. . . . The point is that Karl Marx, Kierkegaard the existentialist, John Dewey, Bertrand Russell, and G. E. Moore were at one time or another close students of Hegel's thought and some of their most distinctive doctrines reveal the imprint or the scars of previous contact or struggle with that strange genius." Given something of the overwhelming philosophical tide that turned against Hegel and his doctrines, it is easy today to ignore or dismiss the fact that Hegel and some of his doctrines are still propounded.

remained bent on finding God; it does mean that Russell maintained a search for something providing some solace in a world of turmoil and uncertainty, such as had swirled around him in his years at Pembroke Lodge. Mathematics and poetry had been at least in the previous running at Pembroke Lodge; in time they would be joined by philosophy at Cambridge. Nevertheless, the specter of Russell's own warning about believing because one desired to believe was instilled in Russell deeply enough to make him leery of the lucrative offerings of Hegelian philosophy, even as this philosophy enticed him. His overriding desire, moreover, would be to consider a philosophy with some religious promise, however remote. The reasons needed to satisfy the necessary justification for adopting such a philosophy would nevertheless prove elusive. Russell would not acquire the needed reasons; indeed, he encountered some very bad reasoning among the idealists, which he typically would mock later. For now, however, he was largely content to listen. Judgements would come later. Nevertheless, his subsequent disdain for the Hegelians of that period exemplifies Russell's perennial impatience with thinkers skirting sharp reasoning. Although for a while this philosophy held some promise to Russell and thus proved attractive, his adherence to such a philosophy could not be sustained:

> The attitude of these men to religion was not one of which the orthodox could approve, but it was by no means one of hostility. The sort of view that I had previously held, 'either there is a God or there is not, and probably the latter,' seemed to them very crude; the correct opinion, they would say, was that from one point of view there is a God and from another there is not. Being myself naturally 'crude', I never succeeded in reaching this pitch of mellowness.[5]

Such is a typical piece of critique by Russell to indicate his nononsense approach to what he regarded as sophisticated sophistry. In such a stance, Russell, somewhat like G. E. Moore, appealed to common sense as part of the crux of his argument against idealism. For Russell, the philosopher need not resort to complicated subtleties to undermine the opponent when the opponent hardly presented an argument requiring much of a sophisticated counterargument at all.

Idealism nevertheless sustained Russell, at least for a time. Too, his earlier appetite for the romantics, though also only for a time, had

---

5. Russell, "My Religious Reminiscences," 34.

derived from this same impetus. Still fresh from battles with indefensible religious beliefs from Pembroke Lodge, Russell was inclining, as he says, toward a surrogate religion of sorts, which idealism in the beginning seemed to offer. However, Russell was undoubtedly suspicious of his own move toward idealism, as suspicious as he always was of what might be called vested interest philosophy.[6] In his seminal essay, "Seems, Madame? Nay It Is," produced in 1897 and first read before the Apostles, the young Russell indicates the position he is moving toward. His contention is that nothing in philosophy is capable of providing religious repose and that religious motivations, though understandable, produce bad philosophy. Thus, Russell is already moving away from idealism as a philosophy of comfort, and still more toward the idea that no philosophy, in principle, can perform such a function or service. In this youthful essay, Russell writes that:

> The view which I have advocated is, no doubt, not an inspiring one, nor yet one which, if generally accepted, would be likely to promote the study of philosophy. I might justify my paper, if I wished to do so, on that maxim that, 'where all is rotten, it is a man's work to cry stinking fish'. But I prefer to suggest that metaphysics, when it seeks to supply the place of religion, has really mistaken its function. That it can supply this place, I admit; but it supplies it, I maintain, at the expense of being bad metaphysics. Why not admit that metaphysics, like science, is justified by intellectual curiosity, and ought to be guided by intellectual curiosity alone? The desire to find comfort in metaphysics has, we must all admit, produced a great deal of fallacious reasoning and intellectual dishonesty. From this, at any rate, the abandonment of religion would deliver us. And since intellectual curiosity exists in some people, it is probable that some attempts would still be made to understand the world, and it is possible that they would be freed from certain hitherto persistent fallacies.[7]

The task of undertaking the "abandonment of religion" would not come easy for Russell, any more than the youthful Plato could manage to

---

6. In a letter of September 28, 1911, Russell writes to Ottoline, "Even when I accepted Hegel, however, I found flaws in most of the comfortable consequences." Document no. 199, Box no. 255, Bertrand Russell Archives, McMaster University Library/ Ottoline Morrell Collection, Box 19, Folder 5, Harry Ransom Center, University of Texas, Austin.

7. Russell, *CP* 1:110–11.

give up poetry as a requirement to study philosophy with Socrates. Thus, even if religious inclinations could not be thoroughly banished for Russell, the courtship with idealism as a viable candidate could. Though Russell relates that his abandonment of idealism was instigated by a disbelief in its doctrines, the suspicious comforts of much idealist philosophy played an equally significant role. For Russell, a truth that was pleasing as one desired the truth to be, was by that very association suspect. Insufficient arguments by idealists were hardly found insufficient by aspirants wanting to believe, however. In other words, protected beliefs were assured safety by the specious reasons defending the guarded belief. This is why the reasons provided were hardly convincing. More importantly, it was a desired belief which affirmed a rather pleasant picture of reality, and one that leaned, as idealism did, toward a comforting metaphysic.

Russell often spoke of his giving up of the idealist philosophy as an emancipatory experience, and one with which, like his departure from the religious beliefs of his family, he was only too glad to be finished. Nevertheless, we recall that a decade earlier in life, Russell had recorded in his "Greek Exercises" for May 27, 1888, "It is very difficult for anyone to walk aright with no aid from religion, by his own internal guidance merely. I have tried, and I may say, failed. But the sad thing is that I have no other resource. I have no helpful religion."[8] Such feeling was not simply or only the remorse of a youngster. When Russell later tries to come to some temporary spiritual understanding with Lady Ottoline Morrell, mixed in with his impatience and frequent denunciations of religious belief are his laments over lacking a religion that he could embrace. Religion may be a sorry affair, but for Russell his resolve sometimes was to pull one out of the fire for use. Moreover, for all the aspiration to salvage something from religion and the occasional lament amidst the greater but differing sentiment of rewarded emancipation, one does not find in Russell any such lament for the idealism he gave up after his rejection of that philosophy. In 1918, Russell affirmed that "My bias remains: I still wish to rescue the physical world from the idealist."[9] The hostile undertone in Russell is evident. Though Russell hardly achieves his goal of a religion, the frustrated desire remains a part of his life, but there is never a wish for nor a trip backwards to idealism. To my knowledge Russell never expressed any regret over his abandonment of the idealistic philosophy

---

8. Russell, "Greek Exercises," *CP* 1:15.
9. Russell, "On Sensations and Ideas," *CP* 8:255.

and certainly none over leaving Hegel behind. Idealism would thus absolutely fail as a surrogate religion. Mathematics would too with Russell's retreat from Pythagoreanism, though with much admitted pain by Russell. Any such pain seems entirely lacking in Russell's flirtation with idealism.

B. MATHEMATICS IN THE EARLY RELIGION OF RUSSELL

In his third year at Cambridge Russell met G. E. Moore. Together, these two men would in subsequent years bring down the reigning idealist tradition at Cambridge. Very different in personality from one another, the two nevertheless developed an intellectual bond of stiff resistance and argument against idealism by their method of analysis. With the breaking down of large problems or issues into smaller chunks for more minute analysis and an insistent clarity of thought and meaning, both men bequeathed a new tradition to Anglo-American philosophy. This philosophical tradition still remains strong today among their intellectual heirs and with few signs of ebbing.

After two years of study of mathematics and around the same time he met the younger Moore, Russell had become impatient with mathematics and wanted time to devote study to philosophy. The philosophy he was acquainted with, that of his godfather John Stuart Mill and other empiricists, was viewed at Cambridge as an outmoded tradition and looked down upon by the reigning philosophical idealism then in command at Cambridge. So as to lessen his worry over his perceived meager knowledge of current philosophy, Russell was provided with coaching and a reading list by an Oxford philosopher named Harold Joachim. With tangible direction for his new study, Russell showed tenacity in managing to make great gains in plowing through a list of philosophical books, while resenting the time necessary for preparing for his mathematical exams. So eager was Russell's appetite for philosophy at the time, that he was given warning by his tutor James Ward not to let philosophical interests usurp the necessary preparations for his upcoming mathematics exams. In the end, however, he passed his mathematical exams, but sold his books on mathematics. This event, or transition, was a milestone in Russell's life.

Meanwhile, a significant break with idealism came when Russell substitute-taught a course on Leibniz in early 1899 for the idealist McTaggart, a friend of Russell's until World War I. In Russell's reading and research in preparation for lectures on Leibniz, which eventually culminated in his book *The Philosophy of Leibniz* in 1900, Russell argued that Leibniz's metaphysics were deduced by him from a subject-predicate logic. Arguing that there were other logical relations besides subject-predicate, Russell went on to claim that this discovery had a "dire effect upon metaphysics."[10] Previous to this discovery he had always been willing "to listen to a metaphysical argument for or against God or immortality," but that willingness now changed: "It was only after acquiring a new logic that I ceased to think such arguments worth examining."[11] The previous desire of a multitude of philosophers for a religious metaphysic, though already constrained if not repudiated by Russell earlier in his 1897 essay, "Seems, Madame? Nay It Is," now seemed assuredly doomed on Russell's estimation, though he still found some solace in mathematical entities, when cast in a platonic world of ideas. Thus, writing in 1902 (though not published until 1907), Russell's quasi-religious if not mystical admiration for mathematics is still evident:

> But mathematics takes us still further from what is human, into the world of absolute necessity, to which not only the actual world, but every possible world, must conform; and even here it builds a habitation, or rather finds a habitation eternally standing, where our ideas are fully satisfied and our best hopes are not thwarted. It is only when we thoroughly understand the entire independence of ourselves which belongs to this world that reason finds that we can adequately realize the profound importance of its beauty.[12]

Russell was later to admit with regret that "this kind of mathematical mysticism, which Plato derived from Pythagoras, appealed to me. But in the end I found myself obliged to abandon this doctrine also, and I have never since found religious satisfaction in any philosophical doctrine that I could accept."[13] Even though the Apostolic essay "Seems, Madame? Nay It Is," of 1897 had seemed to weaken if not sever any such alliance between philosophy and religion, Russell had apparently been

---

10. Russell, *1872–1914*, 212.
11. Russell, "My Religious Reminiscences," 35.
12. Russell, "Study of Mathematics," *CP* 12:91.
13. Russell, *Portraits*, 18.

unable to abide by his own warning completely, particularly exempting his warning when it came to mathematics. Russell, moreover, had believed that mathematics promised an untainted world beyond ourselves and relief from a world of teeming contingencies. Russell yearned to occupy a world like this, and for as long as such seemed possible, he revered mathematics.

However, the later influence of Wittgenstein and Russell's own earlier realization of Leibniz's conception of logical realities provoked him to abandon the previous hope: "In the years from 1894 to 1898, I believed in the possibility of proving by metaphysics various things about the universe that religious feeling made me think important."[14] Nonetheless, as earlier recalled, Russell's essay written for and delivered to the Apostles in 1897 had already suggested the uncomfortable impossibility of deriving comfort from metaphysics or for that matter, in principle, any philosophical doctrine. Russell contends in this very early essay what he will reiterate time and again in future decades—that philosophy is out to find the truth, not to produce or vindicate desired comforts. And thus he writes in that essay, "And this brings out the essential difference between the aesthetic satisfaction, which I allow, and the religious comfort, which I deny to philosophy."[15] However, for as long as Russell could retain his platonic view of mathematics he could conceive of a realm of mathematical sureties preferable to all else.

In his 1902 essay, "The Study of Mathematics," Russell was still affirming an inspiring world outside ourselves and distinct from the transient and beleaguered human world. A consideration of pure mathematics introduces one to a realm where the human only visits, without any needed revamping. In other words, the house of mathematics is already built; it only awaits discovery. Thus, mathematics simply awaits our visitation. This, indeed, is a world for unmatched inspiration. The link of the human world to the world of pure mathematics provides an oasis to those humans desirous of a realm whose realities cannot be destroyed. It is not a world brought into being by humans. The marvels of pure mathematics are then for Russell an exhibition of a world thoroughly non-human, and as such an aspiration for those humans anxious to glimpse such a reality. Though too suggestive of a word to describe Russell's veneration of mathematics, study of the subject nevertheless provides a "heaven" of

---

14. Russell, *Basic Writings*, 43.
15. Russell, *CP* 1:110.

sorts. Illustrative of a world remote from the variables and contingencies that afflict the besieged human, and in a stellar passage from the 1902 essay, Russell contends that in

> The contemplation of what is non-human, the discovery that our minds are capable of dealing with material not created by them, above all, the realization that beauty belongs to the outer world as to the inner, are the chief means of overcoming the terrible sense of impotence, of weakness, of exile amid hostile powers, which is too apt to result from acknowledging the all-but omnipotence of alien forces. To reconcile us, by the exhibition of its awful beauty, to the reign of Fate—which is merely the literary personification of these forces—is the task of tragedy. But mathematics takes us still further from what is human, into the region of absolute necessity, to which not only the actual world, but every possible world, must conform; and even here it builds a habitation, or rather finds a habitation eternally standing, where our ideals are fully satisfied and our best hopes are not thwarted. It is only when we thoroughly understand the entire independence of ourselves, which belongs to this world that reason finds, that we can adequately realize the profound importance of its beauty.[16]

Unlike Russell, Whitehead, though also a mathematician and collaborator with Russell for a decade, did not find metaphysical solace in mathematics, but pursued metaphysics from his scientific understanding—a method of which Russell would be highly critical. In Russell's case, when the brief comforts of idealism failed, further hopes in the direction of a consoling philosophy also failed, though mathematics notably survived as a possibility until Wittgenstein. Russell was enamored of the otherworldly character of mathematics as immune from the usual skeptical corrosives undermining philosophy and religion, for mathematics abstained from pain and suffering and the manifest contingencies of the world in which humans live. This was in Russell's mind the reward mathematics gave to humans who studied such a world. That study, at its deepest level, glimpses the mind of god, though of course Russell would never state the matter in such a fashion. Galileo's statement that "God wrote the universe in mathematical characters" is closer to Russell's notion, though Russell would prefer wording conveying that reality as conscripted according to mathematical artifices that no one built. Russell

16. Russell, "Study of Mathematics," CP 12:91.

sought for metaphysical solace in his quest for a strong soul, so strong as to live almost indifferently toward the struggles of life, which the human directed to mathematics almost disdains to notice. This is the philosopher, or more accurately, the mathematician, whose head, because it is figuratively firmly planted in the clouds is more strongly planted on a shaking earth. However, just as the "consolations of philosophy" gave little satisfaction to Russell, so too the "consolation of mathematics" fails when Wittgenstein conveys to Russell that mathematics is a tissue of tautologies rather than a bastion of immovable eternal truths to which we might cling. This disappointment was not the result of a sudden illumination, but a slower process, in evidence in Russell after his experience of World War I. Perhaps the most informative account of that transition comes from Russell's chapter in his book, *My Philosophical Development*, entitled "The Retreat from Pythagoras."[17]

C. RELIGION IN THE EARLY MARRIAGE OF RUSSELL

As Russell studied philosophy from the list of books furnished by Joachim, at the same time he began working to distance his family from the center of his young and maturing life. He would begin to take steps to remedy a conflict growing each year for as long as he was at Pembroke Lodge. This distancing was now possible—he was twenty-one years of age. Years of silence and muzzled thinking with muffled argument and secret diaries were about finished. As Russell would later write in his *Autobiography*, not the least of pent up emotions was that "I held my tongue on religion until I was twenty-one."[18] Russell was about to be free of people for whom he had affection, but of whom he was also only too glad to be free. Moreover, Russell had met an attractive American Quaker who lived close enough to Pembroke Lodge for the two to strike up an acquaintance, and then, for a relationship to develop between them—or at least a hope for one lodged in Russell's heart.

---

17. Russell, *My Philosophical Development*, 158: "I have no longer the feeling that intellect is superior to sense, and that only Plato's world of ideas gives access to the 'real' world. I used to think of sense, and of thought which is built on sense, as a prison from which we can be freed by thought which is emancipated from sense. I now have no such feelings."

18. Russell, *1872–1914*, 57.

The woman who would become Russell's first wife, Alyssa (Alys) Pearsall Smith, was a Quaker. Her mother, and Russell's future mother-in-law, Hannah Whitall Smith, was a prominent Christian of some notoriety and following, and the author of a popular book of Evangelical piety entitled *The Christian's Secret of a Happy Life*. Marrying into a Quaker family and one of some reputation, might suggest that Russell would set aside his early hostility toward religion upon entering into such a marriage. However, how Russell negotiated the religious element with Quaker Alys is illuminating for glimpses of how unflinching were Russell's reservations toward religion during this time with the woman who would become his first wife. Among the circle of Russell's Cambridge friends, a heritage of Quakerism was not uncommon. Roger Fry and Lytton Strachey, for example, also members of the Apostles, were of vintage English Quaker families, though both had rejected Quaker belief by the time of their friendships with Russell.

The Quaker tradition, going back to the seventeenth century in English religious history, had to endure, as did other Christian bodies, severe questioning of religious beliefs in the nineteenth century. Indeed, the Victorian crisis of faith provoked substantial reformation of English religiosity, particularly among intellectuals. Many now deemed religious beliefs as simply untenable, perhaps even farcical, in the face of alternative and competing explanations that severely tested traditional theological beliefs. New currents of thinking, therefore, swirled around this situation, with various efforts to deal with the crisis.

During the nineteenth century, Amberley, Russell's father, had consciously moved away from Christian orthodoxy for a variety of reasons, first calling himself a deist, somewhat indicative of the soul-searching that besieged persons like Amberley. However, the Quakers were not in the main threatened by the tumult of theological questioning as were other groups, for Quakers placed their theological focus on the social world, contending that the real work of the Christian Gospel belonged more on the street than in the study. Moreover, the Quakers deemed the sins and wrongs of the world to pour forth from human hearts unreceptive to the Gospel message rather than issuing from an intellectual stalemate sparked by philosophical conundrums or scientific discoveries. In Lowes Dickinson's *Modern Symposium*, the Quaker speaker compares his vision for the world with other voices: "For you have all spoken from the point of view of the world. You have put forward proposals for changing society and making it better. But you have relied, for the most part, on external means to accomplish such changes. You have spoken of extending or limiting the powers of government, of socialism, of anarchy, of education, of selective breeding. But you have not spoken of the Spirit and Life, or not in the sense in which I would wish to speak of them."[19] The Quaker speaker continues to articulate his understanding of the good: "That Good is the love of God, and through the love of God the love of man.... Now, as of old, in the midst of science, of business, of invention, of the multifarious confusion and din and hurry of the world, God may be directly perceived and known. But to know Him is to love Him, and to love Him is to love His creatures, and most of all our fellow-men.... And if that love were really spread abroad among us, the questions that have been discussed tonight would resolve themselves. For there would be a rule of life generally observed and followed; and under it the conditions that make the problems would disappear."[20]

Understandably, then, the work of the Quakers, despite their "quietism," was most apt to be visible in their social and community work. Coupled with this emphasis is the fact that many Quakers and similar groups also placed emphasis upon living a fervent religious life, such that from such groups evolved what was called the Holiness Movement. In such circles, and falling within what religious historians refer to as Pietistic traditions, the heart tends to matter more than the head or intellect. Such traditions, moreover, and Quakers included, tended to assess the theological tumult of the crisis of faith in the nineteenth century with less pain than, for example, more overtly Christian theological traditions that desired to wed thinking with believing, rather than relegating Christian witness to principally and perhaps only a Social Gospel.

19. Dickinson, *Modern Symposium*, 146.

20. Dickinson, *Modern Symposium*, 147–48. A mere page later, and now indicating more of why such problems will disappear, the speaker adds, "But we have God to rely on, who gives His help not according to the measure of our powers. A man cannot by taking thought add a cubit to his stature; he cannot increase the scope of his mind or change the range of his senses; he cannot, by willing, make himself a philosopher, or a leader of men. But drawing on the source that is open to the poorest and the weakest he can become a good man; and then, whatever his powers, he will be using them for God and man. If men do that, each man for himself, by the help of God, all else will follow" (149). Perhaps most interesting, however, is how the speaker on the same page concludes this point by exhibiting how this moral consciousness is not necessarily Christocentric: "So true is it that if ye seek first the kingdom of heaven all these things shall be added unto you. Yes, that is true. It is eternal truth. It does not change with the doctrines of Churches nor depend upon them. I would say even it does not depend on Christianity. For the words would be true though there had never been a Christ to speak them. And the proof that they are true is simply the direct witness of consciousness."

For this reason, in the nineteenth century Quakers more easily accommodated new currents of thought in the nineteenth century that seemed to undermine previous orthodox Christian thinking for other religious groups. Quakerism was familiar to many for its work in alleviation of social ills, and with it, a recognition that theological finesse was hardly the strong suite of Quakers. Thus, Quakerism did not first find its theological staples or leanings called to account as severely in the tumultuous crisis of faith in the nineteenth century, as did many other religious groups. To the degree that the broader nineteenth century crisis of faith produced, as it did, a significant theological swing toward theological liberalism, this liberalism relegated the proclamation and work of the Christian Gospel to what became known as the "Social Gospel" in the twentieth century. In such circles, Christian belief moved from creeds and confessions to a more active social and in time political engagement with the culture.

Though the religion at Pembroke Lodge had not been Quakerism, the Russells historically had embraced a kind of liberalism that could rather easily find association with a religious group like the Quakers. So, for example, in his later opposition to England's entrance into World War I, Russell found himself often rubbing elbows with Christian and other pacifists. Many of these individuals were Quakers with whom Russell shared few theological convictions. So too with Alys. That is, though Russell scarcely shared any theological beliefs with Alys, their engagement with social and humanitarian issues provided significant common ground between them for a time. Indeed, there was at Pembroke Lodge a strenuous belief in social and political progressivism, in addition to generally theologically liberal religious convictions. This is why after all of his annoyance with the religious atmosphere of Pembroke Lodge, Russell can nevertheless approvingly comment, referencing his Grandmother Russell and Aunt Agatha, that they "could always be relied upon not be illiberal."[21]

Nevertheless, Alys's religion, however liberal or socially-minded the nucleus might be, was still an obstacle, not to say an offense to Russell. Confrontations with Alys would be inevitable, because for Russell religion should never get a free pass, not even for potential family members. Furthermore, though Russell as a youngster endured the religious atmosphere of Pembroke Lodge, his judgements against the religion of that household, and his wider negative judgements on religion upon leaving

21. Russell, *1872–1914*, 197.

of Pembroke Lodge now began to surface out loud. Though he was unable to move any of the members of the household at Pembroke Lodge to his religious position, there could be no such impasse with the woman he was about to take as his wife. Moreover, his demeanor toward Alys's religion is further testament to Russell's strong feelings toward religion and particularly religious belief, even at this juncture in his early adult life. Thus he writes in his "A Locked Diary," for October 6, 1894, that "We have met each other half way in our theories, and I am more and more impressed by Aly's power of developing and broadening and abandoning long-cherished theories. There only remains religion, and in that there are signs of our soon coming into sympathy, which *would* be a joy to me."[22]

However, in a previous letter of October 29, 1893, Russell had put Alys on notice that they must have some theological reconciliation between them over the matter of religion, and warns her that "I am sorry because I shall unavoidably appear in a rather brutal light as I am so utterly out of sympathy with Christianity."[23] As an example, he references his inability to believe that deity can be conceived as a person, as in orthodox Christianity. However, he also adds in the same letter that religion is nevertheless not ruled out for him, though it requires revision: "But I do not mean to put nothing in its place: on the contrary I am convinced that as soon as we begin to reflect seriously on religion we shall find Pantheism a far finer, a far more inspiring faith," although "the idea of Pantheism is rather difficult."[24] Noticeable here is the fact again, that while Russell has rejected virtually every plank of orthodox belief belonging to Christianity, the matter of religion is not finished or abandoned; a revision of thinking is possible, though not in the spirit of overturning or rescinding his prior rejection of orthodox religious beliefs; furthermore, he concedes the difficulty of such a task. Continuing in this same letter, Russell already reveals some of the direction of his later notable essays, those written under the strain of the later breakup of his marriage to Alys. In the later essays, as in his letter here, Russell is groping for something to strengthen him to persist and indeed triumph against discouragements, and while he concedes a role to faith, it must be understood that:

> ... the faith required is not belief in this or that dogma, but rather in the perfectibility of the world and in the ultimate attainment

---

22. Russell, *CP* 1:67.
23. Russell to Alys Pearsall Smith, October 29, 1893, in Griffin, *Letters*, 1:30.
24. Russell to Alys Pearsall Smith, October 29, 1893, in Griffin, *Letters*, 1:31.

of such perfection. But no amount of faith will I think make one happy without some more substantial source of joy: I have seen the very purest and strongest faith completely powerless against misfortune, and I think it would be so in my own case probably. But there is about great happiness something eternal which is satisfying even when this immeasurable cause of happiness is removed. The fact that such a thing is possible is such a revelation that it seems to make everything else endurable: especially when one is convinced that this feeling is not mere sentiment but can be supported by reason.[25]

Notable here is Russell's notion of the "perfectibility of the world and in the ultimate attainment of such perfection" as an item of reasoned faith that he wishes to uphold. It is this posture and resolve that can account for some of Russell's impatience and anger in later decades when the world around him seemed in danger of collapsing although the solution and means to the solution seemed so self-evident to him. Nevertheless, frustrations aside, the political belief in this perfectibility would unite Russell with Alys for a while in some joint social causes, with Russell continuing to be insistent that on the matter of religion the two needed some resolution. Russell could not accommodate beliefs which seemed to him utterly unbelievable.

In a letter of January 28, 1894, Russell writes to Alys, trying to come to agreeable terms on one matter of religion that could not be avoided as they considered marriage.[26] "But when I told him [Amos] another time in answer to a question of his, that thee was a Christian, he seemed to think that difference important: and indeed I am sure it is and we ought to keep it in mind. It would only become very serious I think if we had children to bring up: I could hardly reconcile it to my conscience to have children of mine brought up as Christians."[27] Softening the letter somewhat, Russell goes on to add that "I cannot argue well with thee, for when I am with thee thy religion seems so right that I lose all wish to change

---

25. Russell to Alys Pearsall Smith, October 29, 1893, in Griffin, *Letters*, 1:31.

26. Reference is made to "Amos" in this letter, who was Maurice Sheldon Amos. Russell describes Amos in his *Autobiography* as "my only link between Cambridge and Friday's Hill." Russell, *1872–1914*, 223. According to Russell, Maurice had a sister named Bonte, whom Russell and Alys befriended and aided. They also took her on their trip to America in 1896. Russell then comments, somewhat wryly, "Both brother and sister refused to know me when I ceased to be respectable, but the brother relented in the end. The sister remained adamant." Russell, *1872–1914*, 223.

27. Griffin, *Letters*, 1:51–52.

it: and yet at other times I am so strongly anti-religious that I am afraid I might in future become serious." However, in the very next sentences of this letter, he states matter-of-factly his charge against religious beliefs, a charge that he would present to Lady Ottoline in years to come, for in Ottoline he would encounter another religious believer with whom Russell clashed over the subject: "I suppose thee would admit that thy beliefs are not founded on reason, indeed that they are not founded on reason, indeed that they are in flagrant contradiction to it: that they are in fact founded only on thy wishes, which thee would not accept as sufficient ground for an opinion at anything else."[28]

Typically, however, and again as with Ottoline many years hence, Russell usually presents an effort afterward to soften some of his vehemence. Thus, he writes to Alys that

> I realized in expressing it to thee the other day, how *very* unreasonable my prejudice against religion is, and how very far beyond reason I went in what I then said—For indeed it is only an intellectual objection I have a right to; morally I am not at all sure whether religion may not be a real help, thou' I *think* it makes very little difference. I have been looking at my old speculations on theology when I was 15; they amuse me now, especially the tremendous struggle I made to free myself from sentiment in forming my opinions. But I was a shocking materialist, and some of the opinions there make me shudder now. Thee ought to be glad I have done some philosophy, as it is that alone which has worked the change.[29]

This last sentence refers to Russell's prior hope that philosophy of some kind might afford him a believable religion of sorts, however unorthodox, and at least provide a way around the materialistic beliefs that had besieged him at Pembroke Lodge. Nevertheless, Alys probably felt little consolation from Russell's commendation of the work of philosophy on him, for Russell had in earlier letters struggled to assuage Alys's lack of enthusiasm for the skeptical tendency of philosophy.[30]

---

28. Griffin, *Letters*, 1:52.

29. Russell to Alys Pearsall Smith, April 12, 1894. Document no. 300067, Box no. 6.52, Bertrand Russell Archives, McMaster University Library.

30. "I don't see why thee doesn't believe in Moore's enthusiasm for skepticism." Russell to Alys Pearsall Smith, February 21, 1894. Document no. 300049, Box no. 6.52, Bertrand Russell Archives, McMaster University Library. In a letter three days previous, writing of Moore's debut in the Apostles, Russell relates, however, that "I had said (we were discussing the Cambridge education) that our training has produced such

Coupled with opposition from the Russell household at Pembroke Lodge to any upcoming marriage, Russell's friend Sanger also had feared that under the influence of Alys, Russell might become more accepting of religion. However, Russell writes to Alys in a letter June 4, 1894, that "I was able to assure him I was as bitter against religion as ever . . . ." Russell, moreover, does not relent with Alys regarding religion and writes to her in a letter of July 8, 1894, that "I am very glad thee has read Mill's *Autobiography*. . . . It is at the bottom of a great deal in me. I am particularly pleased thee should understand better what I feel about religion, as there has always been rather a want of comprehension in both of us on that . . . ."

By September the tenor of letters between the couple evidences more movement of Alys toward Russell on the question of religion and Russell expresses something of this change when he writes that

> I am glad from thy letters to gather thee has been thinking about religion—though now that we're not going to have children it is less unfortunate thee should lose thy religion. I only wish it now because it is a lack of perfect sympathy, and may, in the course of my work or thine, make a disagreeable strain someday—besides that I cannot get over a sort of contempt for a Xtian in our generation, and it is annoying to feel that about thee.[31]

If Russell and Alys were coming closer to terms on the subject of religion, Russell nonetheless found more formidable obstacles from his family to his planned marriage to Alys. Russell, however, pushed back against their resistance, though at the same time he accommodated some of the requests intended by Pembroke Lodge to delay and ultimately weaken any plan for marriage. While Russell was clearly in love with Alys, additional motivation to marry was to escape from the grip of a family whose divergences from the emerging adult Russell were starkly clear to him. Certainly not a few children have experienced such tensions as they journeyed to adulthood, though in Russell the obstacles encountered from the household at Pembroke Lodge became increasingly excruciating to him. Russell wanted to be on his own, and financially he could now do so, but more importantly he wanted freedom from a household with whom he shared so few beliefs and even fewer of their Victorian aversions.

---

a profound skepticism about everything that many of us are unfit for practical life." Russell to Alys Pearsall Smith, February 18, 1894. Document no. 310048, Box no. 6.52, Bertrand Russell Archives, McMaster University Library.

31. Russell to Alys Pearsall Smith, September 22, 1894. Document no. 300151, Box no. 6.52, Bertrand Russell Archives, McMaster University Library.

The woman with whom he made this move and departure from family was certainly not a matter of indifference to him; but the alliance of a marriage would permit him to be free of the onerous shackles of the Russell family living on whispers at Pembroke Lodge. It was not that any marriage partner would do; again, between him and Alys there was every sign of genuine affection. Nevertheless, the differences of thinking between the two started to show in the engagement, reflecting the beginnings of rifts between them that would later strike at the heart of their marriage. Said another way, temperamentally the two were significantly unsuited for one another, a fact that took some time before becoming clear to Russell and to the couple's acquaintances.

Alys's older sister Mary—who would have needed little convincing from Russell about the implausibility of Quaker or Christian theological tenets—would seem to have been more compatible with Russell. However, differences on religion between the two sisters did not differentiate the two sisters as much as Mary's flamboyant and rebel streak, compared to Alys's quiet and deferential manner. Alys possessed little of the audacity and confidence of her more vivacious sister. Russell, moreover, seemed to enjoy time spent with Mary, and for example, was something of a willing participant in a near triste with Mary one evening in November of 1894 in Paris. Russell would later have to provide to Alys some details of what had transpired during that evening so naively suggested earlier by Alys.

The opposition from the Russell family at Pembroke Lodge over Russell's engagement to Alys would have had more principle and potency if Mary, rather than Alys, had been the sister betrothed to the youthful Russell. Quiet and agreeable Alys could hardly have provoked even small quibbles from the Russell family, and certainly nothing compared to her sister Mary, except for the fact that Alys's five more years in age than Russell provoked the charge from Lady Russell that the bride-to-be was simply taking advantage of a younger man who had not the maturity nor experience to realize he was being used for her own gain. Russell was later largely though not entirely correct about the surrounding motivations involved in the opposition from Pembroke Lodge to his engagement. That is, Russell contended that the offensive from Pembroke Lodge was simply one that would have come at any potential wife for Russell. In other words, the particulars of Alys, age and otherwise, were hardly leading the charge against Alys; probably truer was that Alys was removing Bertie not only from Pembroke Lodge, but from the possibility of another Russell being Prime Minister. If such a surmise is accurate, virtually any marriage partner stood to jeopardize Granny's ultimate hope for her grandson as a future statesman. The particulars of Alys were thus somewhat beside the real point of opposition to her from Lady Russell. This surmise is partially proved by the fact that while Aunt Agatha joins Lady Russell in opposition to Russell's engagement to Alys at the time, Agatha became quite fond of Alys later.

Nevertheless, Pembroke Lodge from the beginning stood opposed to the couple's plans to marry, and in reading Lady Russell's letters in particular, one senses that the letter writer feels she has tragically lost a grandson in whom she had placed so much expectation and for whom she had provided great affection. Perhaps equally disappointing for her, he seemed to exhibit only callous indifference toward her. This of course is not true, or certainly not entirely true, for Russell did not wish to inflict pain upon his family with his decision, though at the same time if they were going to be pained by his decision, they would have to endure. Russell, in other words, was resolute in his decision and I think never seriously wavered in that decision. Moreover, and as indicated before, his resolve was not only to take Alys for his wife, but also to be freed from the staid atmosphere and shackles of interfering relatives at Pembroke Lodge.

Russell encountered a host of different characters and a different culture when he moved out of Pembroke Lodge on July 15, 1894, and into Friday's Hill, the home of the Pearsall Smith family. After three months of frustratingly mundane work at the Paris embassy—devised by Lady Russell to put geographical distance between Russell and Alys—on his return home, the couple married on December 13, 1894. Not a single Russell from Pembroke Lodge attended. The Stanley side of the family, as might be expected, were present in good supply, most noticeably Grandmother Lady Stanley and her son and Bertrand's uncle, Lyulph, who had been instrumental in undermining Russell's mother's religion and with notable success.

Indicative of the feeling at Pembroke Lodge less than six months after the marriage, in a letter of May 18, 1895, written to Bertrand's Uncle Rollo's wife, Gertrude, Lady Russell writes, "Our Bertie's birthday—would that I could feel quite entirely happy about him—but no more of that—"[32] And in a letter of November 24, 1895, she writes to Gertrude in the midst of her daughter Agatha's sickness, that "Agatha has been making progress & is all the better for that visit of Dr. Lane, but Bertie weights

---

32. Oxford, Bodleian Libraries, MS. Eng. lett. e. 115, fols. 16–17.

upon her heavily, poor child & I have to go very nearly beyond the truth of what I feel, in trying to cheer her—"[33]

However, sometimes the situation and the relationship between Russell and the Russell family could mollify, at least a bit. In a letter of February 21, 1896, to Gertrude, temporary jubilation is mixed with the silence that had to be kept between Lady Russell and her household when Bertie was her company for the inevitable variant opinions among them: "We were greatly pleased by his attitude of mind. Some days ago when he was here—an attitude of suspended judgement on various knotty subjects—he was so nice altogether, and may we be forgiven for having enjoyed him alone."[34] This is a clear reference to the absent Alys at Russell's visit. Moreover, if Alys were suspect to the Russells, so too were the Pearsall-Smith family, especially Alys's mother, about whom Lady Russell asks daughter-in-law Gertrude in a letter of April 15, 1894, "Do you think there is humbug under that nice Quaker bonnet of the mother?"[35] Moreover, Lady Russell had found Alys easier to bear than her mother Hannah, even as Lady Russell shares with Gertrude that "I always liked the old Lady in spite of her nonsense on several subjects, on one of which, spiritualism, the daughter is quite different with her."[36] However, Lady Russell could make an effort toward Alys, despite the dire

---

33. Oxford, Bodleian Libraries, MS. Eng. lett. e. 115, fols. 44–45.

Agatha certainly reciprocated in her respect and love of her mother, and in a letter of May 17, 1898, shortly after Lady Russell's death, she writes in a manner reflecting Agatha's sense of disappointment with Bertrand: "I shall think of you very much tomorrow and of happy birthdays long ago when she was with us to guide counsel and inspire to all good and when you were still the child brightening our home and filling us with hope of what you might some day become dear dear Bertie has it been an upward growth since those days? Have the joys of life which are now yours helped you to be not less but more loving, more helpful, more thoughtful, for those whose lives may be full of sorrow illness pain and loneliness." In Russell, *1872–1914*, 218–19. What is only implied here, years later, in a letter of August 1926 to Russell concerning Alys and their earlier separation and eventual divorce, she explicitly states with evident disappointment, but also anger: "Do not imagine for a moment that I ever forget, and did not feel most acutely, your own unhappiness, which I know must have been very real and deep:—but to those who truly loved you, it is heart-breaking that you have not grown nobler, stronger, more loving and tender through suffering, but in every way the reverse.—You do not at all realise how you have changed. We ought all to change and grow as life goes on; but it should be upwards, not downwards." Agatha Russell to Bertrand Russell, August 1926, Box no. 6.29, Bertrand Russell Archives, McMaster University Library.

34. Oxford, Bodleian Libraries, MS. Eng. lett. e. 115, fols. 58r-59v.

35. Oxford, Bodleian Libraries, MS. Eng. lett. e. 114, fols. 116–19.

36. Oxford, Bodleian Libraries, MS. Eng. lett. e. 114, fols. 116–19.

situation, and so writes in a letter of September 1, 1894, to Gertrude and prior to the opposed marriage, "Oh dear can we ever manage to love her after all she has done?"[37]

Worse, moreover, Lady Russell believed her anger justified. In a letter of May 1, 1894, she fulminates in writing, "We have allowed ourselves to be outwitted.... Don't tell me not to be angry—I am, and I have a right to be and I don't know when I shall have come down enough from the hipocrisy necessary when I see her again."[38] In a letter of despair to son Rollo of July 24, 1894, she laments, "I often feel this is a nightmare from which we shall awaken—for was there ever a boy in whom duty was more paramount than in Bertie? & was there ever in this world a duty more clearly pointed out than his...."[39] The grave disappointment of her political aspirations for her grandson are evident.

However, even as she lamented her defeat, with Bertie now removed from Pembroke Lodge, Lady Russell did not desire to feel animosity. Indeed, one can see on occasion that she did desire to be accepting of this woman now joined to her beloved grandson's life. Writing to Rollo on April 29, 1897, "I can't help feeling much sadness about him which cannot be written—It would be so delightful to love her with all my heart—not with 3 quarters of it only, as is now the case—do you think the other quarter will come when I see her next?"[40]

D. RELIGIOUS ASPIRATIONS IN A DETERIORATING MARRIAGE

Alys and Russell married on December 13, 1894. The couple would afterward enjoy some years of felicity, though these years were few compared to the long lifespans of each partner after their separation. They parted in 1911, with the marriage nevertheless extending until 1921, when they were finally divorced, enabling Russell to marry his second wife, Dora Black.

While still happily married, Russell and Alys enjoyed the company and also for a time shared a house with the Whiteheads, Alfred and Evelyn, to the point that over time Russell counted this couple among the closest, if not the very closest of friends. The Whiteheads were aids and

---

37. Oxford, Bodleian Libraries, MS. Eng. lett. e. 114, fols. 130–31.
38. Oxford, Bodleian Libraries, MS. Eng. lett. e. 114, fols. 122–31.
39. Oxford, Bodleian Libraries, MS. Eng. lett. e. 113, fols. 81–83.
40. Oxford, Bodleian Libraries, MS. Eng. lett. e. 113, fols. 130–31.

confidants for Russell, in good times and bad, though their relationships were sometimes strained, as when Alfred Whitehead objected to Russell's pacifist stance during World War I. At the same time, Russell shared in their grief when their son North, of whom Russell was very fond, was killed in that war.

The ten-year task of writing their monumental work *Principia Mathematica* might have sufficed for the making of a close relationship between Russell and Whitehead. However, the relationship deepened to the point of revealing another aspect of Russell's character. Unlike few other friends and acquaintances of Bertrand and Alys, the Whiteheads were also particularly close to the collapsing marriage of Russell and Alys, and indeed Evelyn Whitehead had many conversations with Russell about the strained and eventually separated relationship of the estranged couple. Alfred Whitehead was temperamentally unsuited to fulfill this advisory role that his wife apparently provided for Russell.

Among Russell's close and life-long friends, Whitehead was distinctively different. Aside from the rather normal idiosyncratic traits of a lifelong academic indifferent to and uncomprehending of many mundane matters, including imminent dangers such as walking across streets with no thought of oncoming traffic, Whitehead was something of a loner. Though it was Whitehead who had alerted the Apostles about Russell as a newcomer to Cambridge in 1890, and though Whitehead maintained membership in the group, there is very little information about his tenure in that organization.[41] To Russell, however, he was friendly and helpful. Russell reciprocated that kindness in his alliances with Evelyn, Whitehead's wife, when the unworldly Alfred, for example, resorted to a propensity of unrestrained spending and she informed Russell of her worry. Aside from the rather rampant rumor and speculation about a romantic relationship between Russell and Evelyn, it does seem clear that just as Alfred was something of a father to Russell, so too was Evelyn something of a mother. The couple were almost like parents on occasion, in trying to reel in the wayward Russell, and this especially so on the part of Evelyn in Russell's marriage to Alys and in Russell's later romantic but marriageless relationship with Ottoline. It might also be said with some justification

---

41. Paul Levy writes that "It is somewhat curious that Whitehead does not figure at all in the biographies and memoirs of the Apostles who were contemporary with him. He does not seem to have formed any close friendships even with his fellow Apostles, and seems to have been known, if at all, as a mathematician, without much influence until the time of Moore and Russell." Levy, *Moore*, 95. Perhaps the overtly skeptical culture of the group put Whitehead off.

that Russell's character took on some of his trademark propensities and behaviors during this time and that the interventions of the Whiteheads might have lessened the collateral damage of some of Russell's actions.

It is clear from Russell's writings that he had great respect for Whitehead, despite some volatile disagreements they had, particularly over differing positions they took over the First World War mentioned already, and despite the rather wide divergences in their later work. One might say that in the humanity and in some of the intellectual predilections of Whitehead, Russell found much to praise. This is particularly so in the succinct phrase of description when Russell wrote of his friend, "He was at all times deeply aware of the importance of religion."[42] Of course when the two men wrote on the subject, and matters close to the subject, such as science and religion, their differences were glaringly apparent. Thus, Russell writes of Whitehead, "His later philosophy gave him some part of what he wanted from religion."[43] On his own admission, Russell had been on something of the same quest, but Russell took severe issue with the efforts of philosophers and even scientists who Russell deemed engaged in directions he thought devious and unfruitful. Indeed, Russell turned back to writing on religion yet again in the 1930s with annoyance and hostility toward these faulty attempts. In a letter to his publisher W. W. Norton of October 27, 1930, he is incensed that "There is at the present time a terrific outburst of Godism among scientific men—Whitehead, Eddington, J. B. Haldane, General Smuths, etc. It drives me wild, as it is composed entirely of sophistry. I should like, in some part of the book, to show them up, but am doubtful whether you would like the book to be such as all parsons will curse."[44] Numbered among the guilty here, Whitehead is also elsewhere judged negatively by Russell in reviewing Whitehead's book *Science and the Modern World*, where Russell insisted that "Dr. Whitehead has a thesis for the intellect and a thesis for the emotions. The validity of the latter depends upon the validity of the former which must therefore be examined first."[45] From the time of his adolescent questioning, Russell had not allowed himself what Whitehead and others had permitted themselves: a coupling of the two in skewed

---

42. Russell, *Portraits*, 103.
43. Russell, *Portraits*, 103.
44. Russell to W. W. Norton, October 27, 1930. Box no. 636, Bertrand Russell Archives, McMaster University Library.
45. Russell, Review of *Science and the Modern World*, 206. CP 9:312–15.

order. Russell never tired of repeating this familiar charge and in a kinder way contends the same tendency evident in Whitehead's work.

> In the last months of the war his younger son, who was only just eighteen, was killed. This was an appalling grief to him, and it was only by an immense effort of moral discipline that he was able to go on with his work. The pain of this loss had a great deal to do with turning his thoughts to philosophy and with causing him to seek ways of escaping from belief in a merely mechanistic universe. His philosophy was very obscure, and there was much in it that I never succeeded in understanding. He had always had a leaning toward Kant, of whom I thought ill, and when he began to develop his own philosophy he was considerably influenced by Bergson. He was impressed by the aspect of unity in the universe, and considered that it is only through this that scientific inferences can be justified. My temperament led me in the opposite direction, but I doubt whether pure reason could have decided which of us was more nearly in the right. Those who prefer his outlook might say that while he aimed at bringing comfort to plain people I aimed at bringing discomfort to philosophers; one who favored my outlook might retort that while he pleased the philosophers, I amused the plain people.[46]

Rumors of the nature of the relationship between Russell and Evelyn aside, Russell seemed to prefer the companionship and the confidence of women over men. Whatever the advice or counsel exchanged between Russell and Evelyn, the end result, as it concerns the faltering relationship between Russell and Alys, seemed in Evelyn's estimation due to deficiencies on the part of Russell. Setting aside the possibility that this assessment of Russell may have been a vindictive jab at him and due to an element of sour grapes on Evelyn's part, perhaps she was simply noting a character trait of Russell with women and lovers that perpetually strained and often broke relationships between them and Russell. Indeed, something like this might partially explain the rather frosty meetings of Lady Ottoline with Evelyn in late March of 1911, on Russell's recommendation, aside from Evelyn's own and perhaps powerful sympathy for the plight of Alys. That is, Evelyn apparently had little sympathy for the kind of relationships that were not infrequent in the circles of Ottoline and Russell.

Nevertheless, the tumult involved in the breakup of Russell's marriage to Alys did prompt if not push Russell to give words to his pains

46. Russell, *Portraits*, 100–101.

and perplexities through something more than private conversations with trusted confidants. Consequently, Russell turned to what he knew and used best—the written word. However, now Russell would try to somewhat appease his existential predicament by providing some salve in the form of some remarkable and very notable essays where he clearly sought for some relief and understanding of his suffering and predicaments. Though the essays have the flavor of religious writing, we recall that Russell had given up on any orthodox theology some years earlier; his quest for something freeing him of the tumult of a decaying marriage, nevertheless, did send him down something of a parallel tract that religions of various sorts had plotted. In these efforts, Russell is therefore not attempting to return or recoup something rejected or lost, even as he on occasion bumps into ideas of a more orthodox nature than his own. Rather, he is seeking to find some way of living in the face of an overwhelming despair that threatens to eviscerate. No element of orthodox theology is marshalled by Russell as a life raft, though partial similarities—alongside the more striking differences—are notable in these essays. Thus, however slightly conciliatory Russell may at times seem toward some traditional religious notions, his unflinching atheism prompts him toward a different course for the modern unbeliever who cannot be expected to return to unbelievable and therefore discarded beliefs of the past. Russell will therefore continue to deviate from traditional or orthodox notions that he sees as no longer viable in a modern age lived without god and without a juried moral universe providing vindication of and retribution for rights and wrongs, respectively.

Perhaps the most astonishing fact about these particular essays is that a philosopher of such worldly eminence, but more, with an almost unmatched vehemence against most things religious, should have put into print compositions that give at least some legitimacy and to show some sympathy for religion. In another manner of speaking, Russell might have been the last intellectual suspected of writing such pieces, given his so often unmovable allegiance to reason. However, as noted by virtually every scholar studying Russell with something of a comprehensive net around the man and his writings, Russell is not all or only a rationalist. Furthermore, even Russell's later and lesser estimations of some of these written pieces, particularly his "Free Man's Worship," did not erase in Russell's mind the warrant or need for concern about the matters discussed within these essays. The lowered and later estimations by Russell of his own writing, I think, are more of the nature of a frustration, not with what the essays were crafted for, but with their unsatisfactory execution. One may become pessimistic toward the effort after too many unsuccessful attempts. That is to say, Russell could not provide the answer or kind of answer he sought. Nevertheless, and though unwilling to reevaluate orthodox doctrines he deemed false and therefore unbelievable, Russell struggled for some way to coalesce modern unbelief on such matters with something he could will himself to believe. To get beyond lament and languish would be Russell's goal. The effort required in doing that, however, was simply too great for Russell. No successful candidate or program came forward from his pen, though without any forthright admission of defeat.

"Free Man's Worship" is Russell's most reprinted and anthologized essay. Within this short piece Russell both expresses the plight of modern scientific man and offers something of a way to negotiate the reality to which we are subject. The author indicates some safe ground to perch on, at least for a season. Ultimately, however, nothing is forever or entirely secure in the indifferent world to which we find ourselves affixed. Russell is admittedly only able to offer some temporary respites, but holds them up as affording some protection from the reality that assails our human world. The human who is free, in the sense in which Russell intends that word, however, is adamant to maintain the dignity of the human against the formidable and tempting pessimism that could be our unmaking, unless we hold up our own world in a world that is not ours. Defeat need not be admitted until it truly overwhelms us and even then, if we go down in defiance, it is ourselves who will have the last word. In this defiance will be our subtle victory over a finish that never hears even a whisper or whimper from us conceding our doom. However tempting under such harsh conditions to admit the superiority of our opponent, we concede nothing, least of all ourselves to the voracious appetite of time that can wear us and our resistance down. Against time, however, we are as vulnerable as everything else. This thought we conceal from ourselves by refusing even mention of it, to an indifferent world which savors hearing our cry of defeat, but never will. We humans are therefore the real master of the universe, because we never give it the subservience that it anticipates and indeed expects from us. We are stalwart because we never bow to submit. We therefore are the victors, and our enemy is defeated in our dedication and courage to never lay down the fight and so surrender. The essence of man, and therefore, the strength of besieged humans, is in their rebellion against the real. On this humans can stand with unswerving and virtually timeless hope.

It is rather obvious that for Russell no deity clears our path for us or stands with us in this struggle. We in effect act as our own god in the absence of "God," and while obedience traditionally has been deemed the appropriate human response to God, the only respectable relationship we offer to a world that threatens to crush us, is defiance, whereas the prior and traditional responses to the presumed God of the past were indicative of a loathsome cowardice on the part of humans.[47] Russell does not indicate whether respect and subservience would be an appropriate response to a humane God, but because the world we live in is monstrously unfitted for us we properly loathe its purported creator for presenting us with the kind of world we find ourselves struggling against. Thus, Russell writes: "The savage, like ourselves, feels the oppression of his impotence before the powers of Nature; but having in himself nothing that he respects more than Power, he is willing to prostrate himself before his gods, without inquiring whether they are worthy of his worship."[48]

A barbaric conception of God is therefore manifestly unworthy of worship. In time and with a cultural shift to a scientific understanding of the universe, the power of forces indifferent to our desires and plight remain, but moral creatures will not prostrate themselves before mere power. This is in part why Russell calls upon renunciation as necessary to come to terms with the kind of world in which we live. That is, the admission of the inevitability of some losses in our struggle for maintaining a certain kind of life is necessary if we are to persist in our journey without conceding overwhelming defeat. This concession is necessary for a maximal life because "Freedom comes only to those who no longer ask of life that it shall yield them any of those personal goods that are subject to the mutations of Time. Although the necessity of renunciation is evidence of the existence of evil, yet Christianity, in preaching it, has shown a wisdom exceeding that of the Promethean philosophy of rebellion."[49] Resignation, therefore, has pride of place over rebellion because

> Yet, by death, by illness, by poverty, or by the voice of duty, we must learn, each one of us, that the world was not made for us,

---

47. Interestingly, in a letter to Alys of January 31, 1894, Russell writes: "It is not illogical to regard God as almighty in spite of the evil, only then he must be regarded as an almighty Fiend; he cannot even be viewed as partly good and partly bad, like the world he has made, but must be regarded as wholly and infinitely wicked, having done wrong without temptation, for omnipotence cannot be tempted." Griffin, *Letters*, 1:55.

48. Russell, *CP* 12:67.

49. Russell, *CP* 12:69.

and that, however beautiful may be the things we crave, Fate may nevertheless forbid them. It is part of courage, when misfortune comes, to bear without repining the ruin of our hopes, to turn away our thoughts from vain regrets. This degree of submission to Power is not only just and right: it is the very gate of wisdom.[50]

Lest it be thought that here resignation replaces rebellion to the point of denying it position, Russell contends rather that an interface between the two provides the means by which we not only endure the world, but overcome it. For Russell, the exhibition of such a restful peace is best shown by the tragedians, for "Of all the arts, Tragedy is the proudest, the most triumphant; for it builds its shining citadel in the very centre of the enemy's country.... Honour to those brave warriors who, through countless ages of warfare, have preserved for us the priceless heritage of liberty, and have kept undefiled by sacrilegious invaders the home of the unsubdued."[51] The outcome of the art of the tragedians was "To take into the inmost shrine of the soul the irresistible forces whose puppets we seem to be—Death and change, the irrevocableness of the past, and the powerlessness of man before the blind hurry of the universe from vanity to vanity—to feel these things and know them is to conquer them."[52]

However, into this crucible of freedom still smolders something of the promethean spirit that Russell had disciplined earlier for the sake of needful renunciations, the latter necessary to admit for a life denied many of its desires. Thus, however much the majority of the essay by the end offers up something like Stoic-type prescriptions in the face of adversity, the essay culminates on a note of defiance, rather than acceptance. In the overall posture of the free man of "Free Man's Worship" against an indifferent universe, the reader is uncertain whether Man is in retreat and bracing against surrender, or rather, advancing a frontal assault toward subtle if not silent victory.

Near the very end of the essay, Russell contends that knowledge of human history buttresses a life besieged by the troubles of the present. The particular "magical power" that the past can have for us is in the fact that the world of the past has no more contingencies; the swirl of change is absent from our predecessors from the past. Therefore, the solace of the past issues from the fact that it possesses a fixity in the Herculean streams that

50. Russell, *CP* 12:69.
51. Russell, *CP* 12:70.
52. Russell, *CP* 12:71.

permeate the present. In giving attention to things no longer a part of our turbulent world, Russell evokes the image of the human past as something of a consolation for the tumultuous present. This idea is most forcefully and eloquently presented in Russell's essay "On History," written in 1904. Coming close to his final sentences, he writes in majestic prose:

> The past alone is truly real: the present is but a painful, struggling birth into the immutable being of what is no longer. Only the dead exist fully. The lives of the living are fragmentary, doubtful, and subject to change; but the lives of the dead are complete, free from the sway of Time, the all-but omnipotent lord of the world. Their failures and successes, their hopes and fears, their joys and pains, have become eternal—our efforts cannot now abate one jot of them. Sorrows long buried in the grave, tragedies of which only a fading memory remains, loves immortalized by Death's hallowing touch—these have a power, a magic, an untroubled calm, to which no present can attain.[53]

Mathematics once gave Russell something analogous to the contemplation of the historical past, for both provide access to a world unstained by the restless human, given the turbulence and transistoriness of this life and the human world. The quiet stillness of history, like that of mathematics, can give one something of a respite from the obstacles and struggles besetting present human lives:

> Gradually, by the contemplation of great lives, a mystic communion becomes possible, filling the soul like music from an invisible choir. Still, out of the past, the voices of heroes call us. As, from a lofty promontory, the bell of an ancient cathedral, unchanged since the day when Dante returned from the kingdom of the dead, still sends its solemn warning across the waters, so their voice still sounds across the intervening sea of time; still, as then, its calm deep tones speak to the solitary tortures of cloistered aspiration, putting the serenity of things eternal in place of the doubtful struggle against ignoble and transient pleasures.[54]

Knowledge of history can, therefore, intuit to us a realm of being capable of diminishing desire for trivial pleasures; contemplation of history lifts us to a loftier plane. The virtually mystical Past draws us into association and something of communion with a realm of unchanging persons, no longer susceptible to the struggles that are now ours, for they

53. Russell, *CP* 12:81.
54. Russell, *CP* 12:80.

are deceased: "Their failures and successes, their hopes and fears, their joys and pains, have become eternal—our efforts cannot now abate one jot of them."

6

Religion in Early Friendships of Russell

A. LOWES DICKINSON

In Russell's correspondence with Lowes Dickinson, some of which is included in the first volume of Russell's *Autobiography*, an attempt to retain religion in a modern context is a habitual subject between the two. "Goldie" (as he was called by friends) and Russell visited the subject often. Added to the congeniality of Goldie's personality, another reason for the amiability between the two men was that Russell found in Goldie not a grim religious antagonist nor a triumphalist apologist for Christianity. Goldie defended no orthodox or insistent religious stance that would have occasioned at some early point a confrontation with Russell—as occurred with Lady Ottoline and some other religiously inclined people. Moreover, religious discussions with Goldie were on a noticeably different plane because the two men were not just naysayers on religion; they also considered that religion might be beneficial in modernity and Russell found in Goldie something of a kindred spirit, despite significantly different personalities. Both were undoubted critics of much religion— Russell more vehemently so than Goldie. Nevertheless, Goldie, like Russell, somewhat despaired of any realistic possibility of a contemporary version of religion being capable of avoiding many of the past and sordid associations of religions. For example, after a trip to India, which Goldie, like many others, conceded as the home of religion, he expressed both amazement and annoyance. According to his biographer E. M. Forster,

"It was a revelation to him that men could take such constant and passionate interest in the unseen, and less of a revelation that neither their conduct nor their art seemed to benefit thereby."[1] All the same, Goldie was possibly the most sympathetic conversant on the subject of religion that Russell ever had, and that perhaps to a fault. Harold Taylor, who wrote the foreword for the 1967 edition of Dickinson's *A Modern Symposium*, contended that in his "extraordinary capacity for detachment and objectivity Dickinson both represented the character of British intellectual life at its best and achieved within his own life a special kind of integrity. So intent was he on being fair to every idea, no matter how alien to his own, that he took endless pains to study the views of others in order that he might present them convincingly, sometimes more convincingly than those who held them."[2]

While such a picture is fitting in describing Dickinson, Russell displays an opposite tendency, to give offense. In his writing this can be observed easily enough in his translation of circumlocutory prose. From his essay "How I Write" Russell begins

> Take, say, such a sentence as the following, which might occur in a work on sociology: 'Human beings are completely exempt from undesirable behavior patterns only when certain prerequisites, not satisfied except in a small percentage of actual cases, have, through some fortuitous concourse of favorable circumstances, whether congenital or environmental, chance to combine in producing an individual in whom many factors deviate from the norm in a socially advantageous manner.' Let us see if we can translate this sentence into English. I suggest the following: 'All men are scoundrels, or at any rate almost all. The men who are not must have had unusual luck, both in their birth and in their upbringing.'[3]

Such example of finessed and economical prose distills the essential point with blunt force and arresting brevity. In other cases of muddled argument, Russell's predilection was not only for clarity, though that too was necessary on the problem or issue, but also on occasion to provoke the reader to feel the indignation that Russell felt. In doing this, Russell could make the rival position appear loathsome enough to prompt

---

1. Forster, *Dickinson*, 41. In a letter to Goldie of February 13, 1913, Russell writes: "I am interested to see that India is *too* religious for you." Russell, *1872–1914*, 364.
2. Taylor, "Foreword," 6.
3. Russell, "How I Write," 213.

Mad about Belief

audiences to share his outrage. Such a tactic was foreign to Dickinson's personality and Russell was aware of it. In noticeable contrast to Russell, Proctor notes of Dickinson, "For he always did more than justice to the importance of other people's emotions and convictions: it was one of his most enduring qualities."[4] Dickinson himself, in speaking of his *Modern Symposium*, later wrote, "As to the book, I take it as a characteristic of me that I felt impelled to state, as far as I could, from inside, what seemed to me the most important of the radically different attitudes about political questions. For I have never been able to rest in an external and merely partisan appreciation of an opponent's view."[5] It is safe to say that Russell had less difficulty in such matters.[6]

After some study of medicine, Dickinson had received a fellowship to King's College Cambridge in history and is properly described as a thoroughgoing humanist.[7] He had interest in and wrote on such notable figures as Plotinus and Savonarola, though eventually and predominantly on Plato. The family did not seem overtly or even assumedly religious, as had been the case for Russell at Pembroke Lodge. Russell's comment about Dickinson's inclination to despair and unhappiness in response to upsetting conversations and circumstances is particularly noteworthy,[8] compared to Russell's own penchant or "practice of de-

---

4. Proctor, *Dickinson*, 30. Interestingly by way of comparison, Russell might even be put in the camp of Nietzsche with the comment of the latter that instead of having the courage of one's convictions, rather the reverse, should be true. That is, one should have the courage to challenge and if necessary, disbelieve one's convictions.

5. Proctor, *Dickinson*, 172.

6. Katharine Tait writes that fair-mindedness and objectivity were not always easy for her father to manage: "My father dealt with the problem by a sort of intellectual conjuring trick: when he wanted to be indignant over evil, he temporarily put away objectivity in some other compartment of his mind." Tait, *My Father*, 92.

7. He remarks in his autobiography that his mother, should she have known it, "would have been distressed at the line my thinking took at Cambridge." Proctor, *Dickinson*, 57. In his time at Cambridge, he speaks of the emancipation that occurred in him: "It was exciting, to a degree that no modern young man of intelligence could comprehend, to discover that Christianity was not, as it were, an inextensible box, very small, in which the whole world was packed, but that an immense world extended quite outside of it" (61). Forster notes that "We can trace the tradition of the Christian Socialism in which he was brought up, and he was in his own way to continue that tradition, though Frederick Denison Maurice would disown him, and Charles Kingsley turn in his grave." Forster, *Dickinson*, 28.

8. Speaking of religious questions in a letter of March 17, 1932, to friend Herbert Corner, Dickinson writes: "I expect you don't know how provocative and irritating your treatment is certain to be to those who fundamentally disagree. The question is, whether you do good or harm by stirring them up even to anger and indignation. And

scribing things which one finds almost unendurable in such a repulsive manner as to cause others to share one's fury."[9] In further contrast to many of the seventy books that Russell would write, virtually none of Dickinson's "have had any great lasting influence."[10] Nevertheless, indicative of how much respect Russell accorded this friend was the fact that on the death of Russell's brother Frank in 1931, Dickinson was asked to officiate or speak at the ceremony, though he declined.

that is a question hard to answer. I can only say now that I regret all the provocative things I have said in my books about the war. It seems as if they only please those who agree with one, put off the others. . . . My main point, however, about all this is that so deeply are people's religious beliefs entangled in their traditional church teaching, that one can't tear down the one without the other. Hence a certain reticence, which I feel more and more as I get older. When one is actually talking to a given person one can feel one's way. But when one writes a book one hardly knows what one is doing." Forster, *Dickinson*, 212. Such a perspective by Dickinson stands generally (though certainly not always) in great contrast to Russell's feeling about speaking his mind, particularly so on questions of religion.

9. Russell, *Portraits*, 71. This observation by Russell is confirmed in an obituary of Dickinson, found in *The Howard Journal* of January 1, 1932: "He was a man of deep feeling, to whom the knowledge of human stupidity and cruelty caused the acute suffering which more selfish natures feel only for their personal troubles. So, though his life was lived in the pleasant places of beauty, friendship and clear thought, it was dominated by an almost tragic sense of struggle. He was never willing passively to 'lament what man has made of man', but gave himself ungrudgingly in the effort to build a freer, happier and saner world. His gentle and sympathetic nature saved him from falling into the reformer's besetting sin of making the present intolerable for the sake of improving the future. He enriched life for a circle even larger than that of his friends—and he had an extraordinary genius for friendship."

10. Proctor, *Dickinson*, 4. Proctor, however, does not attribute this to any deficiency of Dickinson's writings, but rather to the disruption of the beginning of WWI. Nevertheless, Proctor writes, "But they [the works of Dickinson] occupy, it seems to me, rather a special place in our social history. They were exactly contemporaneous with the first beginnings of the Bloomsbury group; yet their purport was something very different from the characteristic ethos of that essentially inward-looking elite. Though its members, with the exception of Dickinson's lifelong friend, Roger Fry, were born the best part of a generation later than he was, he saw deeper below the surface of modern society, and further into the future, than most of them did." All indications are that Russell would probably wholeheartedly concur with Proctor's analysis of his friend Dickinson and Bloomsbury. Interestingly, another close Cambridge friend of Russell, Desmond MacCarthy, is spoken of by David Cecil as not one evidencing great adulation for the Bloomsbury group: "At Cambridge he had made some lifelong friends who were later to found the nucleus of the so-called Bloomsbury circle. Desmond is sometimes spoken of as belonging to it. This was not so. As he himself said, 'Bloomsbury has never been a spiritual home to me.' Its characteristic attitude to the world was alien to him; its exclusiveness, its intellectual pride, the inability of its members to feel at ease with anyone but each other." Cecil, *MacCarthy*, 15.

Dickinson more than occasionally makes clear his departure from Christianity, a point not lost on Russell.[11] In his biography of Dickinson, Forster contends that Dickinson's mind as well as manner was such that "When a man is modest, gentle, unselfish, and generally decent, and confessed, as he did, to possessing and valuing certain instincts, there is a disposition among people who have formalized such instincts to annex him as one of themselves. They want him—and no wonder. Christians often said he was a Christian, and when he went to India he was hailed as a devotee of Krishna."[12] In fact, he was neither. "He was a great heretic though a quiet one,"[13] as described by Forster, and thus much unlike Russell. Russell seemed comfortable in discussing religion with the milder-mannered Dickinson; nonetheless, at the same time, Russell would not shrink from a disagreement over religion, even with a friend as valued as Goldie. This shows in Russell's letter to Goldie of September 22, 1904, where Russell concedes something to religious faith rarely admitted elsewhere in his writings, though Russell places considerable if not severe qualifications upon that religious faith:

> I agree that 'faith in some form or other seems to be an almost necessary condition, if not of life, yet of the most fruitful and noble life.' But I do not agree that faith 'can be legitimate so long as it occupies a region not yet conquered by knowledge.' You admit that it is wrong to say: 'I believe, though truth testify against me.' I should go further, and hold it is wrong to say: 'I believe, though truth do not testify in my favour.' To my mind, truthfulness demands as imperatively that we should doubt what is doubtful as that we should disbelieve what is false. But here and in all arguments about beliefs for which there is no evidence, it is necessary to distinguish propositions which may be fairly allowed to be self-evident, and which therefore afford the basis of indirect evidence, from such as ought to have proofs if they are to be accepted. This is a difficult business, and probably can't be done exactly. As for faith, I hold (a) that there are certain

---

11. The Catholic apologist G. K. Chesterton in his book, *Paganism and Mr. Lowes Dickinson*, writes that Dickinson, though more astute than thinking that paganism only a celebration and enjoyment of the material world, was nevertheless too optimistic in thinking that a resurgence of paganism in modernity would sideline the Christian error of austere asceticism. Chesterton argues that the distinguishing trait of Christianity was instead its inculcation of humility and that the modern pagan is apt to loathe that trait more than even the asceticism that a critic such as Dickinson detests.

12. Forster, *Dickinson*, 116.

13. Forster, *Dickinson*, 117.

propositions, an honest belief in which, apart from the badness of believing what is false, greatly improves the believer, (b) that many of these very propositions are false.[14]

Interestingly, in these words Russell permits something of the religious pragmatist's point that what one believes on the basis of a religious faith may positively advance the life of that believer. Russell is insistent elsewhere and often in his writings that even if that is true of the religious believer, that fact does not guarantee the argument that what the believer believes is true, simply because the former is true. This is a point that is often encountered in Russell's writings, but what is noticeable is something of the admission here, grudging though it may be, that what may turn out to be a false belief may nevertheless contribute to a fulfilling life. However, so as to place much of this in proper perspective, it is notable that Russell continues the letter by statements that resonate with what Russell had written in "The Free Man's Worship" a year earlier. That is, the faith that is possible, though it be secular, manages to be virtually as fulfilling as anything the religious believer possesses. Russell continues in this letter:

> But I think that faith has a legitimate sphere in the realm of ethical judgments, since these are of the sort that ought to be self-evident, and ought not to require proof. For practice, it seems to me that a very high degree of the utility of faith can be got by believing passionately in the goodness of certain things which are good, and which, in a greater or less degree, our actions are capable of creating. I admit that the love of God, if there were a God, would make it possible for human beings to be better than is possible in a Godless world. But I think the ethical faith which *is* warranted yields *most* of what is necessary to the highest life that is possible. Like every religion, it contains ethical judgments and judgments of fact, the latter asserting that our actions make a difference, though perhaps a small one, to the ethical value of the universe. I find this enough faith to live by, and I consider it warranted by knowledge; but anything more seems to me more or less *untruthful*, though not demonstrably *untrue*.[15]

The attempt to adjudicate a secular ethical faith is positioned beside a religious faith from which it derives, though without of course the unwarranted beliefs of the religious. However, Russell clearly desires to

14. Russell, *1872–1914*, 307–8.
15. Russell, *1872–1914*, 308.

place the revised ethical faith as high as possible in any comparison of the two. The last statement in our quotation, moreover, demonstrates the tenacity of Russell in maintaining ultimate allegiance to truth, whatever the fate of faith or beliefs before that indifferent taskmaster. Somewhat like his nemesis Kant, Russell seems to make something of an appeal to the admission that the chief components of our ethical faith have not been demonstrably proven to be false. In this admission, presumably we can have some hope. However, unlike Kant, Russell makes no boast that he has removed knowledge so as to make room for faith. Rather, Russell always lent a watchful and suspicious eye toward faith, intent that it not claim too much for itself. In a letter of October 1, 1904, Russell continues the debate over faith with Goldie:

> I believe hope to be essential to the best life, but not Faith: there is all the difference that there is between courtship and marriage. I agree that it is desirable that the possibility of better things than science has yet discovered should be a living possibility in the imagination; at least to those who have the strength to endure hope. For my part, I am apt practically to take up with despair as being less exhausting and less disquieting; but that, I think, is cowardice, or at best a piece of practical prudence. I am too skeptical, at bottom, about the finality of our experience; but it is a skepticism which enters little into my ordinary thoughts, probably too little. I feel strongly, however, that Faith ought not be applied to an attitude which is not one of actual belief.[16]

Almost a decade later in writing to Goldie, Russell expresses more skeptical sentiment that will vitiate his effort to construct a religion he could adopt: "I feel as if one would only discover on one's death-bed what one ought to have lived for, and realize too late that one's life had been wasted. Any passionate and courageous life seems good in itself, yet one feels that some element of delusion is involved in giving so much passion to any humanly attainable object. And so irony creeps into the very springs of one's being."[17] It was this perceived irony that badgered Russell often, causing him to walk a tight rope in working between a tragic view of life and an optimistic humanistic vision. Russell hardly perceived

---

16. Russell to Dickinson, October 1, 1904. Document no. 049235, Box no. 5.12, Bertrand Russell Archives, McMaster University Library.

17. Russell to Dickinson, February 13, 1913. Document no. 049237, Box no. 5.12, Bertrand Russell Archives, McMaster University Library.

himself as offering any successful reconciliation, despite some sustained and fervent efforts toward that end.[18]

Meanwhile, Goldie's humanism drew him toward the Greek way and away from the Christian and particularly, the Puritan view of life[19]; indeed, one of his books is titled *The Greek View of Life*. At notable points in that book, Dickinson claims the difference to lie in the fact that "To the Puritan, the inward relation of the soul to God is everything; to the average Greek, one may say broadly, it was nothing; it would have been at variance with his whole conception of the divine power. For the gods of Greece were beings essentially like man, superior to him not in spiritual nor even in moral attributes, but in outward gifts, such as strength, beauty, and immortality. And as a consequence of this his relations to them were not inward and spiritual, but external and mechanical."[20] According to Dickinson, however, the seeds for disunion were sown into a

---

18 Russell's first attempt with fictional form to broach these two elements occurred in his *The Perplexities of John Forstice*, written in 1912. The format of the story much resembles Dickinson's book of 1907, *A Modern Symposium*, a work that Russell complimented as "quite excellent." Russell, *1872–1914*, 292. Interestingly, though most of Russell's friends, including Russell's literary and esteemed friend Joseph Conrad, thought the work weak and needful of substantial revision as a work of fiction, Dickinson nevertheless gave the work high marks: "The end raises a question constantly up throughout in one form or another. Is there in reality such a world 'another best', or are we led on by a mirage? I am myself unable to believe we are led on by a mirage. It is the point that always came up when we discuss. And it seems to me that you are more tentative about it here than in conversation." Letter of Lowes Dickinson to Russell, July 21, 1912. Document no. 049202, Box no. 5.12, Bertrand Russell Archives, McMaster University Library.

19. Dickinson wrote a little work, called *The Wandering Jew*, however, of which Proctor comments "This is something quite exceptional in Goldie's work. His own saint was Socrates: it was to Greece, not Palestine, that he would have looked for the dawn of the world's great age; and I do not recall any other such salutes of his to the Galilean [Jesus]." Proctor, *Dickinson*, 22–23.

20. Dickinson, *Greek View*, 17–18. Further commenting on this difference, "Of the internal drama of the soul with God, the division of the man against himself, the remorse, the repentance, the new birth, the giving or withholding of grace—of all this, the essential content of Christian Protestantism, not a trace in the clear and concrete vision of the Greek" (27). While that Greek view of the human succumbed to later, largely Christian conceptions, Dickinson looked back nostalgically, "But it is impossible not to perceive that with the decline of the Greek city-state something passed from the world which it can never cease to regret, and the recovery of which, if it might be, in some more perfect form, must be the goal of its highest practical endeavours.... [A]nd when we look beyond the means to the wished-for end, limiting our conceptions to the actual possibilities of life on earth, it is among the Greeks that we seek the record of the highest achievement of the past, and the hope of the highest possibilities of the future" (204).

previous union that was inherently unstable. "The reconciliation of man with nature which had been effected by the medium of anthropomorphic gods was a harmony only to the imagination, not to the mind. Under the action of the intellect the unstable combination was dissolved and the elements that had been thus imperfectly joined fell back into their original opposition. The religion of the Greeks was destroyed by the internal evolution of their own consciousness."[21]

By contrast Russell's respect for the classical Greeks varied, though perhaps most surprising was Russell's occasional willingness to admit that a Christian inheritance had more influence on him than ordinarily presumed. As a notable example, in the last volume of his *Autobiography* Russell recounts within a trip to Greece in 1952 an incident he found surprising, as could too, readers only familiar with the denunciatory essays of Russell's *Why I am Not a Christian*.

> I had never before been in Greece and I found what I saw exceedingly interesting. In one respect, however, I was surprised. After being impressed by the great solid achievements which everybody admires, I found myself in a little church belonging to the days when Greece was part of the Byzantine Empire. To my astonishment, I felt more at home in this little church than I did in the Parthenon or in any of the other Greek buildings of pagan times. I realized then that the Christian outlook had a firmer hold upon me than I had imagined. The hold was not upon my beliefs, but upon my feeling. It seemed to me that where the Greeks differed from the modern world it was chiefly through the absence of a sense of sin, and I realized with some astonishment that I, myself, am powerfully affected by this sense in my feeling though not in my beliefs.[22]

21. Dickinson, *Greek View*, 255. Dickinson, moreover, provides a hint of modulated despair in the final paragraph of this book. "Never again has it been possible for man to believe that harmony is in fact the truth of all existence. The intellect and the moral sense have developed imperative claims which can be satisfied by no experience known to man. As a consequence of this the goal of desire which the Greeks could place in the present, has been transferred, for us, to a future infinitely remote, which nevertheless is conceived as attainable. Dissatisfaction with the world in which we live and determination to realize one that shall be better, are the prevailing characteristics of the modern spirit. The development is one into whose meaning and end this is not the place to enter. It is enough that we feel it to be inevitable; that the harmony of the Greeks contained in itself the factors of its own destruction; and that in spite of the fascination which constantly fixes our gaze on that fairest and happiest halting-place in the secular march of man, it was not there, any more than here, that he was destined to find an ultimate reconciliation and repose" (256–57).

22. Russell, *1944–1969*, 84–85.

Thus, despite some of the similarities between these two men, Dickinson and Russell did not always share the same point of view. And, on occasion, as seen here, the philosopher Russell could mix his rational inclinations with feelings that resonated with the religious.

B. GILBERT MURRAY

As Dickinson had revered the Greeks, so too did Gilbert Murray, though Murray more for the Hellenistic elements of the Greek legacy. The Greek who most attracted Murray's attention—and respect—was Euripides. As an increasingly notable classical scholar, Gilbert Murray rubbed shoulders with fellow Greek classicists, people with whom Russell would also be acquainted, indicative of their circle of shared acquaintances. One was Jane Harrison, the classical archaeologist, whose attempts at understanding the Greeks by anthropological focus particularly interested Murray. Moreover, Murray maintained an interest in Greek figures for their skeptical and rationalistic bents. This stance would undoubtedly have resonated with Russell to a significant degree.

Murray tried his hand at writing plays and, in fact, ventured toward the writing of a modern tragedy, a genre of which Russell often spoke highly in communication with Murray. However, Murray's effort met with only limited success, though with more than Russell's attempts at fiction. Both men desired to put their thoughts in a form beyond the academic forum. Though Russell had not been trained in the Classics, as had Murray (like G. E. Moore), he manifested considerable interest in literature, classical literature being one of his loves. Murray therefore was a natural conversational partner for Russell, each on occasion serving as something of a sounding board for the other. The first significant encounter Russell had with Murray derived from Murray's translation of *The Hippolytus*. On an evening of early 1901, Russell and wife Alys went to hear Murray's reading of this translation. The subsequent effect upon Russell was a "conversion" experience of sorts and provoked illuminations inching toward the traumatic for him. This experience (to be spoken of in more detail in the next chapter) was certainly one of the half dozen most memorable and life-changing events of Russell's long life. Soon afterward, Russell wrote to Murray in a letter of February 26, 1901, to express his congratulations and thanks for a fine piece of work and told Murray he had found the play "almost overwhelming." He thanked

Murray for the portrayal of nobility and beauty within sorrow and indicated this feature as particularly meaningful to himself as one of "those of us who are without a religion."[23] Interestingly, in Murray's letter of thanks for Russell's letter, there is no comment from Murray on Russell's accolades for the tragic element of the work.

As Murray's wife Mary was a cousin of Russell, there are some references to her in Russell's letters to Murray, though Mary sometimes seemed inhospitable toward Russell and not infrequently in his letters to Murray, Russell asked Murray to withhold a piece of information from her. In 1925 Murray's wife became a Quaker, while Murray remained a skeptic. The particulars of Murray's religious position, however, are best described as agnostic.[24] By not a few friends, Murray was viewed as something of a secular saint, and in this respect resembled G. E. Moore. Murray was, with Russell, a hard critic of the established Church in England,

Though raised a Catholic,[25] Murray befriended Charles Gore, an Anglican, at Oxford, with whom Russell would conduct a public debate many years later when he had become Bishop Gore. Russell would recount the event afterward with vehement disdain for Gore and Gore's theology. Russell's intense response was in great part because around the time of the debate, Russell's first child John had become seriously ill after a double mastoid operation. In a letter to Ottoline, Russell described what offended him was that "I was told that suffering is sent as a purification from sin. Poor little John never sinned in his life. I wanted to spit in

---

23. Russell, *1872–1914*, 249–50.

24. Only hours before his death, a Catholic priest attended Murray's bedside. This meeting apparently gave rise to much consternation amongst family members, and particularly so when Catholic daughter Rosalind gave an interview about the meeting between her father and the priest. Interestingly, of course, is that in comparison, Russell continued to the very end of his life to maintain his religious unbelief and no such scenario as occurred at the death of Murray occurred at the death of Russell.

25. A fact somewhat surprising to Russell later on, as he indicates in a letter to Murray: "I had not realized you were brought up a Catholic." Russell to Murray, August 21, 1949. Document no. 053651, Box no. 5.33, Bertrand Russell Archives, McMaster University Library. This realization, however, is not followed by less criticism of the Catholic Church afterward by Russell to Murray. In a letter to Russell of June 13, 1951, however, Murray writes "But evidently my experience has not been the same as yours about the inhibitions of gloom and Puritanism and fear. I was given a very easy time as a child, hardly ever called naughty or punished, and perhaps I had an advantage in my father being a Catholic and my mother Protestant, and neither minding very much." Murray to Russell, June 13, 1951. Oxford, Bodleian Libraries, MS. Gilbert Murray adds. 8, fols. 54–55.

their faces—they were so cold & abstract, with a sadistic pleasure in the tortures their God inflicts."[26]

Murray's interest in politics and political issues comported with Russell's involvement in the social arena. Though Russell and Murray would have their political standoffs between each other, the liberal political bent of both men more often put them in compact rather than confrontation. Murray had a familial history rooted in the expropriation of the Irish in the seventeenth century, and a suspicion of English government persisted in his thinking. Toward the end of his student days he engaged in speeches naturally supportive of home rule for Ireland, a cause which the Russell household at Pembroke Lodge supported. When Murray married Lady Mary Henrietta Howard, the marriage was performed by Benjamin Jowett, the classical scholar, a visitor of the Russell family during Russell's childhood at Pembroke Lodge.[27]

Murray's family, including Murray himself, suffered from poor health. After Russell remarked perhaps too casually to Murray in a letter of September 16, 1902, "I have scarcely had a day's illness in my life," some difference between how the two men assessed their plight in the world seemed evident, when Murray wrote of poor health, "I could describe it, pretty accurately, in language which would make it seem as if life was incessant torment to me which it isn't. No by no means. But how odd it

---

26. Russell to Ottoline, February 17, 1929, quoted in Clark, *Life*, 413.

27. Russell recounts the following incident as it concerns Jowett (and himself) in Russell's education at Pembroke Lodge: "Having no one with whom to compare myself, I did not know for a long time whether I was better or worse than other boys, but I remember once hearing my Uncle Rollo saying goodbye to Jowett, the Master of Balliol, at the front door, and remarking: 'Yes, he's getting on very well indeed,' and I knew, though how I cannot tell, that he was speaking of my work." Russell, *1872–1914*, 41. On the occasion of the death of Russell's father Amberley, Jowett wrote a letter of condolence to Lady Russell. Some of the sentiments expressed in the letter further reveal something of the theological mindset of the circles around Pembroke Lodge. "I will not intrude upon your sorrow, but I would like to tell you what I thought of him. He was one of the best men I ever knew—most truthful and disinterested.... Some persons may grieve over them [Amberley and his wife Kate] because they had not the ordinary hopes and consolations of religion. This does not add to my sorrow for them except in so far as it deprived them of sympathy in these times, when everything is made the subject of inquiry with many good persons. God does not regard men with reference to their opinion about Himself or about a future world, but with reference to what they really are. In holding fast to truth and righteousness they held the greater part of what we mean by belief in God. No person's religious opinions affect the truth either about themselves or others." Professor Jowett to Lady Russell, January 14, 1876, in MacCarthy, *Lady John*, 248.

must be never to be ill."[28] Indeed something of this kind of difference between the two men is also perhaps noticeable in Murray's friendly critique of Russell's "The Free Man's Worship," where Murray writes, "Man's natural state is to be dead. It is an extraordinary privilege to be for a while alive."[29] For his part, Russell found the world too overlaid with pain for its inhabitants and sought for relief from the world in mathematics, as reflected in a letter to Murray of April 3, 1902:

> It seems to me now that mathematics is capable of an artistic excellence as great as that of any music, perhaps greater; not because the pleasure it gives (although very pure) is comparable, either in intensity or in the number of people who feel it, to that of music, but because it gives in absolute perfection that combination, characteristic of great art, of godlike freedom, with the sense of inevitable destiny; because, in fact, it constructs an ideal world where everything is perfect and yet true.[30]

The deaths of three Murray children, the third in 1937, made for understandable grief in the Murray household. Such tragedy revealed some religious conflicts within the family, which had probably been building for some time, since Murray's wife Mary had become a Quaker in 1925. Furthermore, in 1933 daughter Rosalind was received into the Catholic Church, having married the historian of note Arnold Toynbee twenty years earlier in 1913. In 1939 Rosalind wrote a book entitled *The Good Pagan's Failure*, in which the author did not spare her parents in a critique of the rationalist assumptions often at the foundation of utopian hopes.[31]

---

28. Murray to Russell, September 16, 1902, Oxford, Bodleian Libraries, MS. Gilbert Murray 165, fols. 35–37.

29. Murray to Russell, February 24, 1903, Oxford, Bodleian Libraries, MS. Gilbert Murray 165, fols. 161–64.

30. Russell, *1872–1914*, 254. Even more pointedly Russell praises mathematics to Murray in the earlier letter of September 16, 1902: "It is an immeasurable comfort to have one department in this smirched and ragged world where one can touch perfection—even if all else one loves has to be abandoned on the threshold of the Temple as is the case with mathematics—the very sternest and most austere of the gods."

31. Typical of the sentiment expressed by the author in that work is a paragraph near the final page of the book: "We have ascribed the failure of the Good Pagan civilization, through all its varying and degenerating phases, to the one primal fault from which it sprang, the denial of God and all that went with God, the rejection of the Supernatural Order and all its bearings, inner and outer, both in the human soul and in the world." Rosalind Murray, *Good Pagan*, 176. None of the works of her father Gilbert are cited or discussed in this book, though a passage from Russell's *A Free Man's Worship* is quoted at some length. Indicative of the thesis of *The Good Pagan's Failure*, Herbert Schlossberg in *Idols for Destruction*, 82, writes "As Rosalind Murray said, it is

The book bears some resemblance, in intentions, to the book that Katherine Tait would write five years after the death of her father Russell.

As it turned out, Murray's chief point of disagreement with Russell over "The Free Man's Worship" was how the essay separates human values from nature when humans are inarguably a part of nature. Murray therefore contends that human ideals are to be found in the world, even in the world of physical nature, while objecting to Russell's contention of an isolation of the human from the world in which he finds himself a part. Russell's dichotomy is thus exaggerated or too pronounced for Murray. In his letter of December 20, 1902, he writes to Russell, "I have a feeling—rather mystical—like this; that there is, really existent, a Glory, a thing like Heaven or God, of which one can get glimpses in many different ways—music, poetry, mathematics, heroic conduct...."[32] In Russell's reply, only days later, he contends, "I do not think this Glory is actually existing: it seems to me the finest product of our own minds."[33] Russell's extended letter concedes that in some way these things we rightly uphold are "outside us," though they are also "the finest product of our own minds." Russell therefore gives some concession to a transcendentalism, coupled with an admitted admission of a needed humanism. The result is an uneasy relationship between the two. Despite such specific differences between Murray and Russell, Murray was still an agnostic, though not with the vigor and high volume of Russell, and so Russell's habitual jabs at religion probably were not offensive to Murray, though Russell seemed a bit cautious at times. Within the next year, however, Murray gave a more extended critique to Russell's essay on "The Free Man's Worship." In Murray's letter of February 24, 1903, he offers that "I can't help thinking that you want the world to be Perfect, (or in some respects Perfect—e. g. Eternal) before you will call it Good."[34] Murray's observation seems on target.

In the 1940s and 1950s Murray became more of a political and social conservative, and reading the exchanges between the two men on the state of the world during these times allows one to see a Russell who

---

the Enlightenment man—the 'good pagan'—and not the Christian who is surprised at the barbarism that results when Christian principles are despised."

32. Murray to Russell, December 20, 1902, Oxford, Bodleian Libraries, MS. Gilbert Murray 165, fols. 57–60.

33. Russell to Murray, December 28, 1902. Document no. 053580, Box no. 5.33, Bertrand Russell Archives, McMaster University Library.

34. Murray to Russell, February 24, 1903. Oxford, Bodleian Libraries, MS. Gilbert Murray 165, fols. 161–64.

is not quite the fire-breathing free-thinker or only the inveterate radical he is usually personified as, and indeed most often was. This is not to say, however, that one finds Russell retracting earlier and largely negative positions on religion, though there is on occasion a milder tone in his interchanges with Murray, even when a negative point is being made. Such, for example, is the case in Russell's letter to Murray of December 26, 1956: "I haven't read Toynbee's *Historian's Approach to Religion*. I imagine I should disagree with it. I become increasingly anti-religious with advancing years."[35] Though expressing of course negative sentiment against religion here, such sentiment is remarked on in a rather matter-of-fact fashion. The sentiment of the statement might suggest that Russell is done with any hope that a religion is possible in subduing some of the ills of modernity and that is that. The door is essentially shut and he would rather not reopen it, not even to Toynbee for whom Russell had significant respect and liking.[36] Indeed, Murray himself had expressed some displeasure with the turn of Toynbee's writing in a letter of November 28, 1954: "I have been a good deal grieved by the last four volumes of Arnold's History. They are amazingly learned, of course. But a sort of religiosity seems to have run away with him; an after effect, I think, of his love for Rosalind and the influence of her Catholicism."[37]

While Murray became more socially conservative in the 1940s and 1950s, his religious agnosticism seemed to remain for the most part steadfast. However, Murray's admission around this time of his growing social conservatism was perhaps prompted by conceding a political naiveté when younger. While Russell admits feeling attraction for that conservatism, lacking in Russell is any admission of naiveté when he was younger, as Murray had suggested for himself. In a letter to Russell of April 23, 1941, and thus written during the War, Murray had expressed this inclination: "Another Conservative view to which I have come

35. Russell to Murray, December 26, 1956. Document no. 00000004, Box no. 11.14, Bertrand Russell Archives, McMaster University Library.

36. Antecedently, Murray also, for he writes in a letter of July 29, 1913, to Russell, "You have heard of course, of Rosalind's engagement to Arnold Toynbee. He is not the man we should have guessed, though we like and admire him greatly. Fellow of Balliol, radical and, as far as I can make out, a quite satisfactory free thinker with no nonsense about the Absolute." Oxford, Bodleian Libraries, MS. Gilbert Murray 165, fols. 137–39.

37. Two years previously, however, Murray had written to Russell to ask, "Have you seen Arnold Toynbee's An Historian's Approach to Religion? I mean the separate book, not the rather unfortunate last three volumes of the "Study of History." I think in some ways it is awfully good." Letter of Gilbert Murray to Russell, 14 December 14, 1956, Oxford, Bodleian Libraries, MS. Gilbert Murray 166, fol. 155.

around is a great belief in a classical education and the maintenance of what they call the 'Christian tradition.' It is really a tradition of a civilization coming from Athens, Jerusalem, and Rome, and it is almost the only thing which holds Europe together. I mean a belief in the supremacy of law, in the rights of the citizen, the duties of conquerors and all kinds of valuable irrational taboos—women and children first, the Captain to go down with the ship, etc., etc."[38]

While admitting "I have been feeling the attraction of conservatism myself," Russell rather truncates agreement with Murray, offering examples of such ideals being weakened in countries like America that lack the longer and stronger history of such associations. In a further and also rare kind of admission for Russell, who most of the time regarded himself as a socialist, he nevertheless also contends, "I should regard Socialism in its milder forms as a natural development of the Christian tradition." He correspondingly laments the fact that "Marx belongs with Nietzsche as an apostle of disruption and unfortunately Marxism won among socialists."[39]

A decade later Murray returns to the subject, though now he expresses an even stronger desire to preserve an endangered Christian civilization. Russell responds with some mild agreement, but also with some of his usual sarcasm:

> I do not feel argumentative about the points you raise in your letter. That is to say I only disagree with them sometimes. I am sure Christian civilization is a grand thing. I read a book the other day about the Southborough Case, and I have, of course, an enthusiastic wish to support Franco, that 'Gallant Christian gentleman' as Winston called him. I like, too, the censorship of books in Eire and Boston. Seriously—I like all these things better than Stalin, but I find it hard to be very enthusiastic about them.[40]

---

38. Letter of Gilbert Murray to Russell, April 23, 1941, Oxford, Bodleian Libraries, MS. Gilbert Murray 166, fol. 50–51. With reference to this letter of Murray, Russell writes to Constance Malleson on June 1, 1941, "Gilbert Murray says he is turning Conservative, feeling that the Christian tradition was important and something of it should be preserved. I partly agree, but am struck here [America], more than elsewhere, by the evils of the Catholic church." Griffin, *Letters*, 2:388.

39. Russell to Murray, June 18, 1941, in Russell, *1914–1944*, 384.

40. Russell to Murray, January 20, 1951. Document no. 053653, Box no. 5.33, Bertrand Russell Archives, McMaster University Library.

Along the same line, Russell made clear to Murray in his letter of May 18, 1951, that while he might concede something to Christian civilization, as one counter example, he regarded the real impediment to effective birth control issuing from missionaries in Africa and Asia funded by "Catholics and Baptists" and that without such opposition, success could be forthcoming.[41] Murray, however, gives pause if not rebuke to Russell's contention, though he blunts his counter point with his last two sentences, hand written at the end of the typed letter. Nevertheless, Murray suggests in this letter that his own earlier and youthful vision for changing the world no longer took the form of what he once thought, with the unstated underline that Russell might consider the same.

> In thinking over your last letter, there came back to me in a flood the sort of emotions for the Shelley-and-Godwin view of the world which I had when young: that if only you could get rid of superstitions and bad customs and kings and priests, and be really in the full sense enlightened, that Paradise would come. I think what has upset me is partly the study of anthropology, showing the incalculable value of fixed customs, and what the Greeks called themis and the Romans fas, and a sort of framework of society; partly experience of life; partly intellectual decay, and the lack of energy that makes people go Conservative. Of course it is not always true that 'these D—-Fools were right.' Perhaps not often.[42]

Russell makes no response for the time being to Murray's shifting point of view. However, in a letter of June 25, 1951, Murray remarks to Russell, "It is rum how our points of view seem to have shifted; also that in a way you and E. H. Carr ... come to a similar, rather nihilistic, result. He starts by explaining that the fundamental Liberal beliefs—in human rights, in a harmony of interests in society, and in reason as a guide—are all exploded. ... I find myself more inclined to say that I do believe in those obsolete Liberal principles."[43] In Russell's response, penned only a

---

41. Russell to Murray, May 18, 1951. Document no. 053655, Box no. 5.33, Bertrand Russell Archives, McMaster University Library.

42. Murray to Russell, May 21, 1951, Oxford University, Bodleian Library, MS. Gilbert Murray 166, fol. 94. In a letter of Murray to Russell of May 21, 1954 Murray writes: "I forget all names and I vote for Winston—yes, positively Conservative. I do want to Conserve the Greco-Judaeau civilisation." Oxford University, Bodleian Library, MS. Gilbert Murray adds. 8, fols. 74–75.

43. Murray to Russell, June 25, 1951, Oxford, Bodleian Libraries, MS. Gilbert Murray adds. 8, fols. 56–57.

day after Murray's letter, he corrects Murray: "I do not at all agree with E. H. Carr, and I still hold the fundamental Liberal beliefs as strongly as ever...."[44] Clearly, Murray had hit a nerve with Russell.

Nevertheless, in a letter of two years later, Murray returns to his earlier point. He writes, "Would you say, roughly, that you and I and many like us, really started life as believers in Shelley and Godwin, thinking you could go straight to virtue and happiness as the crow flies by means of a few perfectly clear abstract principles? Then gradually we got to see that the abstract principles were not quite true, and that custom was what mostly held society together &c &c. An exaggeration, but I think something like that is true of me. Of course you had your real philosophy; I had only some vague and changing discipleships."[45]

Russell's response, coming only three days later, is illuminating, as Russell contrasts himself as having moved in something of a reverse trajectory, compared to Murray: "I think there was a difference owing to the impact of the First War upon me. Until 1914 I was not a rebel and quite expected the Liberal Party to do the sort of things I wanted done. My outlook became more like that of Shelley and Godwin after 1914 than it had been before. Since then I have been gradually calming down. But I do not think I agree with you about custom. Russia and Japan have persuaded

44. Russell to Murray, June 26, 1951. Document no. 053440, Box no. 5.32, Bertrand Russell Archives, McMaster University Library. Russell recommended his forthcoming book, *Human Society in Ethics and Politics*, to Murray, for a fuller presentation of his views on the matter. In his letter of July 23, 1954, Murray tells Russell how much he is enjoying the work, in part because it does "full justice to the absurdity of mankind." At a few points, however, Murray voices disagreements, as, for example, where he writes that "One place where I disagree a good deal, is in your belief that wars are caused by hate." Murray to Russell, July 23, 1954, Oxford, Bodleian Libraries, MS. Gilbert Murray adds. 8, fols. 76–78.

45. Murray to Russell, July 22, 1953, Oxford, Bodleian Libraries, MS. Gilbert Murray adds. 8, fols. 68–69. As noted in chapter 4, however, in writing the preface for the new edition of W. K. Clifford's influential book in 1946, Russell had admitted that his later life had dissolved some of his previous rational optimism for the future of humanity, best expressed in his phrase that "the ghosts of old hopes rise to mock me." Nevertheless, Russell is not prepared to walk away from Clifford's program, and thus he also writes in that preface: "Difficult as it is to maintain the beliefs that inspired the best men of the nineteenth century, there is, I still think, every ground for regarding the old virtues of tolerance and enlightenment as the basis for the hopes that are possible. If the men of that time were too optimistic, it is easy for us to be pessimistic, for bad periods are no more eternal than good ones, though while they last they may seem so." [ix-x] In the letter of May 18, 1952, Murray had written to Russell that his upbringing had in part consisted of being "fanatically devoted to Shelley and Godwin and rebellion generally." Murray to Russell, May 18, 1952, Oxford, Bodleian Libraries, MS. Gilbert Murray adds. 8, fols. 60–61.

me that custom is less powerful than I thought."[46] Though Russell in this letter prefaced these words by indicating that what Murray had said, was "true in the main," the contention by Russell that he had "been gradually calming down," masks Russell's hardly relinquished belief that the world, for all its horrors, could be fixed—as Murray had charged: "by a few perfectly abstract principles." In Russell's belief, he showed himself to resemble the naïve French *philosophes* of the eighteenth century.[47]

C. HELEN FLEXNER AND LUCY DONNELLY

In autumn of 1896, the newly married Russell couple ventured to Philadelphia to visit the American Quaker relatives of Alys Russell, including her cousin Helen Thomas. Russell's relationship with Helen Thomas began with Helen's visits to see her cousins at Friday's Hill, the home of the Pearsall Smiths, which was rather close to Pembroke Lodge. Russell had also seen Helen and her friend Lucy Donnelly in Paris, while doing his exasperating diplomatic work there in November of 1894.[48] Helen

---

46. Russell to Murray, July 25, 1953. Document no. 0000004, Box no. 11.13, Bertrand Russell Archives, McMaster University Library. Murray responds to Russell, "You started from an atmosphere of Whig Prime Ministers, and distinguished Radicals and found in 1914 that their gospel wasn't enough. Of course this is only one element, but it explains some things." Murray to Russell, July 27, 1953. Oxford, Bodleian Libraries, MS. Gilbert Murray, fol. 106.

47. "I may have thought the road to a world of free and happy human beings shorter than it is proving to be, but I was not wrong in thinking that such a world is possible, and that it is worth while to live with a view to bringing it nearer." Russell, "Reflections on My Eightieth Birthday," 58. In a revealing passage from his essay, "First Efforts," included in Russell's *My Philosophical Development*, 27, he wrote of the questioning he undertook at Pembroke Lodge, "After a time, however, I came to disbelieve in God, and advanced a position much more like that of the eighteenth-century French *Philosophes*. I agreed with them in being a passionate believer in rationalism; I liked Laplace's calculator; I hated what I considered superstition; and I believed profoundly in the perfectibility of man by a combination of reason and machinery. All this was enthusiastic, but not essentially sentimental. I had, however, alongside of this, a very vivid emotional attitude for which I could find no intellectual support. I regretted my loss of religious belief; I loved natural beauty with a wild passion; and I read with sympathetic feeling, though with very definite intellectual rejection, the sentimental apologies for religion of Wordsworth, Carlyle and Tennyson." He ends the essay with "Gradually during these three years my interest in theology grew less, and it was with a genuine sense of relief that I discarded the last vestiges of theological orthodoxy" (28).

48. In her opposition to her grandson's plans to marry Alys, Lady Russell had successfully garnered from him a willingness to agree to a period of six months in Paris. Russell more or less loathed his duties as an embassy attaché, while keeping up an active correspondence with Alys. The time in Paris was the occasion for the visit of Mary

was a younger cousin of Alys, while Lucy was an almost inseparably close friend of Helen until Helen Whitall Thomas married Simon Flexner in 1903, becoming Helen Flexner (as she will hereafter be called). Because Flexner and Donnelly resided in America, letter writing was one means whereby they kept up with English relatives, along with some visits Flexner and Donnelly made to England, coupled with Russell's visits to America.

Flexner and Donnelly both had ties to Bryn Mawr College in Pennsylvania, where Helen's older sister Carey Thomas, a highly respected though also a generally feared person, was President. One component of the Russell's visit in 1896 was that both Russell and Alys received invitations to lecture at Bryn Mawr. All might have gone well, save for the fact that to the consternation of Bryn Mawr president Carey and not a few others, cousin Alys offered up an endorsement of what amounted to free love in her talk. Even for an institution as relatively progressive as Bryn Mawr, this was simply too much and Carey Thomas never invited Russell nor Alys back to Bryn Mawr.

Because Helen, like Lucy, was making preparations as a teacher of English literature, literature and literary themes were typical topics of the letters between the two women and Russell. In addition, the topic of religion surfaces fairly often in their correspondence. The overt negativity of Russell on the subject is noticeably less in these letters, though often found with other correspondents and abundant in the popular essays of Russell.[49] With Helen, Russell at times would admit the genuine loss to him from a lost religion.

Cognizant that people within a close friendship might share private matters the letter writer preferred the public not to know, Russell writes to Helen, "By the way, I hope you remember that my letters are only for you and Lucy: it is a comfort to me to let out my depression and discouragement, and to speak of what consolations the wreck of religion has

---

Berenson, Aly's sister, spoken of previously.

49. For example, in Russell's letter to Helen of May 16, 1905, he writes: "I think all the serious things of life make one feel the lack of religion a very great deprivation; I am not one of those who think it can ever be other than a very serious loss." Forte, *Letters*, 48. Only a few months later, however, in his letter to Helen of September 28, 1905, he seemingly has arrived at something of a working solution, however difficult it may be to swallow: "For my part, I have at last grown acclimatized to the planet, and it has ceased to seem to me strange. I find, on looking into what used to seem strangenesses, that they all seemed so because one couldn't divest one of the notion that there must be some purpose in things." Forte, *Letters*, 52.

left me; but the condition of my writing frankly is that you do not repeat things . . . . as it is part of my business to be always cheerful."[50] Indeed such caution was needed, for Russell will write in another two years, "I write no franker letters than those I write to you."[51]

The initial letters of Russell with both Helen and Lucy, beginning in 1900 and 1902 respectively, correspond to some years of a weakening marriage of Russell and Alys after only a few years together. Russell makes not infrequent comments on the health and state of Alys, to include various treatments she was undergoing. The treatments were an attempt to bolster the frail condition of Alys from anxieties over the degenerating marriage.[52] Russell presumably made these kinds of reports because of the kinship between Alys and Helen. Somewhat surprisingly, Helen is not dismissive or castigating of Russell in light of circumstances that were not particularly favorable to Russell in the crumbling marriage.

In Russell's letter to Helen of December 30, 1901, he exhibits one way in which the conversation turned to the subject of religion. "The mood in which I wrote to you last was very transient; the next day I went back to Cambridge in frost and fog, and found no cause of happiness awaiting me. Some sorrows can only be met by patience, and the reflection that life is both short and unimportant. This is a consolation not open to the Christians, and it is one which gives us a real advantage

---

50. Russell to Helen, November 11, 1902. Forte, *Letters*, 33–34. In his very lengthy letter of 19 September, 1904, to Lucy Donnelly he writes: "This letter is full of Self: you will of course understand that it is very private." Forte, *Letters*, 53.

51. Russell to Helen, May 13, 1903. Forte, *Letters*, 44.

52. In his letter of July 24, 1911, he writes to Helen to "Thank you very much for your kind words about Alys & me. There has been much pain, spread over a long time. No one knows one's thoughts resolutely to the future. For my part, I find so much work that I wish to do that I have no difficulty in avoiding vain regrets over what is inevitable." Forte, *Letters*, 110. In the same letter Russell speaks to some points raised in Helen's previous letter to Russell concerning religion and religious belief, beginning with the implications of determinism. Indicating agreement with her over indicting the responsible deity, he writes, "I agree with you in feeling fury at the idea of a God of love who created such a world as this." Russell then shows again, that for all of his frequent vehemence against religion and religious belief, he could hardly or would not set the subject aside. As an indication of Russell's sympathy for the spiritual struggle giving rise to her questions, Russell writes: "I find that religion & the religious attitude to life occupy a very great deal of my thoughts. I am glad to hear your view of life has simplified. I find year by year I grow simpler—I think all the important truths are simple. I should immensely like to hear more of your 'spiritual adventure'. You are certainly right in counting upon my sympathy. There is nothing simulated in it, nor should I ever simulate an interest I do not feel." Clearly Russell wants Helen to know she is not conversing with only a mocker on the subject.

over them."[53] In the same letter, moreover, mathematics is commended as worthy of adulation because "it has nothing to do with life and death and human sordidness, but is eternal, cold, and passionless. To me, pure mathematics is one of the highest forms of art; it has a sublimity quite special to itself, and an immense dignity derived from the fact that its world is exempt from change and time."[54]

However vaunted and idolized mathematics might be, Russell also highly valued great literature. While mathematics allows one to peer into a world absent of humans, great literature informs the human having to overcome the fractured human world: "I commend to your attention the fact that all the greatest literature is concerned in some way with the inevitable: faith or destiny, the flight of time, death, the magic enchantment that gives beauty to the eternally motionless and unchangeable past— these are the true themes of great poetry. These things, being inevitable, are the true Gods of the world of nature; and it is only by making them into Art that we become greater than they are, and can triumph over 'Death & chance & thee, O Time!'"[55]

Though the difficulties and trials of human life are rarely few in number and often overwhelming, Russell nevertheless concedes their necessary value: "Let us admit that the sense of exile from which we suffer has its uses in quickening our interest in the invisible home of the soul."[56] In other words, while life is hardly felicitous, and instead full of pain and trouble, from these experiences the truly virtuous life makes positive use so as to sharpen and correct one's life. Such an admission, however, is very rarely conceded or admitted elsewhere in Russell's writings. Nevertheless, the point persists in Russell's letters to Helen: "The great gift that comes through sorrow nobly borne is wisdom, and from wisdom comes at last serenity, the peace which passeth all understanding. This peace, if we live rightly, will not be refused us at the last."[57]

---

53. Forte, *Letters*, 6. Indicative of his perennial negativity on religion, Russell sometimes felt the necessity of combating God or the belief in God, and so writes to Helen in a letter of February 10, 1910, "I have to write a lecture on the Deity to be delivered publicly at Cambridge to undergrads, but as I was asked to do so, I feel it a duty. I think the Deity does a lot of harm now-a-days, & it is necessary that those who can should speak out about him." Forte, *Letters*, 95.

54. Forte, *Letters*, 6–7.

55. Russell to Helen, March 31, 1902, Forte, *Letters*, 10–11.

56. Russell to Helen, September 16, 1902, Forte, *Letters*, 28.

57. Russell to Helen, October 14, 1902, Forte, *Letters*, 31.

On Russell's own admission, he found Helen the more interesting of the pair of women, and in the beginning of his correspondence with Lucy, the time taken for Russell to turn philosophical with her, as compared to Helen, is noticeably more. Furthermore, Russell seems at times hesitant to speak of philosophical questions with her, even irritated on occasion, as in his letter of August 19, 1904. Thus, he begins with "I wish I knew the thing to say in answer to your letter, but it seems to me I said almost the same as you say when I wrote to you the other day. I really know little in the way of a philosophy of life beyond the end of 'Dover Beach.'"[58] Managing nevertheless to provide a labored answer to her question, Russell seems dutiful or even sterile in his wording, as opposed to inspirational: "I believe the true solution lies in thinking very seldom & very little about things in general, about whether good or evil preponderates in the world or in the lives of those one cares for. The gospel to me has been a cold one, but yet a very useful one; to think almost wholly of what is to be *done*, & hardly at all of evils one cannot remedy, or of goods one cannot create."[59] One might consider such advice hardly up to the daunting heights of Russell's earlier "Free Man's Worship" of 1903. However, something not found in that famous essay does show up in this letter, as Russell writes: "And when one has admitted all the evil of the world, it remains true that there are great & shining things in it: there are heroisms & loves & devotions which redeem it, & which warm all the recesses of the heart like spring sunshine. Learn to think of them: let your contemplative life be filled full with them; let them inspire daily courage, & the faith that, come what may, the good really is good, & makes the long toil worthwhile."[60] Here Russell encourages and gives something of a

58. Russell to Lucy, August 19, 1904, Forte, *Letters*, 45.
59. Russell to Lucy, August 19, 1904, Forte, *Letters*, 45.
60. Russell to Lucy, August 19, 1904, Forte, *Letters*, 46–47. However, in a previous letter of May 5, 1902, he writes to Helen of something of a different "gospel": "The great secret of virtue, & of whatever still leaves pardonable, is to abandon all internal demand for happiness, to realize that happiness is only for the frivolous, & that life, to those who have eyes to see, is filled with tragedy & compassed round with spectres. And then courage! There is my gospel for you. There are no intellectual problems in morals: any child, with honesty, can see the truth. All the tangles are caused by people's obstinate determination to prove the truth of obvious falsehoods, because the opposite is so cruel." Forte, *Letters*, 13. In a letter of October 19, 1906, Russell writes to Helen: "The people you have in mind seem to be devoted, not to ideals, but to a picture of themselves as idealists. This, like other forms of egoism, is certainly to be condemned by the casuist. There is no moral health in people unless their lives are given to objects outside themselves, & this is something quite different from 'high standards', 'ideals', 'devotion to virtue' & all the rest of the buncombe." Forte, *Letters*, 56.

sanction to an optimistic view of the world, or at least evidences a preference for one over its opposite.

As Russell finished up the magnum opus on mathematics with Whitehead, he writes to Lucy in 1909 more or less admitting that having sought for refuge in something such as his work on mathematics testifies to a failure to find satisfaction in human things of which the human should be capable:

> I have made a mess of my private life—I have not lived up to my ideals, and I have failed to get or give happiness. And as a natural result, I have tended to grow cynical about private relations and personal happiness—whether my own or other people's. So all my idealism has become concentrated on my work, which is the one thing in which I have not disappointed myself and in which I have made none of the compromises that destroy faith. It is a mark of failure when one's religion becomes concentrated on impersonal things—it is monkish essentially.[61]

In a letter eight years earlier, Russell had attempted to correct Helen's estimation of himself as veering toward the romantic, a subject about which he would show some inclination, though much more often, as here, he shows himself an adamant opponent. Thus, Russell demurs over Helen's charge and proceeds to explain:

> But the fundamental error of romanticism lies in the fact, which it shares with Christianity, that it places the end of each man's life within himself—personal holiness, or personal excellence of some kind, is what is to be achieved. Leaving quite aside the whole daily mechanism of life, which must absorb most people's activity, this theory misconceives radically the purposes which should be aimed at by those who are free to choose their own ends. And it is here, I think, that classicism is infinitely more in the right. There are great impersonal things—beauty and truth—which quite surpass in grandeur the attainments of those who struggle after fine feelings. Mathematics, as a form of art, is the very quintessential type of the classical spirit, cold, inhuman, and sublime. But the reflection that such beauty is cold and inhuman is already romanticism—it gives a shiver of feeling in which Self has its share. The true classical spirit loses itself in devotion to beauty, and forgets its relation to man.[62]

---

61. Russell to Lucy, October 18, 1909, Forte, *Letters*, 150.
62. Russell to Helen, June 10, 1902, Forte, *Letters*, 16–17.

A comparison of these two letters reflects something of Russell's conception of the conflict between classicism and romanticism. Furthermore, though Russell's depiction of the deficiency of the Christian end of life is overly stated in this letter, it reflects Russell's predominant inclination to think of the place of the subject or person in the Christian metaphysic as unduly anthropomorphic, putting Russell ultimately in the camp of the classicist and not the romantic. However, at other times, such as in a 1904 letter to Lucy, Russell gives a positive account of the human tendency, anthropocentric as it is, to affirm ourselves and our values against all odds in terms of the hostile world we encounter.

> Every tiny village has a huge Gothic church, usually very beautiful; many churches stand quite by themselves, facing the sea as relics of ancient courage. At first I wondered how anyone could believe in God in the presence of something so much greater and more powerful as the sea; but very soon, the inhumanity and cruelty of the sea became so oppressive that I saw how God belongs to the human world, and is, in their minds, the Captain of an army in which they are soldiers: God is the most vigorous assertion that the world is not all omnipotent Matter. And so the fishermen became and have remained the most religious population in the world.[63]

Without objection or rancor, Russell makes an observation that others might make, though this kind of concession is very rarely found in the writings of the polemical Russell. That is, typically Russell impugns religious belief or more simply the religious quest, as evidence of the weakness of people unable to face a world of ruthless and blind matter indifferent to humans. Issuing from this weakness, humans postulate a God for themselves. In these few sentences of this letter, however, Russell does not state his point in a negative vein, but in a matter-of-fact and almost salutary way. That is, there is a muted respect shown for such resilience, inasmuch as they refuse to be bested or beaten because of inferior physical strength. The writer of these sentiments holds up the courage of such people, whereas Russell on most occasions castigates such a response as cowardice. Indeed, Russell rarely spoke as neutrally on the origin of religious belief, for he more often claimed that the genesis of religion lay in motivations hardly to be seen as courageous, but rather as despicably seized by and giving way to fear.

63. Russell to Lucy Donnelly, October 3, 1904, Russell, *1872–1914*, 282.

On Russell's own admission, his appetite for mathematics issued from the wearisome vulnerabilities of human life, of which Russell—and the fishermen—were well acquainted. So, the resolve of the fishermen is hardly to be categorized as lacking courage but rather as adapting to a world or environment, in this case a hostile one, for the sake of desired health and life and indeed life at all. The fishermen's displayed belief in God is evidenced in their church. When mathematics was king with Russell, it too was a kind of refuge, though unlike the Gothic church, not made by human hands, but found by human minds. Russell, however, rarely spoke of religious belief in this fashion, which is to say, yet again, that most of the time when he spoke and wrote on the subject, he was negative and habitually castigated religious motivations as born of fear and cowardice. And yet they need not be.

When Russell did not have a point to be proved, but was instead considering possible answers, he could sometimes show an objectivity often lacking elsewhere. This trait, more often than not, is noticeably evident in his letters to Helen and Lucy.

D. D. H. LAWRENCE

Lawrence comports oddly with the friendships of Russell already surveyed within this chapter, for Russell's relationship with the Welsh novelist, though seemingly promising in the beginning, instead proved to be nasty, brutish, and short, to use Hobbes's famous words. In the second volume of his *Autobiography*, writing of his tempestuous and uncongenial relationship with Lawrence, Russell dismissively recounts of that relationship that "My acquaintance with Lawrence was brief and hectic, lasting altogether about a year."[64]

To understand what initially drew Russell to Lawrence, but then drove them apart with such acrimony (shared equally between the two) requires some description of the tumult in Russell's life in the time leading up to World War I, for a definite and virtually seismic change occurred. In his own words: "The period from 1910 to 1914 was a time of transition. My life before 1910 and my life after 1914 were as sharply separated as Faust's life before and after he met Mephistopheles.... I have therefore got into the habit of thinking of myself as a non-supernatural

---

64. Russell, *1914–1917*, 10.

Faust for whom Mephistopheles was represented by the Great War."[65] Russell's later insistence that he was acting on principle in opposition to that war, is indicated when he writes: "I never had a moment's doubt as to what I must do. I have at times been paralyzed by skepticism, at times I have been cynical, at other times indifferent, but when the War came I felt as if I heard the voice of God. I knew that it was my business to protest, however futile protest might be."[66]

Partly the fatigue of finishing the *Principia*, and the need for something different, had turned Russell in the direction of political work. Indeed, Russell contended that in the years from 1902 until 1910, during time spent away from work on *Principia*, he was increasingly occupied with political questions. In this period, Russell would begin a career of public speaking, something rather new for him and also a necessary and eventually mastered skill. More significant for consideration concerning Russell and the matter of religion was that being drawn into politics would expose Russell's religious unbelief. This fact would matter for the public and political context, in contrast to the academic environment at Cambridge, where religious views or lack thereof drew considerably less attention. Nevertheless, even in charged political settings, Russell steadfastly guarded his unorthodox stance on religious matters, with little to no room made for accommodation to the requirements of political office, any more than he had accommodated Alys's Quaker religious beliefs before their marriage. Thus, when asked about his religious belief and their pertinence to holding political office, Russell recounts the "catechism" he was subjected to:

"Q. Are you a member of the Church of England?
No, I was brought up as a Nonconformist.
Q. And have remained so?
A. No, I have not remained so.
Q. Are we to understand that you are an agnostic?
A. Yes, that is what you must understand.
Q. Would you be willing to attend church occasionally?
A. No, I should not.
Q. Would your wife be willing to attend church occasionally?
A. No, she would not.
Q. Would it come out that you are an agnostic?
A. Yes, it probably would come out."[67]

---

65. Russell, *1914–1917*, 3.
66. Russell, *1914–1917*, 7.
67. Russell, *1872–1914*, 331–32.

Such frank admissions proved only momentary in curbing Russell's political interests, for Russell soon threw his support behind the Liberal candidate Philip Morrell, whose wife was Lady Ottoline, with whom Russell would shortly have an intense romantic relationship. However, in the beginning Russell evidenced no strong attachment to Ottoline, and indeed, he was not impressed with either of the pair, explaining later that Ottoline at the time "offended my Puritan prejudices by what I considered an excessive use of scent and powder."[68] The initial aversion toward Ottoline, however, soon diminished, as Russell began to have as much interest in Ottoline as in her husband's political cause. For her part, Ottoline began to peel back some of Russell's initial misgivings about her and, as importantly, about himself. Russell contended in his *Autobiography* that Alys's Quakerism had exerted its own ascetic proclivities upon him, and that he thus had a double dose of Puritan plainness and judgementalism to overcome from his first marriage and, before that, from his upbringing at Pembroke Lodge. Under Ottoline's influence, Russell labored to extricate himself from his prior shell and prejudices, as Ottoline loosened the crusty Puritan shield she and Russell presumed had previously strapped his inner emotions. Ottoline was as liberating as she was refreshingly enjoyable, even captivating, as she encouraged Russell in what he had been lacking. Because Ottoline was enthralling to Russell in the beginning, his usual contentiousness toward religion softened for a season with her, but he soon proved to be as combative with her over the topic of religion as he was with most others.

Ottoline had a network of notable friends, some of whom became friends with Russell. In time, Ottoline would introduce Russell to noteworthy acquaintances, among them Joseph Conrad, in September of 1913, and D. H. Lawrence in February of 1915. Russell meanwhile was becoming better acquainted with Ottoline, as the two began having significant conversations, starting in March of 1911.

Conrad and Lawrence appealed to Russell on opposite ends. Russell, like Lawrence, was adamant to refashion the present world into something better, whereas and by contrast to Lawrence what Russell found congenial in Conrad was a depth of feeling Russell shared, and which I earlier referenced in Russell as a tragic view of life. However, Conrad was no rebel or revolutionary, which better described Lawrence, and also Russell. In Russell's depiction of Conrad, "He was, as anyone

---

68. Russell, *1872–1914*, 333.

may see from his books, a very rigid moralist and by no means politically sympathetic with revolutionaries. He and I were in most of our opinions by no means in agreement, but in something very fundamental we were extraordinarily at one."[69] Thus, as the clamor for war seemed almost unstoppable, Russell found himself as an opponent of that war in a revolutionary mode lacking in Conrad, though present in Lawrence. Russell's respect and soon near adulation for Conrad gripped him, so the Russell connection with Conrad was personal, in the best meaning of that description. Indicative of Russell's feeling for this writer, he named his third child Conrad Russell after his Polish friend; Russell's first child had received the name John Conrad Russell in 1921.

With political inclinations now revived in Russell he found his political footing in the looming tensions prior to World War I and then during that War. As indicated, this new adventure provided Russell with some new friendships and romances, such that both were found in Ottoline and Constance Malleson, but Russell's stance on England's entry into the war also could imperil previous friendships, among them Whitehead and McTaggart. McTaggart and Russell never reconciled over their disagreement concerning that War. With others, including Whitehead and Gilbert Murray, Russell recovered friendships.

In August of 1914 Russell learned that Ottoline's husband Philip would make a speech arguing for pacifism for which Russell gave strong support. However, the speech had little to no lasting effect and with the near certainty of war expected, Russell fell into days of despair, but intertwined with something of a new understanding about himself and the society in which he lived. Conversing with the woman who had begun to show Russell that he had another side to himself beyond the straight and rational temperament, he now also observed something eerily numbing about others: "The prospect [war] filled me with horror, but what filled me with even more horror was the fact that the anticipation of carnage was delightful to something like ninety per cent of the population. I had to revise my view on human nature. At that time I was wholly ignorant of psychoanalysis, but I arrived for myself at a view of human passions not unlike that that of the psychoanalysts. I arrived at this view in an endeavor to understand popular feeling about the War."[70]

69. Russell, *1872–1914*, 341.

70. Russell, *1914–1944*, 6. Previously, on page 4, Russell writes: "I had fondly imagined what most pacifists contended, that wars were forced upon a reluctant population by despotic and Machiavellian governments." Of all the Russell friendships both

With Russell's prior conception of people as rational now shaken, the occasion of meeting someone like Lawrence seemed promising, for he seemed to have the pensive eye for seeing into souls. His skill in analyzing people therefore might provide opportunity for Russell to understand the underlying causes of war and perhaps to develop greater self-awareness. Thus, Russell's changing view of his fellow humans might benefit from a teacher like Lawrence who could convey what the ravaged rationalism in Russell's prior view of himself and presumed other rational creatures had missed. The virtually voracious appetite for war, moreover, had shown Russell that people were evidencing appetites previously masked and hardly imagined by Russell before. Lawrence seemed to have already gazed into and grasped the nature of the abyss, and the novelist seemed ready to share his visions of what he had seen with Russell. The previously unflappable confidence in reason and logic that was part of Russell had clouded his understanding of people and their motives to action as well as inaction. Lawrence now seemed to be an individual who could help in Russell's revisions, for Russell seemed at first a willing student for what Lawrence was teaching. Interestingly, it was initially Ottoline rather than Russell who expressed possible doubts about whether Lawrence's picture of people was entirely correct. Nevertheless, with Russell poised at the starting line, he was anxious for what seemed like credible wisdom from Lawrence; Russell's turn at a protracted critique of Lawrence would come later. Meanwhile, and particularly regarding England's plunge toward the War, the two men could appear natural allies in their opposition to much of the status quo of a society seemingly anxious to spill blood.

Given the reputation of Russell as the venerable and astute rationalist, the association with Lawrence must appear the most unlikely of human relationships one could imagine for the cerebral Russell. However, in the beginning, both men were joined together by the thought that the world needed to be set aright. Only later does Russell deem Lawrence in another camp and headed in another direction: "Gradually I discovered

---

severed and strained during this time, and in addition to the partial respite gained from the perspective of others, and despite his later more critical stance toward Ottoline as a religious influence, Russell nevertheless concedes in his *Autobiography* a half century later, "Throughout the earlier phases of the War, Ottoline was a very great help and strength to me. But for her, I should have been at first completely solitary, but she never wavered either in her hatred of war, or in her refusal to accept the myths and falsehoods with which the world was inundated" (7–8).

that he had no real wish to make the world better, but only to indulge in eloquent soliloquy about how bad it was."[71]

However, at the beginning of their relationship, matters were different; for example, in the initial planning between Russell and Lawrence there was an idea for joint talks to be presented by both men,[72] Already, however, Lawrence assumed something of the position of a privileged critic and insisted to Russell, "But you must dare very much more than you have done here—you must dare be positive, not only critical."[73] Moreover, already indicative of diverging notions of proper political governance between the two men, Russell contends in his outline of lectures that "Only fear now holds the State together," while Lawrence objects with his contention that "There must be a State, & a government." When only a sentence later Russell writes that one "Can't *worship* the State," Lawrence retorts with "What can I worship?" Russell, however, went on to say, "I feel more allegiance to mathematics than to the State." Lawrence pencils in "Why?"[74] This fragment of an early exchange between the two men displays something of the willingness of Lawrence for an authoritative state and ruler, but a diverging idea in Russell which points humans toward "God or truth or art."[75] Though Russell only briefly expands that thought in this exchange with Lawrence, his words and sentiment will nevertheless express a point of view that he largely held for the rest of his life. He writes:

> Religion, in some form, seems necessary to a good society or a good individual life. By 'religion' I mean devotion to an end outside the individual life, and even, in some sense, outside human life—like God or truth or art. But the Churches consist of certain property only given to those who profess certain beliefs, now known to be false by all who think independently. Because

---

71. Russell, *Portraits*, 113.

72. As Russell was preparing lectures which afterward became his very popular book, *Principles of Social Reconstruction*, he discovered that "He [Lawrence], also wanted to lecture, and for a time it seemed possible that there might be some sort of loose collaboration between us." Russell, *1914-1944*.

73. Moore, *Lawrence's Letters*, 78. Despite this complaint by Lawrence, Russell would indicate that his stance in the lectures was to indicate that impulse had more to do in moulding life than conscious purpose and later wrote: "I took, as examples of embodiments of the possessive impulses, the State, war and poverty; and of the creative impulses, education, marriage and religion. Liberation of creativeness, I was convinced, should be the principle of reform." Russell, *1914-1944*, 10.

74. Moore, *Lawrence's Letters*, 82.

75. Moore, *Lawrence's Letters*, 85.

freedom leads to rejection of these beliefs, churches oppose freedom, and like all forms of unreason—e.g. patriotism and loyalty to sovereigns. In thought, they substitute sentiment for observation, and so encourage subjectivism, which is the root of the trouble. Religion wants as much transformation as marriage and property. Men of science have some elements of a possible new religion. They are the happiest of intelligent men.[76]

In these few sentences we see evidence again that Russell's respect for religion is couched within his warnings of the threats and dangers wrong religion presents for the authentic and creative religious impulse. Nevertheless, while transcendence is almost always a component of viable religion for Russell, the place for spiritual aspiration is couched elsewhere in Lawrence. While Lawrence delights in mocking the reason of any rationalism, and thus rarely felt comfortable with the intellectuals of his day, he sought for a religious consciousness generated from the physical and sensual side of life, not one beholden to any "transcendentals." Indeed, the religious and sexual instinct are often coupled in Lawrence. In Lawrence's thinking, the physical components of life loom large and drive religious aspiration toward the rather bestial side of instinct that provides an untoward identification with an unreflective animal soul or spirit. Lawrence's religion "of the blood," had marks of the grotesque for Russell and issued from an unsavory primitiveness that Lawrence imagined could save humans from what civilization had extracted from many. It is little wonder that the two men ended as great enemies.

The initial move toward Lawrence had been precipitated by Russell's notion of the terrible condition of a world seemingly delighting in the expectation of war. With his recent anthropological and sociological revelations, Russell stood ready to further examine the nature of the human animal. It was indeed this possible "new Russell" of a sort that attracted Russell to Lawrence and possibly Lawrence to Russell. Moreover, perhaps Russell expected or simply hoped that gold might lie within Lawrence. Lawrence thus might present a truthful diagnosis of the terrifying state of the world greater than Cambridge academics had to offer. For now, with some unwillingness and fear of entertaining Lawrence's ideas alone, Russell gave an invitation to Lawrence to visit Cambridge. In Russell's autobiographical account of that event, he writes

---

76. Moore, *Lawrence's Letters*, 85.

I invited him to visit me at Cambridge and introduced him to Keynes and a number of other people. He hated them all with a passionate hatred and said they were 'dead, dead, dead.' For a time I thought he might be right. I liked Lawrence's fire, I liked the energy and passion of his feelings, I liked his belief that something very fundamental was needed to put the world right. I agreed with him in thinking that politics could not be divorced from individual psychology. I felt him to be a man of a certain imaginative genius, and, at first, when I felt inclined to disagree with him, I thought that perhaps his insight into human nature was deeper than mine.[77]

As is evident in this passage, Russell's one-time inclination toward the ideas of Lawrence was partly prompted by his own self-doubts. That is, "What at first attracted me to Lawrence was a certain dynamic quality and a habit of challenging assumptions that one is apt to take for granted. I was already accustomed to being accused of undue slavery to reason, and I thought perhaps that he could give me a vivifying dose of unreason."[78] Lest these last words are weighed as only written in a spirit of vindictive mocking of Lawrence, in the very next sentence and in speaking of his adroit and very popular book *Principles of Social Reconstruction*, Russell nevertheless attributes some gain to himself from his exposure to Lawrence: "I did in fact acquire a certain stimulus from him, and I think the book that I wrote in spite of his blasts of denunciation was better than it would have been if I had not known him."[79]

Not a part of Russell's notion of a remaking of the world was a complete erasure of all thoughts and institutions of the past— as Lawrence seemed only too ready to entertain. Indeed, Russell's differing idea is seen in the wording of the title of his aforementioned book, *The Principles of Social Reconstruction*; that is, Russell wanted to reconstruct, whereas

---

77. Russell, *1914–1944*, 11. After the visit to Cambridge, Lawrence writes to Russell: "It is true Cambridge made me very black & down. I cannot bear its smell of rottenness, marsh-stagnancy. I get a melancholic malaria. How can sick people rise up? They must die first." Lawrence to Russell, March 19, 1915, in Moore, *Lawrence's Letters*, 43. According to Moore, "Lawrence makes a few references to his former friend in his later correspondence," with Moore making reference to Lawrence's letter of December 11, 1916, to Lady Cynthia Asquith where Lawrence speaks sneeringly to Lady Cynthia of 'that old advanced crowd—Cambridge, Lowes Dickinson, Bertie Russell, young reformers, Socialists, Fabians—they are our disease, not our hope.'" In Huxley, *Lawrence's Letters*, 386.

78. Russell, *1914–1944*, 15.

79. Russell, *1914–1944*, 15.

Lawrence was anxious for a needed demolition of the past to make way for a future free and unimpeded by that past. This idea is in great part why Lawrence harangues Russell with vehement criticisms that Russell's plan is full of half-measures and that Russell is still operating with conceptions that must be abandoned in the interest of a completely new start. Russell quotes Lawrence writing to him to protest: "What's the good of sticking in the damned ship and haranguing the merchant pilgrims in their own language? Why don't you drop overboard? Why don't you clear out of the whole show? One must be an outlaw these days, not a teacher or preacher."[80]

However, Russell was a teacher and a scholar, and indeed something of a preacher—if the offensive religiosity of that term to describe Russell is set aside momentarily. This is hardly better exemplified than in a passage Russell wrote in his essay, "History as an Art":

> Sometimes in the moments when I am most oppressed by the fear of coming disaster, I am tempted to think that what the world needs is a Prophet who will proclaim, with a voice combining thunder with the deepest compassion, that the road upon which mankind is going is the wrong road—a road leading to the death of our children and to the extinction of all hope—but that there is another road which men can pursue if they will, and that this other road leads to a better world than any that has existed in the past.[81]

Russell would have excluded Lawrence as a candidate for the office of such a Prophet, simply because Lawrence, in Russell's estimation, wanted a one-man show.[82] The excessive self-absorption Russell observed in Lawrence prevented the novelist from giving status to things outside himself, including other humans. By contrast, Russell admired much from the past, which he viewed as vulnerable and in jeopardy of being lost to a perspective indifferent to and contemptuous of historical knowledge. That is, for all of Russell's radicalness, in great part from his

80. Russell, *Portraits*, 13.

81. Russell, *Portraits*, 208.

82. Russell, *Portraits*, 209: "It is not by the action of any one individual, however great and eloquent, that the world can be saved." Russell is here alluding to his contention, once a point of agreement between him and Lawrence, that not only individuals must be changed, but political institutions also. Russell in some sense might be deemed to have observed that Lawrence increasingly swerved toward only himself and his direction as sufficient cause to remake the world. For Russell of course this was sheer and outrageous vanity that was dangerous.

family background, at the same time he held that worthy ideas and institutions were in danger of being lost with a misguided attempt to turn full circle. A disciplined approach to the study of human history was therefore necessary for the possibility of a desired future: "It is not too late to hope that mankind may have a future as well as a past. I believe that if men are to feel this hope with sufficient vividness to give it dynamic power, the awareness of history is one of the greatest forces of which the beneficent appeal must be felt."[83] Lawrence, however, had nothing beneficent in his plan for the human future according to Russell, and it is therefore little wonder that Russell parted from him or that each by the end of a mere year had a mutual hatred for the other.[84] When Russell began to struggle with his student Wittgenstein as Russell's relationship with Lawrence was collapsing, he commented to Lady Ottoline, "Lawrence is just as furious a critic as Wittgenstein, but I thought W. right and I think L. wrong."[85]

Not surprisingly, Russell placed Lawrence and Lawrence's ideas within the stream of a subjective romanticism for which Russell had little patience. Also not surprisingly, given how the relationship between the two men quickly faded, Russell expressed little to no interest in his former friend thereafter. Six years after Lawrence's death in 1930, his widow Frieda wrote to Russell to say that "If Lawrence hurt you, by saying the things he did, it was love even then. He wanted you to live more fully a whole."[86] Undoubtedly, the reference to "a whole" reflected Lawrence's view of Russell as living cloistered in a mental shell. In the same year, 1936, Russell sold his side of the correspondence with Lawrence, probably indicative of his animosity (or at least indifference) toward Lawrence. In 1945, in a letter to his publisher Unwin, Russell is willing to allow the letters from Lawrence to Russell to be published, though Russell feels

---

83. Russell, *Portraits*, 209.

84. One account of this, referenced in Moore, *Lawrence's Letters*, 25, refers to the autobiography of William Gerhardi, *Memoirs of a Polyglot*, 234, where Gerhadi recounts two conversations, one with each man: "Only when I mentioned D. H. Lawrence's theories did the look of serenity fade in his [Russell's] large wise eyes, and a note of intellectual fastidiousness crept into his voice, and he said 'Lawrence has no mind.' He referred to the letters Lawrence wrote to him during the war, and how, of course, he, Bertrand Russell, was not going to be instructed in wisdom by D. H. Lawrence. A week later, meeting Lawrence, I told him how enchanted I had been by the lucidity, the suppleness and pliability of Bertrand Russell's mind. He sniffed. 'Have you ever seen him in a bathing-dress?' he asked. 'Poor Bertie Russell! He is all Disembodied Mind!'"

85. Russell to Ottoline, July 8, 1915. Griffin, *Letters*, 2:43.

86. Frieda Lawrence to Russell, 1936. Arnold, "Three Unknown Letters," 159.

no inclination to write a preface for the letters.[87] An inquiry from one Mr. Berry in 1960 about possible influences of Nietzsche upon Lawrence, meets with Russell's swipe that "I always thought that Lawrence owed whatever he knew of Nietzsche or Freud to his wife who had a dominant influence upon him. But this was only conjecture."[88]

87. Russell to Unwin, May 15, 1949. Box no. 6.42, Bertrand Russell Archives, McMaster University Library.

88. Russell to P. Berry, January 6, 1960. Box no. 1.20, Bertrand Russell Archives, McMaster University Library.

7

Religion with the Mistresses

A. RELIGION AS IMPROBABLE WITH LADY CONSTANCE MALLESON

Constance Malleson was one of Russell's more lasting and intense female friendships, with the Malleson-Russell relationship initiated and developing during World War I. As one indication of Malleson's affection for Russell, she maintained a practice of annually sending a dozen birthday roses to Russell's (and after his death, Edith Russell's) home in Wales. Though Russell died in 1970, she persisted with the thought and the gift until 1975, the year of her death. When Russell made her acquaintance in 1916, other females were in Russell's circle of friends, though none nearly as exhilarating as Malleson, sporadic and volcanic though that relationship would be on occasion. Katherine Tait perceptively comments about Russell's quest for idyllic romances, "the whole optimistic scheme may have been wrong." That is, Tait's interpretation is that her father sought a utopian world within a human relationship. If religious philosophies as Russell charged to Edgar Brightman were infected with "optimistic bias" in imagining another and heavenly world rectifying the obvious disappointments in the present, then perhaps Russell's own optimistic bias was to surmise such a world attainable between two human beings:

> All his life he sought perfection: perfect mathematical truth, perfect philosophical clarity, certainty of God's existence, a perfect formula for society, a perfect woman to live with in a perfect human relationship. And although he never found them anywhere, he never stopped looking. In his personal life, each new

love roused new hope of an existence of harmonious bliss—and each time the woman proved to have defects which rendered it impossible. Rather than quarrel and compromise and 'settle down,' as people do who stay together, he would leave to search again for the ideal.[1]

While Russell's marriage to Alys had begun fraught with Russell family opposition and ended rather weakly and certainly, to not a few observers, tragically for Alys, Russell's relationship with his second wife Dora Black began strongly and ended bitterly. The relationship with Malleson tended, by contrast and on the whole, to persevere, despite ups and downs. However, when the relationship with Malleson was about three years old and still running, Russell became acquainted with Dora, who became Dora Russell on September 25, 1921, and the mother of two of Russell's children, John, born November 16, 1921, and Katherine, born December 29, 1923. When Dora and Russell began Beacon Hill School in 1927, they hired Patricia "Peter" Spence in 1930 as a nanny at Beacon Hill. In 1936 Spence would become Russell's third wife until a divorce in 1952. Peter would be the mother of Russell's third and last child, Conrad, born April 15, 1937. Malleson never became a wife to Russell, nor did she bear any Russell children or leave her husband, Miles Malleson, to whom she remained devoted. Though Malleson never married Russell, lack of nuptials between the two was not due to lack of effort on Russell's part, with the same true for a time with Russell and Ottoline. Because Malleson did not have the religious appetites that both Ottoline and Russell evidence, the Malleson and Russell relationship is worth some attention for the difference.

Constance Malleson, known to Russell by her stage name "Colette," comes within a period of Russell's life when he is ardent for children, and some commentators have maintained that if Malleson had consented to bear Russell's children, he would not have married Dora Black, who was consenting to having children with Russell. Moreover, Dora had no constraining husband at the time, while Colette did. Though Dora desired children and motherhood, in her early letters to Russell she is noticeably keen to avoid being the lesser Russell in a marriage to the great philosopher.[2] One might contend with some justification that Dora

---

1. Tait, *My Father*, 106.

2. Such a claim in no way implies that Dora in her pre-marriage haranguing with Russell, nor indeed, even after their separation and divorce, was jealous of Russell's successes. However, she did want to maintain a place for herself in a relationship to the great philosopher that would not constrain her to being only an appendage of him.

desired her own life as much as the independently minded and freedom-loving Colette insisted on hers. It is probably fair to say, however, that on this issue, while Dora excised Russell, Russell excised Colette. All the same, Colette managed to rise above Russell's request for marriage to her, while maintaining a fondness for him nevertheless. Colette knew the other significant women in Russell's life over the ensuing years, and though not always friendly nor expressing affection for all, one finds her an adroit observer, particularly of wives Dora and Peter. Her letters to friends are sprinkled with a readiness to size up various people and their situations regarding Russell. Colette also had contact with Russell's fourth wife, Edith, after Russell conveyed to Edith, with obvious affection, the place Colette had in his life. No doubt, partly this was due to the fact that Colette shared more years of friendship with Russell than many other friends who had preceded him in death.

Different women attracted Russell for distinctive reasons.[3] What seemed to attract him most to Colette was her vitality. Reading her autobiography *Ten Years After* abundantly confirms this aspect of her personality, as do the allusions to Colette in Annesley, *As the Sight is Bent*.[4] However, despite Malleson's vivacious nature—something that Russell, again, prized—she seemed to Russell to lack spiritual interests that also mattered to him. Though Russell clearly desired the vitality that Malleson evidenced, he also tried to point her in the direction of impersonal and spiritual things and goals that Russell seemed to infer were weak in

---

3. Katherine Tait contends that "The feeling she [Dora] inspired in my father was quite different from his intense romantic passion for Colette; almost from the start, he wanted my mother to be his wife, and he began to think of divorcing Alys, after almost ten years of separation." Tait, *My Father*, 49.

4. Speaking of her husband Miles Malleson, she writes: "M. and I didn't exactly fall in love: we slipped into it. We got on astonishingly well. We agreed about every single thing that seemed to us important in life. M. had tremendous sincerity—which made up for his lack of drive (and I had drive enough for two). He was anti-church, anti-state, anti-commercial." Malleson, *After Ten Years*, 76. Colette's drive, however, could take unexpected turns, but even these she pursued with vigor: "I was floundering in the depths myself—and perhaps there was more wisdom to be found in the depths than in the shallow places. At any rate, there was strength to be got from fathoming them. The ugliness of the world was as well worth seeing as the joy and beauty of it—B.R. had said. As I walked back to my lodgings, I made a new creed. I believed neither in God the Father nor in God the Son, but in the pity and splendor of all human life. Whatever happened, I'd stick to that faith; I'd live by it" (136). Speaking of her ailing sister's intent to continue riding a horse, Malleson writes: "I did my best to persuade her to go carefully—but in my heart I loved her wild courage. 'Live dangerously'—is as good a slogan as most, it seems to me" (217).

her. There is no mistaking the fact, however, that Malleson's spunk was admirable to Russell.[5]

To observe Russell in the role of something of a spiritual encourager or advisor to Malleson is little short of astounding, though only if the conception of Russell, with reference to religion, remains exclusively one of Voltairean spirit and wit. That is, the relationship between Russell and Malleson provides another and different view of how Russell negotiates religion with someone, like him, who felt negatively toward religion, but lacks his elusive sense of the eternal. In a letter of September 28, 1916, Russell shared with Malleson, that

> In some way I can't put into words, I feel that some of our thoughts and feelings are just of the moment, but others are part of the eternal world, like the stars—even if their actual existence is passing, something—some spirit or essence seems to last on, to be part of the real history of the universe, not only of the separate person—Somehow, that is how I want to live—so that as much of life as possible may have that quality of eternity—I can't explain what I mean—you will have to know.

5. As indication of Malleson's independence and energy, her sister writes, "For two people who have so much in common, my sister and I were about as different as two women could be. She was dark, I was fair. She was modern, I was antediluvian. She was for freedom, I thought discipline needful. She despised the marriage laws, I could not see why the abolition of legal ties would make life better. She had a gushing sympathy for humans. I had not. Though we both enjoyed exploring a countryside, our methods were different. She ranged over an area of thirty miles. My area was nearer three. In high-heeled shoes, she sped along tarmac roads. . . Longer sighted than I, she saw the headlands that thrust out to sea. She looked at a distant hill and in no time she had reached its summit. She always ran where I walked. I fumbled with a pencil to fix my impressions. *She* beat hers out on a typewriter. They were clear, limpid impressions. So, while I plodded carefully round the hill, Colette raced ahead, her eyes on the distant horizon—until she stepped over her ankles into bog. She said it didn't matter. As a child, whatever misfortunes befell her, she had always said it didn't matter. That was her brave philosophy of life." Annesley, *As the Sight is Bent*, 60. Her sister adds in a letter to her granddaughter Margaret, in February 1951, "Do get to know Colette. She has all the brains—and as little sense as all the rest of the family." Annesley, *As the Sight is Bent*, 120; in another letter to Margaret in June 1951, she writes, "Then I'm so glad that you liked your Aunt Colette. The only thing that she completely lacks is a sense of the value of money. In other ways she is the most affectionate and interesting person; and she'd move heaven and earth for you." Annesley, *Bent*, 128.

Such descriptions indicate something of what made Colette impressionable to Russell. However, what made Russell impressionable to Collette? Her description presented him as "A small man, with a fine brow, aristocratic features, silver-grey hair, and a passionate expression. He was conventionally dressed in dark clothes and he wore a high, stiff collar. He sat very still, his hands inert upon his knees. He seemed detached in mind and body—but all the furies of hell raged in his eyes." Malleson, *After Ten Years*, 104.

Of course I don't succeed in living that way—but that is 'The shining key of peace.'[6]

Even more indicative of Russell's striving for something elusive is his letter to Malleson of April 2, 1917: "How I could prostrate myself before God if I believed in him—I long for the repose of some great strength outside me that I could throw myself upon."[7] Though Russell was not sure what that was, he was even less sure he could communicate that feeling to others:

> There is a possibility in human minds of something mysterious as the night-wind, deep as the sea, calm as the stars and strong as Death, a mystic Contemplation, the 'intellectual love of God.' Those who have known it cannot believe in arms any longer, or in any kind of hot struggle. If I could give to others what has come to me in this way, I could make them to feel the futility of fighting. But I do not know how to communicate it: when I speak, they stare, applaud, or smile, but do not understand.[8]

Unlike the earlier relationship with Alys, with whom Russell had to dislodge Quaker religious beliefs, Malleson needed no such debunking of religious belief.[9] Recounting her religious unmaking in an English boarding school in her youth, on the occasion of a walk outside the school, she writes:

> Then, at least, one saw a wide stretch of country and plantations of trees; and in summer, wild flowers: red and yellow poppies, blue cornflowers. But we, poor prisoners, trailed along in a crocodile—wearing heavy purple coats and monstrous straw hats with D.H. embroidered on the front. The letters stood, we said, for *Damned Hell*. They certainly did—for me. There was

---

6. Russell to Malleson, September 28, 1916. Russell, *1914–1944*, 96.

7. Russell to Malleson, April 2, 1917. Document no. 200117, Box no. 6.64, Bertrand Russell Archives, McMaster University Library.

8. Russell to Malleson, July 30, 1918. Document no. 200324, Box no. 6.65, Bertrand Russell Archives, McMaster University Library.

9. For example, when Malleson was asked by some of her neighbors to lend them a hand in producing a village play, she wrote, "I rather took fright at the suggestion. I was afraid it might lead to my getting to know the people in the neighbourhood (not the villagers who were my friends already—but the local gentry and the people at the rectory). I confided to Bert Gallop that I didn't know any of those people and between himself and myself I didn't want to. I also suggested, tentatively, that the rector mightn't approve his choice of producer as I wasn't in the habit of going to church." Malleson, *After Ten Years*, 237.

only one redeeming feature in that Hell: the knowledge that the room I slept in was the room Darwin had slept in. The school had been his house. I didn't know much about Darwin—but I knew he was 'all right': the sort of person who went ahead with truth and didn't bother with the commotion he caused in church and state. I felt that in my bones.[10]

Divested of such religious beliefs as still afflicted many others, Malleson provided Russell with abundant evidence of her "instinctive joy of life,"[11] but she still lacked a religion, an omission that Russell deemed important. That is, Colette seemed to lack the thirst or spiritual appetite Ottoline possessed.[12] Oftentimes expressed in the letters to Malleson is Russell's own spiritual hunger, alongside Russell's encouragement toward spiritual matters for Malleson. In a letter of December 23, 1916, he assures her that her spiritual side "will grow in you with time."[13] In a letter of May 1, 1917, he writes more pointedly: "But personal success is not the thing to live for. Think of the immensity of the world and the vastness of human suffering. . . . I long for you to be happy and to grow to your full spiritual growth."[14] Needless to say, after a time such advice becomes a sore spot with Colette, particular as it seemed to indict her dedication to her craft, which she summarily recounts in her autobiography: "B.R. thought acting was a worthless sort of occupation. He thought it brought out the worst in one's character: personal ambition, love of admiration. He used to write me denunciatory letters."[15]

10. Malleson, *After Ten Years*, 38–39.

11. Russell to Malleson, December 4, 1916, Griffin, *Letters*, 2:92.

12. Colette, however, had a high estimation of Ottoline and in *After Ten Years*, 102, remarks that "Lady Ottoline was always doing kindnesses to tired persons in the [N.C.F] movement." In a letter of May 7, 1950, Malleson writes to her friend Nalle Kielland, "what made me always rather antagonistic to all Ottoline's set: they were always biting the hand that fed them: Ottoline's hand." Box no. 6.71, File 1, Bertrand Russell Archives, McMaster University Library.

13 December 23, 1916. Document no. 200067, Box no. 6.64, Bertrand Russell Archives, McMaster University Library. Indicative of his own spiritual feelings, Russell had prefaced the above letter of April 2, 1917, to Malleson with the admission, "The world is very full of sorrow and I am a poor weak mortal—." Document no. 200126, Box no. 6.64, Bertrand Russell Archives, McMaster University Library.

14. Russell to Malleson, May 1, 1917, Griffin, *Letters*, 2:105.

15. Malleson, *After Ten Years*, 122. In fairness to Russell, and to Malleson, she also writes about their first meeting "It has been said of Burke that 'the evil which caused his mind to blaze was nearly always cruelty' that 'he had a nerve which twitched with a maddening sensitiveness at the sight of suffering.' The same could be said of Russell." Malleson, 104–5. Also, describing her second meeting with Russell among other

In a letter of July 20, 1917, he continues to encourage her: "I can only say again that you must learn to live less personally, to live more for the world and less for success. It is a cold doctrine, but it is the only one by which one can live through the bad times."[16] Some months later, on January 7, 1918, he writes, "The gulf to my mind is between those whose fundamental impulse is to get as much out of the world as they can, and those whose fundamental impulse is to give the world as much as they can... And I want passionately to keep you on the same side of the gulf. I want religion (in some sense) to fill your life."[17] On yet another occasion he writes to her, "Let us forget problems—like theatre, our own future, etc—and live with the sea and sky and eternal things."[18] Such advice to one whose life was cast for the theatre, at times dampened their relationship. Moreover, in her career she maintained a resilience despite unrealized goals. Comparing the years between 1913 and 1925, she wrote:

> Then, I had thought I would become a provincial actress. I hadn't become what I'd set out to become. I had only stuck to my job. I warded off the bitterness of failure by telling myself I might have remained an understudy at two pounds a week. Or I might have been obliged to give up the stage altogether. I had done neither. I hadn't done much, I hadn't climbed very high, but I had climbed ALONE. It didn't make failure any less bitter or defeat any less real. It didn't save me. But it showed me I was still alive. Glamour had gone and high hopes had gone. But I'd be damned if independence had gone. Nor the love of my craft, of my job. I looked at the river and I knew there was still beauty to be found at every bend in the road. Wherever there was country there was beauty. Whereever there was water it reflected the sky. As I stood leaning against the fence that divides the fields from the road, I wished I could find words—as St Francis had found them—to hymn the water and the sky.[19]

---

people at dinner, she remarks, "He was so simple, so humble, a real human being. To know intimately, he was the most complicated of men: a mass of contradictions. But to meet, he was very easy—and, of course, brilliantly witty.... I had an odd feeling that it was perhaps the most important thing that had ever happened to me—or would ever happen to me: this meeting with Russell." Malleson, *After Ten Years*, 106.

16. Russell to Malleson, July 20, 1917. Document no. 2000165, Box no. 6.64, Bertrand Russell Archives, McMaster University Library.

17. Russell to Malleson, January 7, 1918. Document no. 200253, Box no. 6.65, Bertrand Russell Archives, McMaster University Library.

18. Russell to Malleson, October 16, 1918. Document no. 200360, Box no. 6.65, Bertrand Russell Archives, McMaster University Library.

19. Malleson, *After Ten Years*, 232–33.

In an early letter of October 21, 1916, to Malleson, Russell provides something of a summary of his own life aims that is congruent with other such statements, particularly as they come out in his *Autobiography* over a half century later. In this October letter to Malleson, moreover, Russell conveyed his goal and the resultant hardships of his life and work: "the beatific vision—God—I do not find it, and do not think it is to be found—but the love of it is my life—it is like passionate love for a ghost. At times it fills me with rage, at times with wild despair—it is the source of gentleness and cruelty and work, it fills every passion that I have. It is the spring of life within me."[20] Such talk was probably too otherworldly for Malleson, who wanted her feet planted firmly and did not evidence the kind of appetite for metaphysical connections such as seemed to have captured Russell.

When Russell in May 1917 again pointed Colette in a better direction, he received a curt reply to his plea that "my spirit calls out to you to come & seek the mountain tops."[21] Colette clearly did not want to be on the mountain tops, but on the stage, and she let Russell know it. At this time, however, Russell was somewhat diverted from Colette's tart response in light of his expectations for the 1917 political revolution in Russia, to the point of Russell now expressing a desire for the two of them to go to Russia together. Having worked together in the No-Conscription Fellowship, both were allied in enthusiasm for what had happened in Russia.

Meanwhile, Russell became insistent that he would like to have children with Colette but she refused. In his desire for a deeper relationship, and to exacerbate matters, on September 25, 1917, Russell wrote an insulting letter—though unintentionally so—in which he tries to lay her person bare. Russell's letter sent their relationship into a downward spiral with Collette announcing its end. Typical of Russell in more than one of his relationships with females, only days later he yearned for Colette to return.

In January 1918, however, when Russell seemed ready to focus again on technical philosophy, he instead found himself in the middle of confrontational politics, and by the spring of 1918 Russell would

---

20. Russell to Malleson, October 21, 1916. Griffin, *Letters*, 2:85. In a letter of October 25, 1917, Russell is particularly brutal in his self-assessment: "I shall always make every one unhappy who has much to do with me—Such people as I am ought not be left to live. I have spread pain everywhere—because of a devouring hunger which is ruthless and insatiable." Russell to Malleson, October 25, 1917, Document no. 200220, Box no. 6.65, Bertrand Russell Archives, McMaster University Library.

21. Russell to Constance Malleson, May 6, 1917, Griffin, *Letters*, 2:109.

be an occupant of Brixton prison. Russell's political views had been of course aroused by WWI, and the eventual stand he took in opposition to England's entry into the war came from deep within Russell. Indeed, it was in his opposition to entry in the war that Russell had earlier become acquainted with Ottoline and Collette, and also Dora Black. Russell later described his motivations over opposing entry into the war and the necessity of the stance he took:

> I desired the defeat of Germany as ardently as any retired colonel. Love of England is very nearly the strongest emotion I possess, and in appearing to set it aside at such a moment, I was making a very difficult renunciation. Nevertheless, I never had a moment's doubt as to what I must do. I have at times been paralyzed by skepticism, at times I have been cynical, at other times indifferent, but when the War came I felt as if I heard the voice of God. I knew that it was my business to protest, however futile protest might be. My whole nature was involved.[22]

While initially viewing Britain's entry into the war as something of a deliberate and concentrated effort of indifferent politicians to carelessly endanger their population, in time Russell's overriding worry became fear of the loss of civilization; such a fear would also be Russell's greatest worry during WWII. Dreading such a catastrophic loss, Russell became increasingly intrigued with how easily people seemed to welcome such a thing as war; this of course was in conjunction with politicians only too willing to give them their wish. Over such issues, D. H. Lawrence had come into Russell's life. In early 1916 Russell had become alarmed at the instigation of compulsory conscription and threw himself into efforts toward aiding the aims of the No-Conscription Fellowship to support the rights of conscientious objectors to war. Russell recognized that he was not a pacifist in principle and that many of the group were motivated by religious scruples, so he was not precisely well-fitted for the group. When, however, he authored a pamphlet supporting the organization's conscientious objectors, he was brought to court and given a fine. Most importantly, in terms of his future, he was dismissed from his lectureship at Cambridge University in 1916. In retrospect this event was a catalyst in Russell's life and future. That is, the experience pushed Russell toward more public venues and audiences with the attendant exposure that would later give Russell much of his resultant fame.

---

22. Russell, *1914–1944*, 7.

In 1917 Russell, like many other political liberals, enthusiastically welcomed news of the faraway Russian Revolution. When in 1918 Russell, however, wrote an inflammatory piece in *The Tribune* deemed an offense against Britain's American ally, he was hauled into court and this time given a sentence of six months imprisonment in Brixton prison in the same year. Indicative of Russell, this would not be his only stint in prison, for the man did not steer clear of controversy, nor was he averse to making himself culpable by forcing the hand of authority. After some adjustments to prison conditions, Russell resumed reading philosophy and writing again. In time this work would account for two additional books, *Introduction to Mathematical Philosophy* and *Analysis of Mind*. Russell's corpus of books was beginning to mount, and when his prison sentence was commuted by some weeks, he resumed public lectures.

Sometimes in the audience, as she had been for some years previous, though unbeknownst to Russell then, was a female admirer named Dora Black. If Russell's first marriage presented some religious differences to be worked out,[23] with Dora, whom he married in 1921, he welcomed a wife who seemed to share just as much general contempt as he possessed for things religious. Indeed, the years Russell remained with Dora account for some of the peak years of Russell's most vehement writings against religion.[24] Furthermore, according to Katherine Tait, while Russell sprinkled his letters during WWI with evidence of spiritual seeking and appetites, "After the war, finding his life more satisfying, he stopped talking that way; nostalgia for religion was quite absent from our home."[25]

---

23. Russell makes the boast that he had made of Alys by six months of marriage, an atheist like himself.

24. Dora, however, contended that she was hardly the source. In a April 17, 1973 letter to Kenneth Blackwell, the Archivist at the Russell Archives, she writes, "Quite the other way, I am a much less skeptical and cynical person than Russell was." However, in the next sentence of this letter she does express hostilities: "I would have thought that the war and the way religious people behaved and treated Russell was quite sufficient reason in the 1920's for us all becoming atheists or agnostics." Dora to Kenneth Blackwell, Record no. 121754, Box no. 16.57, Bertrand Russell Archives, McMaster University Library. Dora's response was to a letter of Blackwell to her, dated April 12, 1973, in which Blackwell writes, "[Ronald] Jager told me in conversation that he suspected you of making Russell much more militant in his anti-religious writings. Do you think this is so?" Kenneth Blackwell to Dora Russell, Record no. 121747, Box no. 16.57, Bertrand Russell Archives, McMaster University Library.

25. Tait, *My Father*, 185.

While in prison earlier, however, Russell's correspondence included letters to and from Colette and she visited him there. However, as Russell could be rather demanding, what came from her was never quite enough. Nonetheless, Russell maintained strong feelings for her and in letters to Colette religion continues as a not infrequent subject. Time in prison, meanwhile, gave Russell ample opportunity to think over his life and particularly how he desired to spend the rest of it. Some days Russell seemed enthralled with optimistic anticipations of his future, even as he admitted to a bit of superstitious belief that the gods would withhold what they would deem too much happiness for him. Nevertheless, in a most optimistic letter to Malleson penned from prison, Russell wrote: "I must and will do important work: technical philosophy till the war ends, but after that, I think, more the sort of thing Voltaire did for his age. I find I must appeal to a larger public than one can reach by technical philosophy. I want to urge freedom in every direction, and creative energy. I want to be an intellectual power in Europe, and I can be if I can put forth enough vitality. My life is only beginning."[26]

Russell's expectations for his future were joined to his optimism over news of the Russian Revolution of 1917. However, his expectations met with severe disappointment later on his trip to Russia in 1920 in seeing firsthand the Communist experiment, over which Russell had initially expressed much approval, and he had not expected to make the trip without a female companion. In the summer of 1919 and amidst some tumult in his relationships with Ottoline and Colette, Russell developed serious interest in Dora. For a while coldness had descended over his prior relationship with Colette, but the situation became more complicated by the fact that Colette proposed a meeting with Russell which had the effect of reinvigorating the previously rocky relationship between the pair. At the same time, Russell appeared unchecked in reaching out to Dora. Other though smaller differences between the two women aside, Dora's appeal to Russell seemed focused on the desire of both to have children. This was something that Colette would not entertain, whereas Dora was willing. The terms of any marriage beyond the joint affirmation of children, however, remained contentious between her and Russell. Complicating the tension was that Dora, in academic study at the time and recipient of a Girton Fellowship at Cambridge, was considering a career in the theatre, whereas Colette's yearning for larger roles for herself

---

26. Russell to Malleson, August 21, 1918, Document no. 200336, Box no. 665, Bertrand Russell Archives, McMaster University Library.

on stage Russell had judged negatively as a part of her seeming indifference to spiritual matters. However, for the time being a more pressing concern for Russell and Dora was the possibility of a joint trip to Russia.

In May 1920, and with the British Labour Delegation, Russell entered the Soviet Union—without Dora. For Russell it would be something of a life-changing trip. Though the threat of typhus in Russia was one consideration among others that Russell cautioned Dora about, she had remained adamant to go, and when all possibility seemed lost she began to make moves to make the trip on her own. Indeed, she succeeded in that effort, while the separateness of their journeys contributed to the fact of their nearly opposite estimations of what each saw in Russia. As Tait contends, "They went on quarreling about Russia for years."[27]

While in Russia and without either Colette or Dora as a female companion, Russell began to despair of what he witnessed as he feared the Bolsheviks presented not a new dream for the world, but a new horror. His letters to Malleson during this time pointedly reflect his grave disappointment with the Revolution, and typical of Russell, while other fellow travelers placed their observations in a positive context to uphold the Revolution, Russell, virtually alone, demurred. One aspect of the Revolution that clearly troubled Russell was his perception of a lacking spiritual component to the Bolshevik project. The subject of Russell's letters from Russia, to include the future book on Russia written in 1920, is noticeably bleak. Compared to the later trip to China undertaken with Dora in 1921 and the book on China written in 1922, Russell's preference is blatantly obvious. Russell disdained the Bolshevik contempt for things old, while his strong appetite for history welcomed the evident pride of the Chinese in their past, however vulnerable were the old ways in a changing world. Part of this fondness for the Chinese respect for the past was simply Russell's respect for this orientation, while part of his disdain of the Bolsheviks was for the bleak and coarse secularism they vaunted and their disdain for most all of Russia's prior history. Chinese culture, though aged, appeared with a certain magnificence; Russian Bolshevik culture appeared with almost an opposite mundaneness. Furthermore, even the religion of the Chinese, as Russell perceived it, was to his liking; Dora later writes to an inquirer, "What Russell liked about the Chinese was their courtesy, their way of understatement, their wit and humor,

---

27. Tate, *My Father*, 51.

their lack of religion, their love of art and beauty."[28] Russell desired something for his restless soul, so he understandably developed fondness for a culture and civilization that reflected little of the surrounding tumultuous world.[29]

Russell judged the Bolsheviks set on destroying the soul of the Russian people by insistence upon the material conditions of life alone. Furthermore, in a letter to Malleson of May 12, 1920, Russell imagines the Bolsheviks' estimation of him, their critic, and Russell's response: "Come out of your dreams, forget the eternal things. The men you have come among would tell you they are only the fancies of a bourgeois with too much leisure, and can you be sure they are anything more? I come back eternally to the same question: what is the secret of this passionate country? Do the Bolsheviks know its secret? Do they even suspect that it has a secret? I wonder."[30] By contrast the Chinese culture and people Russell would encounter later, he found "lovable and I long to help them."

When Russell arrived back in England on June 30, 1920, Dora was still in Russia, and he was met by Colette and also by a letter inviting him to lecture in China in the autumn. Given Russell's earlier dismissal from Cambridge as consequence of his troubles over his political leaflet and then imprisonment, he welcomed the opportunity to delay any return to Cambridge University by way of a year in China. Awaiting Dora's arrival, part of his time was yet again spent in the company of Colette. As Russell prepared for a Dora deeming the new Russia everything that Russell thought not, an additional consternation for Russell was that he was about to solidify his relationship with Dora, rather than Colette. However, and apparently as some have surmised, the choice for Russell came down to who would be the mother of his desired children. Because Colette said no, he chose Dora. Russell and Dora would proceed together to China in autumn of 1920.

China, quaint and backward by modern standards, possessed almost everything that the new Russia was trying to eradicate. Recognizing

---

28. Dora to David Harley, February 20, 1976, Record no. 121217, Bertrand Russell Archives, McMaster University Library/Dora Winifred Russell Papers, inventory number #53, International Institute of Social History, Amsterdam.

29. Two decades later and now during another world war Russell writes to Malleson that "My work obliges me to read ancient and medieval history, which I find consoling—merely because it makes one feel that these times are not exceptional, and yet the world has gone on." Russell to Malleson, October 7, 1941, Document no. 200820, Box no. 6.68, Bertrand Russell Archives, McMaster University Library.

30. Russell to Malleson, May 12, 1920, Russell, *1914–1944*, 146–47.

this immense country's vulnerability to the encroaching West, Russell knew that in a match of power, which is to say with the power of industrialism in tow, the ways of the West could wipe the old China out. This was the sobering realization that most always accompanied Russell's concern, not to say adulation, for the old ways of China, and this time he and Dora, unlike on Bolshevik Russia, were in agreement.

Moreover, there was some very good news while in China that Russell had long awaited: he would be a parent. He had for so long wanted children, in great part because he saw them, if properly reared, capable of turning the world around. However, returning to England from China in August 1921, he had much business to attend to, for Dora was now five months into her pregnancy. Desiring to be legally free, despite Dora's disdain for legal marriage, he sought a divorce from Alys, so that he and Dora could marry before the birth of their child. An additional complication was his continued entanglement with Colette; however, Colette took the initiative and got out of the way, and Russell and Dora were married on September 25, 1921. John Conrad Russell was born on November 16, 1921.

While in China, Russell and Dora had felt no compunction about Dora's pregnancy outside marriage. Life as he had tolerated it at Pembroke Lodge provoked him to be a prolific critic of conformity and pious obedience and what he regarded as nonsense. His insistence on following reason made Russell in the eyes of some of the public a radical exponent of devious doctrines that would undermine the very stability and well-being of society. For some, he could be a maker of mayhem, and for others his mocking of the authorities during his World War I opposition to conscription had provided evidence that Russell was a dangerous and clever adversary. For his part, however, and from the beginning of England's declaration of war on Germany in August 1914, Russell had been astounded at the jubilation among many that had accompanied a plunge into warfare. Was reason's opposite in charge of the human person? This consideration provoked Russell to consider how one could justify the claims of reason in an irrational world.

Russell had great respect for pacifists, but he was no pacifist in principle and admitted so on many occasions. Furthermore, pacifism was often couched within the pacifist's religion. Russell's objection to the war and conscription had come from something similar and was stated eloquently in a way that carried strong spiritual overtones: "The noblest thing in a man is the spiritual force which enables him to stand firm against the whole world in obedience to his own sense of right; and I will never acquiesce in silence while the men in whom spiritual force is strong are treated as a danger to the community rather than its most precious heritage. I would say to the persecutors: you cannot defeat such men; you cannot make their testimony of no avail."[31]

This rousing call to spiritual arms resembles the defense of the fearless Socrates before impatient and angry accusers. Even if the natural and historical association of spiritual matters with things religious had a checkered history and even if institutional religion and religious hierarchies had often sucked the blood out of the spiritually vibrant and conceived of them as enemies rather than friends, spiritual values must nevertheless be upheld and respected.

Less than ten years later, with his marriage to Dora wearing thin, Russell began corresponding with Malleson again, writing in his letter of January 31, 1931, "The time when you and I were together was the summit of my life, and I no longer possess such fire as in those days."[32] Indeed and again, in those earlier days Russell's religious aspirations were relatively strong, whereas by the 1920s and 1930s one could think with some justification that Russell was solely a critic of religion.

Russell, thereafter, though he became almost entirely a negative critic of religion, still could not leave the subject alone. In this respect, Russell and G.E. Moore diverged significantly. Moore had been reared in a more exacting religious home than Russell, but when he made his break, Moore never looked back, as Russell sometimes would. Indeed, in the Schilpp volume on Moore's philosophy, Moore was in effect silent on the subject of religious belief after he gave it up, while Russell never managed to fully draw the curtain on the subject. With Russell's aversion toward memory of the Victorian atmosphere of Pembroke Lodge, he could rarely refrain from castigating what he viewed as wrong religion. However, I have suggested that Russell set up an impossible situation for himself with reference to religious belief. That is, just as badly as he might desire a religion, he also erected obstacles precluding any viable possibility. With Malleson Russell found a soul-mate of sorts, because she possessed a fire that Russell admired and enjoyed, her zest acting as good medicine for his restless and hungry soul. On the other hand, she lacked something of the penchant for eternal things that Russell so desired.

---

31. Russell, "Courtroom Defence of the Everett Leaflet," *CP* 13:389.
32. Russell to Malleson, January 31, 1931, Griffin, *Letters*, 2:298.

Colette was from the beginning fascinated with Russell, and concludes her autobiography *After Ten Years*, recounting the struggles in her profession of acting and writing. However, she also gives indication that other things besides her craft had occupied her: One was Russell: "For the world took on a very different aspect for me one day in July when I got a letter from B.R. He said he wanted me to know his children: John and Kate. He said they were in Cornwall for the long vacation. Would I come? I took the 10.45 to Cornwall. B.R. met me. The children were the children of one's dreams: happy, fearless, free. We had the evenings together. The wheel had come full circle—after ten years."[33]

B. THE RUSSELL AND LADY OTTOLINE MORRELL ATTRACTION

With Lady Ottoline Morrell we come to the person in Russell's life with whom he struggled most over the subject of religion. While Russell boasts of having converted Alys to atheism only six months into their marriage, he never proves victorious in moving Ottoline from her spiritual beliefs and proclivities, though he does manage to annoy and sometimes infuriate her in his efforts.[34] Strikingly unconventional in ways that Russell found intriguing, Ottoline at first put Russell off by her flamboyance, though she eventually became one of the most influential people in his life.

Religion was part of the glue binding Russell and Ottoline together. Even so, their future could not have looked promising—except Russell was strongly in love and perhaps allowed himself to hope. He would later note that about the same time he was having his courtship with Alys many years earlier, Ottoline and her future husband, Philip Morrell, were also having theirs; the lament of missed opportunity is fairly common in Russell. For now, however, Russell was in great part drawn to Ottoline as she provided an emotional life that Russell clearly desired, but found difficult to negotiate with his relentlessly cerebral nature. With Russell

---

33. Malleson, *After Ten Years*, 311.

34. Miranda Seymour perhaps overstates her point, but contends that "Russell did everything he could in later life to obliterate the most extreme examples of Ottoline's intellectual influence over him as she encouraged him to give voice to the mystical side of his nature.... He praised her in his autobiography for her influence on his character and, in particular, for the way her sense of humour had helped to cure him of priggishness and egocentricity, but he had no wish to recall how far from atheism his love had led him." Seymour, *Ottoline*, 124.

feeling at sea, Ottoline managed to show him his way into the larger world and beyond a chain-saw intellect. Nevertheless, however much Ottoline drew out his emotional side, their interactions over religion fell flat. This is not to say that their confrontations concerning religion had no lasting effect upon Russell, for Russell was genuinely desirous of uniting the intellectual and emotional components of human existence and thought she might help. As he conveys to Ottoline,

> I should like to be able to write things that would say more of what I feel—but hitherto I have found it difficult. I am full of vague plans, but I don't know what would come of them, I feel that you will help me. So much that goes into religion seems to me important, and I want somehow to make people feel what survives [religious] dogmas. Most of the people who think as I do about the dogmas seem to be able to live in the everyday world without windows into a great world beyond. But to me that would be a prison.[35]

Though early on Russell found himself infatuated with Ottoline, he was self-aware enough to warn her about outbursts that might and indeed would arise when conversation turned to religion. When conflict came, Russell's complaint against Ottoline's beliefs was the familiar one. That is, while Russell desired to embrace a religious attitude in life, he refused to ignore or misconstrue factual beliefs about the world. Though reality is uncongenial to the human desires expressed in religious beliefs about the world, many respectable philosophers, Russell contends, are guilty of conjuring up philosophies that are indebted to their emotions while having little to no intellectual credibility. Russell's life with religion, for the most part, was an attempt to keep his guard up against this propensity. What made this difficult was Russell's admission of his own inability to be firmly content in the camp of happy unbelief. That is, he desired a religion that his intellect would not permit. His insistence on the claims of intellect to nullify religious belief left him with religious desires unsatisfied, while Ottoline was credulous in her religious beliefs in his mind.

In the years of his relationship with Ottoline, Russell wanted to offer to his public more than pedestrian philosophy or sermonizing platitudes. Such a desire in part kept Russell close to Ottoline and evidences the

---

35. Russell to Ottoline, April 6, 1911, Document no. 000021, Box no. 2.53, Bertrand Russell Archives, McMaster University Library/Ottoline Morrell Collection, Box 18, Folder 4, Harry Ransom Center, University of Texas, Austin.

point that Russell was willing to work with her for something of the religious perspective she brought to his work. This would include fiction, or at least not only prosaic philosophy, avenues that might open up his vision of a world or reality that philosophy squeezed out. Considering that this form of communication could give his ideas more power, he stood ready to try. Try he did, to the point of asking Joseph Conrad to appraise one of his first attempts to write a fictional piece. Russell's gifts, however, as sparkling as his prose could be and was, were not in fictional writing.

Ottoline in time experienced feelings of both awe and frustration over Russell. He could exhaust her, and at times she thought the relationship overwhelming. Overall, Russell needed her more than the reverse, though by some accounts and in a different way, Ottoline was as needy as Russell. Lawrence judged her as terribly lacking in confidence and unable to rise above her feelings of vulnerability. Lawrence, for all his infuriating behavior toward Russell, could be a keen analyst of people, Russell included.[36] Russell may have for a time thought Ottoline could usher him into a world from which he had largely been self-excluded. If so, there is little wonder Russell veered toward her in an attempt to escape from a rational prison partly or even largely of his own construction.

While Russell would at times attribute something of his demeanor or personality to elements of a Puritan-like upbringing, one could argue that another kind of Puritanism hung on, though in a secular form. Russell welcomed the flamboyant nature of Ottoline's world and freedom from the shackling strictures of Victorianism, but when his intellect held court, it operated from a perspective of austerity and logic. For him a departure from the strictures and rules of a disciplining intellect amounted to indifference to truth.

Ottoline had ties to the Bloomsbury group and brought Russell into that world for a time. Members have been variously described as a cast of free-thinkers, bohemians, gifted intellectuals, artistic and literary writers of various sorts, and social radicals. Not everyone respected this group; Russell was one among others who was critical. In a letter to Lady

36. Or so Ray Monk contends: "For, with the infallible insight for which Russell revered him, Lawrence had put his finger on the central conflict in Russell's nature: the tension between his feeling of alienation from the rest of humanity and his espousal of a selfless identification with it; and the analogous tension between his fierce, dark hatreds and his ideal of universal love. When Russell had tried to see Lawrence's own vehement hatreds as springing from a universal mystical love, he was but trying to foist on to Lawrence his own ideal. Lawrence saw this and resisted it." Monk, *Spirit of Solitude*, 410.

Ottoline in 1915, D. H. Lawrence complained, "They are cased each in a hard little shell of his own and out of this they talk words."[37] Russell's relationship with the group was tenuous at best, and contemptuous at worst. Russell was not disdainful of the artistic temperament the group exuded, admiring that quality in his student Wittgenstein, in whom, for a while at least, Russell reveled in watching him work. Furthermore, to be brought within a literary group such as Bloomsbury surely afforded Russell some glimpse of literary craftsmen at work. Perhaps not, however, as Russell remarked negatively on the fiction of Virginia Woolf, probably the most prominent writer among the group.

Russell judged some of the Bloomsbury group as vain—somewhat as Russell's adversary Lawrence clearly did. Russell also may have deemed the camaraderie among this group somewhat shallow compared to his friendships among the Cambridge Apostles, which he much preferred. To some observers, Russell included, those of the Bloomsbury circle appeared vain to the point of snobbishness. Nevertheless, for members like John Maynard Keynes,[38] Lytton Strachey, and Roger Fry,[39] Russell had some modicum of respect.

Russell's negativity toward the Bloomsbury group of London hardened when he perceived the sniffs of Bloomsbury members for Ottoline. While members were frequently recipients of Ottoline's hospitality and generosity, their later critical reflections on her hardly display gratefulness for her kindnesses toward them. Consequently, Russell tolerated the circle at Bloomsbury—just barely—but he much preferred Ottoline to her critics.

Members of the circle manifested little inclination to religion, and those who did usually moved on. Indeed, Ottoline's religious propensities may have been one reason for the group to afterward criticize her.

---

37. Rosner, *Bloomsbury Group*, 13.

38. Russell contended that "Keynes's intellect was the sharpest and clearest that I have ever known. When I argued with him, I felt that I took my life in my hands, and I seldom emerged without feeling something of a fool." In typical sardonic fashion Russell also attributed something more to Keynes, in that "There are still many people in America who regard depressions as acts of God. I think Keynes proved that the responsibility for these occurrences does not rest with Providence." Russell, *1872–1914*, 102.

39. These three, along with Desmond MacCarthy and E.M. Forster are mentioned as friends in Russell's chapter ""Some of my Contemporaries at Cambridge" in *Portraits*, 73. Forster wrote the biography of Russell's close friend Lowes Dickinson. MacCarthy, along with Russell's Aunt Agatha, edited the volume on Russell's grandmother, entitled *Lady John Russell: A Memoir*. Virginia Woolf, perhaps the most famous member of the Bloomsbury set, wrote *Roger Fry: A Biography*.

Interestingly, early on in her relationship with Russell, and with Russell's intellectual achievements established and growing, Ottoline expressed apprehension over her own abilities compared to Russell's. Ottoline's self-doubt had already registered among the Bloomsbury circle,[40] but Russell was dismissive of her doubts, surely in part because he adored Ottoline, though perhaps equally because of his contempt for the Bloomsbury set.[41] Russell vehemently expressed that contempt to Ottoline in 1918: "I hate all the Bloomsbury crew, with their sneers at anything that has live feeling in it.... They put up with me because they know I can make any one look ridiculous—if I had less brains and less satire, they would all be down on me—as it is, they whisper against me in corners, and flatter me to my face. They are a rotten crew. I wish you had more congenial 'friends.'"[42] However, in fairness to the members of Bloomsbury, Russell might bear some responsibility for less than a congenial relationship with the group; certainly they preferred Moore to Russell, for of the two, Moore was the more affable. Certainly another reason Bloomsbury and Russell did not have a strong relationship was that none of the group, save Keynes, knew anything much about mathematics, where Russell was nearly king. However, as earlier noted, when Russell produced his lectures and then his book, *Social Reconstruction* in 1916, members flocked to hear him and thought highly of the book. Moreover, Russell's vision of a world free from Victorian mores, sexual and otherwise to greater freedom highly resembled Bloomsbury's vision for a new world.

Though the Bloomsbury group was secular-oriented, members included people, like Roger Fry, who had come from well-established Christian traditions, in Fry's case, a Quaker family. The Bloomsbury set, however, was charting new directions in literature and the arts that bypassed things religious. Scarcely surprising, there were no clergy nor any clergy in training among their members. Bloomsbury manifested

---

40. Russell to Ottoline Morrell, May 11, 1911: "No, Darling, I don't think you need be afraid about my finding out your intellect—in fact, you know you needn't—that is all nonsense." Document no. 000063, Box no. 2.53, Bertrand Russell Archives, McMaster University Library/Ottoline Morrell Collection, Box 18, Folder 6, Harry Ransom Center, University of Texas, Austin.

41. In his *Autobiography*, however, Russell comments, "I have known no woman to whom the claims of intellect were as absolute as they are to me, and wherever intellect intervened, I have found that the sympathy I sought in love was apt to fail." Russell, *1914–1944*, 36.

42. Russell to Ottoline, August 1, 1918. Griffin, *Letters*, 2:166.

an overt secular charter.[43] Something of its secular rather than religious leanings is detectable in associates, though non-members, such as T. S. Eliot, whose poetic abilities would have made him an apt candidate for the group, save for his religious inclinations. When these became evident and publicly confirmed with Eliot's entry into the Anglican Church, Russell, as well as some members of Bloomsbury, like Virginia Woolf, expressed both dismay and disdain over Eliot's decision.

As earlier hinted at, one might contend that Russell's attraction to Ottoline brought renewed or sustained interest in things religious only or primarily because Ottoline was religious. However, Russell's appetite for religion was hardly or exclusively motivated by his romantic inclinations for Ottoline. In his letter of May 2, 1911 Russell touches on this point when he writes to Ottoline, "When I spoke yesterday about having found out what pleased you, and then not saying it, I was thinking of all the things that make religion to me. They are very real, but it is a crime against religion to use it to make you love me, so I feel I can only talk about it when the impulse is straight and clean. Fortunately, with you it often is."[44] Certainly Ottoline seemed a lucrative conduit, and Russell's letters to Ottoline reflect something of his regular insistence, that Ottoline had something religious that must be conveyed to him—but without metaphysical religious beliefs. In general, concerning religion, he views himself, at least in the beginning of this relationship, as the needy partner. His insistence upon allegiance to reason and truth are mentioned, though often muted in the early stages of their relationship. In the beginning, moreover, Russell is not insistent upon too much and is prepared to hear Ottoline out, but he does want to to plumb the spiritual side of life with her virtually leading, for which he feels a rather severe need. None of this is because Russell is practicing deceit in his relationship, for he is hopeful that Ottoline can perhaps show him the way to something he has not previously fathomed or figured; his efforts to write fiction derive from this same need, as will be surveyed shortly. His fascination with Ottoline, moreover, does certainly prompt him to exercise as much patience as he can command for himself when the subject of religion is discussed, for he knows that his allegiance to reason will present

---

43. Aldous Huxley is something of an exception. Though for a while a part of Bloomsbury, he eventually withdrew and was pulled to more theological pursuits. Russell had a negative impression of Huxley, particular in his desire to make science and religion compatible. Of such a ploy, Russell was highly suspicious.

44. Russell to Ottoline, May 2, 1911, Griffin, *Letters*, 1:364.

obstacles to going the whole mystical route of Ottoline. In his letter of April 9, 1911, he writes:

> Dearest there is not vital difference between us as regards religion. It is true that I shall sometimes publicly attack things which you believe, but it will be for the sake of other things that you will also believe. It is my business in life to do my best to discover the truth, about such things, and to explain what I have come to think, and why. I do not think it matters so much what people believe, as how they believe it.[45]

The strong epistemological orientation toward belief is evident here as Russell tries to present his motivation as not intentionally combative. What he desires between Ottoline and himself, and just as strongly for himself, is a spiritual life that provides sustenance. The fact that most of Russell's friends and acquaintances exhibited no spiritual appetites or concerns he found disappointing, if not vexing, for Russell was not aloof from spiritual matters. Aside from other factors in Russell's feelings for Ottoline, his spiritual appetite, though cautious and at times confrontational with Ottoline, sought a religious or spiritual interface with a cosmological reality defiant and indifferent to that religious appetite.

Russell had lengthy chats with Ottoline over what he dubbed her mystical orientation to the world, and exhibited some willingness to try for a time the mystical way, until patience wore thin and he demanded she face the challenges of reason. In the beginning of their relationship, however, he tried to tread lightly and his earliest letters are profuse in his contention that he wants something of what Ottoline has in terms of a religion, with his customary caveats conveniently stored safely out of the way, for the moment. Indeed, Russell's desires during this time seem genuine as he strives to be patient. To the cynic, again, it might seem that Russell was simply along for the ride that came with Ottoline, though this change is hardly fair to him, however much his uneasy patience with Ottoline shows through in the beginning.

Conveying some of Russell's awareness of his difficulties with people, in a letter of May 9, 1911, and certainly in light of Ottoline's perception of Russell as "hard," he writes:

---

45. Russell to Ottoline, April 9, 1911, Document no. 000025, Box no. 2.53, Bertrand Russell Archives, McMaster University Library/Ottoline Morrell Collection, Box 18, Folder 4, Harry Ransom Center, University of Texas, Austin.

Yes I should like you to make me more actively tender. I have not hidden it from people in trouble and I think many must have known of it because I have often found that people in trouble trusted me. But in ordinary life it gets thwarted by my critical side. It is more vital that I should be a clear and incisive critic of things and theories than that I should show tenderness, because it is more what I am specially capable of, and it is nearer to the faith I live by. There has always been some difficulty in combining the two.... But it is not impossible to combine them and you will help me. Happiness in itself is a help.[46]

Russell had earlier found some profit in his reading of Spinoza, and he suggests to Ottoline, "If one is in danger of indignation, or of letting desire destroy one's poise, he is just the man to think of. It is difficult digging the good out of his writings, because it is all concealed in a horrible pedantry of geometrical demonstration. Yet even that, in the end, one comes to love—it gives the sense of necessity, and it has the austere impersonal quality that he desires to get."[47]

Meanwhile, grappling with an understanding of proper religion, Russell begins his 1912 essay "The Essence of Religion" with the usual qualifications found when he attempts to breathe viability into a shredded belief that can no longer be maintained, but out of which he hopes something can be extracted for the present, with provisions: "Thus it has become a matter of first importance to preserve religion without any dependence upon dogmas to which an intellectually honest assent grows daily more difficult."[48] The chief unresolvable perplexity for Russell is the presence of evil in a universe where God is deemed to exist. In Russell's view, Christian belief is saddled with a conundrum defying solution, and

---

46. Russell to Ottoline, May 9, 1911, Document no. 000060, Box no. 2.53, Bertrand Russell Archives, McMaster University Library/Ottoline Morrell Collection, Box 18, Folder 6, Harry Ransom Center, University of Texas, Austin.

47. Russell to Ottoline, May 24, 1911, Document no. 081369, Box no. 2.37, Bertrand Russell Archives, McMaster University Library/Ottoline Morrell Collection, Box 19, Folder 1, Harry Ransom Center, University of Texas, Austin. Russell goes on to add in this letter, "When I was young, I had a good deal of cruelty in my nature—it goes, I think, with an incisive habit of thought. I was aristocratic, like Nietzsche—there were important people, and unimportant people—most people bored me and I thought them contemptible. That attitude fell away from me ten years ago—and what I learnt then I have not forgotten since." The latter is undoubtedly a reference to the mystical experience of 1901.

48. Russell, "Essence of Religion," *CP* 12:115.

for which neither his Grandmother Russell nor Ottoline had any fragment of a valid answer:

> Christianity effects this by the belief that, since the apparent evil is in accordance with the will of God, it cannot really be evil. This view, however, demands a falsification of our standard of good and evil, since much that exists is evil to any unbiased consideration. Moreover, if pursued to a conclusion, it destroys all motive to action, since the reason given for acquiescence, namely that whatever happens must be for the best, is a reason which renders our efforts after the best superfluous. . . . For these reasons, though Christianity is in fact often more effective both in causing acquiescence and in providing a religious motive for action, yet this effectiveness is due to a confusion of thought, and tends to cease as men grow more clear-sighted.[49]

To Russell, the often observed indignation over "the blind empire of matter" is without beneficial consequence. Moreover, the utter purity of love is necessary for the kind of love that can persist in any situation: "It is love, contemplative in origin, but becoming active wherever action is possible; and it is a kind of love to which there is no opposing hatred."[50] Referring to this subsequently as the "boundlessness of love," from it, Russell explains, there comes divine love. Using the prison image, Russell further contends that "More than anything else, divine love frees the soul from its prison and breaks down the walls of the self that prevent its union with the world."[51] This process is essential because "it is important to discover a form of union with the universe which is independent of all beliefs as to the nature of the universe."[52] Because we do know, according to Russell, that the universe is indifferent to our desires, we must come to terms with this brutal and unflinching reality without wasted indignation. The older forms of religion had no such task, but we do. Coming to terms with this reality, asks much of us, as Russell avers in the essay's conclusion:

> It is not the strength of our ideals, but their weakness, that makes us dread the admission that they are ours, not the world's. We with our ideals must stand alone, and conquer, inwardly, the world's indifference. It is instinct, not wisdom, that finds this difficult and shivers at the solitude it seems to entail. Wisdom

---

49. Russell, "Essence of Religion," *CP* 12:117–18.
50. Russell, "Essence of Religion," *CP* 12:120.
51. Russell, "Essence of Religion," *CP* 12:120.
52. Russell, "Essence of Religion," *CP* 12:121.

does not feel this solitude, because it can achieve union even with what seems most alien. The insistent demand that our ideals shall be already realized in the world is the last prison from which wisdom must be freed. Every demand is a prison, and wisdom is only free when it asks nothing.[53]

Russell received varied reactions to this essay and while it produced nothing like the acclaim of his prior "Free Man's Worship," a comparison of the essays and the years between them, (1902–1912) are indicative of how the matter of religion, particularly a desirable and livable religion, shorn of past theological beliefs, continued to preoccupy Russell. However, what might be called the different tones of the two essays is evident, with "The Essence of Religion" displaying less stridency than the former essay, a feature perhaps due to Ottoline's influence. Russell, however, has not relinquished anything significant from the former essay: the notion of an indifferent and amoral reality pinching moral creatures who strain for human meaning in a meaningless cosmos is still the human lot. Additionally, "The Essence of Religion," contains no call to arms, as can be seen in portions of "Free Man's Worship." In fact, the later essay, while not attempting to coach the human into something resembling a surrender, does articulate a proposed peace whereby we may end up with no enemies. The net effect of such a peace, however, has no tincture of gain or gratification, but simply the solemn backing of "wisdom." Here the philosopher Russell has found some rest akin to the consolation mathematics had provided for some time in his life. About this time, too, literature will be tried as a way to build a fortress for needful humans, particularly as mathematics was not the fortress it had once been for Russell.

At Pembroke Lodge in May 1911, Russell and Ottoline took a walk around his childhood home, and he wrote to Ottoline the next day that his grandmother would have liked her. He continues: "You would have liked her, I think, because she was deeply religious and utterly unworldly. She was very full of anxious morality, and you might have felt her stuffy."[54] However, Russell had become largely unsettled with his grandmother for precisely the larger reason Ottoline might have appreciated the

---

53. Russell, "Essence of Religion," *CP* 12:122.

54. Russell to Ottoline, May 2, 1911, Griffin, *Letters*, 1:365. For something of a more sober assessment by Russell of his grandmother—and not one as seemingly indifferent as his comment that when she died, he "did mind at all," in this letter to Ottoline,—he writes "She opposed my marriage bitterly, and it produced a certain coolness during her last years. When she was dead I felt remorse, but on looking back I don't think I was *much* to blame."

woman—Lady Russell's religiosity. Nevertheless, Ottoline and Russell were in general agreement about modern morality, in a way that would have appalled and flabbergasted Lady Russell—as she had been on discovering sexual improprieties with Russell's parents after their death.

C. THE FICTIONAL EFFORT WITH RELIGION

A decade prior to that walk with Ottoline around Pembroke Lodge, Helen Flexner had written to Russell "that for a mathematician you are far too literary . . . ."[55] In response Russell speaks of what drew him to mathematics, giving the answer often given—it is above human suffering, it encapsulates perfection, and for such reasons mathematics is the summit of knowledge, and most importantly, without human alloy. Flexner and Russell sought to examine how to manage life when full of ordeals and various trials, and they often turned to consider literature. However, Russell dismisses some misconceptions and writes, for example, "to burn always with a hard, gem-like flame is not the purpose of life."[56] Nevertheless, while Pater's idea strikes Russell as mistaken, Russell now sought a literary path for his work. As indicated by Richard A. Rempel and Margaret Moran, editors of volume 12 of *The Collected Papers of Bertrand Russell*: "Russell was at his most self-consciously literary and confessional during the period 1902 to 1914. Not before and never again would he try so hard to shape the materials of personal experience into literary statements. If the search for a literary form to embody views of self eluded him, it was not for want of repeated attempts."[57] Some of the writings of these early years of Russell are reminiscent of Augustine's *City of God*, and also his *Confessions*, for Russell is likewise out to provide a sizing up of human aspirations and to expand on the need of humans for something transcendent.

In a letter to Flexner in the next year, Russell writes:

> Berenson says that literature is the most inexpressive of the arts: this is a very profound remark to my mind. Essentially, literature deals only with those relations of man to the inevitable and irresistible, which you may call God or Devil as you choose. This theme has above all two forms: Death and Time; there

---

55. Helen Thomas to Russell, December 10, 1901, in Forte, *Letters*, 25.
56. Russell to Helen Thomas, June 10, 1902, in Forte, *Letters*, 16.
57. Rempel and Moran, "Introduction," in Russell, *CP* 12:xv.

are others, for example, in Milton's Satan, but these two are the chief. And Time is either the Past or the transitoriness of what is present. To humanize the irresistible was formerly the province of Religion; now it must be left to Literature. And it is to be done no longer, as before, by fashioning God in our own image, but by enlarging our souls that we can absorb and enfold the whole great Universe, and conquer Nature by thoughts greater than her greatest works.[58]

Indeed, within the writings of these years one discovers something of a Russell largely unknown to both his advocates and his critics. These readers have encountered much more of what Russell wrote in subsequent decades on the subject and from which his reputation on religion became established, though distorted. In these relatively brief and few writings from this earlier period, the reader witnesses the seriousness and sincerity of Russell with his subject. There is considerably less flippancy, and the consuming fire Russell is so well known for by the aforementioned readers burns low.

That being said, it is helpful to remember that Russell's broad views on religion were still in some transition at the time he went up to Cambridge. That is, the prior judgements he had brought forward against the religious beliefs of Pembroke Lodge had left something of a vacuum, for a short while filled at Cambridge by the Hegelianism then prominent at the university. Russell continued to admit a legitimate place for religion in life, but writes to Ottoline in April 1911, "You make me feel fretful and small, for you achieve what I only aim at, and achieve by moments: I wonder whether what you achieve is possible without religious beliefs which are not open to me."[59] Indeed, the question put at the end summarizes the sticking point when the subject was religion, for Russell's quest never extended backward to reconsider "religious beliefs which are not open to me." Nevertheless, in most of the notable essays of these years, Russell tried to varying degrees to find a way to fill a religious vacuum in a modern secular world.

Russell's significant essays during these handful of years express such struggle admirably. When he aspired to a literary format, his subject was still the same: what to make of life, conceived both cosmically and

---

58. Russell to Helen Thomas, August 2, 1902, Forte, *Letters*, 23–24.

59. Russell to Ottoline, April 12, 1911, Morning letter, Document no. 000029, Box no. 2.53, Bertrand Russell Archive, McMaster University Library/Ottoline Morrell Collection, Box 18, Folder 4, Harry Ransom Center, University of Texas, Austin.

existentially. Thus the issue of religion remained with Russell, however much he had put behind him any sort of theological orthodoxy. Just as science had replaced theology as the pinnacle and judge of all aspirants to human knowledge, so too literary figures had replaced theologians.

Russell's desire was to become such an author and thus authority, just as his grandfather Lord John Russell had had his own "strong literary proclivities."[60] The problem, however, was frustratingly more or less always the same—how to construct a religion that was not incongruous with how science understood ourselves and the world. In other words, Russell insisted that one could not violate his knowledge of reality by embracing a religion that denied that knowledge, so as to illicitly have a religion by sacrificing truth. Such a failure, indeed cowardice, he would attribute to guilty philosophers, notably among them his contemporaries McTaggart and the Frenchman, Bergson, and even long since dead philosophers, among the guiltiest, Immanuel Kant. Could Russell do better than they?[61]

In 1911 Russell sent Ottoline pieces of a work from the years 1902 and 1903 and given the tentative title of "The Pilgrimage of Life." He hardly thought well of the work and made reference to his collapsing marriage as something of the catalyst in which the piece was written. Though the ideas presented in this work resemble portions of his youthful "Greek Exercises," "Pilgrimage" tries to provide consolations for living life in a difficult world.

Near the end of the unfinished work, Russell writes, "True, the good is transitory, and truth permits no mysticism which would render its value eternal; but in its little moment, which alone is ours, the good is good, and this must be enough for us."[62] Russell means the human takes up the fight that any presumed God has, from all indications, abdicated, and now makes it his fight as he resists the controlling powers of reality

60. MacCarthy, *Lady John Russell*, 57.

61. Rempel and Moran conceive of the dilemma for Russell in the following manner: "Russell naturally felt tinges of doubt about any benevolence in a universe that permits young life, such as that of his parents, to be so easily snuffed out. But Russell did not become an absurdist or nihilist. He sought to build back lost meaning, to do the work which Christian apologists were unable to do. His excursions into an imaginative review of the past, and into the possibility of caring for humanity in its largest dimension, are evidence of the most positive kind of creativity. Russell's disappointments in the literary results were on a scale with the questions he asked, but the effort, even in its fragmentary remains, was heroic." Rempel and Moran, "Introduction," in Russell, *CP* 12:xxvii-xxviii.

62. Russell, "Pilgrimage of Life," *CP* 12:55.

and the universe. With this understanding, the salutary individual refuses to give any worship to an indifferent and amoral cosmic power simply because the cosmos is greater than the human. According to Russell, the human now resists this God (or matter) greater than himself, and thus this emancipated individual bears similarity to a defiant and rebel devil of older religion.[63] In seeking a religion, among the obstacles to be avoided, we must resist falling into the mindset of a slave. This is why, therefore, true religiosity requires real rebellion, or said more accurately, refusal to worship before what is unworthy of worship. While containing a strong element of reverent acquiescence, real religion consequently manifests an equally strong element of rebellion. That rebellion is rooted in the refusal to be cowered by a reality where matter, in the end, will win out over us. Thus, an appropriate religion issues from a position of conceded but managed weakness and rightly refuses to be subjugated to what is, simply because that reality is materially more powerful. By this means, the impetus to religion is aligned with an appropriate response to our condition. Russell, however, does make a concession:

> But in the face of facts it becomes difficult to retain this conviction unless by the aid of some kind of mysticism. The individual life, it seems plain, is extinguished by Death; the life of the human race must be extinguished sooner or later. The only thing of whose eternity we feel fairly assured is matter; before life began, matter calmly went its way; accidentally but inevitably it will again destroy life. Ruthless, inexorable, careless alike of good and evil, matter unceasingly pursues its purposeless journeys to and fro through the blank abyss of space; matter alone is powerful, matter alone seems God.[64]

However, despite Russell's dabbling with mysticism, doubts seemed to have won, for advocates of mysticism always contend for more than can be truly believed. The mystical effort will inevitably be tempted to assert that the universe is on the side of right in some mysterious way. For Russell, however, this flies in the face of fact. At the same time, "So great is the value of human virtue that it alone redeems the universe; it is for us

---

63. Interestingly, in a letter to Constance Malleson, of October 25, 1917, he writes: "I want to see my way straight—I wish there were monasteries for atheists—if there were I would renounce the world and the flesh—but I would never renounce the devil!" Russell to Malleson, Document no. 200220, Box no. 6.65, Bertrand Russell Archives, McMaster University Library.

64. Russell, "Pilgrimage of Life," *CP* 12:54–55.

to protest, seriously and sadly, against the evil world which is omnipotent except over our thoughts; the terrible duty is ours of creating, in the brief and painful struggle against the Gods, whatever of excellence the world is to contain."[65] Despite the encouraging aspect of such words, the underlying lament is palpable, for with it comes Russell's admission that

> The love of God cannot be replaced by anything similar in the lives of those to whom belief has grown impossible. For the only love that need never be checked is the love of goodness itself; and when we cease to personify goodness, to believe that it lives and exists eternally, the repose of divine love is lost, and we are left to create, by our own efforts, whatever of good our powers may render possible. In varying degrees, the good is embodied in the things that exists; but all are transient, and human beings, the best of all, are among the most transient.[66]

For such reasons, an abiding humanism and confidence in the consolations of philosophy, while sometimes defended by Russell, were secondary to his love and preference for "the sea, the stars, and the night wind in waste places," a phrase found rather often in Russell. Such things evoked a transcendence that Russell found difficult to live without. At the same time, Russell's notion of intellectual honesty did not permit "truth" that could not or would not run his gauntlet of intellectual rigor. Left with beliefs shorn of metaphysical backing, man has his back against the wall. The individual living in such a universe must hold himself and his values up with recognition that he alone gives rise to them and supports them. Without the transitory humans, there would be nothing to support such values in a universe that denies them.

Russell's hopeful work of "Prisons" of 1911 and 1912 was developed in conjunction with discussions with Ottoline over religion, but never reached a final form, though portions of it found a place in his other works. For example, Russell used elements of the earlier work in his 1912 essay, "The Essence of Religion" of 1912. Likewise, some of the ending paragraphs of Russell's *The Problems of Philosophy*, also published in 1912, incorporated material from "Prisons," though the fusion was hardly seamless. The last chapter of *The Problems of Philosophy*, entitled "The Value of Philosophy," has an existential aura quite distinct from any of the prior fourteen chapters. Nevertheless, this single chapter resonated with many

---

65. Russell, "Pilgrimage of Life," *CP* 12:55.
66. Russell, "Pilgrimage of Life," *CP* 12:39.

university teachers of philosophy seeking to defend their discipline and frequently appears in introductions to the subject. The Russellian verbal eloquence is on exhibit within particular sentences and paragraphs. The main point in the last chapter of *Problems*, lifted from the prior "Prisons," is how the enlargement of the human develops through the study of philosophy: "In contemplation, on the contrary, we start from the non-Self, and through its greatness the boundaries of the Self are enlarged; through the infinity of the universe the mind which contemplates it achieves some share in infinity. For this reason greatness of soul is not fostered by those philosophies which assimilate the universe to Man."[67] The concluding sentence is a cardinal Russell doctrine. That is, provincial and puny human desires will find and should find no place in philosophy and are apt to skew truth for the sake of such paltry desires.

Moreover, in the effort of Russell (and Ottoline) to come up with a philosophy of life that embraced both mystical experience and reason, what might have become a final "Prisons" was shelved in early 1912 as Russell shifted his interest to an aspiring novella, *The Perplexities of John Forstice*.[68] Though largely written in 1912, this work was not printed until after Russell's death on his insistence. Partly this was due to Russell's perception of the flawed fictional writing, but more so in light of his later assertion that the work was "much too favorable to religion."[69] Indeed, he expresses his misgivings about the work as it "represented my opinions during only a very short period. My views in the second part were very sentimental, much too mild, and much too favourable to religion. In all this I was unduly influenced by Lady Ottoline Morrell."[70] The desire to distance himself from any evident sympathies for religion is significant.

Nevertheless, in 1912 in *Forstice*, Russell gave himself the task of finding a way of looking at the world that could take the place of older forms of religion, without the falsity and harmfulness attached to their histories. This would of course require a program that did not stray too far from the reigning authority of reason. Under the influence of Ottoline, he would eventually admit failure, as his later strictures against

67. Russell, *Problems*, 159. This is why Russell does not laud consolations of philosophy.

68. "*Prisons* was wrong I think, simply because it was expository. One must have a more artistic form." Russell to Ottoline, February 12, 1912, Document no. 000341, Box no. 2.56, Bertrand Russell Archives, McMaster University Library/Ottoline Morrell Collection, Box 20, Folder 5, Harry Ransom Center, University of Texas, Austin.

69. Quoted in Clark, *Russell*, 182; *CP* 12:127.

70. Clark, *Russell*, 182; *CP* 12:127.

publishing *Forstice* attest. Past thinkers had tried a similar task, though virtually all took leave of sober reason in order to have their religion. These illicit marriages failed in Russell's eyes, so he set himself to see if, with him writing the vows, he might succeed where others had failed.

In the quest for a viable religion, however, the reassertion of an intellect sparing virtually no one always came back to deny him what he hoped to have. Because Russell felt the burden of religious unbelief in an uncommon way, he most often acknowledged the need for a religion that could sustain in the absence of those religious beliefs that he relentlessly and severely criticized. Russell, known as the rationalist *par excellence* to popular audiences, was searching for something that his tight-fisted intellect denied him. With such a desire, Russell now turned to writing fiction with *Forstice*. For a thinker adept at analysis who could produce dazzling phraseology coupled with succinct and minimal word counts achieving results that mopped up the question with Russell's answer, the different requirements for fiction, for a story, plot, and tone constituted formidable challenges. His habits of mind were hardly suited to writing strong fiction. While Russell could spin words virtually without equal, he failed at fiction.[71] This is why friends who took a look at *The Perplexities of John Forstice* told Russell that he needed scenery, action, and sparkling dialogue in a work too laden with speeches and oratory from characters obscure to the reader except as orators.

There is scarcely any development of Russell's characters in this story. In *Forstice*, the last speaker in the roundtable—distinguished from the other participants by his distance from the ethereal heights of the others—nevertheless expresses his down-to-earth ideas in phraseology every bit as finessed as that of his learned company. He contends, "We common people, who are, after all, the great majority of mankind, are too limited, too full of daily cares, to appreciate the refined delights of your

---

71. "Russell proved too good at 'thinking' his story, little good at all at imagining it into being." Rempel and Moran in Russell, *CP* 12:127. In his book *The Art of Fiction*, 62, John Gardner writes, "But however it may be achieved, in all great fiction, primary emotion (our emotion as we read, or the characters' emotions, or some combination of both) must sooner or later lift off from the particular and be transformed to an expression of what is universally good in human life—what promotes happiness for the individual alone and in society; in other words, some statement on value. In good fiction, this universal statement is likely to be too subtle, too loaded with qualifications, to be expressed in any way but the story's way; it may be impossible, that is, to reduce to any rule of behavior or general thesis. We *understand* the value, understand it with great precision, but even the shrewdest literary critic may have trouble formulating it in words and thus telling us the story's 'message.'"

various heavens. We cannot understand mathematics and philosophy, we are indifferent to poetry, and music only pleases us when we can dance to it. We like novels well enough, but they must be about lost wills or amazing murders, not about the mystic marriage of pain."[72] This advocate for the plight of the common person instances the example of his washerwoman, insisting that none of the advice given by those around him would do anything for this burdened beast of a human being. In other words, his charge is that all these eloquent speech-makers have been preaching to themselves; they offer nothing, or next to nothing, to the rest of humankind. And so, this final speaker, Giuseppe Alegno, challenges his listeners to come back to his washerwoman's world—the world of most humans. The efforts of the thinkers of the world to lift people skyward having failed, Alegno suggests a better way:

> And so the machine goes on, grinding out suffering; and so, I suppose, it will go on till the human race is extinct. I do not believe what is needed is a gospel, but merely courage, and the habit of not reflecting on our own misfortunes. If you ask what purpose is served by human life in general, and whether it would be better it should cease, I can only say I do not know. But if any purpose is served, it must be one that can enter into the daily lives of common men, not a rare and difficult good, realized only by the few, to whom all the other millions are to be ministering slaves.[73]

Despite this character's woeful warning, Russell seems most concerned that Forstice's religious unbelief is maintained and respected as a legitimate and honest quest for truth, though his unbelief had been jarred temporarily over the death of his wife. The honorable nun in Russell's story (modeled after Ottoline) gives deference to Forstice's unbelief while Forstice accords a modicum of respect for her belief: "At length she spoke; her voice appeared to come from far away, as if from another world, yet it had notes of strangely poignant feeling, holding an agony of compassion for all the sorrows of mankind. Her vivid memory of tiny details about his uncle surprised him. Gradually she passed on to speak of the heavenly love, avoiding mention of beliefs which she knew he could not share."[74]

---

72. Russell, *Perplexities of John Forstice*, CP 12:143.
73. Russell, *Perplexities of John Forstice*, CP 12:144–45.
74. Russell, *Perplexities of John Forstice*, CP 12:150.

Forstice, though feeling uplifted by the nun's experience, is still caught in the morass of matter, and with it unbelief remains. Thus, as is commonplace in Russell's writings on religion, Forstice scarcely advances in the attempt to obtain something he lacked before and still lacks. Instead, what he came with is reaffirmed, with nothing more resolved and nothing really modified, except for the fact that in the world of people, there is nevertheless "some hidden beauty buried beneath the visible horror. The new insight which the last hour had brought could not, he felt, be all delusion; yet it was hard to find a place for it beside his other beliefs—the belief that the soul dies at death, that Matter rules the world, that spiritual forces are powerless against natural laws, mere shining bubbles on the surface of the hurrying stream."[75] Logic and reason again overrule any mystical moments.

As for any rapprochement between mysticism and science, Fortice (or Russell) asserts, "But here the verdict of science is absolute: if the vision is to have a real place, to be a source of wisdom, not of illusion, it must accept the every-day world, retaining the mystic's feeling without the mystic's beliefs as to the nature of the universe."[76] So as to justify this partitioning of the ways of knowing, Russell contends through Fortice that "Loyalty to science is not hostile to the vision, but a necessary outcome of it. Indifference to knowledge is a kind of irreverence, an assumption that our ignorant imaginings surpass what really is. All search for truth is a kind of reverence, a kind of worship, and all fear of truth a blasphemy."[77] Russell affirms through Fortice how distant his belief about the world is from that of the nun (Ottoline).

The self-understanding of Fortice is hardly bettered by the end of the story. Did Russell think he could discover or produce something in the fictional form not captured in his expository essays? Even as a fictional story, the tale must not take license with the truth, and this Russell affirms in his story. That is, the story must have a plausibility without any kind of special pleading or resorting to sentimentality. Russell, like his character Forstice, possibly hoped that someone might have seen or witnessed something denied him. As he remarked to Ottoline in his letter of August 14, 1912, "I wish I knew more of the world—it is a dreadful thing to have been a student up to the age of forty!"[78] However, no such

---

75. Russell, *Perplexities of John Forstice*, CP 12:152.
76. Russell, *Perplexities of John Forstice*, CP 12:153.
77. Russell, *Perplexities of John Forstice*, CP 12:154.
78. Russell to Ottoline, August 14, 1912, Document no. 000527, Box no. 2.59,

candidate or revelation comes to Russell or to Forstice. What comes, yet again, is the grim truth that the world is not one with us. Science still holds firm against any pretense that our human condition is otherwise.

D. VEXATIONS WITH MYSTICISM

In the second decade of the twentieth century, Ottoline's mystical strain forced the issue on Russell, with Russell's essay "Mysticism and Logic" being published in 1914 in *The Hibbert Journal*. This essay represents a significant turn from the likes of "Free Man's Worship" and "The Essence of Religion." In this essay Russell brings the subject of mysticism to the feet of his overriding epistemological considerations. For Russell the viability of any contention or assertion always comes down to our grounds or justification for believing.

While conceding the place mysticism holds in the history of thought, Russell is nevertheless committed to little more than an agnostic's admission on its possible legitimacy with reference to truth: "Of the reality or unreality of the mystic's world I know nothing. I have no wish to deny it, nor even to declare that the insight which reveals it is not a genuine insight."[79] Russell's point is that we possess another way of knowing, or perhaps we should say, checking what the mystic propounds, that puts the mystical perspective on the defensive. Our fact-checking abilities permit us, at least in principle, the option of placing in doubt some and perhaps all of what the mystic claims. Mystics, moreover, or at least some of them, have denied any such vulnerability; though Russell admires elements of the work and words of various mystics, he must be persuaded by scientific evaluation.

However, some overlap between the mindsets of the rationalist and the mystic can be considered, and Russell appears ready to consider the possibility:

> I yet believe that, by sufficient restraint, there is an element of wisdom to be learned from the mystical way of feeling, which does not seem attainable in any other manner. If this is the truth, mysticism is to be commended as an attitude towards life, not as a creed about the world. The metaphysical creed, I

Bertrand Russell Archives, McMaster University Library/Ottoline Morrell Collection, Box 21, Folder 5, Harry Ransom Center, University of Texas, Austin.

79. Russell, "Mysticism and Logic," *CP* 12:164.

shall maintain, is a mistaken outcome of the emotion, although this emotion, as colouring and informing all other thoughts and feelings, is the inspirer of whatever is best in Man. Even the cautious and patient investigation of truth by science, which seems the very antithesis of the mystic's swift certainty, may be fostered and nourished by that very spirit of reverence in which mysticism lives and moves.[80]

This division of labor, if one might call it such, however, is hardly very promising, because the mystic works from emotion which ultimately has to give due deference to reason while the truth-wielding procedures of the scientific impetus make judgements. Nevertheless, Russell concedes that a thread of mystical exuberance is present even in the "cautious and patient investigation of truth by science," though in the end all such efforts are subject to the policing of reason. The mystic vision may prompt genius, and thus mystics are permitted some entryway by Russell in the quest for knowledge. However, assertions about reality must be weighed by the mechanisms and procedures of rational thinking and intellect. So, for all of that, mysticism, ultimately couched in emotion from which its vision springs, is not allowed to vindicate itself—it must be vindicated by another; and emotional hypotheses about reality, such as those found in religion, have not fared well under the scrutiny of reasoned adjudication.

Nonetheless, Russell does not completely rule out some contribution of the mystic vision and the guiding lamp it sometimes provides for knowledge. Although mysticism cannot win in competition with science and reason, Russell still permits it to work, though only if this accessory to knowledge knows its place and the constraints of its working environment.

Russell's intellect is his gatekeeper for what he can and cannot believe. Only when wrongly constrained will it make grudging but mistaken exceptions for any candidates who appear at its door. We remember that Russell's intellect grants no privileges or passes to anyone or anything, not even what he may find most endearing, for this unbending requirement is the price paid for truth. A lifelong annoyance to Russell were people who consciously or unconsciously refused to follow this dictum, found among both ordinary mortals and professional philosophers. They simply refused to separate themselves enough from their most cherished beliefs to evaluate those beliefs objectively for truth or falsity. Russell, moreover, attempted to make what was usually a secondary nature in

---

80. Russell, "Mysticism and Logic," *CP* 12:164.

most persons, his primary nature. No wonder, therefore, that he was often perceived as unfeeling and cold toward others. True philosophy, therefore, to a great degree is unnatural in people, and its true spirit must be inculcated and practiced before it can become second nature.

According to Russell, when feeling the pinch of reason one may desire a retreat from reason, rather than enduring the discomfort of watching presumptions and wishes dashed upon the rocks of rational analysis. David Hume, the Scottish philosopher whom Russell occasionally lauds and commends for Ottoline's reading, famously described the fears raised by the comforts of our ordinary world becoming unraveled in philosophical study so intensely, and therefore frightfully, that Hume fled from his study to the parlor to resume living in a safer and not comfortless world. Russell eschews such an attempt to flee from the truth, for flight presumes a weak and cowardly attitude toward the respect due truth. Furthermore, such human frailty exhibits how little natural allegiance people have to truth over their wishes and vested interests. This is why Russell rather regularly in his letters to Ottoline questions what evidence she can marshal for her beliefs. Such a demand on Russell's part caused wrinkles in their relationship more than once, but almost always ended by an apology from Russell for his not infrequent tirades on the matter. On occasion, however, Ottoline would face up to Russell: "I cannot understand why you feel I must be dishonest and why you are so intolerant to my belief. It seems to me as if someone who did not care for music to be intolerant to anyone who cared passionately for it, and to whom it was a tremendous revelation of life. But I suppose it is different."[81]

In writing to Ottoline after a period of intermittent squabbling, he confesses, "What belongs to the most serious part of me can never be wholly happy, because I am not happy enough inwardly in that part, and I know I should give a great deal of pain to any one I cared for as much as I care for you. The only thing that could cure this would be religion—but I am so restless and prone to doubt that it is hard to get a religion that will endure—but if I ever could, no one could help me to it as you could. All that I have been saying is the most absolute sober truth."[82]

So Russell was caught in a titanic struggle in which Ottoline could ultimately be of no help. She could only counter some of his restless

---

81. Ottoline to Russell, December 27, 1911, quoted in Seymour, *Ottoline*, 123.
82. Russell to Ottoline, April 5, 1913, in Griffin, *Letters*, 1:453.

nature by eliciting a temporary peace until his episodic doubts disrupted still waters as he charged her with having bought her religious peace with a price he would not remit. The philosopher Russell could not and would not venture down such a path, though he could sometimes look the other way while Ottoline did. Russell's point of view on religious belief did not exempt even his best friendships from severe squabbles and indeed provoked estrangements in relationships over the subject. In his firm allegiance to truth, Russell very rarely spared himself or others unpleasantries. Russell felt assured that religious belief could not be vindicated from a modern perspective; therefore, the only way to retain something of both was to trim religious belief of those elements that scientific modernity would not permit. Chief of these was the continuing presumption of religious believers that we do not reside in an indifferent amoral cosmos. Because he cared for Ottoline, Russell could only hope that his warnings directed at unjustifiable religious inclinations were not too threatening to her. However, as his insistence on truth became too much for her to bear, Russell tried to explain. He seemed to honestly prefer religious clashes not to happen, though they did happen, sometimes savagely, though Russell had put out his warnings in advance:

> About religion: there is not the slightest importance in the difference of actual beliefs, but nevertheless there is something important, which must be approached some day, and which I rather shrink from approaching. I think the point is that I should consider it more necessary than you would to put away all feeling before considering a religious question. For instance, take a question which does not arouse emotion, such as 'Is there a luminiferous aether?' You would not imagine that you could have an opinion on this question, but you would believe what scientific people said if they were in agreement. Now the question whether there is a God is more difficult, but of the same kind—that is to say, it is just as much a purely intellectual question only there is no agreement. It is true one has feelings about it more than about the aether, but they don't bear on the question whether there is a God. I do not for a moment suppose that you would tolerate believing what you felt might be untrue; but I do believe that a stronger passion for truth would have carried you to a more or less different notion as to what is evidence for a belief. It is because I believe this that there is an element which is important in our differences. I do not want you to think that I don't believe anybody with a strong passion for truth could believe. I think Thomas Aquinas, who founded Catholic

orthodoxy, had probably as great a love of truth as I have. And if you continue to believe everything you believe now, I shall not mind in the least; but as things stand I do not feel your vision quite clear or quite unclouded by desire, tho' I see you are not conscious that this is so, so that I think I may be wrong.[83]

The abiding problem is that the world is not our world; this fact must be squarely faced. However, human dedication to the good of its own creation should persist despite the factual state of the world and our consequent place in it. While this scenario will present reason to fret among our weaker members, the recognition that humans bring something of value to the universe that would be lacking without us, can give sustaining courage despite inevitable defeat. Such an undertaking requires an extraordinary balancing act, with traditional and orthodox religion stripped of virtually all its creedal beliefs. This requires an extraordinary effort at constructing a humanistic religion in a world in which only matter seems abiding.

As if Russell's conflicts with Ottoline over religion were not exasperating enough, the subject took another twist when he encountered Ludwig Wittgenstein. In the beginning of that relationship, Russell's letters to Ottoline are peppered with his enthusiasm for this very bright pupil from Austria, though the relationship between teacher and student changes in time such that after some years Russell became something of a student of Wittgenstein and then an opponent over their differing notions of philosophy. The debate began innocently enough, but gradually something of a religious strain developed. While Ottoline would sometimes dare to push back against Russell's criticisms of her religion, Wittgenstein ultimately became an overt critic of Russell's religious and ethical views.

---

83. Russell to Ottoline, May 13, 1911, Document no. 000066, Box no. 2.53, Bertrand Russell Archives, McMaster University Library, Ottoline Morrell Collection, Box 18, Folder 6, Harry Ransom Center, University of Texas, Austin. The high marks given here to Aquinas are not found elsewhere in Russell's verdicts on the medieval philosopher. Indeed, Russell has been taken to task, particularly by medievalists, for his estimation of Aquinas: "There is little of the true philosophic spirit in Aquinas. He does not, like the Platonic Socrates, set out to follow wherever the argument may lead. He is not engaged in an inquiry, the result of which it is impossible to know in advance. Before he begins to philosophize, he already knows the truth; it is declared in the Catholic faith. If he can find apparently rational arguments for some parts of the faith, so much the better; if he cannot, he need only fall back on revelation. The finding of arguments for a conclusion given in advance is not philosophy, but special pleading. I cannot, therefore, feel that he deserves to be put on a level with the best philosophers either of Greece or of modern times." Russell, *History*, 463.

In the very beginning of his relationship with Wittgenstein, Russell assumed he had a comrade-in-arms who marches only to the beat of reason and logic. On the matter of religion and specifically Christianity, early on Russell makes his boast to Ottoline that if she judges Russell severely critical on religion, Wittgenstein was even more fierce: "He is far more terrible with Christians than I am."[84] Indeed, the ardent rationalism of the early Wittgenstein seemed evident by his great interest in logic and mathematics. In addition, Russell surely felt a bit vindicated in his perception of his student when Wittgenstein showed some approval of Russell's critical essay on Bergson. However, Wittgenstein's dislike of "Free Man's Worship" and of the end of Russell's *The Problems of Philosophy* should have warned Russell that Wittgenstein's conception of philosophy, as well as his ideas on religion, departed and would continue to manifest differences from those of Russell.

In the beginning of the relationship between teacher and student, there was an exquisite beauty in Russell's descriptions of becoming acquainted with a rather odd but unmistakably gifted student, who almost out of nowhere appears at Russell's doorstep in October of 1911. Not a native English speaker, he nevertheless insists on speaking English to Russell, even though Russell, thinking him a German, offers to speak German. In retrospect, this small incident might have been a first clue that this student had a mind and will of his own. Nevertheless, Wittgenstein explains his visit motivated by having heard about Russell's work in mathematical logic, and further expounds to Russell his own interests lying in that area, having come to the subject through the study of aeronautics. Despite this potential student's many oddities, as Russell became more acquainted with Wittgenstein, he pushed aside his initial reservations and the relationship between the two moves ahead.[85]

With a shared interest in mathematical logic, and with Wittgenstein rather frequently visiting Russell in his rooms at Trinity College to

---

84. Russell to Ottoline, March 18, 1912, Griffin, *Letters*, 1:418.

85. "At the end of his first term at Trinity, he came to me and said: 'Do you think I am an absolute idiot?' I said: 'Why do you want to know?' He replied: 'Because if I am I shall become an aeronaut, but if I am not I shall become a philosopher.' I said to him: 'My dear fellow, I don't know whether you are an absolute idiot or not, but if you will write me an essay during the vacation upon any philosophical topic that interests you, I will read it and tell you.' He did so, and brought it to me at the beginning of the next term. As soon as I read the first sentence, I became persuaded that he was a man of genius, and assured him that he should on no account become an aeronaut." Russell, *1914–1944*, 137.

discuss the topic, along with exploring some of his existential anxieties, the pair soon become quite close personally. So striking and gifted is this pupil that in time Wittgenstein begins to gain the attention of others in university. However, because of Wittgenstein's evident brilliance, Russell seems protective to the point of uneasily sharing his prize student with competing teachers at Cambridge. Indeed, perhaps partly because of this protective attitude, Russell's prize pupil is somewhat late in receiving an invitation to the organization of the Apostles. However, in only a matter of a couple months, Wittgenstein withdraws from the Apostles, finding the whole thing not to his liking; it seems apparent that Russell's pupil was hardly fit company for the group. Nevertheless, during this honeymoon season, Russell continues to enjoy his student for the most part.

As Russell indicates to Ottoline, beyond shared interest in logic, Russell quickly notices that Wittgenstein possesses the artistic temperament. Trained in music, Wittgenstein manifests a personality type that Russell revels in watching. This student additionally had traits of mind that most people lacked. One that Russell especially liked was Wittgenstein's glee when something was disproved. Russell noticed that he displayed no lament when a possibility was eliminated or shown fallacious; rather, his desire for truth provoked no remorse when a candidate failed, for the claimants to truth were now narrowed. The opposite response, Russell often contended, afflicted people's inability to bear the scrutiny of beliefs for fear of revealing such beliefs as false. Wittgenstein's notion of truth was thus robust enough for Russell's respect. Wittgenstein's genius was not the only factor that drew Russell to this student, however. Russell also felt a responsibility for his student, in part because of Wittgenstein's vulnerabilities. In Russell's genuine affection for his student, he often remarks to Ottoline that he loves him like a son.

While straining under the need to unearth some possible cogency for Ottoline's religious propensities and mystical inclinations, Russell apparently had not discerned that Wittgenstein might be as mystically inclined as Ottoline. Nevertheless, Russell should have noticed. Some of Russell's most popular essays, such as "The Free Man's Worship" and "The Essence of Religion," were unpopular with Wittgenstein and he told Russell so. Furthermore, and indicating even a deeper chasm between the two philosophers, was Wittgenstein's dislike of the last chapter of *Problems of Philosophy*. There Russell had presented philosophy or the philosophical life as the pinnacle of human achievement in the effort to arrive at the elusive goal of finding truth. However, Wittgenstein would pursue another direction philosophically. When he, for example, writes that philosophy leaves things as they are, this has the effect of calling off the philosophical dogs that had previously and so incessantly badgered belief. Wittgenstein's part in the turn to postmodern thinking is perceptible in much that he later writes.

To Russell, this was to give up the philosopher's *raison d'être* and the opposite of what Russell's method of philosophical analysis was endeavoring to do. Indeed, Russell might say that at least the Hegelians and Idealists had tried to pull back the covers to show what reality was; the new breed of philosophers were only interested in the covers. Russell laid much of the fault for this at the feet of a student he had once thought would maintain Anglo-American philosophy in a Russell-like tradition.

Russell had manifestly failed to see that Wittgenstein, like Ottoline, was leaning in another direction, much of it away from the bent of Russell. A parting of the ways, therefore, was in the future as disagreement intensified while Russell increasingly attributes dubious motivations to Wittgenstein. After Russell detects the mystical motif in Wittgenstein, he blames this on Wittgenstein's lack of motivation toward and disinterest in truth: "He has penetrated deep into mystical ways of thought and feeling, but I think (though he wouldn't agree) that what he likes best in mysticism is its power to make him stop thinking."[86] In this accusation, Russell asserts another of his polemics not only against the mystically inclined, but against religious belief—that is, having recourse to God relieves one of the burden of seeking the real cause or reason of things. However, as the parenthetical phrase above indicates, clearly Russell and Wittgenstein had clashed over mysticism and had come to a disagreement. As with religion, Russell had some qualified sympathies for mysticism, but more often figured as critic than as champion. As mysticism penetrated into regions difficult for words to express, words became fewer and sometimes fell away entirely. Russell certainly had had enough exposure to this strain of seeing the world to understand something of the mechanics of mysticism, but Russell could not tolerate words committing one to silence. If this was the mystic's requirement, then there must be a parting of the ways with mysticism.

In 1901, before becoming acquainted with Ottoline or meeting Wittgenstein, Russell had been jolted by an unforgettable event when he witnessed the suffering of Evelyn Whitehead over what seems a heart

---

86. Russell to Ottoline, December 20, 1919, in Griffin, *Letters*, 2:199.

attack. For Russell this event was little short of a life-changing experience, though in his *Autobiography*, he downplays its permanent effect. At the time, however, Russell felt that a new understanding of the world was given to him.

> One day, Gilbert Murray came to Newnham to read part of his translation of The Hippolytus, then unpublished. Alys and I went to hear him, and I was profoundly stirred by the beauty of the poetry. When we came home, we found Mrs. Whitehead undergoing an unusually severe bout of pain. She seemed cut off from everyone and everything by walls of agony, and the sense of the solitude of each human soul suddenly overwhelmed me. Ever since my marriage, my emotional life had been calm and superficial. I had forgotten all the deeper issues, and had been content with flippant cleverness. Suddenly the ground seemed to give way beneath me, and I found myself in quite another region. Within five minutes I went through some such reflections as the following: the loneliness of the human soul is unendurable; nothing can penetrate it except the highest intensity of the sort of love that religious teachers have preached; whatever does not spring from this motive is harmful, or at best useless; it follows that war is wrong, that a public school education is abominable, that the use of force is to be deprecated, and that in human relations one should penetrate to the core of loneliness in each person and speak to that. . . . At the end of those five minutes, I had become a completely different person. For a time, a sort of mystic illumination possessed me. I felt that I knew the inmost thoughts of everybody that I met in the street, and though this was, no doubt, a delusion, I did in actual fact find myself in far closer touch than previously with all my friends, and many of my acquaintances. Having been an imperialist, I became during those five minutes a pro-Boer and a pacifist. Having for years cared only for exactness and analysis, I found myself filled with semi-mystical feelings about beauty, with an intense interest in children, and with a desire almost as profound as that of the Buddha to find some philosophy which should make human life endurable. A strange excitement possessed me, containing intense pain but also some element of triumph through the fact that I could dominate pain, and make it, as I thought, a gateway to wisdom. The mystic insight which I then imagined myself to possess has largely faded, and the habit of analysis has reasserted itself. But something of what I thought I saw in that moment has remained always with me, causing my attitude during the first war, my interest in children,

my indifference to minor misfortunes, and a certain emotional tone in all my human relations.[87]

When good friend Lowes Dickinson told Russell that he had had no mystical experiences of his own, but nevertheless believed in the cogency of such experiences, Russell, who had just had such an experience as chronicled here, nevertheless relates in a letter to Ottoline of May 15, 1911, that he and Goldie, "had a long discussion as to whether the intellect is the only means of attaining truth—I yes, Goldie No, Major slightly no, but not decidedly. You would have been against me. Goldie, as usual, defended mystical illumination; I said it was mere illusion."[88] Somewhat similarly, in a letter to Lucy Donnelly, Russell comments on how much he has enjoyed reading William James's *Varieties of Religious Experience*, enjoying every bit of it, "except the conclusions."[89] He could affirm no metaphysical experience lacking epistemological assurances. As much as Russell might have wanted to give some guarded legitimacy to mystical illumination, he ended by giving it very little.

Years later and a decade after the conclusion of World War I, when G. E. Moore and Russell are contemplating possible examiners for Wittgenstein at Cambridge, Russell tells Moore in a letter of May 27, 1929, that Wittgenstein was not apt to want Russell as an examiner: "The last time we met he was so much pained by the fact of my not being

---

87. Russell, *1872–1914*, 234–35. Russell makes reference about this event at least twice in his letters to Ottoline. He also contends that his wife Alys at the time was uncomprehending of the effect of this event upon Russell and his subsequent life. It is possible that some of Russell's antagonism toward the Pearsall Smiths, though perhaps lesser so to Alys herself, was a perceived lack of spiritual depth, and may be judged by Russell as the habitual lack associated with persons of traditional religion. If so, this made him distant from Alys and her family, but such an experience as occurred in 1901 also separated him from the mass of people he knew. In speaking of it to Ottoline in his letter of July 21, 1911, he writes, "In spite of many faults and many backslidings I succeeded on the whole in what I undertook then. . . . It was during that year I lernt whatever wisdom I possessed before meeting you." Russell to Ottoline, Document no. 000154, Box no. 2.54, Bertrand Russell Archives, McMaster University Library/Ottoline Morrell Collection, Box 19, Folder 4, Harry Ransom Center, University of Texas, Austin.

88. Russell to Ottoline, May 15, 1911, Document no. 000068A, Box no. 2.53, Bertrand Russell Archives, McMaster University Library/Ottoline Morrell Collection, Box 18, Folder 6, Harry Ransom Center, University of Texas, Austin.

89. Russell to Lucy Donnelly, September 1, 1902, in Russell, *1872–1914*, 268. Russell, of course, is not unique in such a reaction to James's work. With reference to James's *Varieties*, the French Thomist, Etienne Gilson, remarked, "After reading W. James, I still want to know if my religious experience is an experience of God, or an experience of myself." Gilson, *Reason and Revelation*, 97.

a Christian that he has avoided me ever since; I do not know whether his pain on this account has grown less, but he must still dislike me, as he has never communicated with me since."[90] Indeed, Wittgenstein had lost much of his previous affection for Russell and soon, in 1930, family problems for Russell in his marriage to Dora Black and with the running of Beacon Hill School in Cornwall, a school that Russell and his wife had together started, intruded.[91]

90. Russell to Moore, May 27, 1929, Document no. 053037, Box no. 5.31, Bertrand Russell Archives, McMaster University Library.

91. "Given the litany of Russell's troubles at this time, it is surprising that he coped as well as he did with the rigors of examining Wittgenstein's work. For his part, Wittgenstein was a harsh critic of Russell's predicament. He loathed Russell's popular works: *The Conquest of Happiness* was a 'vomative'; *What I Believe* was 'absolutely not a harmless thing.'" And when, during a discussion at Cambridge, someone was inclined to defend Russell's views on marriage, sex, and 'free love' (expressed in *Marriage and Morals*), Wittgenstein replied: "If a person tells me he has been to the worst places I have no right to judge him, but if he tells me it was his superior wisdom that enabled him to go there, then I know he is a fraud." Monk, *Wittgenstein*, 294. The perceivable differences between the two men antedate this time by many years. In 1914 Wittgenstein wrote a letter to Russell expressing his feeling that "You may be right in saying that we ourselves are not so very different, but our ideals could not be more so. And that's why we haven't been able and we shan't ever be able to talk about anything involving our value-judgements without either becoming hypocritical or falling out. I think this is incontestable; I had noticed it a long time ago, and it was frightful for me, because it tainted our relations with one another . . . ." McGuinness and Wright, *Ludwig Wittgenstein*, 79.

8

Russell in Contention over Religious Belief

A. WITH WILLIAM JAMES

Oddly enough, despite his qualified sympathies with religion, Russell was a fervent critic of those seeking to defend something of religion from a total secular victory in the modern world. Moreover, Russell never seemed to meet a religious apologist whom he liked, and he took significant issue with almost all maneuvering by apologists for religion who sought to preserve something of a religion in an increasingly scientific and secular culture. This opprobrium includes the thinkers examined in this chapter—William James, T. S. Eliot, Henri Bergson, and George Santayana. Despite Russell's own advocacy for a personal religion, virtually every religious apologist Russell encounters, again, he strenuously opposes. Russell, nevertheless, ironically shared something of their concern. All the same, Russell's lack of affinity for and indeed harsh criticism of these thinkers and systems of thought is based on his refusal to defend a religious view of the world that in any way presumed to revise (or undermine) reality in the effort to conform reality to religious tenets. Simply stated, for Russell the scientific view of the world cannot be evaded by the desire to maintain a religious view of the world. Essays like "A Free Man's Worship" and "The Essence of Religion" were attempts to establish a psychological or spiritual perspective that could countenance but could not change the amoral and valueless scientific realities of physics and chemistry. For humans living in a world blind and indifferent toward all-too-human values, a religious perspective is still a possibility, but that perspective cannot take the form of imagining that reality is friendly to humans or shares a moral perspective with us. In Russell's perspective, real religion does not issue from servitude to this amoral reality, but from the refusal of humans to accept the heartless indifference of the world that impinges on us throughout life and until death. Courage (or faith in our values) will have to replace the older religious metaphysic and ethic. This new outlook will necessarily differ from the older one as it must protect and defend the values of the human in a morally indifferent universe. Any religious apologist, therefore, who ignorantly or deceivingly jettisons science in order to have religion is a fraud. However, we can adjust ourselves, but not by overturning the scientific picture of the world—rather by coming to terms with it. This much Russell concedes in his understanding of mysticism. He thus writes in "Mysticism and Logic" that "while fully developed mysticism seems to me mistaken, I yet believe that, by sufficient restraint, there is an element of wisdom to be learned from the mystical way of feeling, which does not seem attainable in any other manner. If this is true, mysticism is to be commended as an attitude towards life, not as a creed about the world."[1]

If Bergsonian philosophy proved worthy of disdain to Russell, pragmatism, as it issues from William James, should also receive opprobrium, in great part because pragmatism permitted wishful thinking in the matter of belief, particularly religious belief, though dressed up as enlightened and defensible philosophy. However, before looking at further details of the fault-finding that Russell pronounces over this philosophy, it is notable that Russell regarded James as nevertheless worthy of the respect and dignified reputation this American thinker had earned. Though revered as James was by nearly everyone else, George Santayana thought little of him, and as if by unavoidable reciprocity, James was put off by Santayana. Indicative of the depth of the antagonism between the two men, Russell writes, "There was between these two men a temperamental opposition

---

1. Russell, "Mysticism and Logic," *CP* 12:164. The overriding issue with Russell over mysticism (or instinct or intuition) is epistemological. On the same page in this essay Russell concedes that "Of the reality or unreality of the mystic's world I know nothing. I have no wish to deny it, nor even to declare that the insight which reveals it is not a genuine insight." However, because the means of knowing relies upon science to vindicate what is perhaps first suggested by the mystical route, and though each is thus dependent upon the other, at the end of the day, science is the rightful judge of anything purporting to be knowledge.

which nothing could have overcome."[2] One might say, to borrow James's own terminology, that he was tender-minded, while Santayana was tough-minded. Russell's preference was for James: "His religious feelings were very Protestant, very democratic, and very full of warmth of human kindness. He refused altogether to follow his brother Henry into fastidious snobbishness."[3] Though Russell liked James, he regarded James's philosophy of pragmatism as specious reasoning.

Though James himself admitted to no religion of his own, he found the subject matter fascinating, as is clearly evidenced in his famous little book, *The Varieties of Religious Experience*, published in 1902. However, it had been James's study of medicine that enabled him to see how easily materialism as a doctrine found disciples from scientific fields of study. Russell contends that James by contrast managed to keep materialism at bay and "in check by his religious emotions."[4] Russell of course was highly suspicious of the human emotions.

Philosophy in America during the nineteenth century reflected something of the American religious character, as manifested not only in the case of the Transcendentalists, but also with others willing to grapple with challenges to religion. This was certainly the case with James, who had first been a student of psychology. He was drawn to philosophy by the burden American thinkers were laboring under—science and the implied materialism often accompanying it with reference to human free will. Understandably, it was thought religious belief would grow steadily weaker against the competence and competition of science. However, James had jumped into the fray to argue for the cogency and practical benefit of religious belief even in a skeptical age. To a great degree, James's issue was close to that of Kant: that is, to reconcile a religious and moral view of the world with the view of science. To pre-empt some critics, James conceded in his *Varieties* that religious genius was often accompanied by a personality deemed almost mad on occasion. He made the comparison, moreover, that admired intellectuals in other fields were sometimes similar, but that in an age of natural suspicion toward religion, the religious genius was apt to be regarded as a hopeless crank.

In his book *Will to Believe*, James attempted to show the practical benefits of beliefs working for the believer, as opposed to the skeptic. A

---

2. Russell, *History*, 811.
3. Russell, *History*, 811.
4. Russell, *History*, 811.

part of his pragmatic attempt was to steer clear of metaphysical Hegelianism, which he mockingly referred to as a "block universe." Russell affirmed James's metaphysic, labeled "neutral monism," and also much of James's philosophy known as "radical empiricism." However, as applied to religious belief, Russell was an unmistakable opponent of pragmatism. "It is chiefly in regard to religion that the pragmatist use of 'truth' seems to me misleading."[5] With reference to James's distinction between the tough and tender minded, Russell writes, "It will clear the ground for me to confess at once that I belong, with some reserves, to the 'tough-minded type.'" Not specifying what these "some reserves" might be, Russell goes on to say "I find myself agreeing with the 'tough-minded' half of pragmatism and totally disagreeing with the 'tender-minded' half."[6] The latter is clearly not entirely correct.

On the matter of religious choice, James offers a defense that Russell strongly opposed: "William James proceeds to point out that, in the case of religion, the choice between believing and disbelieving possesses all the characteristics of the options which, according to him, ought to be decided by the emotions. He tacitly assumes that there is no evidence for or against religion, and he points out that by refusing either to believe or to disbelieve we lose the benefits of religion just as much as by deciding to disbelieve."[7] Russell thus charges that James wants to force the issue of belief, particularly religious belief, when the issue need not be forced. The issue need not be settled, Russell contends, because probability figures into most questions, and he charges that probability is something that James ignores. Nevertheless, as Russell writes, "there is almost always some discoverable consideration of probability in regard to any question."[8] Russell charges that James would make it seem as if "the only alternatives were complete belief or complete disbelief, ignoring all shades of doubt."[9] Interestingly, Russell makes the same charge against Blaise Pascal's famous "wager."[10] In fairness to James, however, the noted pragmatist concedes that many things or issues or questions can be decided by attention to the facts, particularly the sensible facts. But what does one do when the question on hand is not of such a type?

5. Russell, *Philosophical Essays*, 24.
6. Russell, *Philosophical Essays*, 113–14.
7. Russell, *Philosophical Essays*, 82.
8. Russell, *History*, 815.
9. Russell, *History*, 815.
10. Russell, *History*, 691.

James thinks questions of ethics and religion for the most part fall into this category. In taking this tack James is placing himself in a tradition reminiscent of Pascal, whom he references with the famous and controversial contention, "The heart has reasons which reason knows nothing of." In his defense, Pascal is not advocating a path away from reason. He is, however, extending the range of knowing to include this thing he calls the heart or emotion or intuition.[11] Russell, as we have seen, is suspicious of restricting reason to allow usurpers to work.

If questions that defy conclusive evidence remain inconclusive for want of that evidence, then what does one do with them? James argues they are simply too important to be tossed aside because the methodologies we have for deciding questions prove inconclusive. Therefore, it is simply wrong on James's analysis to say that all questions are to be decided on the basis of evidence and that if no (sensible) evidence is available, we dispose of the question. James contends that we live our ordinary life all the time on the basis of inconclusive evidence. And in fact if we did not, life would scarcely be livable. Life is full of choices that are made without conclusive certainty. Frankly, the opposite point of view fears risk too much, for the insistence on certainty is completely unrealistic. From the philosophical point of view, moreover, James charges that his opponent is more fearful of error than he cares for truth. Afraid of being mistaken, he refuses to entertain any answer, while all the time appearing to stand on the high ground of appealing to the lack of evidence as supporting his indecision.

---

11. By this route Russell places pragmatism within the traditions of irrationalism: "We have, he [James] maintains, a right to adopt a believing attitude although 'our merely logical intellect may not have been coerced.' This is essentially the attitude of Rousseau's Savoyard vicar, but James's development is novel." Russell, *History*, 814. In his final paragraph from his chapter on James in his *History*, Russell adds more historical genealogy to James's pragmatism: "James's doctrine is an attempt to build a superstructure of belief upon a foundation of skepticism, and like all such attempts it is dependent on fallacies. In his case the fallacies spring from an attempt to ignore all extra-human facts. Berkeleian idealism combined with skepticism causes him to substitute belief in God for God, and to pretend that this will do just as well. But this is only a form of the subjectivistic madness which is characteristic of most modern philosophy." Russell, *History*, 818. In Russell's essay on pragmatism, he adds more genealogy: "The habit of mind which believes that there are no essential impossibilities has been fostered by the doctrine of evolution, with its literary corollary of the *Uebermensch*. Hence have arisen a self-confidence and a pride of life which in many ways remind one of the Renaissance, and establish some affinity between historical humanism and its modern namesake." Russell, *Philosophical Essays*, 108.

Perhaps Russell's greatest objection to pragmatism, however, was its flagrant humanistic orientation: "God the Architect of the Cosmos is forgotten; all that is remembered is belief in God, and its effects upon the creatures inhabiting our petty planet. No wonder the Pope condemned the pragmatic defense of religion."[12] This same point comes across strongly in a letter to Ottoline: "But the worship of my life, as you said, is Truth. That is the something greater than man that seems to me most capable of giving greatness to Man. That is why I hate pragmatism—do read the last paragraph of my essay on pragmatism in my book, where I have tried to express this."[13]

Russell considered the question of the truth of religion to be paramount, coupled with his view that religious belief is harmful, for Russell almost always refuses to separate the two considerations. In Eames summation of one of the squabbles fought over pragmatism between Russell and James, she records that "He [Russell] goes on to say, 'The pragmatic difference that pragmatism makes to me is that it encourages religious belief, and that I consider religious belief pernicious . . . .'"[14]

B. WITH T. S. ELIOT

Eliot, like Wittgenstein, began his relationship with Russell as his student and also like Wittgenstein, came in the end to have some fundamental

---

12. Russell, *History*, 818.

13. Russell to Ottoline, May 16, 1911, Document no. 000069, Box no. 2.53, Bertrand Russell Archives, McMaster University Library/Ottoline Morrell Collection, Box 18, Folder 6, Harry Ransom Center, University of Texas, Austin. The last paragraph to which Russell refers, reads, "To sum up: Pragmatism appeals to the temper of mind which finds on the surface of this planet the whole of its imaginative material; which feels confident of progress, and unaware of non-human limitations to human power; which loves battle, with all the attendant risks, because it has no real doubt that it will achieve victory; which desires religion, as it desires railways and electric light, as a comfort and a help in the affairs of this world, not as providing non-human objects to satisfy the hunger for perfection and for something to be worshipped without reserve. But for those who feel that life on this planet would be a life in prison if it were not for the windows into a greater world beyond; for those to whom belief in man's omnipotence seems arrogant, who desire rather the Stoic freedom that comes of mastery over the passions than the Napoleonic domination that sees the kingdoms of this world at its feet—in a word, to men who do not find Man an adequate object of their worship, the pragmatist's world will seem narrow and petty, robbing life of all that gives it value, and making Man himself smaller by depriving the universe which he contemplates of all its splendour." Russell, *Philosophical Essays*, 110–11.

14. Eames, *Bertrand Russell's Dialogue*, 193.

disagreements with his teacher.[15] Furthermore, as Whitehead had been something of a father figure to Russell, and Russell to Wittgenstein, so for a while was Russell to Elliot. Russell, as he did in the case of gifted students, almost immediately recognized the intellectual potential in Eliot. Interestingly enough, however, Eliot is not included in Russell's informative and sometimes unflattering descriptions of various people found in his *Portraits from Memory*, even though a significant number of those included are literary figures, such as Joseph Conrad, whom Russell adored, and D. H. Lawrence, whom Russell despised. It is difficult to determine with exactness Russell's estimation of Elliot, but we do know that the two men endured a quarrelsome relationship. The paucity of Russell's later remarks on Eliot are in all probability accounted for by the significance (and perhaps the pain) of their disagreements. In earlier and happier days, Russell had great respect for Eliot's intellect and remarked that Eliot's review of Russell's "Mysticism and Logic" expressed an understanding of the piece lost on other reviewers.

Both men came from privileged backgrounds. Eliot's grandfather had founded Washington University in St. Louis. Interestingly, Eliot began his studies in philosophy, whereas Russell restarted with philosophy after mathematics and would try his hand at literature on occasions, though with scant success in that venture.[16] Russell's biographer Alan Wood relates that Eliot read some of early poetry to Russell, a fact undoubtedly supplied to Wood by Russell during the unfinished composition of that biography by Wood. From such indications, and because of the time they lived together, the relationship was surely close at times, as Russell suggests. In fact, Russell in his *Autobiography* conveyed to readers that his love for Eliot was as strong as that of a father, and so the relationship might have been viewed at some points as promising for Eliot's future. Indeed, it was Russell who introduced Eliot to the vaunted Bloomsbury group. However, the friendship between the two men, which included Eliot's wife, was not always harmonious, as Russell concedes more than once in his *Autobiography*.

---

15. "This strange conjunction of personalities could not endure." Kirk, *Eliot and His Age*, 32.

16. John Gardiner, the late American novelist, in his noteworthy book, *On Becoming a Novelist*, advises readers intent on writing fiction to study philosophy as one means toward educating themselves to that end. While this kind of generalization may be good advice for most, it certainly cannot account for the success or lack thereof of all aspiring writers of fiction, as the case of Russell makes clear.

> One day in October 1914 I met T. S. Eliot in New Oxford Street. I did not know he was in Europe, but I found he had come to England from Berlin. I naturally asked him what he thought of the war. 'I don't know,' he replied, 'I only know that I am not a pacifist.' That is to say, he considered any excuse good enough for homicide. I became great friends with him, and subsequently with his wife, whom he married early in 1915. As they were desperately poor, I lent them one of the two bedrooms in my flat, with the result that I saw a great deal of them. I was fond of them both, and endeavoured to help them in their troubles until I discovered that their troubles were what they enjoyed.[17]

At about the same time he was becoming more familiar with the Eliots, he was becoming more disparaging of religion, and noticeably different in attitude than that manifested in previous essays like "The Essence of Religion." When confrontations with disagreeable clergy increased, Russell turned up his volume against religion, while becoming especially agitated by religious officials calling for divine favor or rebuke for rival combatants in World War I. Even his brother Frank, not known for moderation in many things, confronted his younger brother in a letter of November 11, 1915: "I saw some correspondence in the Cambridge Magazine too, from which I gathered you have said rude things about bishops and armaments. I do not like bishops, but I do not think as badly of them as all that, and I doubt if I should say it just now, if I did." Frank went on to add that there was something else that his brother should observe when any criticism of religion is expressed:

> Most of this is really beside the point, because of course I agree that if you have to say it, you must, even now. I would wish that in some ways you would put it a little differently, because in the cold-blooded antagonistic point of view, there is just at the moment something a little jarring, which hurts, much as though J. M. Robertson, contemplating a Christian martyr burnt at the stake, were to spend the time in pointing out that there never was an historical Jesus. Deluded or not, many people have these ideals, and firmly believe in them; and while one would not mind you making them think, I think you do rather unnecessarily affront what to them are great emotions.[18]

17. Russell, *1914–1944*, 9. Russell footnotes at the bottom of the page, "The suggestion sometimes made, however, that one of us influenced the other is without foundation."

18. Frank Russell to Russell, November 11, 1915, Box no. 6.27, Bertrand Russell Archives, McMaster University Library.

With Russell's vigorous free thought aimed against both a religious establishment and religious beliefs that Russell was only too willing to critique, animosity between Eliot and Russell over the subject of religion and, by extension, the foundation and direction of Western civilization, would begin to surface. At the same time, strains in the troubled marriage of Eliot and Vivian escalated every day, though the strain, as it can be tracked through some letters, evidences Russell becoming closer with the pair despite their increasing strife with one another.

In a 1927 talk given by Russell at Battersea Town Hall, the rift between Eliot and Russell became pronounced. Russell's talk and the eventually published piece were provocatively entitled "Why I am Not A Christian." Nothing in this essay attempted to build bridges between modern thought and religion or to diffuse past conflicts.[19] Indeed, this essay posed the two in absolutely antagonistic terms. The Russell who had made some not so faint-hearted attempts to fuse the two for over a decade now for the most part relegated such efforts to the past. The stage was set for Russell and Eliot to part ways.[20]

---

19. In a piece written the year before, 1926, for his *Criterion*, Eliot spoke of trying to ignite a literary revival of sorts, and mentioned positively the works of persons like Hulme, Maritain, and Babbitt for doing so. After these recommendations he adds, "And against the group of books I will set another group of books . . . . which represent to my mind that part of the present which is already dead." Works and authors mentioned are three: H. G. Wells, Bernard Shaw, and Russell's *What I Believe*. Eliot then writes, "I am sorry to include the name of Mr. Russell, whose intellect would have reached the first rank even in the thirteenth century, but when he trespasses outside of mathematical philosophy his excursions are often descents." Kirk, *Eliot*, 105–6. Eliot from this time spearheaded efforts to reinvigorate a Christian presence in a world where it seemed diminishing. In his *Thoughts after Lambeth*, he put the picture in the following way, a picture of course that Russell would take issue with to a very great degree: "The Universal Church is today, it seems to me, more definitely set against the World than at any time since pagan Rome. I do not mean that our times are particularly corrupt; all times are corrupt. I mean that Christianity, in spite of certain local appearances, is not, and cannot be within measurable time, 'official.' The World is trying the experiment of attempting to form a civilized but non-Christian mentality. The experiment will fail; but we must be very patient in awaiting its collapse; meanwhile redeeming the time: so that the Faith may be preserved alive through the dark ages before us; to renew and rebuild civilization, and save the World from suicide." Kirk, *Eliot*, 129.

20. In preceding years, the relationship had not been bitter between the two men. In fact, fearing perhaps some ill feeling from Russell over a piece Eliot had written for a forthcoming issue of Eliot's *Criterion*, he writes to Russell that what "most people would call an attack upon you" is not that, and Eliot explains that "Anyway it is simply a point I am sure you would know that I should disagree with you, but I had rather you saw it before it appeared." Furthermore, and presumably having seen the piece, in a letter to Dora on April 23, 1924, Russell writes from St. Paul, Minnesota, to say, "If you are writing to Eliot tell him I am not at all hurt by his remarks." Russell to Dora, April

The tone of Eliot's letter of June 22, 1927, pointedly reflects changes between the two men. Eliot writes almost scornfully to Russell, "I have just read your little pamphlet on Christianity. With some sadness. All the reasons you advance were familiar to me, I think, at the age of six or eight; and I confess that your pamphlet seems to me a piece of childish folly. But I was brought up as an Atheist, and you were evidently brought up, and in my opinion remain, an Evangelical. Why don't you stick to mathematics?"[21]

If there had been any question on Eliot's part that the two were not advocating something of similar principles before 1927, after Russell's essay was printed there could be no conceivable doubt anymore. In fact, there is indication that Eliot had become aware of just how juxtaposed were he and Russell.[22]

23, 1924, Document no. 250329, Box no. 7.29, Bertrand Russell Archives, McMaster University Library. On June 12, 1924, from Carn Voel, Russell writes to Eliot, "The proof of your article duly reached me in America. There was absolutely nothing in it to vex me. Your opinion is different from mine, but why shouldn't it be?" Almost a year later, in April 1925, writing from Carn Voel, Russell affirms to Eliot that "My affection for you is what it always has been since I got to know you well." In this letter he goes on to encourage Eliot to "pay a visit here." Russell to Eliot, April 23, 1925, Eliot, *Letters*, 2:639–40. The piece, written for the April 1924 issue of the *Criterion*, however, was unmistakably something of a throwing down the gauntlet on the part of Eliot. It seems virtually impossible that Russell missed that, and certainly so after Eliot depicts Russell as appallingly unappreciative of a literary culture for being unconversant with the science of the day, for Russell's tone in his original in *The Dial* certainly does not match his letter to Eliot. Eliot, however, was not finished.

21. T. S. Eliot to Russell, June 22, 1927, Eliot, *Letters* 3: 568. In Russell's response he apparently had admitted that what he had written was a propagandist piece, but to little avail to Eliot, who responded by writing, "I can see a distinction between theological speculation and propaganda; but even in propaganda I don't see a place for bad reasons. But perhaps what I dislike is the smell of the corpse of Protestantism passing down the river." Eliot to Russell, October 5, 1927, Eliot, *Letters* 3: 739–40. In a letter from Russell of December 17, 1927, to Ottoline, Russell laments, "It is a pity Tom Eliot is become so religious—I fear he is definitely a catholic." Document no. 001658, Box no. 2.69, Bertrand Russell Archives, McMaster University Library/Ottoline Morrell Collection, Box 27, Folder 1, Harry Ransom Center, University of Texas, Austin.

22. In a letter written to the Catholic historian Christopher Dawson, Eliot clarifies the nature of a book that Eliot's publishing house, Faber and Faber, is hopeful about putting out against Russell's book *Marriage and Morals*: "What we want is less a dialectical rejoinder to Russell than a positive statement from a point of view which shall clearly be that of a Roman Catholic layman. We wish less a refutation on general grounds, than a positive statement of the Catholic point of view and principles, as they appear to a layman; incidentally, as far as you like, bringing in reference to the views of Russell and Judge Lindsay etc." Eliot to Dawson, January 19, 1930, in Eliot et al., *Letters of T. S. Eliot*, 5:40. In a letter of response of November 5, 1930, to Marguerite Caetani, having been asked about the best books of a host of authors, Eliot writes, "The best books of

While Russell's circle of friends had included mostly contented secularists and very few restless secularists on a religious quest, Russell remained in the latter group. While he had earlier expressed qualified sympathy for some religious aspirations, audiences and readers now imbibing his more frequent critiques of religion might have thought the earlier Russell something of a different man and partly he was.

Eliot understood that Russell was not only attacking errant bishops and pompous popes, but even more so the cultural fabric and Christian undergirding of Western Civilization. That is, in his writings, Russell was now calling for a day when the lingering vestiges of things religious were set aside and when people would with gratitude acquiesce to their deliverance. Russell's expectation, therefore, was that there was an optimistic future possible if the representatives of religion were simply ignored or mocked. In his response to the question of how long religion would persist in society, Russell asserts that it would last for as long as society had problems. In other words, the besetting sin of religion is creating and enabling problems it alone claims to fix.

In light of such ideas, Eliot understood that Russell was not engaged in simple skirmishes or tangential assaults on religion; Russell was fighting a frontal assault against much of the religious elements of Western culture from a stance of clear repudiation of the prior historical and religious ethic. What made the ensuing animosities between the two men so fractious was that Russell and Eliot understood each other in this adversarial way.[23] Nevertheless, despite the earlier ill feeling toward each

---

Bertrand Russell are *The Philosophy of Leibnitz*, *The Principles of Mathematics*, the first volume of the *Principia Mathematica*, and an excellent volume on PHILOSOPHY in the 'Home University Library'. All the other books of his that I have read are bad books. The best books of Whitehead are the remaining volumes of the *Principia Mathematica* (which I have not read and which I do not recommend for the reason that they are very expensive and composed entirely of mathematical formulae); but a book you should read if you are interested in such things is *Science and the Modern World* which is a very brilliant piece of work. If you are interested in Whitehead, I should think you would also be interested in Professor Eddington's book, and possibly in a book by Sir James Jeans, which has just come out, entitled *The Mysterious Universe*." Eliot et al., *Letters of T. S. Eliot*, 5:373. Interestingly, some of these authors and their works cited here by Eliot, particularly Eddington and Jeans, and lesser so, Whitehead, are summarily condemned by Russell.

23. Somewhat in conjunction with Santayana, who was another of Eliot's teachers at Harvard, Eliot championed a well-known thesis that "in the seventeenth century a dissociation of sensibility set in, from which we have never recovered," Eliot, "Metaphysical Poets," 247. Eliot would in all probability instance some of Russell's notable themed essays on religion in the early twentieth century, particularly, *The Free Man's*

other, after almost four decades had elapsed since the incident with Russell's notorious "Why I am Not a Christian" pamphlet, Eliot politely compliments his former teacher after hearing a broadcast given by Russell, writing, "As you may know, I disagree with your views on most subjects, but I thought that you put your beliefs over in a most dignified and even persuasive way."[24]

Worship, as evidence of a titanic struggle with this divorce. In a perceptive essay by James Seaton, "Poetry and Religion in George Santayana and T. S. Eliot" (in Lockerd, *T. S. Eliot and the Christian Tradition*, 239–50) Seaton writes, "For Eliot, attempts to conflate religion with art or anything else were reminders of the bad old days of the late nineteenth century when 'religion became morals, religion became art, religion became science or philosophy; various blundering attempts were made at alliances between various branches of thought.'" Lockerd, *T. S. Eliot and the Christian Tradition*, 244; Eliot, *Selected Essays*, 393. Indicative of the fact that Santayana and Eliot took different routes out of similar critiques of intellectual and specifically cultural romanticism, Seaton observes, "One can understand why Russell Kirk was able to subtitle the first edition of *The Conservative Mind* 'From Burke to Santayana' and later change the subtitle to 'From Burke to Eliot' without radically altering his account of the tradition he was claiming and reaffirming—and reinvigorating." Lockerd, *T. S. Eliot and the Christian Tradition*, 243.

24. Eliot to Russell, May 20, 1964, in Russell, *1944–1969*, 58–59. Eliot finished his short letter with the words: "I wanted you to know this as you are getting on so far, and as I myself am, I hope, somewhat mellowed by age." Eliot had sent Russell a congratulatory note for his O.M. award in 1949, while referencing some of Russell's earlier books, and complimenting Russell as "one of the few living authors who can write English prose." Russell, *1944–1969*, 57–58.

The fact of the matter, however, was that Russell had not precisely mellowed in age, and one could argue plausibly that he grew more radical, with his bouts with religion certainly not an exception. World War II was certainly an exception, in that Russell supported the Allied cause and war against the Nazis, but this foray into agreement, when he was so used to opposition, put him not infrequently ill at ease. He had remarked to Gilbert Murray in 1952, "There certainly is some comfort in such things as the O.M., though I am always a little ashamed of feeling this sort of comfort. And I have been a rebel during so much of my life that conventional recognition makes me a little uncomfortable. What has made me respectable has been my hatreds of Hitler and Stalin, neither of which fits very well into the kind of general outlook that I like. It would be pleasant to be liked for one's virtues, if any, and not only for one's weaknesses." Russell to Murray, May 23, 1952, in Griffin, *Letters*, 2:466. As one sample indicating that Russell had not mellowed on religion, Russell produced a letter exchange between himself and Ernest Jones, the famed psychologist. The occasion was a letter of some rebuke sent to Russell for his sordid life and misused intellect that had been sent by the Anglican Bishop of Rochester in 1957. Russell sent a copy of the bishop's letter to Jones, asking for Jones's comment. Most interesting about the exchange is Russell's response to Jones, after Jones had expressed his utter lack of amazement over the content of the bishop's letter, remarking "I should have thought you received many such, and indeed I even wonder how many masses are already being said for your soul." Russell's response shows that no fire has gone out of his soul regarding religion, and specifically clergy: "Thank you for your very pleasant letter of February 4. Ever since I got it, I have been

Indeed, there had been a "culture war" between the two men long before the term became prominent in the American press in the late twentieth century.[25] Cognizant of the increasingly secular voices of thinkers like Russell, Eliot took up the editorship of the conservative journal *The Criterion* for not a few years, from 1922 to 1939. A survey of the essays and articles of those years reveals the looming presence of Russell, for the years of Eliot's editorship of the journal coincide with some of Russell's most vehement writing against religion.

Even earlier, Eliot was headed in a direction different from Russell. In 1911, Eliot had attended some lectures of Henri Bergson in Paris, though three decades later he recalled that any influence of Bergson was only temporary. The main currents of thought of the day Eliot would sample, but he grew dissatisfied with most. Returning from Paris he re-entered Harvard University, his initial meeting place with Russell. Now Eliot would begin some serious study of Eastern thought, portions of which show up in his poetry. In the decade of 1910, he would look at pragmatism, and not unlike Russell, would reject it for its anthropocentric orientation. Though Eliot would begin a dissertation on Bradley's idealism, in time he turned away from it. Like the youthful Russell, Eliot wanted to avoid the scientific determinism increasingly common in intellectual culture. Though Eliot even took stock of some teaching about the occult, he was eventually led more toward English mysticism. The still young student would reflect years later that he had been searching for something to unify the spiritual and material components of reality,

---

luxuriating in the pleasure of seeing myself as a formidable father-figure inspiring terror in the Anglican hierarchy. What surprised me about the letter I sent you was that I had imagined eminent Anglican Divines to be usually fairly civilized people. I get hundreds of letters very similar to the one I sent you, but they are generally from people with very little education." Russell, *1944–1969*, 173–76.

25. As an example of Eliot's thought on the possibility of exchanging one culture for another: "It is in Christianity that our arts have developed; it is in Christianity that the laws of Europe have—until recently—been rooted. It is against a background of Christianity that all our thought has significance. An individual European may not believe that the Christian Faith is true, and yet what he says, and makes, and does, will all spring out of his heritage of Christian culture and depend upon that culture for its meaning. Only a Christian culture could have produced a Voltaire or a Nietzsche. I do not believe that the culture of Europe could survive the complete disappearance of the Christian Faith. And I am convinced of that, not merely because I am a Christian myself, but as a student of social biology. If Christianity goes, the whole of our culture goes. Then you must start painfully again, and you cannot put on a new culture ready made. You must wait for the grass to grow to feed the sheep to give the wool out of which your new coat will be made." Eliot, *Notes Towards the Definition of Culture*, 200.

more usually separated by religious seekers. Slowly the orthodox Christian traditions, as found in, for example, the writings of St. John of the Cross, began to find some footing in Eliot. Upon entering the Anglican Church in 1927, spiritual and religious satisfaction came home to him. As noted by Spurr, "'The conversion to Christianity', Eliot reflected in 1937, 'is apt to be due, I think, to a latent dissatisfaction with all secular philosophy.'"[26] That secular philosophy, moreover, Eliot increasingly placed in his sights after his conversion.[27] One of those sights was Eliot's former teacher, Russell.

As earlier noted, Eliot in subsequent years regarded his former teacher and friend as opposed to the culture that Eliot sought to preserve. On the other hand, and not to be forgotten, Russell was proud of many things that Western culture stood for and thus cannot be counted simply as a wholesale critic of that culture. However, in the 1930s and 1940s, as religion in Russell's hands received fewer and fewer positive mentions, Eliot grew weary of the secularizing direction Russell's writings now evidenced. Eliot's own literary successes might have nudged and qualified the younger man to offer some advice on Russell's literary undertakings, but no such discussion developed between the two men. The philosopher perceived that he and his former pupil were now working at cross purposes.

As earlier indicated, many of the Bloomsbury set had attended Russell's lectures that were printed in *Principles of Social Reconstruction* in 1916. Indeed, in ensuing years, Russell thought well enough of the book to still commend it. With reference to his religious views, he later commented, "As regards my own personal religion . . . . the expression of it which seems to me least unsatisfactory is the one in *Social Reconstruction* (Chapter VII)."

Eliot had written a critique of that work, and in a letter to Russell of March 13, 1917, he writes, "I made no positive objection to the principle

---

26. Spurr, *Anglo-Catholic in Religion*, 26. However, many secularly inclined people greeted Eliot's religious conversion with secular dissatisfaction. Such was undoubtedly much of the impetus for Eliot stepping away from the Bloomsbury circle, to which Eliot had been introduced by Russell. Virginia Woolf had badgered Eliot about his religious conversion, to Eliot's annoyance. Apparently, however, there was ill feeling between the two people for some time prior. Woolf records in her diary of April 6, 1919, "I amused myself by seeing how sharp, narrow, & much of a stick Eliot has come to be, since he took to disliking me." Woolf, *Diary I*, 262.

27. "'We must find our own faith,' he had written in *The Criterion* in January 1926, 'and having found it, fight for it against all comers.'" Spurr, *Anglo-Catholic in Religion*, 26.

of 'reverence'—it merely seems to me inadequate. My chief objection is to the passage on p. 165."[28] For Eliot to take issue with the referred to and famous "Thought" passage from the given page is notable and reflects the fact that in 1917 Eliot is already poised for opposition to Russell's thinking a full ten years before the inflammatory "Why I am Not a Christian" of 1927. The overtly secular tone of the Thought passage was simply too much for the increasingly religiously inclined Eliot. Probably its last sentence Eliot found the most offensive: "Thought is great and swift and free, the light of the world, and the chief glory of man."

Just as Russell's religious side was confined by required secular fences, so also his secular side sought something of a religious spirit, though this might not be apparent to a cursory reading of Russell and indeed remains omitted from those touting only or primarily Russell's loudest denunciations against religion. Moreover, embedded within him was a desire for something more than a secularism that was too self-satisfied. He voices this complaint about the contented secularist many times, as when he writes to Ottoline, "People with whom I have intellectual sympathy hardly ever have any spiritual life, or at any rate have very little."[29] Eliot certainly had the requisite spiritual life, but Eliot's direction was one Russell rejected. Thus, the two men remained for the most part at odds with each other over their differing ideas.

For most of his life Russell was an adherent of socialism, though he told his mistress Colette Malleson (who often referred to her own religion as one of freedom), "I don't like the spirit of Socialism—I think freedom is the basis of everything."[30] Nevertheless, Russell felt an obligation toward society, in great part seeded from his aristocratic background and habits, while also reflecting a prior era. In his societal responsibilities, Russell felt much more aligned with the Victorians for their sense of social responsibility, even as Russell faulted them for a host of other vices. Russell's coolness toward some younger members of the Cambridge Apostles was because Russell observed them ignoring much of the world around them, with a not infrequent air of dismissive arrogance. This was likewise true of some of the Bloomsbury group. They, in effect, were a class of aesthetes unto themselves. In a word, theirs was a world of significant self-absorption.

28. Eliot and Haughton, *Letters of T. S. Eliot, Vol. I, 1898–1922*, 179.

29. Russell to Ottoline, March 4, 1916, Document no. 082581, Box no. 2.45, Bertrand Russell Archives, McMaster University Library /Ottoline Morrell Collection, Box 26, Folder 1, Harry Ransom Center, University of Texas, Austin.

30. Russell to Malleson, September 29, 1916, in Russell, *1914–1944*.

C. WITH HENRI BERGSON

Henri Bergson is perhaps the philosopher of the twentieth century for whom Russell had least respect. Despite Russell's low opinion of the man, Bergson's writing drew considerable praise from readers. For example, William James heralded Bergson's book *Creative Evolution* as marking out a new direction in the old debate between science and ethics/religion. However, the reception of Bergson's work was less enthusiastic among other philosophers (especially English) who had started to imbibe the analytic methodology of Russell and Moore. To this school of critique, the decorative prose of Bergson was a liability in conveying his ideas, even as in 1928 Bergson was recipient of the Nobel Prize for literature. Though Bergson's explanations offended the analytic spirit and school of philosophy, a wider reading public, including Ottoline Morrell, affirmed the seeming possibilities of Bergson's ideas.

A rather frequent countercharge of Bergson as well as James was that Russell was simply buried in his rationalism and too unwilling to entertain their larger and more true-to-life ideas, which, they argued, took in more of the world and human experience than did Russell's narrowly cognitive approach to knowledge. Russell might concede something of this criticism as it issued from James, though only because Russell desired a philosophy that would be advantageous for life, but first and foremost it must embrace truth. In addition, Russell did not want to be only an abstractionist,[31] however much he may have seemed one. And, however intense his disagreements with James, particularly over the application of pragmatism to the questions of religion and religious belief, Russell counted James a worthier intellectual opponent than Bergson. To the latter, Russell gave very low marks.

Russell's strong disagreement with Bergson's philosophy arose from Russell's contention that Bergson's thinking "exemplifies admirably the revolt against reason which, beginning with Rousseau, has gradually dominated larger and larger areas in the life and thought of the world."[32] As background to such a critique, Russell categorizes philosophies by their different inspirations or aspirations: knowledge, feeling, or action.

---

31. This seems only true to a point, however, while the difference shows in another way in the correspondence between Russell and James. Eames notes "He [Russell] comments that while James's first 'demand of God is to love him'; Russell's is to worship him." Eames, *Bertrand Russell's Dialogue*, 193.

32. Russell, *History*, 791.

While applauding his favored inspiration to philosophize, namely knowledge, as "the source of most of what is best in philosophy," Russell relegates the inspiration of the others to a lower status as simply too practical in bent and desire. Russell's additional charge against Bergson is the travesty the French philosopher makes of science and scientific knowledge to avoid the deterministic implications of scientific findings as they concern humans. We may recall that in principle such an effort was evidenced in Russell's youthful "Greek Writings" and the "Locked Diary." However, according to Russell, Bergson is engaged in his effort by dubious means: the manipulation of scientific data. Russell cannot stomach any thinker presenting an alluring and tempting blueprint of nature if he violates the scientific account of nature in the attempt to safeguard humans from a feared reality. Bergson's announcement, that the human person is not bound by determinism as current scientists and philosophers seemed to insist, was greeted with jubilation by his fawning audiences. Russell, however, took exception. He writes to Lucy Donnelly, "Everybody congratulated themselves and each other on their possession of freedom & on their escape from the barren scientific dogmas of the sixties. I still believe in those dogmas, so I felt out of it."[33] In Russell's conception of fusing beliefs, there was simply no room, at least none that he had found, whereby the scientific picture of the world could be suspended or distorted to enable thinkers to indulge themselves in rosy pictures of the human place in the world. In fact, Russell scarcely admits Bergson to the rank of a true philosopher, for to Russell he seems to be carrying the weak-minded away from truth because he fears it unpleasant.

Despite Bergson's popularity, in Russell's mind he had to be critiqued, so Russell, seeing that the Frenchman was carrying many thinkers away with his faulty philosophy, writes to Gilbert Murray to ask, "What do you think of the Bergson books?"[34] For his part, Russell regarded Bergson's philosophy as hardly "more than an imaginative and poetic view of the world."[35] However, perhaps Russell's greatest objection to

---

33. Russell to Lucy Donnelly, October 28, 1911, in Forte, *Letters*, 183. Typical of Russell's ability to mock an opponent, in the same letter, he writes, "They seemed to me like naughty children when they think (mistakenly) that the governess is away—boasting of their power over matter, when matter might kill them at any moment."

34. Russell to Murray, November 9, 1911, Document no. 053512, Box no. 533, Bertrand Russell Archives, McMaster University Library.

35. Russell, *History*, 800. Russell adds, "The number of similes for life to be found in his works exceeds the number in any poet known to me." Russell, *History*, 799. Indicative of Russell's view that argument and reason are scarcely present in Bergson's work,

Bergson is that he claims to find in the mechanisms of evolution a human purpose which can be simply described as action meant only for the sake of action: "Thus we are condemned, in action, to be the blind slaves of instinct: the life-force pushes us on from behind, restlessly and unceasingly."[36] Russell's conception of the human place in nature and the cosmos is entirely different from this. In Bergson's conception, moreover, the human is composed from the fabric of nature and thus finds his home within that agreeable and mothering world. Consequently, there is scarcely any cause for disgruntlement or demurring against the mechanisms of nature giving birth to the human within the natural world. Bergson has made nature friendly and rejected the scientific conception of the world as inhospitable because indifferent toward the human. He opts for a softer view of reality. Russell, however, much in agreement with T. H. Huxley, argued that the human species, though arising from the mechanisms of amoral nature has nevertheless repudiated its mother and in Huxley's words, "We have kicked down the ladder by which we have come up."[37] In other words, we are a species set apart by our moral aversion to the mechanisms of amoral nature that we judge ghastly and cruel. To this degree, we find ourselves odd man out in the context of the rest of the living world. That world manifests an entirely different "ethic" compared to our own. Bergson skates past this difference, while Russell concurs with Huxley. This is not a pretty picture, but it is a true one, Russell contends.

While Bergson finds for the human a comforting home within the natural world, Russell emphatically does not; like Huxley, Russell notes the incongruence of the human and the world in which he lives, as is

---

Russell contends that "as a rule he does not give reasons for his opinions, but relies on their inherent attractiveness, and on the charm of an excellent style." Russell, *History*, 799. Russell's most biting criticism of Bergson's philosophy, however, is probably to be found in Russell's response to Wildon Carr's defense of Bergson against Russell's criticism of Bergson's philosophy: "I hold that much less can be known about the universe as a whole than many philosophers are inclined to suppose; I should not therefore assert dogmatically that the universe is other than it is said to be in this or that system, unless the account in question appeared self-contradictory. What I do maintain is that, in view of the mistakes in Bergson's reasoning, his conclusions remain mere imaginative possibilities, to be placed alongside of the thousand other possibilities invented by cosmic poets." Russell, "Mr. Wildon Carr's Defence of Bergson," *CP* 6:342.

36. Russell, *History*, 810.

37. Typical of Russell's sarcasm for attempts to placate and soften the historical battle between religion and science, in reviewing Julian Huxley's work *Essays of a Biologist* in 1923, Russell writes that in "Huxley's grandfather's day, religion and science were enemies, now they are friends." *Nation and Athenaeum*, 223.

made explicit in his "Free Man's Worship": "A strange mystery it is that Nature, omnipotent but blind, in the revolutions of her secular hurrying through the abysses of space, has brought forth at last a child subject still to her power, but gifted with sight, with knowledge of good and evil, with the capacity of judging all the works of his unthinking Mother."[38] So too, in "The Pilgrimage of Life," Russell writes: "So great is the value of human virtue that it alone redeems the universe; it is for us to protest, seriously and sadly, against the evil world which is omnipotent except over our thoughts . . . ."[39] Russell, therefore, places the greatness of Man outside a hostile environment and positioned from a moral insistence pitted against the amoral natural world. As mentioned earlier, Russell would contend that Bergson's philosophy is representative of a time when thought for the sake of thought was hardly desired and frequently complains that Bergson "thrives upon the errors and confusions of the intellect . . . and to regard every foolish mistake as revealing the bankruptcy of intellect and the triumph of intuition."[40] For his part, Bergson was critical of philosophy when steeped in a Platonism that to him seemed too static and other-worldly. Russell, however, complains, "There is no room in this philosophy for the moment of contemplative insight when, rising above the animal life, we become conscious of the great ends that redeem man from the life of the brutes. Those to whom activity without purpose seems a sufficient good will find in Bergson's books a pleasing picture of the universe."[41]

Russell opposed Bergson's philosophy on essentially two counts. First, Bergson's thinking shared the pragmatist inclination to move philosophy away from its goal of knowledge for the sake of knowledge. Like pragmatists, Bergson prized action and thus these philosophies sidestepped, and indeed showed little respect, for the worthy pursuit of truth in knowledge. Secondly, Russell perceived in Bergson a contemptible and provincial philosophy of feeling, with the dubious aim of portraying one's place in the world with obvious neglect of the scientific picture of humans and the world. For Russell, Bergson's philosophy was simply another attempt to produce a pleasant philosophy by the manipulation of scientific knowledge. Although Bergson was certainly not the first among

38. Russell, "Free Man's Worship," *CP* 12:67.
39. Russell, "Pilgrimage of Life," *CP* 12:55.
40. Russell, *History*, 803.
41. Russell, *History*, 810.

philosophers to engage in such a practice, he had wooed too many blind but faithful followers in his day to be ignored by Russell.

Bergson was opposing the doctrines of materialism and determinism, that, as earlier mentioned, had been a youthful hope of Russell. Nevertheless, Russell could scarcely bear the French philosopher's insistence on intuition and creative evolution. Some of Russell's friends, however, were of a contrary viewpoint on Bergson, among them Ottoline. Ottoline surely found Bergson intellectually less trying than Russell, partly because Bergson's philosophy, however nebulous and outrageous and frustratingly poetic it might seem to Russell, resonated with a wider audience of spiritually hungry readers. Ottoline must have had such a realization of the difference, while Russell seemed to think himself and Ottoline on a similar journey, when they scarcely were. Russell's "no" to Bergson was also a "no" to Ottoline, which she surely recognized at various points in their relationship.

In other words, flirtations with the likes of Bergson were not uncommon among some of Russell's associates, even if, like Ottoline, these were not all card-carrying academics. To Russell, however, the philosophy of Bergson represented a defection from real philosophy. To follow in Bergson's direction, even if not actually sympathetic to Bergson himself, represented giving up on real reason and philosophy for the mystical flight. Bergson was only fanning the flame set in motion by Rousseau and other romantics according to Russell.

Convoluted within Russell's disdain for Bergson was Wittgenstein's charge that Russell's 1912 essay "The Essence of Religion" was "too intimate for print." In Russell's appraisal of Wittgenstein's criticism, he suggestively concedes to Ottoline that his disappointment over Wittgenstein's verdict was "because I half agree with him" and adds that "Wittgenstein's criticisms disturbed me profoundly."[42] For all of Wittgenstein's rationalism, he also manifested a religious or mystical side, and this came between him and Russell, like it did between Russell and Bergson, and like it did Russell and Ottoline. However, it must be remembered Russell had had his own flirtations with mysticism, and in his reaction to Wittgenstein's estimation of "The Essence of Religion," the disappointment expressed by Russell is at least indication that Russell was never content as only the quintessential rationalist.

42. Russell to Ottoline, October 11, 1912, Document no. 000600, Box 2.60, Bertrand Russell Archives, McMaster University Library/Ottoline Morrell Collection, Box 22, Folder 2, Harry Ransom Center, University of Texas, Austin.

Nevertheless, for Russell the drawing line between religion courted and intellectually impossible religious belief must always be drawn, however undesirable and painful for many. Even as hordes of people subverted reason for religion, so too, some close to Russell, fall too. In 1912 Wittgenstein had written to Russell about the value he found in reading James's *Varieties of Religious Experience*,[43] of which Russell thought highly, though with a necessary caveat. In his study of James's book, Wittgenstein surmises in an almost existential manner, that he needs to do some work upon himself. Another book that he becomes enamored with is Tolstoy's *Gospel in Brief*. As we have seen, however, Russell viewed such works as providing recourse to feeling as the primary way of avoiding the question of the truth of religion. Of this penchant for error Bergson was abundantly guilty.

D. WITH GEORGE SANTAYANA

In a 1953 letter from Constance Malleson to her friend Nalle Kielland, Malleson writes of Santayana, "As far as I know, he was as bitter an enemy as B. [Bertrand] ever had. . . . My guess is that B. will be remembered long after S.'s name is completely erased from memory. I don't know MUCH abt S., but my impression is that he was more of a lit. writer than any sort of serious philosopher."[44] Indeed, George Santayana is a figure often difficult for scholars to easily place or position. Moreover, as depicted by Russell, Santayana was a thinker consciously out of step with his times, from which Russell draws both positive and negative estimations. As an indication of Russell's waning friendship with Santayana, he writes, "As I came to know him better I found some sympathy and much divergence."[45]

Like some other intellectual notables such as Benjamin Jowett, Harold Joachim, John Stuart Mill, John Tyndale, and others, Russell also had a connection with Santayana, as Russell's older brother Frank was a close

---

43. Russell thought highly of the work, but took issue with the conclusions, and as usual, that on epistemological grounds.

44. Constance Malleson to Nalle Kielland, May 20, 1953, Box no. 6.71, Bertrand Russell Archives, McMaster University Library. In a letter of October 13, 1953, Malleson writes to Kielland, "The 3rd volume of Santayana's autobiography is just out: "MY HOST THE WORLD" Cresset Press. I gather that it is full of nasty remarks about B.—just as B's recent broadcast (end Sept. or early Oct.) was full of ditto remarks abt Santayana. It is queer that S. was fonder of B's brother than of anybody else in the world. I wonder why."

45. Russell, *Portraits*, 92.

friend of the man, and indeed it appears that each counted the other among the very closest of friends. In terms of personality, Frank was a better fit with Santayana than younger brother Bertrand, for both Santayana and Frank were given to a degree of flamboyance. Russell, despite his rather colorful life, took life and its incidents with a level of seriousness less evident in Santayana. For example, if flippancy could be a trait Russell too sometimes exhibited,[46] he nonetheless regarded Santayana's actions at times as coarse or indifferent when something more was required. Regarding this lack of seriousness, Russell recounts the following: "A few days before the Battle of the Marne, when the capture of Paris by the Germans seemed imminent, he remarked to me: 'I think I must go to Paris, because my winter underclothes are there, and I should not like the Germans to get them. I have also left there the manuscript of a book on which I have been working for the last ten years; but I don't mind so much about that.'"[47]

Russell therefore hardly got on well with Santayana, though he took notice of Santayana's estimation of Russell's philosophy, most notably in Santayana's book, *Winds of Doctrine*, published in 1913. Russell said of the work, "I like Santayana's Winds of Doctrine, & thought his criticism of me not unjust, at least in great measure."[48] In that work Santayana dedicated a whole chapter to Russell and Russell's philosophy and does assert some astute observations on Russell. Notable is Santayana's comment that "Mathematics seem to have a value for Mr. Russell akin to that of religion. It affords a sanctuary to which to flee from the world, a heaven suffused with a serene radiance and full of a peculiar sweetness and consolation."[49] On the matter of religion, moreover, Santayana is also perceptive enough to notice that "The reader will perceive, perhaps, that if the function of philosophy is really, as the saying goes, to give us assurance of God, freedom, and immortality, Mr. Russell's philosophy is a dire failure. In fact, its author sometimes gives vent to a rather emphatic

---

46. Speaking of his "conversion experience" in 1901, Russell wrote of the years before that event, "Ever since my marriage, my emotional life had been calm and superficial. I had forgotten all the deeper issues, and had been content with flippant cleverness." Russell, *1872–1914*, 234.

47. Russell, *Portraits*, 93. In a letter of April 22, 1906, he writes: "I don't think I shall become 'civilized' in Santayana's sense, as I don't wish to, I find his temperament very repulsive." Russell to M.L. [Margaret] Davies, older sister of Crompton and Theodore. Griffin, *Letters*, 1:300.

48. Russell to Lucy Donnelly, July 3, 1913, in Forte, *Letters*, 206–7.

49. Santayana, *Winds*, 117.

pessimism about this world; he has a keen sense for the manifold absurdities of existence. But the sense for absurdities is not without its delights, and Mr. Russell's satirical wit is more constant and better grounded than his despair."[50]

Santayana further compliments Russell (and Moore) when in the same paragraph he concedes, "It is refreshing and reassuring, after the confused, melodramatic ways of philosophizing to which the idealist and the pragmatists have accustomed us, to breathe again the crisp air of scholastic common sense."[51] By identifying himself as no friend of either the idealist or the pragmatist, Santayana might be deemed edging himself toward Russell philosophically. Moreover, when in the same book, Santayana devotes a chapter to consideration of Bergson's thought, and is as scathing in his estimations of Bergson as was Russell,[52] one might think the bond between Russell and Santayana was stronger than Malleson or even Russell admitted.

However, at best the relationship between the two philosophers was virtually always fluid. In January 1911 Santayana had written Russell a letter of thanks for his book *Philosophical Essays*, published the previous year. Santayana advises Russell that he is writing an "elaborate review" of the work, and that "You will not expect me to agree with you in everything, but, whatever you may think of my ideas, I always feel that yours, and Moore's too, make for the sort of reconstruction in philosophy which I should welcome. It is a great bond to dislike the same things, and dislike is perhaps a deeper indication of our real nature than explicit affections, since the latter may be effects of the circumstances, while dislike is a reaction against them."[53]

After reading Santayana's book *Winds of Doctrine*, Russell became convinced that Santayana's criticism of Russell's ethic was sufficient to

---

50. Santayana, *Winds*, 113.

51. Santayana, *Winds*, 114.

52. For example, Santayana writes: "M. Bergson is afraid of space, afraid of the intellect and the possible discoveries of science; he is afraid of nothingness and death. These fears may prevent him from being a philosopher in the old and noble sense of the word; but they sharpen his sense for many a psychological problem, and make him the spokesman of many an inarticulate soul." *Winds*, 63. So too, "But philosophers are either revolutionists or apologists, and some of them, like M. Bergson, are revolutionists in the interest of apologetics. Their art is to create some surprising inversion of things, some system of the universe contrary to common apprehension, or to defend some such inverted system, propounded by poets long ago, and perhaps consecrated by religion." *Winds*, 82.

53. Russell, *1872–1914*, 351–52.

displace Russell's previous belief in moral values as objective, and in Russell's 1966 preface to a reprint of his 1910 book, he writes, "I have not attempted to make such emendations in the texts reprinted in this volume as might be called for by changes in my opinions during the intervening fifty-five years. The chief change is that I no longer believe in objective ethical values as I did when (following Moore) I wrote the first essay in the present volume."[54] This same admission was duly noted by Russell with the later caveat that the famous essay "Free Man's Worship" was written from an ethical stance that he no longer held, painful though the retraction was. Somewhat typically, however, Santayana offered that "I cannot help thinking that a consciousness of the relativity of values, if it became prevalent, would tend to render people more truly social than would a belief that things have intrinsic and unchangeable values, no matter what the attitude of any one to them may be."[55] Though Russell on occasion could be as flippant as Santayana might seem here, Russell found such an attitude on these matters hard to accept.

Both men spent considerable time in America, with Russell making some trips for the purpose of raising money for Beacon Hill School in conjunction with his second wife, Dora. Interestingly, both men shared a generally low view of American culture and often too of the academy in America. Russell remarks, "Santayana enjoyed being aloof and contemptuous, whereas I found this attitude, when forced upon me, extremely painful. Aloofness and facile contempt were his defects, and because of them, although he could be admired, he was a person whom it was difficult to love."[56] However, with the coming of the Second World War, Russell found himself confined in America because of dangers for sea traffic on the Atlantic.

In the same essay, Russell insinuates that Santayana's estimation of him was not always accurate: "And he accuses me, oddly enough, of religious conservatism. I will leave the reader to form his own judgment on this matter."[57] By stating the matter this way, Russell of course implies that Santayana is off the mark. Santayana may assume that Russell judged

---

54. Russell, *Philosophical Essays*, 7.

55. Santayana, *Winds*, 151. Russell by contrast wrote: "When I was young, I agreed with G. E. Moore in believing in the objectivity of good and evil. Santayana's criticism, in a book called *Winds of Doctrine*, caused me to abandon this view, though I have never been able to be as bland and comfortable without it as he was." Russell, *Portraits*, 98.

56. Russell, *Portraits*, 97.

57. Russell, *Portraits*, 98.

that religious life is only viable in the context of, indeed the necessity of, cogent religious belief.[58] Russell, as we have witnessed on multiple occasions, did not think this—if such is Santayana's meaning. Again, if this is Santayana's meaning as pertains to Russell, he is clearly mistaken, though perhaps not entirely. Perhaps he means that Russell is too reticent to incorporate aspects of a cultural religious life after religious beliefs are deemed moribund, for Santayana was not. That is, somewhat like McTaggart, who regarded himself as an atheist but was nevertheless a Hegelian, Santayana is prepared to embrace elements of religiosity in his life and work as distinct from his religious unbelief. That Russell presumably had not followed such a route may signal to Santayana that Russell is too religiously conservative.

Russell in some ways judged Santayana in an opposite manner: as a thinker devoted to the past to a fault. That is to say, Russell judged Santayana's thought as antiquated and indifferent, not to say contemptuous, toward a more modern mode of thought. As lovers of much of the past, particularly the Greeks and Lucretius, and Spinoza, Santayana and Russell might have shared much, but often, and more so than Russell, Santayana placed great weight on and respect for cultural fabric with scant regard for whether such things partook of the truth.[59] Perhaps something of the offense Russell took with the later Wittgenstein was also part of the offense Russell took to Santayana. That is, the traditional role of the philosopher to search for the truth seemed to Russell abandoned for contentment on the part of Wittgenstein for analyzing things as they simply were. For Russell, philosophy undertaken in this manner never rose above all the talk about "ordinary language" and "language games." Santayana, similarly perhaps, found connectedness and contentment in

---

58. The difference between the two men is also observable in different estimations of some acquaintances and friends the two shared. Thus, Joseph Epstein observes, "Santayana found E. M. Forster's friend and philosophical mentor, Goldsworthy Lowes Dickinson, hopeless in his utopianly sentimental moralizing." Epstein, *Partial Payments*, 326.

59. Oftentimes the particulars of the cultural fabric did not seem to matter so much to Santayana. In a letter to Sidney Hook, dated June 8, 1934, Santayana wrote, "But I love order in the sense of organized, harmonious, consecrated living; and for this reason I sympathize with the Soviets and the Fascists and the Catholics, but not at all with the liberals. I should sympathize with the Nazis too, if their system were, even in theory, founded on reality; but it is Nietzschean, founded on will; and therefore a sort of romanticism gone mad, rather than a serious organization of material forces—which would be the only way, I think, of securing moral coherence." Quoted in Epstein, *Partial Payments*, 343.

the culture around him and so required little need of "improvements," very much unlike Russell. Santayana saw little reason for the citizen to entertain self-questioning, for that could undermine culture. Somewhat similarly Wittgenstein took issue with Russell's last chapter in *Problems of Philosophy* for mistakenly prodding people to take up philosophy as a way to guide them to more than trivial concerns. Wittgenstein complained that some people simply took to philosophy and others did not; Russell, however, never regarded it as proper that individuals be shielded from facing up to unsettling questions.

Summing up Santayana, Russell comments, "Although not a believing Catholic, he strongly favored the Catholic religion in all political and social ways. He did not see any reason to wish that the populace should believe something true. What he desired for the populace was some myth to which he could give aesthetic approval."[60] For Russell Santayana was too complacent, and his preference for the aesthetic over the true was illustrative of that failing.[61] Of both men it might be said that they were beholden to the past, though Russell bemoaned much of the past for its errors and cruelties. Russell had his sights set on the future and embraced the socially liberal, not to say utopian, view of what could and should be done in the world. Hence, Russell was a social activist, whereas Santayana was a social conservative. According to Russell, this fact about Santayana sometimes went unnoticed because "The American dress in which his writing appeared somewhat concealed the extremely reactionary character of his thinking."[62]

Russell found Santayana's writing style similarly veiling complications that his prose skates over, and Russell writes, "The impression one gets in reading him is that of floating down a smooth-flowing river, so

---

60. Russell, *Portraits*, 94.

61. This is evident when Russell writes in the same pages, "For my part, I was never able to take Santayana very seriously as a technical philosopher, although I thought that he served a useful function by bringing to bear, as a critic, points of view which are now uncommon." Russell, *Portraits*, 94–95. Nevertheless, there seemed to be always something of a rub between the two men, starting decades earlier, and mentioned, for instance, when Russell wrote to Donnelley, "I admire his mind & his writing, thou' fundamentally I don't like him because he is heartless." Russell to Lucy Donnelly, November 14, 1913, in Forte, *Letters*, 214.

62. Russell, *Portraits*, 95. In the next sentence and as an example Russell offers, "Not only did he, as a Spaniard, side politically with the Church in all its attempts to bolster up old traditions in that country, but, as a philosopher, he reverted in great measure to the scholasticism of the thirteenth century."

broad that you can seldom see the bank . . . ."[63] That being said, Russell charges that "Santayana's merits are literary rather than philosophical." However, it is the perceived complacency of Santayana in his philosophy that Russell finds the greater fault. Santayana's cultural conservatism is most evident in his noteworthy essay "Modernism and Christianity," included in his *Winds of Doctrine*. There Santayana disdains the efforts of modernists "to reconcile the church and the world," as the modernist "forgets what Christianity came into the world to announce and why its message was believed. It came to announce salvation from the world; there should be no more need of just those things which the modernist so deeply loves and respects and blushes that his church should not be adorned with—emancipated science, free poetic religion, optimistic politics, and dissolute art."[64]

Though Santayana was as unbelieving of religious dogma as Russell, Santayana's main argument for retaining religion in modern life was that the comforts of religion, whether rooted in fact or fancy, provide more security for people living in the world than people lacking them have.[65] Thus, Santayana writes:

63. Russell, *Portraits*, 96. In the prior sentences Russell had charged that "His style, to my mind, is not quite what a style ought to be. Like his patent-leather boots, it is too smooth and polished." Note that one might make something of the same charge with much of Russell's popular writings.

64. Santayana, *Winds*, 51. Of "optimistic politics," Santayana could find abundant conformation in Russell's writings. For example, Russell writes, "When I allow myself to hope that the world will emerge from its present troubles, and that it will someday learn to give the direction of its affairs, not to cruel mountebanks, but to men possessed of wisdom and courage, I see before me a shining vision: a world where none are hungry, where few are ill, where work is pleasant and not excessive, where kindly feeling is common, and where minds released from fear create delight for eye and ear and heart. Do not say this is impossible. It is not impossible. I do not say it can be done tomorrow, but I do say that it could be done within a thousand years, if men would bend their minds to the achievement of the kind of happiness that should be distinctive of man." Russell, *Human Society*, 199–200. In his section of Introduction from the same work, Russell confronts the charge of utopianism against what he will have to say in coming pages: "The world in which we find ourselves is one where great hopes and appalling fears are equally justified by the possibilities. The fears are very generally felt, and are tending to produce a world of listless gloom. The hopes, since they involve imagination and courage, are less vivid in most men's minds. It is only because they are not vivid that they seem utopian. Only a kind of mental laziness stands in the way. If this can be overcome, mankind has a new happiness within its grasp." Russell, *Human Society*, xvi.

65. The difference between the two thinkers is not this crisp, however, for in recalling Russell's response to Edgar Brightman, Russell contended that "although I consider some form of personal religion highly desirable, and feel many people unsatisfactory through the lack of it, I cannot accept the theology of any well known religion . . . ."

> Although the prophecies it [Christianity] relied on were strained and its miracles dubious, it furnished a needful sanctuary from the shames, sorrows, injustices, violence, and gathering darkness of earth; and not only a sanctuary one might fly to, but a holy precinct where one might live, where there was sacred learning, based on revelation and tradition, to occupy the inquisitive, and sacred philosophy to occupy the speculative; where there might be religious art, ministering to the faith, and a new life in the family or in the cloister, transformed by a permeating spirt of charity, sacrifice, soberness, and prayer. These principles by their very nature could not become those of the world, but they could remain in it as a leaven and an ideal. As such they remain to this day, and very efficaciously, in the Catholic Church.[66]

Clearly then, what Russell regards as blocking the way to progress, or as an obstacle that prevents improvements whose time has come, Santayana regards oppositely. For Santayana, the components of a religious culture often impugned by critics are in fact integral vessels through which civilization is maintained. The permeation of things religious into culture, despite the dubious dogmas behind them, in Santayana's view, gives some light to a world that would be walking in darkness without them. Most of the time, Russell's view is the opposite, as is evident in Russell's description of an incident at the beginning of his second incarceration: "When, ten years later, I was welcomed by the Chaplain to Brixton Prison with the words, 'I am glad that you have seen the light,' I had to explain to him that this was an entire misconception, that my views were completely unchanged and that what he called seeing the light I should call groping in darkness."[67]

The debate between Santayana and Russell on religion and culture reverberates beyond the particular dispute between these two men,[68] and

---

66. Santayana, *Winds*, 52.

67. Russell, *1944–1969*, 24.

68. Santayana's undue adulation of the past, for Russell, would seem to make for a future never differing from the past for fear that nothing in the present is ever as good as that of the past. In Russell's mind, humankind has borne the pains of its brutal and cruel past to finally begin to emerge in a more sane and now civilized world, which nonetheless was threatened in the twentieth century by a descent backwards and downward to the barbarism from which it had come. In this scenario, there is a possible golden age ahead, and a largely barbarous past to extricate ourselves from, save some residual elements of the Greek and Roman legacies. Contemplating such possibilities, Russell could encourage a retreat to some previous sanity largely absent in the present, but he was no advocate for presuming a prior golden age from which the more lethal wrangles of the present could take lessons. This is to say that Russell's expectation for

reflects differing estimations of the blessing or curse of religion on society. What does Russell add to this debate?[69] Though he very often showed his animus toward religion, he also understood that religion can provide some needed strength in the life of an individual. Conceding this much, therefore, is to admit, however subtly or forthrightly, that religion is not born exclusively or solely from antecedent fear, nor does it only provoke cruelty as an inevitable result. This kind of oscillating posture toward religion, moving from qualified sympathy to venomous animosity, is present in any general survey of Russell's writings, and indeed, to a degree, in his life.[70]

However, as more of the outspoken critic of religion than its defender, Russell would rarely admit the sentiment, such as found in J. G. Herder, that "It is saying nothing to say that fear invented the gods of most peoples. For fear, considered as such, does not invent anything: it simply awakens the understanding."[71] On some occasions, however, Rus-

---

the future is not rooted in the past, save for a modernity whose gains are in an age of conflict greatly susceptible to being lost or destroyed. At the same time, just as in Russell's view harbingers of independent and ultimately secular thinking had to fight against and resist religious forces vying for their continuing power and influence, so too, he was unimpressed by and mocking of religious figures referencing and calling out to God in times of social upheavals.

69. In contrast to Santayana on the subject of religion, Russell can be assessed as a *philosophe* of Enlightenment vintage, particularly and rather obviously, the French Enlightenment.

70. For example, when living in 1901 with the Whiteheads at Grantchester (outside Cambridge), Russell later reflected that "The most unhappy moments of my life were spent at Grantchester. My bedroom looked out upon the mill, and the noise of the millstream mingled inextricably with my despair. I lay awake through long nights, hearing first the nightingale, and then the chorus of birds at dawn, looking out upon sunrise and trying to find consolation in external beauty. I suffered in a very intense form the loneliness which I had perceived a year before to be the essential lot of man. I walked alone in the fields about Grantchester, feeling dimly that the whitening willows in the wind had some message from a land of peace. I read books, such as Taylor's *Holy Dying*, in the hope that there might be something independent of dogma in the comfort which their authors derived from beliefs. I tried to take refuge in pure contemplation; I began to write *The Free Man's Worship*." Russell, *1872–1914*, 240.

71. Herder, *Ideas for the Philosophy of the History of Mankind*, 13:162. Granted, one should not expect Russell to follow Herder, as one who broke with the Enlightenment. Indeed, as earlier seen, Russell habitually portrays the Romantic movement and the Counter-Enlightenment, of which Herder can certainly be counted, as weakening and delaying the progression of humanity to civilized and rational society. The well-springs of human behavior are therefore decidedly different between these positions. This is partially reflected in Gilbert Murray's estimation of Russell's *Human Society in Ethics and Politics*, a book Murray thought well of, but took some issue: "One place where I disagree a good deal, is in your belief that wars are caused by hate. War causes hate

sell ascribes to the sentiment expressed by the psychologist Carl Jung, that "The religious myth is one of man's greatest and most significant achievements, giving him the security and inner strength not to be crushed by the monstrousness of the universe."[72] Russell does concede something of this view, (which places him somewhat alongside Santayana's viewpoint) though the action Russell counsels the human to take in the context of the "monstrousness of the universe" is more often rebellion than reconciliation—though sometimes both. This uniting and also oscillating between the two opposites is most observable in Russell's earliest and best essays on religion. It is Russell's later polemical writings on religion where rebellion against religion takes more center stage and positive thoughts on religion largely move out of the arena.

In the final chapter I venture that aspects of Russell's thinking on religion might be usefully compared and coupled to Nietzsche, while other

---

of course, and is apt to leave hate behind it, but I am sure that in 1914 there was no particular hate on either side. . . . Now also, though we dislike the Russian system, I don't think that is one of the causes that make war likely. I think it is on one side that the Russians have conquered all their neighbors in the hope of feeling more safe. On our side that Russia has for the last two hundred years been always expanding and is now much the strongest power on this side of the Atlantic. My point is that both sides have good reason to be afraid and to think it necessary to take precautions in order to avoid war, though some of the precautions may not be wise ones. I dare say there is among the satellites a good deal of hatred for Russia, but that is just because they are being badly treated. Their chief emotion is probably a wish to escape rather than actual hatred." Murray to Russell, July 26, 1954,Oxford University, Bodleian Library, MS. Gilbert Murray 166, fols. 120–21.

72. Jung, *Symbols of Transformation*, 231. Jung thought religion a natural and somewhat beneficial result of the collective unconscious of humanity whilst Freud contended religious belief a neurosis and in a modern age indicative of essentially human inability to confront reality. Where Russell predominantly falls within this debate is suggested in many passages in Russell's writing: "There is something feeble, and a little contemptible, about a man who cannot face the perils of life without the help of comfortable myths. Almost inevitably some part of him is aware that they are myths and that he believes them only because they are comforting. But he dare not face the thought, and he therefore cannot carry his own reflections to any logical conclusion. Moreover, since he is aware, however dimly, that his opinions are not rational, he becomes furious when they are disputed." Russell, *Human Society*, 183.

In his student days, T. S. Eliot manifested some disagreement with rational critics who deemed fear always an unworthy motivation to belief. Of the years before Eliot's 1927 religious conversion, Spurr notes that "Eliot's dissatisfaction with the theoretical explanations of reality and religion which his studies had proposed, . . . had prompted his somewhat fitful investigation of irrational phenomena in this period. In a manuscript, probably of 1914, Eliot wrote that 'I agree thoroughly with Mr Russell when he speaks of cause as a superstition: I only question whether we could live without superstition'. And, again, in a seminar of March 17, 1914, he asked: 'Can we do without superstition?'" Spurr, *Anglo-Catholic in Religion*, 22.

elements of Russell's thinking bear resemblance to the English Puritans. I will offer these suggestions with necessary caveats, for Russell claimed no fondness and not infrequently expressed opprobrium for both Nietzsche and the Puritans. However, as with his broader thoughts on religion, Russell's expressions of agreement and disagreement must be conjoined for understanding facets of a man not always well known to his public, nor perhaps at times, to himself.

9

Conclusions

A. RUSSELL AS A PURITAN

Russell possesses something of a Puritan mind and as a consequence he personifies aspects of the Puritan aesthetic. That is, Russell reflects the Puritan mind in that Russell's search is for truth that is shorn of all accoutrements and bereft of any human alloy and thus pure. This in great part was the source of Russell's early love of mathematics. Though the "plain style" of the Puritan reflects an aesthetic choice, it antecedently reveals something of a methodical principle suspicious of exuberant or lavish presentation as detracting from what I have termed "naked truth." In his desire for naked truth, Russell's Puritanism becomes more discernable.[1]

Antipathy toward aesthetic elements as detracting from truth is often encountered in the Western world in a religious context, and as an example of this we commonly see the philosopher Plato's views on art anachronistically referred to as "Puritan."[2] The congruence of an overt religious tradition such as Puritanism, intent in the seventeenth century on reforming perceived Anglican excesses in religious practice and devotion, to an older philosophical tradition such as Platonism, itself steeped in religiosity, serves to suggest a seemingly implausible link between Russell and a people, the Puritans, of whom he was highly critical.

---

1. Despite the fact that Russell's grandparents were not precisely crusty Puritans nor Victorian Evangelicals in their day, they nevertheless stood for elements of opposition to Anglicanism from within the historical Puritan tradition, though this is truer of Lady Russell than her husband Lord John.

2 For example, Murdoch, *Fire and The Sun*, 16.

As repeatedly noted in this book, Russell's attempts to formulate a personal religion always encountered objections of his own sufficient to forestall and indeed confound such an attempt. In other words, Russell could not have what he wanted, even though the hurdles presented were of his making on his own admission. (Recall his comment to Murray that "My own doctrine is repellent to me.") With a ring of similarity, Edmund Morgan, in his noteworthy book on the subject, *The Puritan Dilemma*, argued that the dilemma of Puritanism was to have aroused passions that its regimen and efforts could never, in principle, satisfy.

In addition, coupled with Russell's largely derisive comments about savants of the Romantic movement, is his negative evaluation of mysticism. Russell's rationalism, as directed to the subject and evaluation of religion, undermines the tenets of religious belief, for the severity of his critique is simply more than the beliefs can bear. Thus, though Russell much appreciates and somewhat envies the religious experience of others, such as Ottoline, he founders on the cognitivism of his approach, although he nevertheless desires (somewhat) to live in the world of the romantic, while insisting that this is only temporarily possible until reason raises its head. Sometimes appreciative of mysticism and religious experience to a degree, he could not envision or accept that one could base the validity of any religious belief upon them. In his mind, they were simply in his mind too weak for that. Russell's evaluation of religious belief occurs in the battle between reason and most everything else, with emotion near the top. In this standoff, he again resembles the Puritans.[3]

Part of the desire of both the Puritans and Russell, was to be in the presence of an unmediated truth. The Puritans wanted Christian worship purged of unnecessary elements and forms they found in excess in Anglicanism. Reflecting this insistence, Richard Sibbes, a prominent seventeenth century Puritan preacher, contended that "'Truth feareth nothing so much as concealment, and desireth nothing so much as clearly to be laid open to the view of all: When it is most naked, it is most lovely and powerful."[4] Russell shared some of this Puritan propensity as governing his search for truth. Though from a secular (or rather a presumed neutral) perspective, he desired to grasp truth as it was, that is, uncompromised and unsullied by anything—most importantly unmediated by

---

3. Eugene White has written of Puritanism, that "Its tragic flaw was the issue of emotion in religion. Its chief legacy may be the continuing conflict between emotion and reason." White, *Puritan Rhetoric*, 64.

4. Haller, *Rise of Puritanism*, 140.

anything. From that perspective came Russell's lifelong harangue against thinkers who employed compromising methods to salvage religious beliefs. Russell, like the ardent Puritans, wanted his truth unwrapped and free from any husk. Russell, therefore, exhibits in his person something of an insistent quest for "naked" truth. The desire on occasion pulled him toward mysticism, but for Russell mysticism presented epistemological problems, as attractive as that option might be for him otherwise. As mentioned earlier, his love affair with mathematics evidences his great desire to look on pure unsoiled and unsullied form. Russell wants to seize truth that is outside human hands, and for that matter, human minds—thus, Russell's dislike of Kant's humanistic philosophy.

Visitors to Russell's beloved home in Wales, Plas Penrhyn, frequently commented on the plainness of the rooms. That is, decorations seemed minimal and the rooms dominated by dullness.[5] Interestingly, in a paper read to the Apostles on February 11, 1899, Russell appears to not divest himself entirely of what he refers to as a "radical Puritanical view" concerning art; that view he describes as "that beauty is good neither as means nor as end, but is an invention of the fiend to tempt us to damnation. This is a view I have much sympathy with, and should like, outside the Society to advocate."[6] Aspects of this paper initially read before the Apostles are reiterated in Russell's letter to Gilbert Murray of April 3, 1902. In this letter to Murray, Russell reveals more of his Puritan affinities, and lets his friend Murray know that pleasure and pain are not fundamental for him, not in ethics nor in a consideration of beauty. What is? "Also I reflected that the value of a work of art has no relation whatever to the pleasure it gives; indeed, the more I have dwelt upon the subject, the more I have come to prize austerity rather than

---

5. "After Edith Russell's death in 1978, one of her husband's political admirers visited Plas Penrhyn, the Russell's home in North Wales, and was surprised by the lack of taste in the furnishings and décor: the ungainly furniture (some of which was sent to the Russell Archives at McMaster University to re-create an ugly shrine); the shabby buff-coloured walls; the vulgar wall hangings and embroidered tributes; the cold linoleum-floored bathroom with its chipped enameled tub. Only a reproduction of Piero della Francesca's Holy Ghost, supposedly above Russell's bed, helped to relieve the cheerlessness. The visitor concluded that Russell's many struggles had not affected his brain but had dulled his eye. The philistine who appreciated literature (and music and architecture, to a lesser extent), loved nature, and revered mathematics might have accepted that conclusion." Spadoni, "Bertrand Russell on Aesthetics," 76. As indicated, elements of the Apostle's paper referenced are reiterated in Russell's letter to Gilbert Murray of April 3, 1902.

6. Russell, "Was the World Good before the Sixth Day?" *CP* 1:114.

luxuriance."[7] Meanwhile, Russell extolled the beauty of mathematics, for "it constructs an ideal world where everything is perfect and yet true." Physical beauty usually gave Russell little of such an experience, though he had many opportunities among his friends and acquaintances for such experience—his aesthetician brother-in-law Bernard Berenson (married to Alys's sister Mary), not the least among them. Russell remarks to Murray about the beauty of the setting and house at I Tatti, Settignano, that

> The house has been furnished by Berenson with exquisite taste; it has some very good pictures, and a most absorbing library. But the business of existing beautifully, except when it is hereditary, always slightly shocks my Puritan soul—thoughts of the East End, of intelligent women whose lives are sacrificed to the saving of pence, of young men driven to journalism or schoolmastering when they ought to do research, come up perpetually in my mind; but I do not justify the feeling, as someone ought to keep up the ideal of beautiful houses. But I think one makes great demands on the mental furniture where the outside is so elaborate, and one is shocked at lapses that one would otherwise tolerate.[8]

Coupled with such Puritan hesitations is Russell's admission of a complicating love/hate relationship with Plato,[9] for "His austerity in matters of Art pleases me, for it does not seem to be the easy condemnation that comes from the Philistine."[10] It has certainly been common among philosophers to categorize Plato as a Puritan, particularly for his views on art and artists. This is not difficult to understand, as Plato is one of the most stalwart advocates for the rigorous discipline required by philosophy. Further warning comes from Plato that the philosopher is in perilous danger of compromising truth when courting the artist who may have little of the required discipline necessary for searching for and

---

7. Russell, *1872–1914*, 254.

8. Russell to Gilbert Murray, in Russell, *1872–1914*, 260–61. In this letter it is notable that Russell finds mathematics supreme as regards beauty. So he writes concerning the forthcoming volume of *Principia*, "The later mathematical volume, which will not be ready for two years or so, will I hope be a work of art; but that will be only for mathematicians."

9. Russell to Gilbert Murray, September 24, 1947, "My own feeling to Plato is ambivalent: I love him, but think I ought to hate him." Document no. 053645, Box no. 5.33, Bertrand Russell Archives, McMaster University Library.

10. Russell to Gilbert Murray, November 27, 1902, in Russell, *1872–1914*, 257.

defending truth. The artist, therefore, is scarcely to be trusted with truth, as he is habitually drawn more to pleasure.

As we have seen and according to Russell, a significant reason that truth is so rarely encountered is the fear of coming upon an unwelcome or unwelcoming truth. Furthermore, in examining religious beliefs, from the perception of how much is at stake, the faint-hearted inquirer is apt to fudge his investigation in order to claim an agreeable outcome. Russell, however, wants to abide by truth in its sovereignty, like the Puritan desires to allow God his sovereignty. Russell emphatically contends that fear of truth, rather than unflinching allegiance to truth, frequently biases the results of investigation. This kind of shortcut may satiate a fear or fears, but it hardly qualifies as a legitimate quest for real knowledge.[11]

What provokes an inquirer to take a cowardly retreat, rather than pursue the arduous high road? In a single word, Russell says, fear. That is, when truth appears too austere for comfort, the inquirer turns his ship around. However, this kind of inquirer compromises his investigation so as to preclude undesirable answers, while Russell believes one should strive to accept whatever result one finds. What is found may not be comforting, but equally important is realizing that when findings are comforting, and particularly so if they seem simply too comforting, there is reason to be suspicious.

However, is it always appropriate to view a finding as suspicious if we deem it agreeable? We can ask the question in a Jamesian way, and in fact note the manner in which James asked it of Russell: "Surely, *other satisfactions being equal* in two beliefs, Mr. Russell himself would not adopt the less emotionally satisfactory one, solely for that reason. It seems to me a man would be a fool not to adopt the more satisfactory one."[12] However, the congenial nature of purported religious truth was virtually always problematic for Russell.[13]

11. "Scepticism may be painful, and may be barren, but at least it is honest and an outcome of the quest for truth. Perhaps it is a temporary phase, but no real escape is possible by returning to the discarded beliefs of a stupider age." Russell, *Scientific Outlook*, 100.

12. Quoted in Eames, *Bertrand Russell's Dialogue*, 193.

13. Referencing Freud's theory of religion, Hick contends that "Perhaps the most interesting theological comment to be made upon Freud's theory is that in his work on the father-image he may have uncovered the mechanism by which God creates an idea of deity in the human mind. For if the relation of a human father to his children is, as the Judaic-Christian tradition teaches, analogous to God's relationship to mankind, it is not surprising that human beings should think of God as their heavenly Father and should come to know God through the infant's experience of utter dependence and the

Though far from being a Puritan in the ordinary and usual usage of that word, and indeed he distanced himself from what might be called a Puritan ethic, he exhibits intellectual inclinations for a reality of the kind Puritans sought in God. Though Russell is also arguably a romantic at heart,[14] his is not the traditional religious soul. In shades akin to Puritanism, Russell desires to grasp a truth possessing sovereignty over human subjects. Like the sovereign God envisioned by the Puritans, Russell sought for a truth independent of us and sought it with something of a restless Puritan temperament, for some time finding it in mathematics. Moreover, Russell's commitment to the supremely rational man sometimes made him something of a caricature of such a persona as found in literary works by Eliot, Huxley, and Lawrence, while the tagging of Russell as a Puritan of sorts has had currency with some Russell acquaintances and scholars, though usually without the needed caveats concerning the meaning of the term sufficient to make the label correctly applicable to Russell.

The common characterization of an individual as a Puritan usually references one who maintains an ardent focus and is usually presumed, though not always, to be dour and narrowly focused—without necessarily being narrow-minded. Puritans are often adamant about right and wrong and hold strict to very strict mores. Grandmother Russell would fall into such a category for the most part, and Russell paints a picture of his grandmother accordingly: "She was a Puritan, with the moral rigidity of the Covenanters, despising comfort, indifferent to food, hating wine, and regarding tobacco as sinful."[15] Life as a Puritan is accordingly strictly regimented, with discipline that may seem excessive to the critic preferring a more relaxed life. Such is Russell's comment that his grandmother would not sit in a soft chair until after 6:00 in the evening, and Russell's contention that in the final analysis the reason the Puritan will not smoke is the aversion to doing anything for mere pleasure.[16]

---

growing child's experience of being loved, cared for, and disciplined within a family. Clearly, to the mind that is not committed in advance to a naturalistic explanation there may be a religious as well as a naturalistic interpretation of the psychological facts." Hick, *Philosophy of Religion*, 36.

14. Leithauser, 47, writes, "Despite his analytic judgment, something of the romantic consciousness remained unrelinquished."

15. Russell, "My Mental Development," 38.

16. However, in Morgan's *The Puritan Dilemma*, 10, the author writes, "No Puritan objected to recreation as such; indeed it was necessary for a man to indulge in frivolous pleasures from time to time, in order that he might return to his work refreshed. But to

The Puritan tendency to brush aside superfluities suggests a regimented life somewhat resembling the Spartan, who desired a toughness providing resilience in the face of difficulty and who exercised the necessary discipline to achieve it. Therefore, indifference to some things in the world and a certain contempt for them may be evident in the life of the Puritan. Russell claims to find something of this trait again in his grandmother: "Although she lived her whole life in the great world until my grandfather's retirement in 1866, she was completely unworldly. She had that indifference to money which is only possible to those who have always had enough of it. She wished her children and grandchildren to live useful and virtuous lives, but had no desire that they should achieve what others would regard as success, or that they should marry 'well.'"[17] The regimen of religious life as lived at Pembroke Lodge Russell in time expunged from himself, with Russell in adulthood contributing a plethora of derisive comments about Puritans and Puritanism in his writings.[18] That is, in time Russell became undeniably distant and different in significant ways from the pious household at Pembroke Lodge.[19]

However, one need not be religiously minded to share facets of the Puritan mentality or personality, for Russell would direct his energies for the select purpose of ascertaining the truth as the truth, while rejecting the temptations threatening to add compromise to the goal of truth he observed upending so many other and less careful thinkers. With keen intent to avoid this weakness and to confront truth as truth, no matter how stark, Russell and the Puritan mentality come close together.

---

serve the purpose, recreation had to be fun and not exhaust a man physically or bore him or frustrate him."

17. Russell, "My Mental Development," 38.

18. Concerning himself he wrote, "The War of 1914–1918 changed everything for me. I ceased to be academic and took to writing a new kind of books. I changed my whole conception of human nature. I became for the first time deeply convinced that Puritanism does not make for human happiness." Russell, *1914–1944*, 36.

19. Russell, *Bolshevism*, x: In a comparison of communism to Puritanism, Russell contends that "Both tried to compel their countries to live at a higher level of morality and effort than the population found tolerable. Life in modern Russia, as in Puritan England, is in many ways contrary to instinct. And if the Bolsheviks ultimately fall, it will be for the reason for which the Puritans fell: because there comes a point at which men feel that amusement and ease are worth more than all other goods put together." In the previous paragraph, Russell had written: "These views are the familiar consequences of fanatical belief. To an English mind they reinforce the conviction upon which English life has been based ever since 1688, that kindliness and tolerance are worth all the creeds in the world."

Puritan leanings of another stripe had been present within the Russell family at various historical junctures and among various Russell family members. Those holding political position supported the English Reformation of the sixteenth century, while in the seventeenth century others maintained the Puritan side by insisting on further measures of Reformation in England. Russell's grandfather, Lord John Russell, clearly places himself on the side of the Puritans regarding the cause of Parliament as against the English king in the battles of the seventeenth century. Lord John's position, poised from the nineteenth century, however, reflects more affinity for the political than the religious cause, the latter so important to earlier Puritans. Moreover, by the time of the eighteenth century, the developing Whig faction of Parliament is mixed in make-up between traditional Church of England Anglicans and dissenters. Furthermore, the political liberalism belonging to the Whigs almost necessarily drew them into opposing the older Tory traditions of allegiance to the King and respect for the State Church. With the Puritan insistence on the need for further religious reform, it is noticeable that the Russells, like other gentry families in the nineteenth century, are arguing for religious toleration in the context of ever-widening political freedom. Therefore, though the Puritan desire for further religious reform may have advantaged the political cause of freedom, the political cause of freedom becomes increasingly its own impetus, however much earlier religious roots may be discernable.

Of special note in English history for the Russells was the figure of William Russell (1639–1683), of whom succeeding members of the Russell family would be rightly proud. William was adamant for the cause of political liberty when it seemed a Catholic king might be in England's near future, and if his depictions of Catholicism have a caustic sound, this was because he believed the Catholic religion inimical to political freedom. To a significant degree, the accolades from the Russell family for their notable ancestors begins with this man, particularly as other Russell ancestors increasingly become men of wealth. However, and by notable contrast, this William, and two centuries later, Lord John Russell, are men of political principles and resultant motivation. In John Russell and some of his successors, the Russells manifest an increasingly evident independent streak. Bertrand Russell was therefore understandably proud of ancestors who bolstered the cause of personal liberty, like his ancestor William Russell, who would be martyred for the cause of political liberty. Comparisons of William and his fate to the trial and execution of Socrates were not amiss. In his opposition against Charles II, William perceived simply too many Catholic sympathies and affiliations issuing from the crown, coupled with Russell's disdain for the harassment of Protestant dissenters.

As the rising tide of the Whig perspective grew in England, the Russell ancestors maintained their rightful place in that advancing tradition, but no indication of the antecedent religious links to that political tradition are later drawn by Russell from his ancestors of Puritan persuasion. In Russell's typical neglect of this subject, we find in him a general hostility toward the suggestion of any causal nexus between religious beliefs and advancing civilization.[20]

Today Puritanism is more often associated with a plain and even bland aesthetic than with the cause of advancing political liberties. Indeed, the latter may even be forgotten as an historical legacy of Puritanism, though not by Lord John Russell. That point aside, and regarding the lean aesthetic of Puritanism, Lady Ottoline Morrell early on observed how Russell did evidence in his Puritan lineage an overt Puritan aesthetic, as earlier asserted. In Ottoline's stroll with Russell one May afternoon at Bolsover Castle, a place of childhood fascination for Ottoline, she noted how Russell remained aloof from her talk of the alliance of beauty and truth.[21] While friends and acquaintances of Russell on oc-

---

20. Such is the case concerning the historical question of religious and specifically Christian origins in the inception of Western science in the sixteenth and seventeenth centuries. That is, religious elements that may have contributed are usually minimized or even denied by Russell, with Russell often attributing to religion hindrance rather than help on the scientific front. As an example, we find the following passage in Russell's chapter entitled "The Rise of Science" in his *A History of Western Philosophy*: "There is an interesting book by E. A. Burtt, called *The Metaphisical Foundations of Modern Physical Science* (1925), which sets forth with much force the many unwarrantable assumptions made by the men who founded modern science.... The general purpose of the book is to discredit modern science by suggesting that its discoveries were lucky accidents springing by chance from superstitions as gross as those of the Middle Ages. I think this shows a misconception of the scientific attitude: it is not *what* the man of science believes that distinguishes him, but *how* and *why* he believes it. His beliefs are tentative, not dogmatic; they are based on evidence, not on authority or intuition." Russell, *History*, 527.

21. "Bertie and I wandered in and out of the ruined banqueting hall and the many rooms adjoining, looking up at the tall doorways, and the deep empty fireplaces, and then we sat on the steps where King Charles and the courtiers had sat and watched Ben Jonson's masque and William's cream horses. We pondered on many things, on Kings and Parliaments and Civil Wars, and Loyalty and Beauty. 'You certainly would have been a Roundhead, Bertie. There is no doubt about that! Yes, and you would then have led the prayers and called upon God to smite the enemy hip and thigh, and you would

casion remarked on his "Puritanism," Ottoline not excepted, rarely have any ventured to relate something of his philosophical inclinations to a particular Puritan root. For starters, one might suggest that Russell's Puritanism is detectable in his almost unceasing insistence that truth as sovereign is to be guarded from any intrusion or influx of human hopes or preferences. As noted by Griffin, "There are times, indeed, when I think he saw a situation as bleaker than the facts would warrant, as if he thought optimism was plain evidence of self-delusion."[22] Indeed, to Russell, naïve expectations of truth as friendly toward the human inquirer, must be expunged, so that one respects the sovereignty of truth, as the religious Puritan does God, in effect, alone. Secondly, Russell's inveterate insistence on reason, deriving from his rationalistic nature, is somewhat akin to Puritan rationalism. That is, as Professor Haller noted of Puritan sermonizing, however rich in imagistic allusions such sermons might be and often were, these tools of the preacher were meant to serve in the interest of truth, though they could tickle the ear much like the eye had been in medieval sensual religious culture— that is, without drawing the listener to Christ. These flourishes, therefore, were and should be temporary, lest they be idolatrous, for "Truth feareth nothing so much as concealment, and desireth nothing so much as clearly to be laid open to the view of all: When it is most naked, it is most lovely and powerful."[23]

---

have helped the Lord in his work too, and smitten as well as prayed.' Bertie laughed one of his loud laughs, thinking of himself smiting hip-and-thigh. 'But you would have been a Roundhead too,' he asked, 'wouldn't you?' 'I always wonder,' I replied. 'I hope I should, but how hard it would have been to be disloyal, and how hard it would have been to see those strong, determined, fierce, fanatical, self-righteous men and women, battering down and destroying the fragile beauty that my ancestors had loved and built up, and to have heard them denouncing innocent beauty as wicked, fit only to be cast out and trodden underfoot with the roses from my grandparent's tomb . . . But I know they were in the right, and stalwart and noble and very good, and I expect one side of me would have been quite happy singing psalms with Lady Fairfax and Cromwell's daughters, although I might have shed a tear when I thought of being parted from my charming Cavendish cousins, and of having to wear grey wool dresses instead of lovely yellow satin ones. That civil war never ends, does it, Bertie? The war between beauty and Puritanism? I know I always feel those two sides fighting in myself. Sometimes I believe I have made peace, but it soon begins again. Is beauty after all but a temptress from the straight and narrow way of goodness? Is she but a wanton Circe that leads people on to wallow in luxury and selfishness and depravity? There must be something in beauty that stirs men to fury and intolerance and instigates them to have a desire to destroy. It sometimes seems to me as if it were a magnet to drive men mad.' Bertie sucked away at his pipe and only silently nodded his head." Gathorne-Hardy, *Ottoline*, 288–89.

22. Griffin, "Russell as a Critic," 52.

23. Haller, *Rise of Puritanism*, 140. Interestingly, in Russell's 1961 preface piece

In other words, the relationship and traffic in religious experience is between minds and words, not to be grasped in pleasing flourishes that tickle the emotions. Perhaps a legacy of rationalism derived from a Puritanism not commonly identified with Russell can go some distance regarding his stark view of truth.

B. RUSSELL AS A NIETZSCHEAN

Despite Russell's overtly negative estimation of Nietzsche and Nietzsche's philosophy, he shares some common ground with Nietzsche on the subjects of religion and religious belief. However, one also notices that when Russell does give some concession to a point made by Nietzsche, he usually couples this with a rebuke. For example, in his *Portraits from Memory*, Russell writes, "The only nineteenth-century writer who foresaw the future with any approach to accuracy was Nietzsche, and he foresaw it, not because he was wiser than other men, but because all the hateful things that have been happening were such as he wished to see."[24] Russell, moreover, is hardly one for name-calling, whereas Nietzsche refers to Russell's godfather, John Stuart Mill, as a "blockhead." As another example, though Russell will occasionally make a mild to mocking reference to St. Paul, he sometimes expresses agreement with that Apostle, whereas Nietzsche is viciously antagonistic to this figure in Christian history. Nietzsche's negative estimation of the Apostle rivals the diatribes he heaps on his former friend Richard Wagner, about whom Nietzsche fashioned a scathing essay which he entitled *Nietzsche Contra Wagner*.

---

to Egner and Denonn's edited volume *Basic Writings of Bertrand Russell*, 7–8, Russell contends, "I should not wish to be thought in earnest only when I am solemn. There are many things that seem to me important to be said, but not best said in a portentous tone of voice. Indeed, it has become increasingly evident to me that portentousness is often, though not always, a device for warding off too close scrutiny. I cannot believe in 'sacred' truths. Whatever one may believe to be true, one ought to be able to convey without any apparatus of Sunday sanctification."

24. Russell, *Portraits*, 129. Reflecting his disdain for both Nietzsche and romanticism, Russell concludes his chapter on Nietzsche in his *History* this way: "I dislike Nietzsche because he likes the contemplation of pain, because he erects conceit into a duty, because the men whom he most admires are conquerors, whose glory is cleverness in causing men to die. But I think the ultimate argument against his philosophy, as against any unpleasant but internally self-consistent ethic, lies not in an appeal to facts, but in an appeal to the emotions. Nietzsche despises universal love; I feel it is the motive power to all that I desire as regards the world." Russell, *History*, 772–73.

CONCLUSIONS

As noted earlier in Russell's lament of T. S. Eliot entering the Anglican Church, Russell particularly bemoaned such a decision from highly gifted people such as Eliot. Russell likewise sees in Blaise Pascal's religious conversion from the seventeenth century a waste of considerable intellectual talent lamentably given by Pascal to God rather than to science. Moreover, what Russell finds offensive in Pascal is the particular religious personality he manifests, and in this Russell is willing to concede substantial agreement with Nietzsche's harsh words on Pascal:

> It must be admitted that there is a certain type of Christian ethic to which Nietzsche's strictures can be justly applied. Pascal and Dostoevsky—his own illustrations—have both something abject in their virtue. Pascal sacrificed his magnificent mathematical intellect to his God, thereby attributing to Him a barbarity which was a cosmic enlargement of Pascal's morbid mental tortures. Dostoevsky would have nothing to do with 'proper pride'; he would sin in order to repent and to enjoy the luxury of confession. I will not argue the question how far such aberrations can justly be charged against Christianity, but I will admit that I agree with Nietzsche in thinking Dostoevsky's prostration contemptible. A certain uprightness and pride and even self-assertion of a sort, I should agree, are elements in the best character; no virtue which has its roots in fear is much to be admired.[25]

With this kind of objection to the Christian ethic, Russell edges closer to agreement with Nietzsche in identifying the real culprit within the Christian tradition, and thus writes:

> There is a very eloquent passage about Pascal, which deserves quotation, because it shows Nietzsche's objections to Christianity at their best: 'What is it that we combat in Christianity? That it aims at destroying the strong, at breaking their spirit, at exploiting their moments of weariness and debility, at converting their proud assurance into anxiety and conscience-trouble; that it knows how to poison the noblest instincts and to infect them with disease, until their strength, their will to power, turns inwards, against themselves—until the strong perish through their excessive self-contempt and self-immolation: that gruesome way of perishing, of which Pascal is the most famous example.'[26]

---

25. Russell, *History*, 768.

26. Russell, *History*, 766. Russell writes to Lady Ottoline, "But something in me rebels against the glorification of sinners. I have more joy over one just man who needs no repentance than over 99 sinners who repent—it is part of my wish for perfection.

In comparing not only reprehensible individuals, but also the ideal individual, the two thinkers, despite very significant differences elsewhere, are not miles apart. Thus, Russell writes:

> The best individual, as conceived by Aristotle, is a very different person from the Christian saint. He should have proper pride, and not underestimate his own merits. He should despise whoever deserves to be despised. The description of the proud or magnanimous man is very interesting as showing the difference between pagan and Christian ethics, and the sense in which Nietzsche was justified in regarding Christianity as a slave-morality.[27]

Nonetheless, one substantial point on which Nietzsche and Russell widely differ is the responsibility of the individual to others. Even here, however, close examination of the difference does reveal some alignment between them. Nietzsche's contempt for socialism (as well as democracy) was well-nigh shrill, whereas Russell was for most of his life a socialist of sorts, though always hesitant over the circumscription of freedom it required. By contrast, Nietzsche had no desire to see the strong individual subjugated by obedience before anyone or anything but himself. With Nietzsche there is nothing and there should be nothing more powerful than the strong individual.

In further contrast, Russell regards this kind of individualism as a crass and egotistical self-absorption to the point of dangerous lunacy. By the end of a fractious relationship with D. H. Lawrence, Russell probably perceived some such traits in the Welsh novelist. Russell may have also detected something of such an arrogant mindset—though in a much milder form than would be agreeable to Nietzsche—in some members of the Bloomsbury group. Life for the majority of members of this near cabal is about them, Russell would charge, as earlier noted. While Nietzsche contends that the strong man should will for himself an indifference to others, by contrast Katherine Tait observed of her father Russell:

And I feel I can do the virtuous-sinner business myself, so it doesn't impress me. I confess that just men usually bore me, because they are usually very limited. But that is accidental—they need not be. And when they are not, they are restful and give one hope for mankind as no one else does. I always want the best better than the worst less bad. If a fairy offered me a gift, I should ask for more brains, but if I were a stupid saint, I should ask for more saintliness." This sentiment bears some similarity to Nietzschean thought. Russell to Ottoline, December 6, 1911. Document no. 000192, Box no. 2.55, Bertrand Russell Archives, McMaster University.

27. Russell, *History*, 175.

> All the yearnings of his powerful nature were directed to the future, to a golden age to come, if not in heaven, then on earth. All his life, he felt the old necessity to devote his best efforts to achieving future goals, at no matter what cost to himself, for the coming happiness of mankind meant more to him than his present pleasure. More than that, it was the *purpose* of his present actions. He taught us to feel the same way. Our personal desires were to be considered less important than the good of the human race, our talents and energies devoted to improving the lot of mankind.[28]

Despite the obvious difference of the two men on obligations to others, there is another and not unrelated point of comparison between Nietzsche and Russell. Russell desired individuals to be rational; Nietzsche desired a very few candidates to be extraordinary *ubermensch* or overcomers. Both thinkers acknowledged the odds and opposition they faced, though in Russell's case, this was perhaps not so evident to him until the time of World War I. In Nietzsche, repudiation of the herd of men is most pronounced in the self-absorbed "last men." These individuals of the present and probable future represent a cultural species of decadence for Nietzsche in which appetites for what is comfortable and easy have absorbed them to the point that they desire nothing more than paltry satisfactions. Any notion of the presence of significant obstacles to be overcome is repugnant to such persons, for last men are utilitarians of the narrowest sort. The only reason they exert any effort is simply and only to satisfy their continual appetite for material staples and pleasures.

In comparison, Russell's perceived obstacles to a better world are capable of requiring a less contentious remedy, for the injunction to live by reason presumes a kind of respectable self-reliance. However, such a life and world seems extraordinarily difficult for many people, as indicated in Russell's pithy contention, "Most people would rather die than think. In fact, they frequently do."[29] Thus, the person skirting reason

---

28. Tait, *My Father*, 183.

29. Russell, *ABC of Relativity*, 166. Indicative of the susceptibilities of reason is Russell's statement in *The Prospects of Industrial Civilization*, 219, that "To save the world requires faith and courage; faith in reason, and courage to proclaim what reason shows to be true." At the same time, there is a selfish vanity that some men are careless about to the point of indifference to others. Into this category Russell places many British politicians who crafted England's entry into World War I. In his letter to *The Nation* of August 15, 1914, Russell contends that the wartime situation "has been brought about because a set of official gentlemen, living luxurious lives, mostly stupid, and all without imagination or heart, have chosen that it should occur rather than that any one of them

may have little desire to be or act reasonably. Speaking to this dilemma in his *History*, he offers explanation for this resistance to reason:

In one form or another, the doctrine that will is paramount has been held by many modern philosophers, notably Nietzsche, Bergson, James, and Dewey. It has, moreover, acquired a vogue outside the circles of professional philosophers. And in proportion as will has gone up in the scale, knowledge has gone down. This is, I think, the most notable change that has come over the temper of philosophy in our age. It was prepared by Rousseau and Kant, but was first proclaimed in its purity by Schopenhauer.[30]

Nietzsche, however, as one of the accused romantics here, has his own list of reprehensible accused. High on his list are the last men who can manage only a paltry will for maintaining their comforts. Indeed, when Zarathustra encounters the "last man" he finds a culminating man living at the end of modernity.[31] Zarathustra is understandably profoundly disappointed, and so too is his advocate Nietzsche.

Nietzsche's anxiety over this cultural phenomenon may be misconstrued unless we consider the fact that for all of Nietzsche's chiding and mocking, and for all of his contempt for a dubious concept known as truth, Nietzsche nevertheless manifestly takes the possibilities of life seriously. The last men, however, appear to have lost any goal for life, except for their own material pleasures. How could this have happened? Nietzsche seems strangely aloof from considering that his own criticisms of the spiritual focus of prior Western culture have produced an unintended consequence in last men who are so thoroughly at home in a material world as to desire nothing greater. They certainly do not want to be any kind of *ubermensch*. Nietzsche, however, may be partially responsible for these last men. Now fully clothed in their autonomy, they are content when their material wants are satisfied and evidence wanting nothing more. By comparison, Russell hardly ever springs for a defense

---

should suffer some infinitesimal rebuff to his country's pride." Russell, "Rights of War," *CP* 13:7.

30. Russell, *History*, 759.

31. In a letter of March 19, 1903, Russell writes to Helen Flexner, "I have been reading Nietzsche's Zarathustra: it is well-written & contains some clever aphorisms, as 'He who loveth his God chasteneth Him'. But it is fundamentally shallow. Like all creeds that make our own greatness the essence of virtue, it forgets that we live in a society, & that the excellence of others should be as much our aim as our own. No refinement of Self can ever replace the ultimate necessity of altruism; & whoever has not submitted to the yoke of the world has not crossed the threshold of the moral life." Forte, *Letters*, 42.

of autonomy, though he clearly affirms the secular and scientific picture of individuals and society, and frequently complains that religion and the residue of religion still continue to hinder secular advance. However, as we have seen, Russell also maintained that science and the inventions of science could mask an unacknowledged but persistent spiritual hunger which science, on Russell's own admission, could hardly alleviate. This lament, however, though poignant in Russell, was a quieter and less frequent voice than Russell's castigations of religion, religious institutions, and religious beliefs that continued, he contended, to stand in the way of secular and scientific progress.

Thus, while my contention is that Nietzsche's "last men" are in part accounted for by a culture having imbibed something of the secularizing Nietzschean spirit, particularly the exalting of matter over spirit, I further contend that while Russell's admissions about the limitations of science in aiding "the good life" are most certainly in evidence in his writings, his general haranguing of the sins and missteps of religion prevents most readers from recognizing his religious sympathies, a situation partly of his own making, not to say intention. Russell in great part advocated for a secular mindset in ways that undermined the pursuance of a sufficient personal religion, though he had written, "I consider some form of personal religion highly desirable, and feel many people unsatisfactory through the lack of it."

Russell was too frequent and severe a critic of religion to draw attention to positive aspects of his thinking that go in the other direction. Moreover, Russell the famed critic of religion contributed to the blows against something that he still upheld to some degree. That is, he so critiqued wrong religion with an escalating reputation for that kind of critique—and very often with zinging prose—that he was only rarely recognized for giving voice to his contention for the need for a religion.

Russell would certainly agree with Nietzsche's insistence for living the robust life that is unafraid. This was evident as Russell found himself working alongside pacifists during World War I, for Russell could not fully embrace the pacifists nor they him. Though they and he agreed on the war, most lacked the robustness that Russell upheld, not to say idolized—but he was not of their stock, and he more than once describes them as so "Sunday-schoolish." Russell, of course, was never "Sunday-schoolish."

On occasion, however, the pacifists could be the very models of fortitude that Russell sought to encourage among the fainthearted. After one night meeting of the No Conscription Fellowship [NCF], he proudly reported back to Ottoline, "The spirit of the young men was magnificent. They would not listen to even the faintest hint of compromise. They were keen, intelligent, eloquent, full of life—vigorous courageous men, full of real religion, not hysterical at all—not seeking martyrdom, but accepting it with great willingness. I am convinced that at least half will not budge an inch for any power on earth."[32] Russell saw in them no Nietzschean herd animals.

For Russell, spiritual concerns or focus could be so eroded and eclipsed by material concerns, and then so practically obscured by material plenty, that the individual becomes spiritually void and indifferent. Any religious inclinations were often forgotten by a society impatient for the newest scientific discoveries and inventions. Such a societal culture often exudes optimism and in time possesses what could be worrisome power, as weightier matters are often neglected. That is, lest we make too much of Russell as a twentieth century Voltaire, we note again that Russell pointed out to friends how people even close to him frequently possessed an erroneous estimation of himself. The same friends and acquaintances were capable of misreading Russell on religion, and he was aware of it. In a letter of January 1, 1912 to Ottoline, Russell writes, "I do not agree with the run of Cambridge people. Ask Lytton what he thinks of my religious views and he will tell you I am a Xtian. They don't care for religion—I care for it more than for anything else in the world. Without it the whole world would seem dross. With it, there are strange possibilities, glimpses that blot out complacency, and leave one in almost prostrate wonder, revelations of values that are infinite—everything that makes human life worth enduring." At the same time and in the same letter he desires Ottoline to be aware of the strictures he places around his desire for religion.

> I do think the spiritual things—the things that make religion, are the great things; they are what make life infinite and not petty. And I feel the need of worship just as much as you do. But I long to free these things from dependence on belief that this or that exists, and that the world is such and such, so that they may be secure. But Darling don't think that I should wish for even the very smallest lessening of the importance of religion in your life.[33]

32. Russell to Ottoline, February 24, 1916. Document no. 001354, Box no. 2.66, Bertrand Russell Archives, McMaster University Library/Ottoline Morrell Collection, Box 26, Folder 1, Harry Ransom Center, University of Texas, Austin.

33. Russell to Ottoline, January 1, 1912, Document no. 000306, Box no. 2.56,

This insistent distinction by Russell is the basis of his view that any apologist for religion who presumes to manipulate the findings of science so as to mesh with pious wishes reveals that he is not a man of science nor a viable advocate for the defense of religion. Therefore, Russell's argument is not one of fear of an advancing science overturning tomorrow what one believes today (though he often puts forth that argument when challenging religious belief from the perspective of scientific belief), but rather that spiritual things or truths should uphold and affirm the truths of science. Thus, Russell does not wish to see "the spiritual things" bound to "dependence on belief that this or that exists, and that the world is such and such." He desires independence for those things "so that they may be secure." In effect, Russell wants to provide permanence for spiritual things, for the security of spiritual things should not be susceptible nor shattered by scientific convolutions.

Indeed, what Russell himself desired from the company of spiritual things to include mathematics, was the calming presence of certainty and perfection. As aptly characterized by Katherine Tait, "All his life he sought perfection: perfect mathematical truth, perfect philosophical clarity, certainty of God's existence, a perfect formula for society, a perfect woman to live with in a perfect human relationship. And although he never found them anywhere, he never stopped looking."[34] As earlier noted, Tait concedes that though Russell prior to and around the time of WWI provided abundant evidence of his spiritual seeking and appetites, "After the war, finding his life more satisfying, he stopped talking that way; nostalgia for religion was quite absent from our home."[35] While this was true, it was also true that during this time Russell began to make his way increasingly as a public figure, with more and more of his attention given to considering how the ills of society might be ameliorated. With that mission, Russell was quick to target the failings of religion as contributing to the story of human unhappiness and the ills of society. Contrary to much of his previous striving for a viable personal religion came his critique against religion in various forms and bombastic critiques. This man seemed and seems to many no friend nor defender of religion.

Bertrand Russell Archives, McMaster University Library /Ottoline Morrell Collection, Box 20, Folder 4, Harry Ransom Center, University of Texas, Austin.

34. Tait, *My Father*, 106.
35. Tait, *My Father*, 185.

C. RUSSELL AS THE RATIONAL CRITIC OF GOD AND RELIGIOUS BELIEF

Russell seems to judge that to the degree a belief is desirable our reasons for claiming it as true are proportionally dubious. Any coincidence of what is desired to what is found is simply too great. While in Russell's view this constitutes a justified suspicion of religious belief, this criticism is not unique to Russell, though very often repeated by him. Nevertheless, it is part of a general criticism of religious belief found most notably in Freud, Marx, and others. To take Freud as one instance, in his book *The Future of an Illusion* he writes, "We shall tell ourselves that it would be very nice if there were a God who created the world and was a benevolent Providence, and if there were a moral order in the universe and an after-life; but it is a very striking fact that all this is exactly as we are bound to wish it to be. And it would be more remarkable still if our wretched, ignorant and downtrodden ancestors had succeeded in solving all these difficult riddles of the universe."[36] Critics contend that neither life nor Freud's dichotomy are as simple as that, for living a Christian religious life is sometimes extraordinarily difficult and as such scarcely enviable to nonbelievers. As one instance, Tertullian's quip that the blood of the martyrs is the seed of the church is one indication of how costly religious commitment can be. The "pie in the sky" estimation of religious life and belief is only part of the story of religion.

While giving ready assent to Freud's point, Russell would nevertheless balk at Freud's contention that "The moment a man questions the meaning and value of life he is sick."[37] Though Russell at times would exhibit his own mocking tone referencing such a question, at the same time he saw the value of philosophy in the raising of such questions, and judged dismissal detrimental.

In his overt hostility to religion Russell has frequently been compared to Voltaire and to the spirit of eighteenth-century thought. Russell did indeed express his sympathies for that era and for the rational critique of religious beliefs prominent during the Enlightenment. In further comparison of Russell to Voltaire, one notices that both nevertheless concede with qualifications a warranted place for religion in life. As seen, Russell concedes something of value to the religious emotion, though when in the mode of the *philosophe*, Russell gives scant voice to this kind

36. Freud, *Future of an Illusion*, 42.
37. Freud, *Letters of Sigmund Freud*, 436.

of admission. For Russell the harms caused by religious belief and institutions rival the benefit of religion for the individual and even more for any society infused with religious values.[38]

Russell usually will take issue with Voltaire on the Frenchman's adage that even if God does not exist, it would be necessary to invent him, because for Russell, accepting any candidate for truth that is dubious compromises intellectual integrity. At most places in his writings, Russell can be found condemning any suggestion to the contrary. On the other hand, Russell does make some concession to the need for something outside oneself to provide desired direction. Much of his positive remarks on religion, particularly as they appear in his writings in the first two decades of the twentieth century, acknowledge such an appetite and need, even if the ideals put forward issue from "a world of our imagining." Indeed, some of Russell's most beautifully written prose of that period as it concerns religion reflects the need in human life for something transcendent.[39]

Still, wider perusal of Russell's denunciatory writings against religion and religious belief reveals the passion of an Enlightenment *philosophe*, castigating the world of religion and religious beliefs with scarcely

---

38. As another example and from a 1911 letter, Russell wrote: "I read the other day of a man who got 6 weeks for kicking his wife to death when he was drunk—he habitually ill-treated her but gave no ground for divorce. I sat next to a parson in Hall the other night, who said he had turned against Women's Suffrage because most suffragists were in favour of freer divorce—so I began to argue divorce with him. As I expected, he lied, pretending it was on secular grounds that he opposed divorce. Of course he said divorce was bad for the children, so I instanced the above drunkard. Thereupon he said life is greater than logic. I suppose drink is greater than either since it destroys life, but otherwise I failed to see the relevance of his remark.—Margaret Davies is working hard for divorce, & starting a movement among working women, with great success. Of course religion is the enemy. Ecrasez l' infame should still be our motto." Russell to Lucy Donnelley, June 16, 1911, in Forte, *Letters*, 176–77.

39. Perhaps the most stellar such passage is a paragraph from his *Principles of Social Reconstruction*, where he writes, "If life is to be fully human it must serve some end which seems, in some sense, outside human life, some end which is impersonal and above mankind, such as God or truth or beauty." Two sentences later he adds the caveat that "Contact with this eternal world—even if it be only a world of our imagining—brings a strength and a fundamental peace which cannot be wholly destroyed by the struggles and apparent failures of our temporal life." Russell, *Principles of Social Reconstruction*, 169. Here of course, Russell is denying for these thoughts any metaphysical connection of the sort that Aristotle and Augustine and Averroes had conceived. In other words, even with this kind of concession to the need for something to set in front of us—*something not us*, Russell emphatically asserts, he is also scrupulous in how one is to understand that thing or those things to which we give such gravity and therefore adulation.

even a hiccup, while seeking to bring into being the heavenly city of the eighteenth-century philosophers, that but for the obstacles of religion could already be resident. Writing in 1969 to a correspondent who had inquired into some details of the running of Beacon Hill School by Russell and wife Dora, Dora responds to her questioner that "Russell's views are surely plain enough in all that he has written? He wants to create individuals capable of living the 'good life' in all senses, and thus bring about the diminution of war, violence, etc. [sic] within and between nations. However, although he writes of creative and destructive impulses, he is basically a rationalist in his approach and stems straight out of the 18th century. But in his emphasis on the individual he has always been at variance with those who think everything can be done by government and technology, like the dunderheaded 'socialists' of our time."[40]

One may note also that as a *philosophe* of sorts, Russell on religion resembles much more a thinker of the French Enlightenment than the English one.[41] The radicalism in Russell as a negative critic of religion shares little with Locke or similar English thinkers, though something perhaps with the Cambridge Platonists.[42] In other words, Russell's stance

40. Dora Russell to Mr. Terry Philpot, March 2, 1969. Record no. 121277, Bertrand Russell Archives, McMaster University Library/Dora Winifred Russell Papers, inventory number #75, International Institute of Social History, Amsterdam.

41. Himmelfarb writes, "The British did not have *philosophes*. They had moral philosophers, a very different breed. Those historians who belittle or dismiss the idea of a British Enlightenment do so because they do not recognize the features of the *philosophes* in the moral philosophers—and with good reason: the physiognomy is quite different." Himmelfarb, *Roads*, 25. Further distinguishing the British and American Enlightenments from the French, she writes, "In a sense, the French Enlightenment was a belated Reformation, a Reformation fought in the cause not of a higher or purer religion but of a still higher and purer authority, reason. . . . This was not, however, the Enlightenment as it appeared either in Britain or America, where reason did not have that preeminent role, and where religion, whether as dogma or as institution, was not the paramount enemy. . . . A book on the British or American Enlightenment could never bear the subtitle that Peter Gay gave to the first volume of his work on the Enlightenment: *The Rise of Modern Paganism*." Himmelfarb, *Roads*, 18–19.

42. The Cambridge Platonists were odd men out in their day, and though religious, largely unamenable to the currents of Puritanism in England while also resistant to the perceived increasingly mechanistic viewpoint of early modern science. In regard to the latter, the Cambridge Platonists are perhaps most famous in the figures of Ralph Cudworth and Henry More, who in their opposition to the new picture of nature, posited a "plastic nature" and tried to configure reality without the feared determinism suggested in the scientific picture of nature. My allusion to this group with reference to Russell is that, like them, Russell early on tried to find his philosophical and mathematical footing within a largely platonic framework providing for something of a bulwark religion and thus avoiding any complete freefall into something like an indifferent atheism.

toward religion appears to lack a particularly English tone. Indeed, for the most part the deists of England in the eighteenth century, by way of contrast to the French, reflected a desire for a natural religion, and more often without excessive rancor, unlike the French *philosophes*. Furthermore, even in the case of Russell's godfather, John Stuart Mill, (who according to Russell, provided for him the pronouncement of death upon the cosmological argument for God's existence) there is an admission that religion has some utilitarian value, as unwelcome as that was to some of Mill's critics when his *Three Essays on Religion* were published posthumously in 1874. Indeed, if one looks behind Mill, to his father, J. S. Mill, one finds a thinker significantly more hostile to religion than his son, and particularly critical of Christianity's contribution to human morality and, by extension, to human civilization. The junior Mill's more moderate tone on religion reflects the difference between father and son, for in Russell's account of James Mill, as aided by Mill's son's comments, Russell writes that "he objected to the modern stress laid upon feeling. Like the whole utilitarian school, he was utterly opposed to every form of romanticism. He thought politics could be governed by reason, and expected men's opinions to be determined by the weight of evidence."[43]

Notably, when Russell surveys the seeds of the English so-called "Philosophical Radicals" of the nineteenth century (principally the Utilitarians), he observes that "in general, there is complete silence about the Germans."[44] That is, the German Romantics represent a category of thinkers that the English Philosophical Radicals would scarcely even call philosophers. With the Radicals, English philosophy therefore did not take a turn through German Philosophy, in notable contrast to the later arriving of German idealism on English shores. The pertinence to Russell is that before Russell's acquaintance with German philosophy early on at Cambridge, he had by contrast at Pembroke Lodge already imbibed something of the school of the Philosophical Radicals and the skeptical spirit of W. K. Clifford.

Unlike these thinkers and their notion of "plastic nature," Russell was averse toward manipulating the scientific picture of reality so as to present a softer or friendlier version of the world for religious purposes. As discussed earlier, Russell presented any apologetic for religion in the direction of changing the human to accord with the scientific picture, rather than to presumptuously change the scientific picture so as to accord with the human.

43. Russell, *History*, 777.
44. Russell, *History*, 773.

Speaking of what they stood for, Russell contends that the English Philosophical Radicals were part of

> [a] profound revolt, both philosophical and political, against traditional systems in thought, in politics, and in economics, [and] gave rise to attacks upon many beliefs and institutions that had hitherto been regarded as unassailable. This revolt had two very different forms, one romantic, the other rationalistic. . . . The romantic revolt passes from Byron, Schopenhauer, and Nietzsche to Mussolini and Hitler; the rationalistic revolt begins with the French philosophers of the Revolution, passes on, somewhat softened, to the philosophical radicals in England . . . .[45]

One need look no further than W. K. Clifford for one of the most unsparing critics of religion in nineteenth century England and one whose influence on the young Russell was earlier noted. However, and also noted, in writing the preface to the second edition of Clifford's main work in 1946, Russell concedes he evidenced a youthful appetite for Clifford's championing of the rightful place of reason that seemed to hold no sway at Pembroke Lodge. Nonetheless, the adjustments of nearly a half century should not be exaggerated, for Russell is hardly any less keen to champion and exonerate reason in all things at the later date. Russell continued to share affinity with James Mills's notion that men can be rational, though it appeared falsified by a great mass of humanity who seemed scarcely rational at all. Russell, like James Mill, did not defer to romantic opinion, even when Russell on occasion walked along its path.

Clifford's manifesto for reason and against religious belief had to weather substantial criticism from opponents in Clifford's day. William James, as might be expected, disputed Clifford's contentions. James, by way of his critique, asks if it is not appropriate that our will influence our decision making, and insists that excessive fear of error could produce in a purported empirical philosophy a strong penchant to indecision and inaction. However, Russell in contrast to James, was not ready to march unless he could know what was leading him, while Whitehead, somewhat similarly to James, contended that "Panic of error is the death of progress; and love of truth is its safeguard."[46] Russell, who wanted truth

---

45. Russell, *History*, 719.
46. Whitehead, *Modes of Thought*, 22.

as much as he wanted anything, could not abide with James's or Whitehead's point of view.[47]

While Russell maintains agnosticism on the question of God's existence, he admits the inability to disprove God's existence, though on the matter of that existence, he insists that "there is not faintest reason to think so."[48] However, Russell at times can be ambiguous in what he means by "reason," aside from the fact that reason appeals to argument for the position taken and not to faith or intuition. That being understood, does "reasonableness" indicate a truth–claim such as is non-contradictory and such as agrees with the facts of our empirical experience, or is by "reasonable" meant doctrines such as we find acceptable to our moral sensibilities? While Russell most often speaks of religious claims or beliefs as "unreasonable," in other contexts Russell argues against the sufficiency of what one regards as "unreasonable" as a trustworthy criterion

---

47. The general critique of Clifford's insistence about the use of reason is that on most everything that comes our way, we are de facto left having to presume much more than we can ever hope to produce by way of the required evidence. In other words, though Clifford's requirement for evidence at first seems blindingly apparent or true, not much of our life could be lived at anything more than a snail's pace if anywhere and everywhere we find ourselves, we must undertake the work of unearthing the evidence, so as to make a proper decision and move forward. However, and on the other hand, Clifford's requirement might seem absolutely appropriate with reference to religious beliefs, commonly held to receive justification by faith and not by reason. To hold them without any further investigation beyond simple religious faith, Clifford would contend, results in moral mischief which can be dangerous enough to be deadly. What possible objection could any rational person have to examining evidence for religious beliefs before permitting believing?

A twist in this issue arose some decades ago (though earlier with Scottish philosopher Thomas Reid [1710–1796]), with a school of thinking among religiously Christian philosophers, referred to as Reformed Epistemology. Prominent proponents are Alvin Plantinga, Nicholas Wolterstorff, and William Alston. Proponents argue that some intractable issues in philosophy, such as the problem of induction, the existence of other persons, etc., are indicative of the fact that one can still be "rational" and reasonable without any absolute proofs, for no such proofs are forthcoming. The rationality of moving to religious or philosophical belief, though failing the insistence of Clifford for the requisite reasons beforehand, is simply that our receptors with reference to our impressions of the world are supported by the deliverances of our cognitive faculties. Similarly, we should trust those faculties that elicit from us belief in God. Such contention does not equate to any kind of admission that belief in God is groundless, because it is grounded in ordinary and sometimes spectacular human experience that prompts belief in God, without overt proof, and lacking in proof of the kind that Clifford insists upon. Of course, the inference to God from such experience will be wanting in those denying having any such experience. However, much like William James contended, familiarity with God is more like familiarity with other people than familiarity with atoms. Consequently, relationship between these two different things will of course be different.

48. Russell, *My Philosophical Development*, 49.

for making ontological pronouncements. Russell's claim is simply that what we can conceive as "reasonable" or not is hardly an infallible guide to determinations of truth and falsity, but perhaps reflects the limitations of the human intellect. If this be conceded, certain religious doctrines, such as the incorporeal soul, are hardly to be rejected because they seem inconceivable or unreasonable to the human reason.

As often noted in this study, Russell was not quite like the wholesale negative critic of religion or religious belief. That is, he left some room for religion serving a positive purpose, despite the pointed criticisms for which he is much better known. However, as I have maintained, though Russell was hardly able to let religion go out of his life, the matter of truth and falsity could not be ignored with any subject. That is, though Russell had strong desire for religion, he had a stronger and more abiding allegiance to reason that would not admit much of anything that seemed incredible in relation to Russell's conception of reason. If Russell had any hope at all of coming away with a religion of his own and with more than simply a base in emotion or feeling, it must co-exist with chain-saw intellect. Moreover, the head of reason would raise itself often in Russell to the detriment of Russell's stated and hardly doubtable wish to couple a religion of some sort with a commensurate respect for reason. This he would never be able to do, though he made fervent attempts. To him most efforts that he observed in others involved some form of illicit "escape from reason" that Russell simply could not endure. In Ottoline Morrell he had his brightest hopes when his romantic relationship with her was strongest. In the beginning of the relationship, moreover, Russell seemed poised to try for something with Ottoline that he had been unable to fashion alone. Russell had, after all, something of a similar hope with D. H. Lawrence. It was not implausible, therefore, for Russell to think at the time (but not so later) that reconciliation with religion might be possible with Ottoline.

Russell's early technical work in philosophy required incredible energy and left him for a time exhausted and thus distanced from any spiritual purposes he was wont to achieve. As much as he had enjoyed the earlier technical work he sometimes alluded to other work he desired to do: "So much that goes into religion seems to me important, and I want somehow to make people feel what survives dogmas."[49] Indeed,

---

49. Russell to Ottoline, April 6, 1911. Document no. 000021, Box no. 2.53, Bertrand Russell Archives, McMaster University Library/Ottoline Morrell Collection, Box 19, Folder 5, Harry Ransom Center, University of Texas, Austin. The paradox with Russell

it is within some of Russell's letters to Ottoline that we often observe the religious side of the philosopher, though a side that virtually disappears when he turns polemical against religion. The letters and Russell's interaction with Ottoline portray a man in quest of something that always proves elusive, though there are moments when he seems slightly hopeful he may seize it. Nevertheless, Russell's letters to Ottoline provide ample evidence that Russell was not for the most part the happy atheist. In fact, Russell oftentimes found himself alone with his spiritual appetites in most friendships, and remarks to Ottoline, "Most of the people who think as I do about the dogmas seem able to live in the every-day world without windows into a greater world beyond. But to me that would be a prison."[50] At the same time, he commends to her his own preference for Spinoza, his favorite philosopher, as something of a spiritual savant.[51]

Though Russell often exults in the decay of religious beliefs, he does so from an historical frame of reference, as, for example, ". . .when I reflect upon the cruelties and errors which man has owed to religious dogma, I feel the gain outweighs the loss if men come to feel that their destiny is in their own hands."[52] However, when Russell spoke of religion in more existential terms he could acknowledge a real loss incurred by fading religious beliefs. In reviewing McTaggart's *Some Dogmas of Religion* he wrote:

---

is that while he has this distinctive and differing desire among his secularized circles, he, much more than virtually any of them, writes and is much more known for his secular vehemence than they. In his morning letter of April 12, 1911, Russell writes to Ottoline: "My world is full of 'clever' people—most of them so clever that they have seen the folly of everything of value. Serious people are not 'clever', inside. If they seem so, it is only a mask. What matters is how one feels about the things that are important. And your way of feeling is much better than mine, and just what I should wish to be." Russell to Ottoline, Document no. 000414, Box no. 2.58, Bertrand Russell Archives, McMaster University Library/Ottoline Morrell Collection, Box 18, Folder 4, Harry Ransom Center, University of Texas, Austin.

50. Russell to Ottoline, April 6, 1911. Document no. 000021, Box no. 2.53, Bertrand Russell Archives, McMaster University Library.

51. Interestingly, though Russell regards Spinoza and Leibniz as perhaps his two favorite philosophers, his preference for Spinoza over Leibniz is seen in the positive though guarded religious uses Russell makes of Spinoza's thought, while to my knowledge Russell never cites material from Leibniz to make a positive point religiously. Spinoza is often recommended reading by Russell, as it was to Ottoline. In further contrast to Russell's praise of Spinoza, Leibniz is not infrequently charged by Russell as a thinker who hardly maintains his religious beliefs with any integrity. Russell is also merciless with Leibniz's notion of this as the best of all possible worlds.

52. Russell, "Confession of Faith," 4.

I cannot but think also that the author underestimates the loss incurred in losing the love of God. By love, he says, he means something quite different from reverence and admiration and gratitude; and, though the love of God must go, others remain to be loved (pp. 289–290). This view of the emotions is surely too atomic. A love which is mingled with reverence and admiration and gratitude which has an object that is unchanging and sinless and always strong enough to help, is something different from any love which is possible towards a human being. Love of God may seldom be as vivid as love of other human beings; but it is sustaining as no other love can be. Dr. McTaggart appears to value love of bad people as much as love of good people (p. 73, note), and this too perhaps makes him not realize the restfulness of love of God of those who suffer from the imperfections of human beings.[53]

The fixedness of God in being and essence, then, supplies something desired on the part of humans. Likewise, though written many years previously, Russell had told Lucy Donnelly, that "in ordinary times one builds up a world in which there is some degree of reason, and then something of this sort [accident] shatters one's edifice. I am sure the religious notion of a 'judgement' is a real comfort, because nothing is so alien as sheer irrationality."[54] But of course a reality unordered by the judgements of human reason was the irrevocable reality humans faced. The desire by the great majority of people for religion and religious belief was understandable in the wake of a perceived irrationality of the world. However, and again, for Russell, one cannot manipulate religious expectations and scientific belief so as to accommodate religious wishes. As he wrote with some show of vehemence in 1931:

> Academic philosophers, ever since the time of Parmenides, have believed that the world is a unity. This view has been taken over from them by clergymen and journalists, and its acceptance has been considered the touchstone of wisdom. The most fundamental of my intellectual beliefs is that this is rubbish. I think the universe is all spots and jumps, without unity, without continuity, without coherence or orderliness or any of the other properties that governesses love.[55]

---

53. Russell, Review of *Some Dogmas of Religion*, by J.M.E. McTaggart, CP 12:324.
54. Russell to Lucy Donnelly, June 13, 1905, in Forte, *Letters*, 79.
55. Russell, *Scientific Outlook*, 94–95.

After a parting of the ways with Hegelianism, and then Pythagoreanism, Russell increasingly saw himself with few resources from which to construct a personal religion. Nevertheless, Russell on some occasions wanted to keep the door open to possibility and acknowledged something of this frustrated desire in a letter of October 1, 1904, to his friend Dickinson:

> I agree that it is desirable that the possibility of better things than science has yet discovered should be a living possibility in the imagination; at least to those who have the strength to endure hope. For my part, I am apt practically to take up with despair as being less exhausting and less disquieting; but that, I think, is cowardice, or at best a piece of practical prudence. I am too skeptical, at bottom, about the finality of our experience; but it is a scepticism which enters little into my ordinary thoughts, probably too little.[56]

Years later, and upon reading Russell's *Forstice*, and speaking of it admirably—as very few others did—Dickinson writes, "You are the only man I know well who seems like myself to be aware of being on a pilgrimage. I feel often the wish it were not so; that one ought not to be so side-tracked from the normal more or less instinctive life as I feel myself to be and as I think you feel yourself to be."[57]

Despite Russell's usually derisive remarks regarding religion in a general sense, we might ask if any of Russell's religious sympathies, such as they are, reflect a stance that even a philosophical perspective cannot completely overturn. It is notable in Kant, as an example, that though this philosopher remains a critic of the arguments for God's existence, Kant nevertheless expresses sentiments indicative of the influence of the design argument and the moral argument upon him. Most famous in this context is Kant's admission that "Two things fill the mind with ever new and increasing admiration and awe, the more often and steadily we reflect upon them: the starry heavens above me and the moral law within me." For his part, however, Russell oftentimes berated the suggestions people gave to account for their moral consciousness, to include his Grandmother Russell as well as Kant. However, with Kant's motivation to acknowledge the effect of the "starry heavens above" we might consider

---

56. Russell to Dickinson, October 9, 1904. Document no. 049235, Box no. 5.12, Bertrand Russell Archives, McMaster University Library.

57. Dickinson to Russell, July 21, 1912. Document no. 049202, Box no. 5.12, Bertrand Russell Archives, McMaster University Library.

and compare Russell's not infrequent allusion to "The sea, the stars, the night wind in waste places." These things, moreover, according to Russell, "mean more to me than even the human beings I love best." They seem, therefore, the closest things to God that Russell encountered in his "vain search for God."[58] While neither Kant nor Russell intends such sentiments to be understood as any kind of proof, they do regard the things mentioned as in some sense standing above and outside humans enough to warrant particular notice.[59]

Russell could on occasion evidence the part of the sinner with remorse for any wrongdoing. As one example of not merely pious religious talk, in August 1913 Russell went on a walking holiday with his Cambridge friend Charles Sanger in the Alps of Italy, with some intention of resting his thoughts from Ottoline, who was proving her powers as an astute critic of Russell enough for him to have become annoyed with her, as she was with him. The exchange of letters between the disgruntled pair hardly bettered their battered relationship this time, until Russell, as he was wont to do on occasion, took to severe pleading. "I know there is a great calm place where we could live together in peace and perfect spiritual union—but the flesh is weak—O Dearest help me help me . . . Life is hard for me—but I must try to live in the spirit and not in this wretched turmoil of self-seeking. I have reached the nethermost pit of pain—Dear dear love don't let me destroy our love. . . . O help me Dearest have mercy on a struggling Sinner."[60]

However, Russell rarely appeared as penitent as this. He more often posed as the rebel contrasted to the reverent. He could be extraordinarily defiant, even when near death, as when Russell's sense of the kill-joy Deity canvassing him with trouble and near catastrophes could provoke him to brazen mocking. On the occasion of a dental appointment only days after he had initiated his love affair with Ottoline, he was told he might have cancer, and his first thought on such news was to congratulate the deity "on having got me after all just as happiness seemed in sight. I suppose that in some underground part of me I believed in a Deity whose

58. Russell, *1914–1944*, 36.

59. This is not precisely true of Kant, however, according to Russell: "I hated the stuffiness involved in supposing that space and time were only in my mind. I liked the starry heavens even better than the moral law, and could not bear Kant's view that the one I liked best was only a subjective figment." Russell, *My Philosophical Development*, 48.

60. Bertrand Russell to Ottoline Morrell, August 18, 1913. Document no. 000850, Box no. 2.62, Bertrand Russell Archives, McMaster University Library/Ottoline Morrell Collection, Box 23, Folder 4, Harry Ransom Center, University of Texas, Austin.

pleasure consists of ingenious torture."[61] When Russell did lay close to death in China in early 1921, wife Dora later recounted, "I swore that he should not die and shook my fist at the foul universe, and I rejoiced all the time to find that he did too."[62]

When Russell found himself spiritually restless, as was intermittently often the case, he went looking for some relief from his restlessness, but it seemed with no satisfying result. Indeed, he admits almost the opposite. In effect, he complained that he chewed people up, as noted in his October 25, 1917, letter to Malleson where he writes: "I shall always make everyone unhappy who has much to do with me—such people as I am ought not to be left to live. I have spread pain everywhere because of a devouring hunger which is ruthless and insatiable."[63] He had given this same warning or indictment to Lady Ottoline early in their relationship, and she felt the brunt of it on occasion as their relationship aged.

Often to his public Russell exuded confidence as well as much happiness, and he frequently made the argument that vitality was the key to human happiness, whereas he observed that too much of life was committed to a lethargic drudgery derived from moral principles suffused with negativity. Certainly this was the impression of Russell's publisher W. W. Norton, who was prepared to print books about subjects Russell thought important, not least among these subjects being Russell's combativeness toward religion.[64] Moreover, one might speculate that as Russell increasingly soured on religion in the 1920s and 1930s, his view of the world became bleaker. In other words, and certainly with more needed caveats, perhaps Russell gave up much of his hope for the world

61. Russell, *1872–1914*, 336.
62. Dora Russell to her mother, April 13, 1921, in Russell, *Tamarisk Tree*, 137.
63. Russell to Malleson, October 25, 1917. Document no. 200220, Box no. 6.65, Bertrand Russell Archives, McMaster University Library.
64. Indicative of Russell's tone on the subject, even with a sympathetic publisher, was his letter of October 27, 1930, to W. W. Norton: "There is at the present time a terrific outburst of Godism among scientific men—Whitehead, Eddington, J.B. Haldane, General Smiths, etc. It drives me wild, as it is composed entirely of sophistry. I should like in some part of the book, to show them up, but am doubtful whether you would like the book to be such as all parsons will curse." Box no. 6.36, Bertrand Russell Archives, McMaster University Library. In a letter of November 22, 1930, after making comment about the book with Norton, Russell adds more vitriol in his words to Stanley Unwin: "This last section will be a pillory of those whom the public believe to be men of science.... It makes me sick to see the hogwash in which Eddington and Jeans *et hoc genus omne* are causing the public to wallow, and I should like to give the public a nice clean sty." Griffin, *Letters*, 2:297.

as he increasingly ceased from portraying religion in any positive light. Of course one would want to be wary of contending that such a shift rose to the level of consciousness in Russell. Furthermore, such a shift is possibly and simply a consequence of his frustration with religion, coupled with the dashing of hopes he had once had. As the state of the world prodded him toward more negativity, so too Russell conceivably witnessed the gargantuan, not to say impossible, task of interfacing a scientific view of the world with the kind of personal religion he had hoped to formulate. Any such suggestion of this kind of dogged determination persisting, however weakly, in Russell may sound completely outlandish to the Russell admirer who has been fed nearly exclusively a diet of Russell's derisions of religion. However, as this work has tried to show, Russell had more to say about religion than his almost too easy polemical posture suggests. He certainly judged a critique of religion and religious belief an easier thing to do than to create a personal religion that he simply could not work out in sufficient or satisfactory detail, leaving him frustrated to the point of giving up. Thus, Russell's comment to Gilbert Murray in 1956, "I become increasingly anti-religious with advancing years," may not presume only heightened judgments against religion, but also cynicism about his own efforts to secure one.

D. RUSSELL AS DOGGEDLY DEVOUT

In Ray Monk's suggestive biography of Russell, he surmised that a fear of madness was a relatively constant worry for the adult Russell. Monk's theory is at the very least partially borne out by ample quotations Monk supplies from Russell's own hand over a feared precipice dooming him to madness if he came too close. However, in my analysis of Russell, I have indicated something different, though still familial, as dominating Russell. That is, Russell largely formed his adult life in conscious and unconscious opposition to his upbringing, particularly his Victorian religious upbringing at Pembroke Lodge. His reflection on that experience, though not of course entirely negative, nevertheless supplies some explanatory material for understanding Russell's critique of religion and religious belief in his later life and writings. Before Cambridge, Russell's adolescent life at Pembroke Lodge, coupled with grandmother Stanley, was either a frustrating or a frightening experience, dependent partly on which grandparent the youngster Russell kept company with at the time. Beyond that, wider experience of people in the world nevertheless seemed to make him further disgruntled with those he encountered, in high Puritan fashion.[65]

Moreover, from his experience of living at Pembroke Lodge, in time Russell plotted his departure from the Russell family and their religious beliefs, for "after the age of fourteen I found living at home only endurable at the cost of complete silence about everything that interested me."[66] Remarking on these largely unsettling years, he wrote that "Throughout this time, I had been getting more and more out of sympathy with my people. I continued to agree with them in politics, but in nothing else. . . . It appeared to me obvious that the happiness of mankind should be the aim of all action, and I discovered to my surprise that there were those who thought otherwise."[67]

In his efforts toward marriage to Alys, he again encountered significant resistance from his family at Pembroke Lodge, though he endured their obstacles and resisted to the point of defying them and marrying Alys anyway. As I have contended, part of Russell's impetus to marry was simply to escape from the brooding Russell family. Furthermore, as Russell pulled free from Pembroke Lodge, he decreasingly identified with the family there, as he increasingly upheld and identified with the radical motivations of his deceased parents. Such knowledge of his parents, however, took some time in coming to Russell, due to the secrecy maintained about them and against which other family members, chiefly Lady Russell, had tried to shield him during the youngster's formative years. During his courtship with Alys, moreover, and in combination with the more open culture of Cambridge, he began to move away from the influence of his grandmother. In a letter of 1914 to Lucy Donnelly, Russell indicated something of what he was about, or wanted to be about, with reference to others. It is drawn in notable contrast to the atmosphere at Pembroke Lodge:

---

65. The experience of attending an Army crammer with virtual ruffians shortly before his sixteenth birthday for purposes of preparing for the scholarship examination at Trinity College, Cambridge, stoked the youngster's Puritan inclinations. As Russell admits concerning the topic of sex: "In spite of my previous preoccupation with sex, contact with it in this brutal form deeply shocked me. I became very Puritanical in my views, and decided that sex without deep love is beastly. I retired into myself, and had as little to do with the others as possible." Russell, *1872–1914*, 52.

66. Russell, *1872–1914*, 57.

67. Russell, *1872–1914*, 55.

> I try to make people realize that there is a lot to be found out, & that anybody can find it out if they will free their imaginations & live boldly & adventurously; I try to make them feel that thinking is delightful, & that it is not impossible to build up the Cosmos from the very beginning, provided people can forget the authority of parents & guardians & the sages of former times. Reverence for the aims & minds of great men, contempt for their opinions & results, is what I aim at; to make people like them, not imitators of them. Revolution tempered by reverence—do you like that as a watchword?[68]

The motivations expressed do not allow placing Russell into the camp of the revolutionary and nothing more, for he shows here and elsewhere that he is beholden to some wisdom of the past, with part of that motivation properly characterized as "reverence."[69] Furthermore, for all of Russell's insistence that change was the ultimate component of reality—underlined with Russell's expressed affinity for Heraclitus and for Chang Tzu—he desired something not susceptible to change. For a time this was mathematics, and, though not quite equally, history. Each gave some rest and repose from the tumultuous present and maintained a sense of solidity in a world full of change and contingency. However, comporting revolution with reverence was no easy task—and that on Russell's own admission.[70]

Russell did not want to be known simply for radicalism, and in a premature obituary he wrote in 1937 about his life and work, he strongly

---

68. Russell to Lucy Donnelley, February 20, 1914, in Forte, *Letters*, 218. Interestingly, though much Chinese thinking appealed to Russell, he wrote to Donnelley on October 31, 1915, "I like their philosophy & poetry & art; I could do with them very well. Their literary style is exquisite. The only thing I know against them is their belief in filial piety." Two years previously he had written to Donnelley, "I don't care for the applause one gets by saying what others are thinking; I want actually to *change* people's thoughts. Power over people's minds is the main personal desire of my life; & this sort of power is not acquired by saying popular things." Russell to Donnelley, February 10, 1916, in Russell, *1914-1944*, 70.

69. During the War when he felt most desperate he wrote to Donnelly that "When the war is over I shall vanish from the world & devote my time to solitary contemplation. There are still mathematics, & the stars, & the wind at night—" Russell to Lucy Donnelley, March 23, 1917, in Forte, *Letters*, 259.

70. Indicating the problem in a religious context, Russell wrote, "A long short story that I published with *Nightmares* is called 'Zahatopolk' and concerns the hardening of what begins as a career of freedom of thought into a hard persecuting orthodoxy. This has hitherto been the fate of all the great religions; and how it is to be avoided in the future I do not know." Russell, *1944-1969*, 33. Granted, Russell's usual notion of any "Wisdom of the Past" was expressed as the account of the follies and cruelties of the past, and hardly presented any honorific account of stellar accomplishments and achievements.

insinuates this desire. He faults some of his public for falsely construing him simply as a mischief-maker and irreverent sort of fellow,[71] and seems, moreover, to take exception with those who thought him lacking in what he implies he in fact possessed. Russell located himself largely, once again, in the glorious past of the eighteenth century and wrote of himself and an idealized past that, "His historical writings, by their style and their wit, conceal from careless readers the superficiality of the antiquated rationalism which he professed to the end."[72] A man of the past he was, but underneath it all, unrepentant. Moreover, referencing his love of China, he indicates that "he enjoyed the rationalism of the traditional civilization, with its still surviving flavor of the eighteenth century." However, looming just as important as his rationalistic temperament is Russell's conception of himself evident in the comparison he made between Whitehead and himself as concerns what Russell calls "spiritual depth":

> Whitehead, a man who, as his subsequent writings showed, was possessed of that insight and spiritual depth so notably absent in Russell; for Russell's argumentation, ingenious and clever as it is, ignores those higher considerations that transcend mere logic. This lack of spiritual depth became painfully evident during the First World War, when Russell . . . perversely maintained that, war being an evil, the aim of statesmanship should have been to bring the war to an end as soon as possible, which would have been achieved by British neutrality and a German victory.[73]

This comparison with his onetime mentor and then colleague and most always close friend is expressed facetiously of course. Indeed, the suggestion by Russell here is that he in fact possessed more "spiritual depth" than presumed. As the reader may remember, Russell was extremely critical of Whitehead's "subsequent writings," though not because his older friend wrote positively of the religious impulse, for that much Russell

71. If so, this perhaps vindicates Gilbert Murray's contention to Russell, noted in Chapter 1, that an autobiography by Russell is needed because "You have been much misunderstood and attacked."

72. Russell, *Unpopular Essays*, 174. It was, however, this ardent rationalism in her father's thinking that provoked Katherine Tait during the time of her religious conversion to contend that Russell had not sufficiently taken stock of human sin and guilt. Perhaps Tait's point is somewhat similar to Kant's statement that "Of the crooked timber of humanity, nothing was ever made straight." Russell, however, would not have agreed with such a statement, anymore than he liked Kant's philosophy, and indeed, perceiving that his daughter had a self-conception as mired in a sinful state, Russell took issue with her estimation of herself.

73. Russell, *Unpopular Essays*, 174.

agreed with, but because in Russell's view Whitehead illegitimately tried to present the fields of science and metaphysics, understood in a certain way, as congenial to a religious metaphysic. Likewise, Russell cautions his daughter Kate in a letter of October 3, 1946, "As for yourself, try to separate the ethical & dogmatic aspects of religion. Belief that the universe is such-&-such, if it goes beyond what physics says, is irrational, & to adopt an irrational belief because it is comforting is infantile & cowardly. But the ethical aspects of religion are a different matter."[74] As pointed out already, it was maintenance of this separation that always dogged Russell's religious efforts, but so too created the impression of a thinker largely void of spiritual insight or principle, particularly as he ranted about misuse of scientific knowledge for purpose of religious apologetic. Given the predominance of the latter, there is hardly reason for wonder that Russell was perceived as lacking in "spiritual depth."

Regarding British participation in World War I and Russell' months spent in jail, it is sufficient to recall again Russell's impetus to take up the issue: "I never had a moment's doubt as to what I must do. I have at times been paralyzed by skepticism, at times I have been cynical, at other times indifferent, but when the War came I felt as if I heard the voice of God. I knew that it was my business to protest, however futile protest might be."[75] In other words, what he should do was self-evident to him, so that not even his own habitually skeptical intellect could divert him from his duty. Thus, Russell presents himself not as any saint, though not as a spiritual lightweight either. However, and again, to see that Russell is anything more than a mocker of religion and religious belief, one has to read outside the rancor of essays in the popular book *Why I am Not a Christian*.

As British politicians contemplated entering World War I, Russell encountered, both intellectually and romantically, Lady Ottoline Morrell. As influential as she was upon Russell, Ottoline did not put Russell back in the religious camp from which he had come, though the pair sought something of an understanding on religion. Russell's "Greek Exercises" and time at Cambridge had laid to rest the religious beliefs Russell as a youngster had grappled with while at Pembroke Lodge.[76] Nevertheless, what Ottoline succeeded at was some easing of Russell out of the

---

74. Russell to Kate, October 3, 1946. Box no. 8.36, Bertrand Russell Archives, McMaster University Library.

75. Russell, *1914–1944*, 7.

76. "From the moment that I went up to Cambridge at the beginning of October 1890 everything went well with me." Russell, *1872–1914*, 78.

enclosure of his prior priggish self—a word his brother Frank had used to describe younger brother Bertie in his pre-Cambridge days. Ottoline opened up Russell's emotions. She was his liberator from a fear of himself, and part of that fear was the familial insanity he thought might break him. However, and significantly, on other matters Russell was already demolishing the remaining fences of prohibitions that Pembroke Lodge had earlier instilled in him. That is, other inclinations were already loosed and resident in Russell before Ottoline. During his courtship with Alys, Russell had felt and enjoyed some attraction to and from Alys's sister, Mary, who rather took charge of Russell for an evening, while Russell seemed the willing partner. Afterwards, his attempt to explain the situation to Alys proved less than satisfactory.

As public a figure as Russell became, he rather frequently felt himself something of odd man out or even a loner for whom not even Ottoline could effectively close the distance. As earlier noted, he speaks of this most poignantly in the second volume of his *Autobiography*, where he references the wind and the sea and waste places as sometimes stronger and even more desirable companions than the people he earnestly but distantly loved. We might even venture the ironic suggestion that this philosopher felt spiritual estrangement with most other people when he perceived spiritual indifference on their part. A careful reading of Russell's obituary of 1937 certainly suggests such a surmise. While Russell did not feel close to the Bloomsbury group, he did feel at home at Cambridge as one of the Apostles. However, the underlying spiritual camaraderie that Russell sought but rarely found was a matter Russell and his friend Goldie frequently discussed, for they belonged to a small minority of essentially secular intellectuals who nevertheless continued to inquire about spiritual matters that fellow free thinkers and secularists presumed a dated and dead subject. Russell, however, should not be portrayed as an evangelist on this matter, though he does not stay silent on the need for a personal religion, even as he is insistent to keep what he considered unbelievable beliefs outside consideration. Russell was sure to inform any inquirer of what could not be believed. However, one might conclude that too much is being made of Russell's contention about the need for a personal religion, for such a point of view might be deemed as generic or platitudinal as former American President Eisenhower's statement that every person needs a religion. Though Russell could be interpreted in such a way with some legitimacy, despite some of his language at the same time, such an interpretation does not encapsulate all of

Russell. That is, though there are in Russell hostile and at times unqualified castigations of religion and religious belief, there are slighter but also deliberate threads in Russell on religion leading to what one might call an opposite purpose. This tension is most evident in Russell's essay "Mysticism and Logic," where the strife between mysticism and logic is laid bare and any hopeful expectation for the mystical point of view succumbs to the relentless march of logical and scientific considerations that cannot be silenced and must be acknowledged. This essay, however, does evidence the effort, intermittent though it is, of trying to assimilate each to the other, however much the outcome is apparent before the final summation of a conclusion. Noticeably however, and as also earlier noted, at virtually the same time as the writing of this essay, in his broader philosophical efforts Russell began to insist that philosophy can be more productive only as it takes up and models the scientific method. This point of view would tend to moderate and even undermine the already fragile suggestions found in an essay like "Mysticism and Logic." In fact, the ferocity of Russell in his insistence upon use of the scientific method in philosophy might cast him as a highly unlikely author for a piece like "Mysticism and Logic." To the same point, in Russell's hands the mystic and the mystical inclination are so severely disciplined as to provide the mystical view and vision scarcely room for any kind of substantive role in the pursuit of knowledge. Certainly the whole mystic venture is given no ready endorsements and only light suggestions are made for occasions when it might be permitted to come out of its corner. This means that for Russell the viability of any contention or theory comes down to weighing our justification for believing. Thus, while at brief times in that essay Russell remains cautiously respectful of the mystic and the mystical vision, he is nevertheless hesitant to commit more than an agnostic's admission on its possible legitimacy, meaning fruitfulness, with reference to coming closer to the thing called truth. The dazzling nature or even promise of the mystic's contention, therefore, is undercut by the epistemologist's insistence that the mystic fails at the requisite obstacle course for any and all claimants to truth. Thus, the hope of a possibility of any kind of union between mysticism and logic is vaporized, not to say suffocated, just as religious belief is squeezed out of the realm of valid belief because science might quickly show it as false. So the religiously inclined person must rely upon, or retreat to, religious feeling or emotion, if he is to have any religion at all. Thus, with Russell the mystic and the logician in the end have a falling out, for their competing differences are simply too great for any significant partnership. However, any hope, like the hope for a personal religion in Russell, uneasily combines with Russell's insistence on the inevitable fate of religious belief. The beliefs of religion, like the mystic vision, are not competent, or competent enough, to withstand, much less survive, rational and scientific scrutiny. If one ask on what grounds this is so, Russell makes reference to the Copernican and Darwinian account of the world: that is, to science.

Despite the occasionally respectful nod toward the inclinations of the mystic or religionist, the critique and rebuke both receive is nevertheless not fatal to the observation that Russell concedes the rightful, indeed, the needed place of religion in human experience, though always with the necessary caveats.[77] Writing to his friend Dickinson in 1903, he expresses his usual posture toward traditional Christianity:

> It seems to me that our attitude on religious subjects is one which we ought as far as possible to preach, and which is not the same as that of any of the well-known opponents of Christianity. . . .But what we have to do, and what privately we do do, is to treat the religious instinct with profound respect, but to insist that there is no shred or particle of truth in any of the metaphysics it has suggested: to palliate this by trying to bring out the beauty of the world and of life, so far as it exists, and above all to insist upon preserving the seriousness of the religious attitude and its habit of asking ultimate questions.[78]

Despite Russell's admitted failure to undergird those religious feelings with any metaphysics, his concern with and the importance he attached to religion hardly diminished, though it certainly had seasons and corresponding droughts. This concern for how to configure religion is evident in his abortive attempt around 1912 to write a book essentially on the philosophy of religion, which never reached publication, though the last chapter was incorporated into his "The Essence of Religion" of 1912. In the same year he began another work, this time a novel, published after his death and entitled *The Perplexities of John Forstice*. This work,

---

77. Russell's brother makes the following observation about the Russell family in his autobiography, which would equally well apply to Bertrand: "There must, however, be something in the Russell blood which prevents their being indifferent about religion and makes it impossible for them to avoid concerning themselves with it. My grandfather wrote a *History of the Christian Religion*, my father wrote *The Analysis of Religious Belief*, and I have myself been guilty of a religious work." Russell, *My Life*, 334.

78. Russell, *1872–1914*, 303.

described by biographer Clark as "thinly disguised autobiography"[79] is, as told in fictional narrative, the story of Russell's spiritual pilgrimage, though we note again that Russell was later to describe the fictional story as "much too favourable to religion," and that "due to Ottoline."[80]

It is perhaps evident in this study of Russell and religion that though Russell speaks primarily in a negative vein about this subject, he nevertheless values a religion, as he puts it, "in proportion to its austerity,"[81] and not in a mentality governed by endless strictures and attention to frivolous matters. Russell's adulation of St. Francis of Assisi is indicative of the type of religion that Russell envied:

> In the matter of saintliness, Francis has had equals; what makes him unique among saints is his spontaneous happiness, his universal love, and his gifts as a poet. His goodness appears always devoid of effort, as though it had no dross to overcome. He loved all living things, not only as a Christian or a benevolent man, but as a poet. . . . He felt a duty to lepers, for their sake, not for his; unlike most Christian saints, he was more interested in the happiness of others than in his own salvation. He never showed any feelings of superiority, even to the humblest or most wicked. Thomas of Celano said of him that he was more than a saint among saints; among sinners he was one of themselves.[82]

Russell thus values a religion capable of creating and sustaining a human strength that by itself might or would fail. His remarks on the religious leaders of Christianity at the sack of the Roman Empire, though somewhat critical, illustrate this point:

> It is no wonder that the Empire fell into ruin when all the best and most vigorous minds of the age were so completely remote from secular concerns. On the other hand, if ruin were inevitable, the Christian outlook was admirably fitted to give men fortitude, and to enable them to preserve their religious hopes when earthly hopes seemed vain. The expression of this point of view, in *The City of God*, was the supreme merit of Saint Augustine.[83]

Conversely, Russell recognizes that the religion he admires is a rarity among most individuals, who, though they may be religious, have

---

79. Clark, *Life*, 179.
80. Clark, *Life*, 182.
81. Russell, *1872–1914*, 301.
82. Russell, *History*, 450.
83. Russell, *History*, 344.

nothing in their nature "that deserves to be called religion in the sense in which I mean the word."[84] In this vein, Aristotle is a disappointment for Russell, who finds him "not passionate or in any profound sense religious."[85] Russell finds the Chinese thinker Confucius also rather wide of the mark.[86] Good manners and prudence are not the nucleus of real religion for Russell.

The respect for passionate religious feeling sometimes abates Russell's critical attitude towards religious belief, as seen in a partial way in the instance of St. Augustine just referenced, but in another manner in Russell's estimation of Mohandas Gandhi. Though Russell was an admirer of Gandhi, he had serious reservations about some of Gandhi's ideas, and was particularly pointed in his criticism of Gandhi's views on sex, which he described as "superstitious and harmful."[87] Nevertheless, in an article written for the *Atlantic Monthly* in 1952, Russell goes so far as to say, concerning Gandhi's personal decision to stay celibate while married, "Probably for him the decision was a right one." For anyone acquainted with Russell's views on sex, such a statement will appear little short of incredible. Presumably, Russell conceded the point because of his respect for what, in the same article, he termed Gandhi's "deep religious convictions."[88]

---

84. Russell, *Principles of Social Reconstruction*, 142. It bears notice that Russell from an early age observed the discrepancy between the adherence to religious teaching and actual practice. He notes in reference to his brother, who became a Buddhist, that "from what I could tell of esoteric Buddhism from my brother's conversation, it did not offer me anything that I found of service," Russell, *1872–1914*, 57. Russell's first mother-in-law, who was also the author of the best-seller *The Christian's Secret of a Happy Life*, he described as "one of the wickedest people I had ever known. Her treatment of her husband, whom she despised, was humiliating in the highest degree. She never spoke to him or of him except in a tone that made her contempt obvious. It cannot be denied that he was a silly old man, but he did not deserve what she gave him, and no one capable of mercy could have given it." Russell, *1872–1914*, 238.

85. Russell, *History*, 161, 184.

86. Russell, *Problem of China*, 190. Russell complains, "I must confess that I am unable to appreciate the merits of Confucius. His writings are largely occupied with trivial points of etiquette.... When one compares him, however, with the traditional religious teachers of some other ages and races, one must admit that he has great merits, even if they are mainly negative." This negative estimation was not true of other Chinese traditions that Russell enjoyed: Lao Tzu and Chuang Tzu.

87. Russell, "Gandhian Way," 34.

88. Russell, "Mahatma Gandhi," 39. I do not mean to convey the impression that Russell had a respect for deep religious feeling or emotion that was indifferent to content. On the contrary, he said of the romantics, "It is not the psychology of the romantics that is at fault: it is their standard of values. They admire strong passions, of no matter

Russell's religious quest sought an elusive justification for the strong emotions he felt in the presence of such things as the sea and the night wind in waste places,[89] though on Russell's view man is the arbitrator of value in the world by default, for Russell believes as much as any modern secularist that the discoveries of the modern age, via Copernicus, Darwin, Freud, and others, have dethroned man from his privileged position as the summit of all creation, and in consequence the human is now understood as an accidental visitor to an accidental universe. For Russell the modern and scientific view of man must be acknowledged in any honest weighing of religious belief, which means an absence of any conception of the human being as a privileged cosmic creature or of the world as providing a spiritual network. However tenacious Russell's desire to ascertain value in something other than the human heart, he nevertheless reluctantly admits, "Not the starry heavens, but their effects on human percipients have excellence; to admire the universe for its size is slavish and absurd; impersonal non-human truth appears to be a delusion. And so my intellect goes with the humanists, though my emotions violently rebel."[90] The problem is, however, this is a weight the emotions cannot easily bear.

Russell made a constant point to chastise modern philosophers—religious or secular—whose view of reality inordinately located the human world as the center of attention: "Marx's purview is confined to this

---

what kind, and whatever may be their social consequences." Russell, *History*, 681. Similarly, Russell's praise of Gandhi is tempered in another article in which Russell writes, "You have to ask yourself a question here that is of fundamental importance; which is better for mankind, a saint or an intelligent man? . . .For my part, I don't think that the saintly type is the one that is most useful. It is useful in generating enthusiasms, but, on the other hand, it generates enthusiasm that always goes too far. We saw how Gandhi's non-violent campaign led into violence, and we know how the Sermon on the Mount eventually led to the burning of hundreds of thousands of people at the stake. That is the sort of thing a pure saint produces in the world, even though it is not the effect he intends. . ..Therefore, I cannot put Gandhi on a level with a good many other men of our time who seem to me to be perhaps morally inferior, but, nevertheless, greater forces for good than he is." Russell, "Medieval Mind of Gandhi," 89.

89. This desire to embrace something felt to be greater than our own existential contingency is evident in Russell's remarks in a review of a work on Spinoza: "To a certain type of mind there is something sublime about necessity: it seems that in the knowledge of what is necessary we place ourselves in harmony with what is greatest in the universe. This constitutes, to those who feel it, a great part of the value of mathematical demonstration." To those who are aware of Russell's love of mathematics, to which he was initially drawn by its claim "to prove things," these remarks are obviously autobiographical. Russell, Review of *Spinoza*, by W. Hale White, 280.

90 Russell, *Basic Writings*, 49.

planet, and within this planet to Man. Since Copernicus, it is evident man does not have the cosmic importance formerly thought. No man who has failed to assimilate this fact has a right to call his philosophy scientific."[91] Russell's indictment of William James's pragmatism is most severe for lending the false impression that the way we understand the world should be congruent with our human interests. By way of contrast, Russell applauds the Anglican clergyman and Prelate Dean Inge in the clergyman's refusal to confine his attention to "this petty planet and the groveling animalcules that crawl upon its surface."[92]

From such sentiments Russell contends that the human must maintain courage along with his acknowledgement of living in the presence of a world that ignores him. To preserve some dignity, the human bystander is permitted recognition and respect for non-human truths, though their existence is, admittedly, in "a world of our imagining." Russell spoke to how this sense of proportion might be achieved (however uncomfortably at times) in one of his frequent pieces on the subject of how to right the world:

> If I had the power to organize higher education... I should seek to substitute for the old orthodox religions... something which is perhaps hardly to be called a religion, since it is merely a focusing of attention upon well-ascertained facts. I should seek to make young people... profoundly conscious of the minuteness of the planet upon which we live and of the fact that life on this planet is only a temporary incident; and at the same time with these facts which tend to emphasize the insignificance of the individual, I should present quite another set of facts designed to impress upon the mind of the young the greatness of which the individual is capable, and the knowledge that throughout all the depths of stellar space nothing of equal value is known to us.[93]

Russell thus pits himself against virtually any religious believer whom he deems so naïve or ignorant as to think that traditional and orthodox religious beliefs are sustainable in the modern world. For Russell, this stance most often spared neither friend nor foe.

91. Russell, *History*, 788.

92. Russell, Review of *Outspoken Essays*, by Dean Inge, 309.

93. Russell, *Conquest of Happiness*, 164. It is probably the attribute of stability that Russell cherishes the most in his adulation of non-human truth. This desire for something stable is one source of Russell's love of history, which for him is a description of events and persons no longer subject to the sway of time or to living human interference.

Some of Russell's reasons for his confident unbelief have been suggested in these pages, though an equal aim of this study has been to explore Russell's variegated tone toward religion in general, because he clearly pursued and at times passionately desired a religion of sorts. This fact about Russell distinguishes him from most of his secular compatriots, a fact noted both by himself and by some family, friends, and acquaintances. Sometimes comfortable with what he had lost by consequent unbelief, he was at the same time saddled with a desire for a religion that made him for the most part a stranger to many unbelievers who seemed perfectly able to live without what Russell sought to have.

To fully assess the cogency and validity of Russell's case against religious belief would require another and greater book, though some surmises toward that end have been suggested in prior pages. Intriguing about Russell's critique of religion, moreover, and also made evident in these pages, is the confident charge of incredulity that Russell rather constantly lays at the feet of religious believers. This is why I think he had little hesitation with extending his critique of religious belief all the way to the top, so to speak. Perhaps a fitting example of that kind of critique is Russell's contention that if God exists, this Being must be faulted for not providing evidence sufficient to settle debate about that existence. The thought of Russell lecturing God about the matter, however, and God being brought low, rather than the reverse, seems as parochial to this writer as James's pragmatism did to Russell.

There were times when Russell's life, as almost all lives sometimes do, seemed to hit bottom. Perhaps the gravest time for him intellectually occurred when Russell admitted Wittgenstein's criticisms of his technical work in mathematical philosophy—an admission that Russell had been putting off for some time. Compounding this devastating realization, Russell was simultaneously begging a recalcitrant Ottoline to reunite in their relationship while he agonized over the possibility that their relationship might be severed, for Ottoline was irritated with Russell for more than one reason. In her diary she wrote: "He seems like a delicate, fine, electric instrument, but not fed by ordinary life, only by theories and instincts. And yet at times he has visionary power, but that mood is rare; usually the vision is abstract and mathematical or, if gazing upon humanity, passionate, tragic and pessimistic."[94]

---

94. Quoted in Gathorne-Hardy, *Ottoline at Garsington*, 281.

CONCLUSIONS

Such was the person and polymath philosopher, Bertrand Russell. As a petulant and continual critic of religious belief and believers, he manifests a resemblance to other modern thinkers in Western philosophy, particularly those of the French Enlightenment. Unlike thinkers of that era, however, Russell numbers among the rare secular-minded thinkers of the twentieth century who still carried "the burden of God" even in an age of science. Alas, he is scarcely known for that posture, but as the virulent critic of religion. Neither religious belief or secular unbelief were easy matters for Russell.

In some expurgated form, Russell desired to be a romantic despite his very severe and frequent criticisms of romanticism for allowing human emotions to rule the head rather than the reverse. He was at times tempted to do the same, but Russell could not justify rationally the impulses upon which the romantics fashioned a notion of reality or took offense with the mechanistic and deterministic implications inferred from much of modern science. Beginning with the writing of the "Greek Exercises" and continuing as Russell began to struggle with this conflict, it became apparent to him in time that the tensions between the two could not be resolved by any dubious compromises of the scientific picture, and so any hopeful "reconciliation" between them was ultimately impossible, either by the romantic or the religious.

Russell was doggedly persistent in trying to achieve such a reconciliation for himself, however, though not by compromising science, as did Bergson and others. Russell needed to find a way that a personal religion, bereft of any claim to a metaphysical grounding, could endure with the scientific account of the world and not sacrifice science as the price for maintaining a religion. His efforts toward a coupling of logic and mysticism, rationalism and romanticism, for a time spurred by his friendship with Ottoline, was a valiant attempt to make peace with the bristly and envious combatants: the end of the matter was as the beginning for Russell. Humans are on their own. This kind of humanism was not of the type Russell could exult in, however much he insisted upon it to religious adversaries. He would have preferred to go another direction, and in that desire we find Russell unlike many of the modern thinkers of his time. An essential point for understanding Russell's non-contentedness in the world, and what makes of him at times nearly an existentialist, is the divorce he sees between human reality and the world in which the human lives. Russell, like most if not all humans, needed to define or situate himself—his being even—in relationship to something beyond himself.

This is why in his most sober moments, lacking that, Russell was only rarely a happy humanist.

Thus, Russell's frequent tendency to mock religious belief as cowardice requiring a security blanket is easily misunderstood, with Russell himself contributing to that misunderstanding. That is, Russell himself sought for security for much the same reason as the religious, however far removed from the common man might be the heights to which the philosopher Russell dared to climb to find what he wanted and needed. With the religious beliefs at Pembroke Lodge jettisoned, mathematics was a candidate for such a role in Russell's mind and life for a while, but that proved, again, and with Wittgenstein, to fail. In Russell's turn to philosophy, there was hope for other candidates, chief among them the later berated Idealism, and in the end Russell wrote by way of summary, "I have found in philosophy no satisfaction whatever for the impulse toward religious belief."[95]

Often modern people seem perfectly content, and are usually insistent to supply their own life purpose for themselves. For their life they desire no template afforded them from outside themselves. Such persons therefore typically live a life of desired autonomy; any question raised about the meaning of life sounds archaic to them or as belonging to a previous epoch when humans did not do their own thinking for themselves, nor self-construct themselves. These autonomous persons will themselves to be as they wish themselves to be. The watchword of such a culture is freedom, that is, freedom to live in such a self-supervised manner, without any interfering metaphysics deigned to bring them to heel.

While modern people essentially want to maintain a freedom against what may be perceived as constriction, Russell by contrast moves in something of the other direction, and in so doing, his resemblance to strains of the existentialists has been noted by some observers. Curiously enough, and as modern as Russell certainly is, he does not fully share some of the prior sentiments mentioned above as belonging to modern people. For all of his ideas, radical and otherwise, "autonomy" is not one of Russell's most frequent watchwords or even ideas. That is, however much Russell reflects the Enlightenment ideal of coming out from beneath a "self-incurred tutelage," to use Kant's words, for Russell the resultant freedom is for the purpose of being able to think for oneself, and to do this, one hopefully learns, among other things, how to reason properly.

---

95. Russell, *Portraits*, 11–12.

CONCLUSIONS

Though possessing the freedom of self-determination, the modern individual may presume himself capable of finding fulfillment first and foremost because he functions as his own master—impediments from the outside are removed or reordered within him so as to make the individual master of himself. This scenario is to a great degree what Russell finds most loathsome in Nietzsche's philosophy, which Russell regards as springing from Rousseau's romanticism. For Russell as well as others, to include this author, the program for the human forming himself requires a reference to something other than himself: Russell's referenced "God or truth or beauty." However, in the thinking of some romantics and most moderns, that which is outside of and to some degree independent of the individual is skirted so that the autonomous individual has no competition. This individual has placed himself in charge of his self and a thorough humanism is the result. In Russell's negative estimation of Kant's philosophy, his epistemology by implication likewise conceives of the human mind as configuring reality and idealism gains a foothold in Britain, until Russell and Moore broke from that philosophy at Cambridge.

Moreover, as steeped as Russell was in emulating and adoring of the eighteenth century and the rabid and largely irreligious French thinkers of the Enlightenment, here too, Russell was different. This is most evident when Russell's thoughts on religion turn positive, evidencing a thinker very unlike many other secular associates, both past and present. Russell still desired a religious way of being, even when the world of modern science configured reality and was to be respected in how it maps the domain of knowledge. Russell, therefore, could be something of an odd man out on the subject of religion, also because while he somewhat shared the emotion of the romantic, he wanted to be, and worked hard at maintaining himself, as a rationalist. Unfortunately, it is as the latter that Russell on religion will continue to be remembered, however much I have indicated that Russell was both, and that he was frustrated with each viewpoint as it allied with or impugned religion. Neither the giving up of religious belief or embracing secular unbelief were easy matters for Russell. In great part this was because he tried to have both.

Russell acknowledges aspirations for things that are not "real," in that spiritual hunger in his view finds no resonance with a reality void of religious or spiritual purpose. Having to acknowledge this incongruence, I think, provoked resentment in Russell. For Russell, human values deemed absent in larger reality reflect a discrepancy between the world as it is and how we should wish it to be. This admission, though required for modern people, was never easy for Russell. Beyond that, and however clever Russell's answer to an interviewer's question about what Russell might say to God in the afterlife ("You did not provide us with sufficient evidence for your existence"), this response possibly reflects Russell's dismay and disappointment, not to say anger, over the fact that there is little in his estimation of the world from which to satiate religious appetites. This is one reason Russell is mad about a religious belief he could never have.

Bibliography

1. PRIMARY WORKS BY RUSSELL

a) Books by Russell

(i) alphabetical order

Listed below are the individual books authored by Russell and drawn upon in the research and writing of this book. Russell's books are given in alphabetical order by title. For most books I have a second date when I have used a later edition, as usually the later edition is easier and cheaper than the original to access and acquire.

Russell, Bertrand. *Atheism, Collected Essays, 1943-49.* Edited by Madalyn Murray O'Hair. New York: Arno, 1972.
———. *The Autobiography of Bertrand Russell, 1872-1914.* London: George Allen & Unwin, 1967.
———. *The Autobiography of Bertrand Russell, 1914-1944.* London: George Allen & Unwin, 1968.
———. *The Autobiography of Bertrand Russell 1944-1969.* New York: Simon and Schuster, 1969.
———. *The A B C of Atoms.* New York: E. P. Dutton, 1923.
———. *The A B C of Relativity.* 1925; London: George Allen & Unwin, 1958.
———. *The Amberley Papers.* 2 vols. Co-edited with Patricia Russell. London: George Allen & Unwin, 1937.
———. *Authority and the Individual.* London: George Allen & Unwin, 1949.
———. *The Basic Writings of Bertrand Russell.* Edited by Robert E. Egner and Lester E. Denonn. New York: Simon and Schuster, 1961.
———. *The Conquest of Happiness,* NY: Horace Liveright, 1930.

BIBLIOGRAPHY

———. *Education and the Social Order*. London: George Allen & Unwin, 1932; Unwin Paperbacks, 1977.
———. *Essays in Skepticism*. New York: Philosophical Library, 1963.
———. *Fact and Fiction*. New York: Simon and Schuster, 1962.
———. *Freedom versus Organization: 1814–1914*. New York: W. W. Norton, 1934.
———. *German Social Democracy*. 1896; London: George Allen & Unwin, 1965.
———. *A History of Western Philosophy*. New York: Simon and Schuster, 1945.
———. *How to Be Free and Happy*. New York: Rand School of Social Science, 1924.
———. *Human Knowledge: Its Scope and Limits*. New York: Simon and Schuster, 1948.
———. *Human Society in Ethics and Politics*. 1955; New York: Mentor, 1962.
———. *The Impact of Science on Society*. New York: Simon and Schuster, 1953.
———. *An Inquiry into Meaning and Truth*. 1940; Baltimore, Maryland: Pelican, 1962.
———. *Justice in War-Time*. London: National Labour, 1916.
———. *Let the People Think*. London: Watkin, 1941.
———. *Logic and Knowledge*. Edited by Robert Charles Marsh. London: George Allen & Unwin, 1956.
———. *Marriage and Morals*. 1929; New York: Liveright, 1970.
———. *My Philosophical Development*. London: George Allen & Unwin, 1959.
———. *Mysticism and Logic*. 1917; New York: Doubleday Anchor, 1957.
———. *New Hopes for a Changing World*. London: George Allen & Unwin, 1951.
———. *On Education, Especially in Early Childhood*. London: George Allen & Unwin, 1926; Unwin, 1960.
———. *Our Knowledge of the External World*. 1914; New York: Mentor, 1960.
———. *An Outline of Philosophy*. 1927; New York: Meridian, 1974.
———. *The Perplexities of John Forstice*. In *The Collected Stories of Bertrand Russell*, edited by Barry Feinberg, 17–43. George Allen & Unwin, 1972; also published in Russell, *Collected Papers* 12, 123–54.
———. *Philosophical Essays*. 1910; New York: Simon and Schuster, 1966.
———. *Political Ideals*. 1917; London: Unwin Paperbacks, 1963.
———. *Portraits from Memory*. New York: Simon and Schuster, 1956.
———. *Power: A New Social Analysis*. New York: W. W. Norton, 1938.
———. *The Practice and Theory of Bolshevism*. 1920; New York: Simon and Schuster, 1949.
———. *The Problem of China*. London: George Allen & Unwin, 1922.
———. *The Problems of Philosophy*. 1912; New York: Oxford University Press, 1959.
———. *Proposed Roads to Freedom: Socialism, Anarchism, and Syndicalism*. Cornwall, NY: Cornwall, 1918.
———. *The Prospects of Industrial Civilization*. Co-authored by Dora Russell. 1923; London: George Allen & Unwin, 1959.
———. *Religion and Science*. 1935; Oxford: Oxford University Press, 1961.
———. *The Scientific Outlook*. New York: W. W. Norton, 1931.
———. *Unarmed Victory*. London: George Allen & Unwin, 1963.
———. *Unpopular Essays*. London: George Allen & Unwin, 1950.
———. *What I Believe*. New York: E. P. Dutton, 1925.
———. *Why I am Not a Christian*. Edited by Paul Edwards. New York: Simon and Schuster, 1957.

(ii) date order

Russell's books above are listed below in chronological order of initial publication.

Russell, Bertrand. *German Social Democracy*, 1896.
———. *Philosophical Essays*, 1910.
———. *The Problems of Philosophy*, 1912.
———. *Our Knowledge of the External World*, 1914.
———. *Justice in War-Time*, 1916.
———. *Principles of Social Reconstruction*, 1916.
———. *Political Ideals*, 1917.
———. *Mysticism and Logic*, 1917.
———. *Proposed Roads to Freedom: Socialism, Anarchism, and Syndicalism*, 1918.
———. *The Practice and Theory of Bolshevism*, 1920.
———. *The Problem of China*, 1922.
———. *The Prospects of Industrial Civilization* (co-authored by Dora Russell), 1923.
———. *The A B C of Atoms*, 1923.
———. *How to Be Free and Happy*, 1924.
———. *The A B C of Relativity*, 1925.
———. *What I Believe*, 1925.
———. *On Education, Especially in Early Childhood*, 1926.
———. *An Outline of Philosophy*, 1927.
———. *Sceptical Essays*, 1928.
———. *Marriage and Morals*, 1929.
———. *The Conquest of Happiness*, 1930.
———. *The Scientific Outlook*, 1931.
———. *Education and the Social Order*, 1932.
———. *Freedom versus Organization: 1814–1914*, 1934.
———. *Religion and Science*, 1935.
———. *The Amberley Papers* (co-edited with Patricia Russell), 1937.
———. *Power: A New Social Analysis*, 1938.
———. *An Inquiry into Meaning and Truth*, 1940.
———. *Let the People Think*, 1941.
———. *A History of Western Philosophy*, 1945.
———. *Human Knowledge: Its Scope and Limits*, 1948.
———. *Authority and the Individual*, 1949.
———. *Unpopular Essays*, 1950.
———. *New Hopes for a Changing World*, 1951.
———. *The Impact of Science on Society*, 1953.
———. *Human Society in Ethics and Politics*, 1955.
———. *Portraits from Memory*, 1956.
———. *Logic and Knowledge*, editor Robert Charles Marsh, 1956.
———. *Why I am Not a Christian*, editor Paul Edwards, 1957.
———. *My Philosophical Development*, 1959.
———. *The Basic Writings of Bertrand Russell* (edited by Robert E. Egner and Lester E. Denonn), 1961.
———. *Fact and Fiction*, 1962.

———. *Essays in Skepticism*, 1963.
———. *Unarmed Victory*, 1963.
———. *The Autobiography of Bertrand Russell, 1872–1914*, 1967.
. ———. *The Autobiography of Bertrand Russell, 1914–1944*, 1968.
———. *The Autobiography of Bertrand Russell, 1944–1969*, 1969.
———. *Atheism, Collected Essays, 1943–49* (edited by Madalyn Murray O'Hair), 1972.
———. *The Perplexities of John Forstice*, in *The Collected Stories of Bertrand Russell* (edited by Barry Feinberg), 1972.

b) The Collected Papers of Bertrand Russell

Every student of Russell is immensely indebted to the labors of the Bertrand Russell Editorial Project, which has undertaken the formidable task of publishing all the writings of Russell, save his books and letters, under the title *The Collected Papers of Bertrand Russell*. For purposes of the present book, individual volumes referenced from *The Collected Papers of Bertrand Russell* are abbreviated as Russell, CP, along with volume number. These volumes include both published and previously unpublished pieces by Russell, making this collection invaluable and extraordinarily time saving for research on Russell. Volumes 1 and 12 are particularly resourceful for study of Russell and religion. Volume 1 presents the earliest writings of Russell both as an adolescent and from his earliest days at Cambridge and provide ample picture of his earliest struggles with religious belief. Volume 12 presents some especially memorable and vigorous pieces written on religion before Russell became best known and oftentimes only known as a most severe critic of religious belief. When the collection is completed there will be over thirty five volumes in this huge publishing project. Below are listed the various volumes of *The Collected Papers* I have consulted and used in the writing of the present book.

Russell, Bertrand. *CP 1, Cambridge Essays, 1888–99*, edited by Kenneth Blackwell et al., London: George Allen & Unwin, 1983.
———. *CP 6, Logical and Philosophical Papers, 1909–13*, edited by John G. Slater with the assistance of Bernd Frohmann. London: Routledge, 1992.
———. *CP 8, The Philosophy of Logical Atomism and Other Essays, 1914–19*. Edited by John G. Slater. London: George Allen & Unwin, 1986.
———. *CP 9, Essays on Language, Mind and Matter, 1919–26*. Edited by John G. Slater with the assistance of Bernd Frohmann. London: Unwin Hyman, 1988.
———. *CP 10: A Fresh Look at Empiricism, 1927–42*. Edited by John G. Slater with the assistance of Peter Kollner. London: Routledge, 1996.

———. *CP* 11, *Last Philosophical Testament, 1943–68*. Edited by John G. Slater with the assistance of Peter Kollner. London: Routledge, 1997.
———. *CP* 12, *Contemplation and Action, 1902–14*. Edited by Richard A. Rempel et al. London: George Allen & Unwin, 1985.

c) Published and Other Collections of Letters of Russell

Below are listed various collections of letters written by Russell which I have consulted and used in the writing of the present book.

Feinberg, Barry, and Ronald Kasrils, editors. *Dear Bertrand Russell... A Selection of His Correspondence with the General Public, 1950–1968*. Boston: Houghton Mifflin Company, 1969.
Forte, Maria, ed. "Bertrand Russell's Letters to Helen Thomas Flexner and Lucy Martin Donnelly." PhD diss., McMaster University, 1988. http: hdl.handle.net/11375/15946.
Griffin, Nicholas, ed. *The Selected Letters of Bertrand Russell: Vol. I, The Private Years, 1884–1914*. Boston: Houghton Mifflin Company, 1992.
Griffin, Nicholas, ed. *The Selected Letters of Bertrand Russell: Vol. II, The Public Years, 1914–1970*. London: Routledge, 2001.
Perkins, Ray, Jr., ed. *Yours Faithfully, Bertrand Russell: A Lifelong Fight for Peace, Justice, and Truth in Letters to the Editor*. Chicago: Open Court, 2002.

d) Articles, Essays, Book Reviews by Bertrand Russell

The following items written by Russell were used and consulted in the writing of the present book. A youthful journal, diary, articles, essays, book reviews, interviews, papers read, book blurbs, and other pieces by and with Russell are listed below in alphabetical order by title and also referenced to the volume within *The Collected Papers of Bertrand Russell*, when so published. Previously unpublished pieces are solely referenced to *CP*. Some few pieces are referenced from inclusion into a later book.

(i) alphabetical order

Russell, Bertrand. "Adaptation: An Autobiographical Epitome." In *Portraits from Memory*, 1–12. New York: Simon and Schuster, 1956.
———. "Bertrand Russell's Confession of Faith." *The Jewish Daily Forward* (1927) 3, 11; *CP* 10:194–201.
———. "Bertrand Russell on the Afterlife." *The Humanist* (1968) 29.
———. "Bertrand Russell Reflects." *The Listener* (19 March, 1959) 503–5.
———. "The Essence of Religion." *The Hibbert Journal* (1912) 46–62; *CP* 12:110–22.

———. "The Existence and Nature of God." (1939) *CP* 10:253–68.
———. "The Free Man's Worship." *The Independent Review* (1903) 415–24; *CP* 12:62–72.
———. "From Logic to Politics." In *Portraits from Memory*, 32–37. New York: Simon and Schuster, 1956.
———. "The Gandian Way: Replies to the Editor's Questionnaire." *Illustrated Weekly of India* (1965) 34.
———."Greek Exercises." (1888–1889) *CP* 1:3–21.
———. "History as an Art." In *Portraits from Memory*, 190–209. New York: Simon and Schuster, 1956.
———. "How I Came by My Creed." *The Realist* 1 (1929) 14–21; *CP* 10:11.
———. "How I Write." In *Portraits from Memory*, 210–14. New York: Simon and Schuster, 1956.
———. "A Locked Diary." (1890–1894) *CP* 1:41–67.
———. "Mahatma Gandhi." *Atlantic Monthly* (1952) 35–39.
———. "Man's Peril." *The Listener* (1954) 135–36; in *Portraits from Memory*, 233–38. New York: Simon and Schuster, 1956.
———. "The Medieval Mind of Gandhi." *Bulletin of the Institute of Social Studies* (1952) 88–89.
———. "My Mental Development." In *The Philosophy of Bertrand Russell*, edited by P. A. Schilpp, 3–20. Evanston, IL: Northwestern University, 1944. In *Basic Writings of Bertrand Russell*, 37–50. New York: Simon and Schuster, 1961.
———. "My Religious Reminiscences." *The Rationalist Annual* (1938) 2–8; In *Basic Writings of Bertrand Russell*, 31–36. New York: Simon and Schuster, 1961.
———. "Mysticism and Logic." *The Hibbert Journal* (July 1914) 780–803; *CP* 12:155–77.
———. "Nice People." *Harper's Magazine* 163 (1931) 226–30.
———. "On History." *The Independent Review* (1904) 207–15; *CP* 12:73–82.
———. "On Sensations and Ideas." (1918) *CP* 8: 252–55.
———. "The Pilgrimage of Life." (1903) *CP* 12:31–55.
———. "The Place of Science in a Liberal Education." *Mysticism and Logic* (1913) 32–43; *CP* 12:387–97.
———. "Preface." In *The Common Sense of the Exact Sciences* by W. K. Clifford, v–x. New York: Alfred A. Knopf, 1946.
———. "Reflections on my Eightieth Birthday." In *Portraits from Memory*, 54–59. New York: Simon and Schuster, 1956.
———. "Religion and Happiness." *The Spectator* 145 (1930) 714–15.
———. "Reply to Criticisms." In *The Philosophy of Bertrand Russell*, edited by P. A. Schilpp, 681–741. Evanston, IL: Northwestern University, 1946; *CP* 11:18–64.
———. Review of *Essays in Common-Sense Philosophy*, by C. E. M. Joad. *The Athenaeum* (1919) 652; *CP* 9:393.
———. Review of *Essays of a Biologist*, by Julian Huxley. *The Nation and The Athenaeum* (1923) 223–24.
———. Review of *Language, Truth and Logic*, by A. J. Ayer. *London Mercury* (1936) 541–43; *CP* 11:171–72.
———. Review of *Mephistopheles and The Brute*, by George Santayana. *The Nation and The Athenaeum* (1923) 457; *CP* 9:429.
———. Review of *Outspoken Essays*, by Dean Inge. *The New Republic*. (1922) 309–10.

———. Review of *Pagan and Christian Creeds: Their Origin and Meaning*, by Edward Carpenter. *The Nation* (1920) 116, 118.
———. Review of *Philosophy and the Soul*, by J. S. Haldane et al. *The Nation* (1919) 646, 648; *CP* 9:381.
———. Review of *The Principles of Citizenship*, by Henry Jones. *The Athenaeum* (1919) 270; *CP* 9:401–3.
———. Review of *Science and the Modern World*, by A. N. Whitehead. *The Nation and The Athenaeum* 39 (1926) 206–7; *CP* 9:312–15.
———. Review of *Some Dogmas of Religion*, by J. M. E. McTaggart. *The Independent Review* (1906) 109–16; *CP* 12: 319–25.
———. Review of *Spinoza*, by W. Hale White. *The Nation* (1910) 278, 280; *CP* 6: 251–54.
———. "Seems, Madam? Nay, It Is." (1897) *CP* 1:105–11.
———. "The Study of Mathematics." *The New Quarterly* (1907) 29–44; *CP* 12:83–93.
———. "Was the World Good Before the Sixth Day?" (1899) *CP* 1:112–16.
———. "Why I Took to Philosophy." *London Calling* (1955) 9; in *Portraits from Memory*, 13–18. New York: Simon and Schuster, 1956.

(ii) date order

The preceding items—youthful journal, diary, articles, essays, book reviews, interviews, papers read, book blurbs, and other pieces by and with Russell—are below provided in historical order with date of composition or publication.

Russell, Bertrand. "Greek Exercises," 1888–1889.
———. "A Locked Diary," 1890–1894.
———. "Seems, Madam? Nay, It Is," 1897.
———. "Was the World Good Before the Sixth Day?" 1899.
———. "The Pilgrimage of Life," 1903.
———. "The Free Man's Worship," 1903.
———. "On History," 1904.
———. Review of *Some Dogmas of Religion*, by J. M. E. McTaggart, 1906.
———. "The Study of Mathematics," 1907.
———. Review of *Spinoza*, by W. Hale White, 1910.
———. "The Essence of Religion," 1912.
———. "The Place of Science in a Liberal Education," 1913.
———. "Mysticism and Logic," 1914.
———. "On Sensations and Ideas," 1918.
———. Review of *Essays in Common-Sense Philosophy*, by C. E. M. Joad, 1919.
———. Review of *Philosophy and the Soul*, by J.S. Haldane et al., 1919.
———. Review of *The Principles of Citizenship*, by Henry Jones, 1919.
———. Review of *Pagan and Christian Creeds: Their Origin and Meaning*, by Edward Carpenter, 1920.
———. Review of *Outspoken Essays*, by Dean Inge, 1922.
———. Review of *Essays of a Biologist*, by Julian Huxley, 1923.
———. Review of *Mephistopheles and The Brute*, by George Santayana, 1923.

———. Review of *Science and the Modern World*, by A. N. Whitehead, 1926.
———. "Bertrand Russell's Confession of Faith," 1927.
———. "How I Came by My Creed," 1929.
———. "Religion and Happiness," 1930.
———. "Nice People," 1931.
———. Review of *Language, Truth and Logic*, by A. J. Ayer, 1936.
———. "My Religious Reminiscences," 1938.
———. "The Existence and Nature of God," 1939.
———. "My Mental Development," 1944.
———. "Reply to Criticisms," 1944.
———. Preface to W. K. Clifford, *The Common Sense of the Exact Sciences*, 1946.
———. "Mahatma Gandhi," 1952.
———. "The Medieval Mind of Gandhi," 1952.
———. "Reflections on my Eightieth Birthday," 1952.
———. "From Logic to Politics," 1954.
———. "Man's Peril," 1954.
———. "Why I Took to Philosophy," 1955.
———. "Adaptation: An Autobiographical Epitome," 1956.
———. "How I Write.," 1956.
———. "History as an Art," 1956.
———. "Bertrand Russell Reflects," 1959.
———. "The Gandian way: Replies to the editor's questionnaire," 1965.
———. "Bertrand Russell on the Afterlife," 1968.

2. SECONDARY WORKS

The secondary sources listed below are the editions I have used and consulted in the writing of this book, without necessarily being the date of the first publication of that work.

Amberley, John Russell. *An Analysis of Religious Belief*. London: Trubner, 1876.
Andersson, Stefan. *In Quest of Certainty: Bertrand Russell's Search for Certainty in Religion and Mathematics up to The Principles of Mathematics (1903)*. Stockholm, Sweden: Almqvist and Wiksell International, 1994.
———. "A Secondary Religious Bibliography of Bertrand Russell." *Russell* 7 (1987–88) 147–61.
Annesley, Mabel Marguerite. *As the Sight is Bent: An Unfinished Autobiography*. Edited by Constance Malleson. London: Museum, 1964.
Arnold, Armin. "Three Unknown Letters from Frieda Lawrence to Bertrand Russell." *The D. H. Review* 2 (1969) 157–61.
Ayer, A. J. *Bertrand Russell*. New York: Viking, 1972.
Baldwin, Thomas. *G. E. Moore*. London: Routledge, 1990.
Becker, Carl. *The Heavenly City of the Eighteenth Century Philosophers*. New Haven, CT: Yale University Press, 1932.
Bell, Robert H. "Bertrand Russell and the Eliots." *The American Scholar* 52 (1983) 309–25.

BIBLIOGRAPHY

Blackiston, Georgiana. *Lord William Russell and His Wife*. London: John Murray, 1972.

———. *Woburn and the Russells*. London: Constable and Company, 1980.

Blackwell, Kenneth. *The Spinozistic Ethics of Bertrand Russell*. London: George Allen & Unwin, 1985.

Brightman, Edgar Sheffield. "Russell's Philosophy of Religion." In *The Philosophy of Bertrand Russell*, edited by P. A. Schilpp, 539-56. Evanston, IL: Northwestern University, 1946.

Brink, Andrew. *Bertrand Russell: The Psychobiography of a Moralist*. Atlantic Highlands, New Jersey: Humanities, 1989.

Brooke, Stephen. *Sexual Politics: Sexuality, Family Planning, and the British Left from the 1880s to the Present Day*. Oxford: Oxford University Press, 2011.

Candlish, Stewart. *The Russell/Bradley Dispute and Its significance for Twentieth-Century Philosophy*. Houndmills, Hampshire: Palgrave Macmillan, 2007.

Carson, D. A. *The Gospel According to John*. Grand Rapids: Eerdmans, 1991.

Cecil, David, ed. *Desmond MacCarthy: The Man and His Writings*. London: Constable, 1984.

Clark, Ronald W. *The Life of Bertrand Russell*. New York: Alfred A. Knopf, 1976.

Clarke, W. Norris. "A Curious Blindspot in the Anglo-American Tradition of Anti-Theistic Argument." *Monist* 54 (1970) 181-200.

Clifford, W. K. *Common Sense of the Exact Sciences*. New York: Alfred A. Knopf, 1946.

Copleston, Frederick. Review of *The Autobiography of Bertrand Russell, 1872-1914*. *The Month* (1967) 314-15.

———. *A History of Philosophy*, Vol. 8, pt. 2: *Modern Philosophy: Bentham to Russell*. Garden City, NY: Doubleday, 1967.

Cox, Harvey. *Religion in the Secular City*. New York: Simon and Schuster, 1984.

———. *The Secular City*. New York: Macmillian, 1965.

Crawshay-Williams, Rupert. *Russell Remembered*. London: Oxford University Press, 1970.

Dickinson, G. Lowes. *The Greek View of Life*. Ann Arbor: University of Michigan Press, 1958.

———. *A Modern Symposium: Basic Political Viewpoints Debated*. New York City: Hart, 1967.

Eames, Elizabeth Ramsden. *Bertrand Russell's Dialogue with His Contemporaries*. New York: Routledge, 1989.

Eisler, Lee. *The Quotable Bertrand Russell*. Amherst, NY: Prometheus, 1993.

Eliot, T. S. *Christianity and Culture: The Idea of a Christian Society and Notes towards the Definition of Culture*. New York: Harcourt Brace Jovanovich, 1940.

———. "The Metaphysical Poets." In Selected Essays of T.S. Eliot, 241-50. New York: Harcourt, Brace, 1932.

———. Review of "Why I Am Not a Christian." *The Criterion* 6 (1927) 177-79.

———. "'Style and Thought,'" review of *Mysticism and Logic*. *The Nation* 22 (1918) 768, 770.

Eliot, T. S., Valerie Eliot, eds, et al. *The Letters of T. S. Eliot*. Vol. 5: 1930-1931. New Haven, CT: Yale University Press, 2015.

Eliot, Valerie, and Hugh Haughton, eds. *The Letters of T.S. Eliot*. Vol. 1, 1898-1922. Rev. ed. New Haven, CT: Yale University Press, 2011.

———. *The Letters of T.S. Eliot*. Vol. 2, 1923-1925. Rev. ed. New Haven, CT: Yale University Press, 2011.

———. *The Letters of T.S. Eliot.* Vol. 3, 1926–1927. New Haven, CT: Yale University Press, 2012.
Epstein, Joseph. *Partial Payments: Essays on Writers and Their Lives.* New York: W. W. Norton, 1989.
Feinberg, Barry, and Ronald Kasrils. *Bertrand Russell's America: 1945–1970.* Boston: South End, 1984.
Forster, E. M. *Goldsworthy Lowes Dickinson.* New York: Harcourt Brace Jovanovich, 1934.
Forte, Maria. "Lucy Martin Donnelly: a Sojourn with the Russells." *Russell* 7 (1987) 53–59.
Freud, Sigmund. *The Future of an Illusion.* Translated by James Strachey. New York: W. W. Norton, 1961.
———. *Letters of Sigmund Freud.* Selected and edited by Ernst L. Freud and translated by Tania and James Stern. New York: Dover, 1992.
Froude, J. A. *Woburn Abbey and Chenies.* N.d.: J.M. Dent, n.d.
Gardner, John. *The Art of Fiction.* New York: Vintage, 1991.
———. *On Becoming a Novelist.* Repr. W. W. Norton, 1999.
Gathorne-Hardy, Robert, ed. *Ottoline: The Early Memoirs of Lady Ottoline Morrell.* London: Faber and Faber, 1963.
Gilson, Etienne. *Reason and Revelation in the Middle Ages.* New York: Charles Scribner's Sons, 1961.
Grayling, A. C. *Russell: A Very Short Introduction.* Oxford: Oxford University Press, 2002.
Greenspan, Louis. *The Incompatible Prophesies: Bertrand Russell on Science and Liberty.* Oakville, ON: Mosaic, 1978.
Greenspan, Louis, and Stefan Andersson, eds. *Russell on Religion: Selections from the Writings of Bertrand Russell.* New York: Routledge, 1999.
Griffin, Nicholas. "'The Acts of the Apostles.'" Review of Levy, *G. E. Moore and the Cambridge Apostles. Russell* 1 (1981) 71–82.
———. "Bertrand Russell as a Critic of Religion." *Studies in Religion* 24 (1995) 47–58.
———. "Introduction." In *The Cambridge Companion to Bertrand Russell*, edited by Nicholas Griffin, 1–50. Cambridge: Cambridge University Press, 2003.
———. *Russell's Idealist Apprenticeship.* Oxford: Oxford University Press, 1991.
Haller, William. *The Rise of Puritanism.* Philadelphia: University of Pennsylvania Press, 1938.
Hardy, G. H. *Bertrand Russell and Trinity.* Cambridge: Cambridge University Press, 1970.
Harre, Rom. "Wittgenstein: Science and Religion." *Philosophy* 76 (2001) 211–37.
Harrison, Royden. "Bertrand Russell and the Webbs." *Russell* 5 (1985) 44–49.
Hick, John, ed. *The Existence of God.* New York: Macmillan, 1964.
Himmelfarb, Gertrude. *The Roads to Modernity: The British, French, and American Enlightenments.* New York: Alfred A. Knopf, 2004.
Huxley, Aldous, ed. *The Letters of D. H. Lawrence.* London: William Heinemann, 1932.
Ironside, Philip. *The Social and Political Thought of Bertrand Russell: The Development of an Aristocratic Liberalism.* New York: Cambridge University Press, 1996.
Jager, Ronald. *The Development of Bertrand Russell's Philosophy.* London: George Allen & Unwin, 1972.

Kantra, Robert A. *All Things Vain: Religious Satirists and Their Art*. Philadelphia: Pennsylvania State University, 1984.

Kay, William K. "Bertrand Russell and World Religions." *Journal of Beliefs and Values*, 18 (1997) 239–42.

Keynes, *Collected Writings*, Vol. 10, *Essays in Biography*. Edited by Elizabeth Johnson and Donald Moggridge. Royal Economic Society, 1978.

Kirk, Russell. *Eliot and His Age: T. S. Eliot's Moral Imagination in the Twentieth Century*. 2nd ed. Wilmington, DE: ISI Books, 2008.

Kohl, Marvin. "Russell on the Utility of Religion: Copleston's Critique." *International Journal for Philosophy of Religion* 22 (1987) 69–79.

Lawson, Lesley. *Out of the Shadows: The Life of Lucy, Countess of Bedford*. New York: Bloomsbury Academic, 2008.

Leithauser, Gladys Garner. "Spirited Satire: the Fiction of Bertrand Russell." *Russell* 13 (1993) 63–82.

Leithauser, Gladys Garner, and Nadine Cowan Dyer. "Bertrand Russell and T. S. Eliot: Their Dialogue." *Russell* 2 (1982) 7–28.

Levy, Paul. *G. E. Moore and the Cambridge Apostles*. London: Weidenfeld, 1979.

Lockerd, Benjamin G., ed. *T.S. Eliot and the Christian Tradition*. Lanham, MD: Fairleigh Dickinson University Press, 2014.

Lubenow, W. C. *The Cambridge Apostles, 1820–1914*. Cambridge: Cambridge University Press, 1998.

MacCarthy, Desmond, and Agatha Russell, eds. *Lady John Russell: A Memoir with Selections from her Diaries and Correspondence*. London: Longmans, 1926.

Mackinnon, D. M. "Some Aspects of the Treatment of Christianity by the British Idealists." *Religious Studies* 20 (1984) 133–44.

Malleson, Constance. *After Ten Years: A Personal Record*. London: Jonathan Cape, 1931.

Marler, Regina. *Bloomsbury Pie: The Making of the Bloomsbury Boom*. New York: Henry Holt, 1997.

McGuinness, Brian, and G. H. von Wright, eds. *Ludwig Wittgenstein: Cambridge Letters: Correspondence with Russell, Keynes, Moore, Ramsey and Sraffa*. Oxford: Blackwell, 1995.

Miri, Seyed Javad. *East and West: Allama Jafari on Bertrand Russell*. Lanham, Maryland: University Press of America, 2013.

Monk, Ray. *Bertrand Russell: The Ghost of Madness, 1921–1970*. New York: The Free Press, 2000.

———. *Bertrand Russell: The Spirit of Solitude, 1872–1921*. New York: The Free Press, 1996.

———. *Ludwig Wittgenstein: The Duty of Genius*. New York: Penguin, 1990.

———. "The Madness of Truth: Russell's Admiration for Joseph Conrad." *Russell* 14 (1994) 119–34.

Moore, Harry T. *D. H. Lawrence's Letters to Bertrand Russell*. New York: Gotham, 1948.

Moorehead, Caroline. *Bertrand Russell: A Life*. New York: Penguin, 1992.

Moran, Margaret. "Men of Letters: Bertrand Russell and Joseph Conrad." *Russell* 2 (1982) 29–46.

Moran, Margaret, and Carl Spadoni, eds. *Intellect and Social Conscience: Essays on Bertrand Russell's Early Work*. Hamilton, Ontario: McMaster University Library Press, 1984.

Morrill, John. "Russell, Conrad Sebastian Robert, fifth Earl Russell (1937–2004)." In *Oxford Dictionary of National Biography*, 48:n.d. Oxford: Oxford University Press, 2009.

Murdoch, Iris. *The Fire and the Sun: Why Plato Banished the Poets*. Oxford: Oxford University Press, 1977.

Murray, Rosalind. *The Good Pagan's Failure*. New York: Longmans, Green, 1948.

Nietzsche, Friedrich. *The Birth of Tragedy and The Genealogy of Morals*. Translated by Francis Golffing. Garden City, NY: Doubleday Anchor, 1956.

———. *Thus Spake Zarathustra*. Translated by Thomas Common. Mineola, NY: Dover Thrift, 1999.

Pitt, Jack. "Russell on Religion." *International Journal for Philosophy of Religion* 6 (1975) 40–53.

Pringle-Pattison, A. S. "Free Man's Worship: Russell's Views on Religion." *Hibbert Journal* 12 (1913) 47–63.

Proctor, Dennis, ed. *The Autobiography of G. Lowes Dickinson and other Unpublished Writings*. London: Duckworth, 1973.

Randall, John Herman, Jr. Review of Russell's *History of Western Philosophy*. *The New York Times Book Review* (October 21, 1945).

Rice, Cara Elizabeth. "Shelley: A Russellian Romantic." *Russell* 29 (2009) 13–28.

Robson, Ann. "Bertrand Russell and His Godless Parents." *Russell* 7 (1972) 3–9.

Rosenbaum, S. P., ed. *The Bloomsbury Group: A Collection of Memoirs and Commentary*. Rev. ed. Toronto: University of Toronto Press, 1995.

Rosner, Victoria, ed. *The Cambridge Companion to the Bloomsbury Group*. Cambridge: Cambridge University Press, 2014.

Russell, Conrad. "Francis Russell." In *Oxford Dictionary of National Biography*, edited by H. C. G. Matthew and Brian Harrison, 48:241–50. Oxford: Oxford University Press, 2004.

———. *An Intelligent Person's Guide to Liberalism*. London: Duckworth, 1999.

Russell, Dora. *The Religion of the Machine Age*. London: Routledge, 1983.

———. *The Tamarisk Tree*, Vol. 1: *My Quest for Liberty and Love*. London: Virago Limited, 1977.

———. *The Tamarisk Tree*, Vol. 2: *My School and the Years of War*. London: Virago, 1981.

Russell, Edith. "'Clark's Fatuous Book': Comments on Ronald W. Clark's *Life of Bertrand Russell*, Part I." *Russell* (2009) 35–52.

———. "'Clark's Fatuous Book': Comments on Ronald W. Clark's *Life of Bertrand Russell*, Part 2." *Russell* (2010) 31–56.

———. "'Clark's Fatuous Book': Comments on Ronald W. Clark's *Life of Bertrand Russell*, Part 3." *Russell* (2011) 127–41.

Russell, Frank. *Lay Sermons*. London: Heinemann, 1912.

———. *My Life and Adventures*. London: Cassell, 1923.

Russell, Lord John. *Essays on the Rise and Progress of the Christian Religion*, 2nd edition. London: Longmans, 1873.

Ryan, Alan. *Bertrand Russell: A Political Life*. New York: Hill and Wang, 1988.

Santayana, George. *Winds of Doctrine*. New York: Harper Torchbooks, 1957.

Scheler, Max. *Ressentiment*. Translated by Lewis B. Coser and William W. Holdheim. Milwaukee: Marquette University Press, 1994.

Schilpp, Paul Arthur, ed. *The Philosophy of Bertrand Russell*. The Library of Living Philosophers, 1946.
Schlossberg, Herbert. *Idols for Destruction*. Wheaton, IL: Crossway, 1990.
Scott, Frederick J. Down, ed. *William James: Selected Unpublished Correspondence 1885–1910*. Columbus, Ohio State University Press, 1996.
Seckel, Al, ed. *Bertrand Russell on God and Religion*. Amherst, NY: Prometheus, 1986.
Seymour-Jones, Carole. *Beatrice Webb: A Life*. Chicago: Ivan R. Dee, 1992.
Seymour, Miranda. *Ottoline Morrell: Life on the Grand Scale*. London, Hodder and Stoughton, 1992.
Shusterman, Richard. "Russell's Fiction and the Vanity of Human Knowledge." *Modern Fiction Studies* 29 (1983) 680–88.
Skidelsky, Robert. *John Maynard Keynes*, Vol. 1, *Hopes Betrayed, 1883–1920*. New York: Viking Penguin, 1983.
Slater, John. *Bertrand Russell*. Bristol: Thoemmes, 1994.
Smith, Logan Pearsall. *Unforgotten Years*. Boston: Little, Brown, 1939.
Spadoni, Carl. "Bertrand Russell on Aesthetics." In *Intellect and Social Conscience: Essays on Bertrand Russell's Early Work*, edited by Margaret Moran and Carl Spadoni, 49–82. Hamilton, On: McMaster University Library Press, 1984.
Spelman, Henry. *The History and Fate of Sacrilege*. London: John Hartley, 1689.
Spurr, Barry. *'Anglo-Catholic in Religion;' T.S. Eliot and Christianity*. Cambridge: Lutterworth, 2010.
Stone, Peter. Review of Peter H. Denton, *The ABC of Armageddon: Bertrand Russell on Science, Religion, and the Next War. Russell* 21 (2001) 181–85.
———. "Ray Monk and the Politics of Bertrand Russell." Review of Ray Monk, *Bertrand Russell: The Ghost of Madness, 1921–1970. Russell* 23 (2003) 82–91.
Strachey, Barbara, and Jayne Samuels, eds. *Mary Berenson: A Self-Portrait from her Letters and Diaries*. New York: W. W. Norton, 1983.
Sumares, Manuel. "Bertrand Russell's Refusal of the Christian Faith: A Reappraisal." *Revista Portuguesa de Philosofia* 62 (2006) 851–64.
Sylvest, Casper. "Russell's Realist Radicalism." *The International History Review* 36 (2014) 876–93.
Tait, Katharine. *Carn Voel: My Mother's House*. Penzance: Patten, 1998.
———. *My Father Bertrand Russell*. New York: Harcourt, Brace and Jovanovich, 1975.
———. Review of Ronald W. Clark, *The Life of Bertrand Russell. Russell* 21 (1976) 51–56.
Taylor, Harold. "Foreword." In *A Modern Symposium*, by G. Lowes Dickinson. New York City: Hart, 1967.
Thomas, J. E., and Kenneth Blackwell, eds. *Russell in Review: The Bertrand Russell Centenary Celebrations at McMaster University, October 12–14, 1972*. Toronto: Samuel Stevens, Hakkert, 1976.
Turcon, Shelia. "A Quaker Wedding: the Marriage of Bertrand Russell and Alys Pearsall Smith." *Russell* 3 (1983) 103–28.
Watkin, E. I. "Bertrand Russell—Religious Atheist." *Catholic World* 116 (1923) 731–42.
Watling, John. *Bertrand Russell*. Edinburgh: Oliver and Boyd, 1970.
Weidlich, Thom. "Did Russell Have a Personal Religion?" Review of Louis Greenspan and Stefan Anderson, eds. *Russell on Religion: Selections from the Writings of Bertrand Russell. Russell* 2 (2000) 176–81.
White, Morton. *The Age of Analysis*. New York: New American Library, 1964.
Whitehead, A. N. *Modes of Thought*. New York: Macmillan, 1938.

———. *Religion in the Making*. New York: Macmillan, 1926.
———. *Science and the Modern World*. New York: Macmillan, 1925.
Wielenberg, Erik J. *God and the Reach of Reason: C.S. Lewis, David Hume and Bertrand Russell*. New York, Cambridge University Press, 2008.
Wilson, Duncan. *Gilbert Murray OM: 1866–1957*. Oxford: Oxford University Press, 1987.
Wood, Alan. *Bertrand Russell: The Passionate Sceptic*. London: George Allen & Unwin, 1957.
Wood, H. G. "Logic and Pessimism." *Expositor* (1919) 42–63.
Woolf, Virginia. *Diary*, Vol. 1. Orlando, Harcourt, Brace and Co., 1978.
Zinsser, William, ed. *Inventing the Truth, the Art and Craft of Memoir*. Boston: Houghton Mufflin, 1998.

Index

Academic Hesitations with Russell on Religion, 41–48 n32, n40, n42
Apostles, 14, 79, 126–28, 138, 253
Aquinas, Thomas, 60–61, 231–32 n83
Aristotle, 282, 309
Augustine, Saint, 112, 219, 308

Beacon Hill School, 195, 238, 290
Bergson, Henri, 254–59
Black, Dora, 148, 195–96, 202–8, 238, 290
Blackwell, Kenneth, xii, 203 n24
Bloomsbury Literary Circle, 17–18, 98, 126–27, 161 n10, 211–14, 252–53, 282
Bradley, F. H., 61, 79, 81, 84
Brightman, Edgar, 19–20, 63–64
Broad, C. D., x
Bryn Mawr College, 177
Burtt, E. A., 278 n20

Cambridge Platonists, 290–91
Carr, E. H., 174–75
Carson, D. A., 30 n46
Catholics, 107–8, 277
Chesterton, G. K., 162
China, 205–7
Church of England, 184, 277
Christian Civilization, 172–73
Clifford, W. K., 83, 114 n63, 115–16, 291–93
Conrad, Joseph, 185

Conservative, 171–74
Contrasts Between the Russell and Stanley Families, 94 n16, 95–99
Copleston, Fr. Frederick, xi, xxvii–viii, 13, 42–44, 74
Counter-Enlightenment, 72–73, 267
Cox, Harvey, 44–45
Crawshay-Williams, Rupert, 7–8, 11 n17
Cult of Common Usage, 5

Dawson, Christopher, 248
Descartes, Rene, 88
Determinism, 120–21
Dickinson, Lowes, 78, 81, 158–67, 237
Differing Saints, 58–59, 308
Dissenters, 127
Donnelly, Lucy, 176–81
Dostoevsky, Fyodor, 281 n26

Eddington, Arthur, 80
Edwards, Paul, ix, 45–46
Eliot, T. S., 214, 244–53, 268 n72
Enlightenment, 68
Exodus, Old Testament Book of, 89 n2

Fictional Effort with Religion, 219–28, n61
Flexner, Helen, 176, 178–81, 219–20
Forster, E. M., 158–59
Francis of Assisi, Saint, 308
Free Man's Worship, 151–56

INDEX

French *Philosophes*, 176, 290, n41
Freud, Sigmund, 274–75, n13, 288
Froude, J. A., 89–90

Gandhi, Mahatmas, 9–10, n13, 309, n88
Godwin, William, 174–76, n45
Gore, Charles, 168–69
Greenspan, Louis, 47
Griffin, Nicholas, 94, n16, 279

Hegelian Philosophy at Cambridge, 128–33, n4
Hick, John, 274–75
Himmelfarb, Gertrude, 290
Herder, Johann Gottfried, 68, 267 n71
Hobbes, Thomas, 3
Hume, David, 230
Huxley, Julian, 64 n13
Huxley, T. H., 256

Idealism, 4

Jager, Ronald, 39 n42, 47
James, William, 42, 239–44 n11, n13, 254 n31, 274
Joachim, Harold, 133
Joad, C. E. M., 78
Jowett, Benjamin, 169
Jung, Carl, 267–68

Kant, Immanuel, xxvi, 23–25, 63, 164, 221 n61, 297–98 n59
Keynes, J. M., 18, 27–28,

Lady Henrietta Maria Stanley, 94–99 n21, 146
Lady John Russell, (Frances Anna Maria Elliot Russell), xiii, 87, 90–91, 99, 100–112 n33, n34, n35, n46, 114, 147–48
Lawrence, D. H., 183–93, 202, 211–12, 281–82
Leibniz, Gottfried, xxv, 1, 8–9, 43 n29, 134, 295 n51
Lessing, Gotthold, 22–23, 42–43
Logical Positivists, 65–66,

MacCarthy, Desmond, 161
Malleson, Lady Constance, 194–209 n12, n34, 253
Malleson, Miles, 10–11
Marx, Karl, 288, 310–11, n89
Mathematics, 179, 181, 183, 302 n69
Mathematics in the Early Religion of Russell, 133–37
McTaggart, John, 43, 63, 295–96
Mill, James, 291–92
Mill, John Stuart, 44, 90, 92, 124, 133, 280, 291
Monk, Ray, xiii, 26, 300
Moore, G. E., 4–6 n5, 9, 80, 133, 208, 237
Morrell, Lady Ottoline, 17, 20–21, 28, 40, 82, 85, 127–28, 143, 151, 168–69 n24, n25, 185, 187, 192, 195, 199, 209–19, 220, 224 n68, 230–33, 237 n87, 253, 254, 258, 278–79 n21, 281–82, 294–95, 304–5, 312
Morrill, John, 89
Mysticism, 68–72 n33, 222–23, 228–38 n87, 306–7 n77
Murray, Mary, 168–69
Murray, Gilbert, 7, 28, 81, 167–76, 250, 267–68
Murray, Rosalind, 179

Nietzsche's Last Men, 283–85 n31
No-Conscription Fellowship, 202, 285–86
Norton, W. W., 13, 299

Opposition to Marriage with Alys Pearsall Smith, 144–48 n33
Oxford Movement, 108

Pacifists, 285–86
Pascal, Blaise, 281
Pembroke Lodge, xiii, 1, 35, 87–88, 97–98, 101–6, 120, 124, 127–28, 140–41, 146–48, 176 n47, 208, 218, 300–301
Perfectibility of the World, 141–42, 176
Philosophical Belief, 73–79
Philosophical Radicals, 291–92

INDEX

Pitt, Jack, 43, 47–48
Plato and Platonism, 82, 257, 273 n9
Pragmatism, 61, 66, 241–44
Pringle-Pattison, 47
Proctor, Dennis, 160
Proper Beliefs, 79–86
Puritan, Puritanism, 112–13, 185, 211,
Puritan Aesthetic, 272–73
Pythagoras, 82

Quaker Theology, 138–40

Radicalism in the Russell Ancestry, 87–94
Randall, John Hermann, xxvi, 33
Ravenscroft, 90–91
Reason and Religious Belief, 294
Reform Bill of 1832, 88
Religion at Cambridge University, 126–33 n4
Religion in the Early Marriage of Russell, 137–48 n30
Religion as False But Possible in Russell, 54–59
Religion as Harmful in Russell, 48–54
Religion as Negative in Russell, 32–41 n15, n19
Religion as a Blessing or Curse, 266–68 n68
Religion and Human Vitality, 49–50
Religious Aspirations in a Deteriorating Marriage, 148–57
Religion Based on Fear, 12–13, 51, 53
Religion Under Scrutiny by a Favored Grandson, 112–25
Religious Belief, 60–66 n8
Role of Epistemology in Russell's Religious Views, 19–24 n30
Role of Metaphysics in Religious Views, 25–31
Romanticism, 181–82, 192, 267
Rousseau, John Jacques, 61, 68
Russell as Doggedly Devout, 300–316 n72, n93
Russell as an Existentialist, 313–15
Russell as a Nietzschean, 280–87
Russell as Penitent, 298–99

Russell as Public Figure and Philosopher, 1–13
Russell as a Puritan, 270–80 n19
Russell as a Spiritual Seeker, 302–6
Russell as Suspiciously Religious, 13–19
Russell as the Rational Critic of God and Religious Belief, 288–300
Russell's Agnosticism, 39, 42–43
Russell's Cynicism, 299–300
Russell's Retreat from Pythagoras, 16, 21
Russell's Suspicion of Religious Beliefs, 30
Russell's Theologian's Nightmare, 26–27
Russell's Tragic View of Life, 18–19, 23–24
Russell's View of His Parents, 93
Russell's View of the Limitations of Faith, 163–64
Russell's Visit to a Greek Church, 166
Russell, Agatha, 106
Russell, Conrad, 89, 95, 186,
Russell, Frank, 2, 96–97, 100, 161, 246
Russell, Gertrude, 146–48
Russell, John Conrad, 186
Russell, Lord John, 6, 88, 90, 92, 107–8, 221, 277–78
Russell, Rollo, 123
Russell, William, 277
Russian Revolution, 203–6

Santayana, George, 8, 40, 78, 240–41, 259–66
Schiller, F. C. S., 42
Schlossberg, Herbert, 170–71
Scientific Belief, 66–73
Scope of Philosophy, 73–79
Secularism, 68, 312
Shelley, Percy, 121, 174–76
Sins of Organized Religion, 57–58 n88
Smith, Alys Pearsall, 1–2, 142–48, 151–52, 198
Smith, Mary Whitall, 145
Socialism, 173, 253, 282
Spence, Patricia, 9, 96, 195
Spencer, Herbert, 125
Spinoza, Baruch, xxv–xxvi, 216, 295 n51
Stanley, Lyulph, 95

INDEX

Stone, Peter, xiv–xv
Strachey, Lytton, 286
Subjective Bias, 118–19

Tait, Katharine, 3, 9–11, 18, 36, 47,
    56–57, 160, 194–96, 203, 282–
    83, 287, 304
Taylor, Helen, 90
Theological Examinations, 113–14
Thomas, Carey, 177
Toynbee, Arnold, 172
Transcendentals, 55–56

Unitarianism, 122
Unwin, Stanley, 37, 192–93

Victorians, 79–80, 121

Voltaire, 84, 288–89
Voltairean Tradition, 85

Ward, James, 133
Watkin, E. I., 46–47
Whitehead, A. N., 21, 42, 63, 78, 80–81,
    85, 127, 136, 148–51, 292–93,
    302–3
Whitehead, Evelyn, 148–51, 235–37
Wittgenstein, Ludwig, 6, 8, 16, 29,
    42, 136–37, 232–35, 237–38,
    258–59, 312
Wood, Alan, 74
Wood, H. G., 86

Years at Pembroke Lodge with
    Grandmother Russell, 100–112